Discrimination in
Mortgage Lending

Discrimination in Mortgage Lending

Robert Schafer
and
Helen F. Ladd

The MIT Press
Cambridge, Massachusetts
London, England

This is a publication of the Joint Center for Urban Studies

This book was set in VIP Times Roman by DEKR Corporation and printed and bound by The Murray Printing Co. in the United States of America.

Library of Congress Cataloging in Publication Data

Schafer, Robert.
   Discrimination in mortgage lending.

   Includes bibliographical references and index.
   1. Discrimination in mortgage loans—United States.   I. Ladd, Helen F.   II. Title.
HG2040.2.S29   332.7'22   81-11834
ISBN 0-262-19192-X   AACR2

Contents

Acknowledgments   vii

1
Introduction   1

2
Default Risk in Mortgage Lending   14

3
Flow of Funds   33

4
Lending Decision Models   62

5
Decision to Lend in California   83

6
Mortgage Credit Terms in California   137

7
Decision to Lend in New York   185

8
Mortgage Credit Terms in New York   225

9
Appraisal Practices   247

10
Summary of Results   274

11
Recommendations   301

Appendixes

A. Variable Definitions   323

B. Model Estimates for California Savings and Loan Associations   338

C. Model Estimates for State-regulated Lenders in New York   356

Notes   377

Publications of the Joint Center for Urban Studies   389

Index   393

Acknowledgments

The research in this book was conducted over two and one-half years and was supported with two grants that were administered through the Joint Center for Urban Studies of the Massachusetts Institute of Technology and Harvard University. The Savings Banks Association of New York provided a grant during 1977–1978 to study mortgage lending decisions in New York, especially those of savings banks. The United States Department of Housing and Urban Development (HUD) provided a grant during 1978–1980 to study the accessibility to mortgage funds by women and minorities in California and New York. Robert Schafer directed the first grant and shared these responsibilities with Helen F. Ladd on the second grant. The authorship of the various chapters reflects this division of responsibility. We jointly authored Chapters 1, 4, 6, 8 and 10. Robert Schafer assumed primary responsibility for the remainder of the book.

The cooperation and assistance of many persons have aided in the preparation of this manuscript. We owe a special debt to Arthur P. Solomon, Director of the Joint Center, for providing the opportunity to undertake this project and for his support throughout.

The staff of the Savings Banks Association and the officers of the savings banks, commercial banks, and savings and loan associations cooperated in several ways. They provided copies of their Equal Housing Opportunity Lender forms and facilitated the collection of data with our Mortgage Loan Survey. We wish to thank Ira O. Scott, Jr. and Monte I. Radack especially for their efforts to ensure that the project received all the necessary information. The bank officers who assisted are too numerous to thank individually. We are grateful to all of them for their help. Two deserve a special note of thanks: Morris D. Crawford, Jr. and Leonard S. Simon.

Ronald Wienk and Monika Curry at the Department of Housing and

Urban Development provided valuable assistance throughout the HUD-funded study.

The findings, conclusions, and recommendations do not necessarily represent the views of the Savings Banks Association of New York State or the Department of Housing and Urban Development.

We owe a special intellectual debt to Franco Modigliani, John Lintner, and John R. Meyer for their comments on the research methodology and drafts of the manuscript. We are also grateful to Dwight Crane, John F. Kain, Arthur P. Solomon, and Howard Stevenson for their comments on various drafts.

Many residents and members of community organizations provided valuable information about lending practices. We thank the following people for their assistance: Julie Kerksick, Tom Moogan, and Diane Moogan of the Bank on Brooklyn organization; Herb Steiner of the Against Investment Discrimination organization; Richard W. Golden, Marilyn Ondrasik, and Larry Farber of the New York Public Interest Research Group; and Father Dennis J. Woods of the Division of Housing of the Catholic Diocese of Buffalo deserve special thanks.

We are also grateful to Muriel Siebert, William Woodward, Gary Brody, and William A. Volckhausen of the New York State Banking Department, and to William F. Harrison and Kobey Horn of the California Department of Savings and Loan, for their cooperation in making their data available.

We wish to thank John Baer of the New York City Planning Commission and Nancy Minter of the Community Analysis Bureau of the City of Los Angeles for their cooperation in providing information on their respective cities.

Many other persons have assisted in the preparation of this report. Our five research assistants—Stephen E. Erfle, John A. Kirlin, Amy F. Philipson, Gary J. Reid, and Mark S. Roberts—worked assiduously to complete the two research projects, and they deserve special recognition. We also wish to thank Judy Payne who aided in gathering data at a critical time during the first project.

Much of the data had to be transcribed and coded prior to being keypunched for computer-assisted analysis. A staff of over twenty persons carried out this task. We are indebted to Sari Nelinson for her excellent work in supervising the coding operation.

We wish to acknowledge, with appreciation, the assistance of Charlotte B. Moore and Joan Wilson in revising versions of the manuscript, and Victoria Smith for preparing the index.

Several persons assisted in typing the various drafts and the final manuscript: Susan Jennifer Bennett, Elizabeth N. Gleason, Irene F. Goodsell, Christopher L. Roberts, Carolyn Jane Smyth, and Steven P. Stepak.

Robert Schafer
Helen F. Ladd

**Discrimination in
Mortgage Lending**

1
Introduction

Many federal and state statutes currently make it illegal for banking institutions to discriminate in the granting of mortgage loans on the basis of certain characteristics of the borrower such as race, sex, or marital status or on the basis of certain characteristics of the property, such as the arbitrary use of age or location.[1] These laws reflect two social concerns, one relating to individual justice and the other to the viability of urban neighborhoods.

Generally accepted concepts of justice require that individuals not be treated adversely just because they happen to share certain characteristics of a group. Membership in certain groups, especially those defined by the color of a person's skin, has in the past resulted in differential treatment. This concept of justice and its historic violations have led to laws that prohibit discriminatory lending on the basis of certain unacceptable categories while allowing differentiation based on other factors related to the riskiness of the loan such as applicant income or net wealth. The Federal Equal Credit Opportunity Act (as amended, March 23, 1976) embodies this concept of fairness:

It shall be unlawful for any creditor to discriminate against any applicant, with respect to any aspect of a credit transaction:
1. on the basis of race, color, religion, national origin, sex or marital status, or age (provided the applicant has the capacity to contract);
2. because all or part of the applicant's income derives from any public assistance program; or
3. because the applicant has in good faith exercised any right under the Consumer Credit Protection Act.[2]

Laws requiring disclosure of mortgage lending by census tract or zip code, encouraging financial institutions to "help meet the credit needs of the local communities in which they are chartered consistent with the safe and sound operation of such institutions,"[3] or making discrimination on the basis of the age or location of a building illegal,[4] emanate from the concerns of community activist groups. These groups believe that lending institutions contribute to the declining quality of life in certain urban neighborhoods by refusing to grant mortgages even though demand exists, or by granting mortgages with less favorable terms even though the expected yield and risk of loss are the same as in other neighborhoods. Older neighborhoods are usually alleged to be the target of these practices, which are commonly referred to as "redlining." As a consequence, this alleged practice may have its most severe effect on minority groups who tend to be concentrated in redlined areas.

This study uses several different sources of data to examine the extent to which urban mortgage lenders discriminate on the basis of prohibited borrower characteristics and the extent to which allegations by antiredlining groups are valid. It focuses, however, on the lender's decision to lend through the use of mortgage applications data rather than on the aggregate volume of lending by geographic area, an outcome that reflects both supply and demand factors. This focus differentiates this study from most previous studies.[5] Multivariate statistical analysis is used to determine the impact of the discrimination variables on the probability that a loan will be denied or modified and the terms of mortgage credit, controlling for objective measures of risk.

The bankers' mortgage-lending decision is only one link in a chain of decisions that determine the extent to which decent housing is accessible to minorities and women. Other actors in the urban housing market allegedly have major impacts on the ability of women and minorities to buy homes. Among these actors are real estate brokers who may steer buyers away from or toward certain neighborhoods on the basis of race, sex, or marital status; real estate appraisers who may underappraise certain types of property in a discriminatory manner; or insurance companies who may refuse to sell fire insurance in certain geographic areas or to some categories of home owners.[6] The analysis of the role of these actors (with the exception of appraisers) is outside the scope of this study. Their interaction with mortgage lenders must be kept in mind, however, when interpreting our results. For example, a finding that banks do not appear to discriminate against minorities in making mortgage loans might be due to advance screening by real estate brokers who tell their minority clients that they should not even apply for a bank loan.

The Residential Lending Process

A banking institution's decision to make a loan for the purchase of a single-family house and the terms on which that loan is made are part of a complex portfolio decision. At one level, the bank must determine the appropriate portion of its assets to hold in the form of mortgages on residential property. The demand for residential mortgages from the bank influences this decision through its impact on the expected rate of return and risk on this investment compared to others. In addition, liquidity needs, lender attitudes toward risk, and regulatory constraints all play major roles in this decision. Regulatory constraints may affect the portfolio composition directly, as in the case of the requirement that savings and loan associations invest a certain percentage of their assets in real estate, or indirectly, as when a binding usury law applies to certain types of investments such as in-state mortgages on one- to four-family houses but not to other types.

At a second level, the lender must determine which applications for loans on specific properties to accept and the terms on which the loans will be made. Those applications of acceptable quality are approved, as requested or with modification, subject to sufficient funds being available in the portfolio for this type of investment; other applications are rejected.

Both the credit worthiness of the borrower and the security offered by the property influence the quality of the application. The individual's credit worthiness generally depends on such factors as his or her current and expected future income, employment experience and prospects, net wealth, and credit history. The more credit worthy the borrower, the lower the probability that he or she will default on the loan. As a reflection of the market value of the property, the appraised value measures the property's value as collateral. The greater the collateral in relation to the size of the loan, the less the risk of loss to the bank in the event of foreclosure.

Uncertainty plays a major role in the lending decision. On the basis of current and past information about the borrower and the property, the lender must project the ability of the borrower to make timely payments in the future and must assess the probability that the value of the property will fall short of the outstanding loan at some future date. As discussed below, this uncertainty may lead banks to develop operating procedures that have discriminatory effects.

Uncertainty is not the only explanation for discriminatory lending, however. The following sections present the range of allegations commonly made against conventional mortgage lenders. These include allegations of discrimination on the basis of both the characteristics of the mortgage applicant and the location of the property.

Discrimination on the Basis of Characteristics of the Borrower

Although mortgage loans are fully secured by the value of specific properties, banking institutions pay close attention to the credit worthiness of the borrower when evaluating mortgage applications. The quality of the collateral protects the lender against loss in a foreclosure situation, but foreclosure is costly and has the potential for creating ill will in the community. Hence, to reduce the probability of delinquency and to minimize the possibility of foreclosure, banks usually perform thorough credit analyses of mortgage applicants.

This was not always the case; for example, during the 1920s, when short-maturity, balloon-payment loans prevailed, bankers were more concerned with the quality of the collateral than with the credit worthiness of the borrower. Not until the 1930s with the shift to longer-maturity amortized loans did bankers introduce borrower ratings and personal interviews. Since World War II, most banks have recognized that borrower characteristics contribute significantly to the riskiness of the loan.

Banks use objective factors such as income, net wealth, and credit histories to determine the credit worthiness of the borrower. Representatives of women's and minority groups allege, however, that even the application of these objective factors leaves room for discriminatory treatment, especially when banks are not required to explain the reasons for rejection. Banks may, for example, define income differently for different applicants, fail to follow up on adverse credit reports that may be incorrect, or vary the maximum acceptable ratio of monthly payment to monthly income or other criteria depending on certain characteristics of the borrower.

The importance of the applicant's personal interview with the loan officer of the bank leaves additional leeway for subjectivity in the loan evaluation process. Subjective evaluation has a relevant and valuable place in lending decisions. The loan officer is assessing such hard-to-measure qualities as the applicant's strength of attachment to the property, motivation, character, reputation, and stability of family life.[7] This subjectivity of the evaluation process combined with the importance to the lender of borrower characteristics, however, provides a situation in which banks could discriminate, if they wished, against certain categories of borrowers. Whether based on racial prejudice or outdated stereotypes, discrimination against minority, female, or unmarried applicants runs counter to accepted notions of social justice and is now illegal.

Sex or Marital Status

Married Women   Women's groups complain that married women are treated unfairly by traditional mortgage lending criteria related to the measurement of household income. As documented by several surveys in the early 1970s, mortgage lenders often explicitly discounted the wife's income by 50 percent or more when evaluating mortgage applications.[8] Fifty percent discounting means that a banker treats an application from a two-worker household having $20,000 in annual income with 40 percent contributed by the wife as comparable to that from a single earner household having $16,000 in annual income, all other factors held constant. Such a procedure apparently represents a rule-of-thumb solution to the problem of estimating the probability distributions of future income for two-earner households.

Although income discounting was apparently widely used, specific practices varied across banks and across applicants. A 1973 study by the U.S. Commission on Civil Rights found that several Hartford banks, for example, treated wives with professional jobs differently from wives with other jobs.[9] In addition, the study found that banks were more likely to discount the wife's earnings if she was of child-bearing age or if the household contained preschool children. In some cases the bank might require a "baby letter" to count any of the wife's income at all. A "baby letter" is a physician's statement which attests to the wife's or husband's sterility, their use of approved birth-control methods, or their willingness to terminate pregnancy.[10]

The view that the possibility of pregnancy increases the riskiness of the loan is not restricted to the lenders of conventional mortgages. Indeed, pre-1973 standards for Veterans Administration (VA) loans state clearly that the mere possibility of pregnancy is a reason for discounting a wife's income.[11] Federal Housing Administration (FHA) policy traditionally has been less restrictive than VA policy; the FHA criterion for fully counting the income of working wives states that "income and motivating interest may normally be expected to continue throughout the early period of mortgage risk." [12] It is, however, somewhat vague, leaving room for individual interpretation.

The practice of income discounting is not only discriminatory and inconsistent with generally accepted concepts of social justice, but is unwise bank policy. Changing social conditions and liberal maternity-leave policies probably render obsolete the assumption implicit in income discounting that married women have little long-run commitment to remaining in the labor force. [13] A recent study sponsored by the U.S. Department of Housing and Urban Development (HUD) provides statistical evidence in support of this argument. Using the Parnes data on household incomes between 1966 and 1970, the study found that the 50 percent rule represents overdiscounting of second-earner incomes. [14] This would be even more true today in light of continued changes in the role of women in the labor force during the 1970s. [15] In addition, a simple rule of thumb calling for 50 percent or any other fixed discount is not likely to incorporate fully the differences in both the expected level and the variance of income for different household types.

The Equal Credit Opportunity Act (ECOA) prohibits sex-based classifications and makes income discounting illegal under federal law. The Federal Reserve Board's Regulation B, which implements the Equal Credit Opportunity Act, explicitly rules out the use of "assumptions or aggregate statistics relating to the likelihood that any group of persons will bear or rear children or, for that reason, will receive diminished or interrupted income in the future." [16] The Federal Home Loan Bank Board's nondiscrimination guidelines rule out income discounting even more explicitly:

A practice of discounting all or part of either spouse's income where spouses apply jointly is a violation of section 527 of the National Housing Act. As with other income, when spouses apply jointly for a loan, the determination as to whether a spouse's income qualifies for credit purposes should depend upon a reasonable evaluation of his or her past, present, and reasonably foreseeable economic circumstances. [17]

Single Women Women's groups believe that lenders discriminate against the single woman (single, divorced, widowed, or separated) because of prejudicial attitudes toward women. It is alleged that these attitudes are based on outdated myths that women are inherently unstable, are incapable of conducting their own affairs, and need the protection of a male; that the divorced woman must be emotionally unstable; and that the inability of an unmarried woman to find a man demonstrates that something must be wrong with her.[18]

In addition to outright denial on the basis of sex, illegal under ECOA, women's groups believe that banks discriminate in more subtle ways such as imposing so many additional requirements on female applicants that they either withdraw their applications or suffer unacceptable financial burdens. These requirements include the payment of all outstanding debts, the purchase of mortgage insurance, the taking of monthly payments directly from the applicant's paycheck, and the cosigning of the mortgage by an appropriate man.[19]

Female applicants may also be adversely affected by lender evaluation policies that, although not necessarily designed to discriminate against women, have the effect of doing so. The exclusion from the loan evaluation process of alimony, child-support payments, and public assistance is one such policy because of the importance of these income categories to single female applicants. According to the Federal Reserve Board's Regulation B, a lender must now "consider alimony and child support payments as income to the extent that they are likely to be consistently made."[20] The Federal Reserve Board Regulations also explicitly state that public-assistance income must be fully counted as income.

Women may also be treated unfavorably because of insufficient credit records. An unmarried woman, for example, may have no credit record because of past discrimination against her by consumer credit companies, and a divorced woman may have no credit record in her own name.[21] Thus, unmarried, divorced, or separated women may not qualify for mortgages even though they have adequate income and wealth.

Finally, banks have been criticized for discriminating on the basis of marital status.[22] ECOA makes discriminatory-lending behavior on the basis of marital status illegal independent of the sex of the applicant.[23] One interesting question is whether banks discriminate against applications involving any unmarried or separated applicants, whether such applicants be men or women or both applying jointly.

Race

In the past, racial prejudice has clearly been a factor in the lending decisions of banks.[24] Mortgage lenders played a key role in the racial discrimination practiced by all segments of the real estate industry, including the enforcement through 1948 of a restriction in the deed on the race of future purchasers. Racial discrimination in mortgage lending is clearly illegal under the 1968 Civil Rights Act. However, recent studies employing multivariate statistical techniques on individual applicant information indicate that this law has not eliminated racial discrimination in mortgage lending.

For example, Lowry's study, based on a six-metropolitan area sample of mortgage applications from the summer and fall of 1977, supports the hypothesis that some subgroups of the nonwhite population are discriminated against.[25] In particular, Lowry found that nonwhites seeking to purchase very expensive homes and nonwhites with tenuous financial positions seeking to buy modest homes suffered significant disadvantages compared to similarly situated whites. He also found evidence of wide variation in lenders' treatment of racial minorities both across regions and among lenders within a given region.

Geographic Discrimination

At the heart of the current redlining debate is the allegation that lenders sometimes evaluate loan applications on the basis of the property's location without looking at the applicant's credit worthiness or the value of the specific property as collateral. In its simplest form, redlining refers to the delineation of whole neighborhoods within which lenders refuse to grant mortgage credit. Although outright refusal to lend is one form of redlining, antiredlining groups point to several indirect tactics such as unfavorable terms and systematic underappraisal of property that could have the same effect.

The terms of the loan (loan-to-value ratio, maturity, interest rate, discount points, and closing costs) can be made so unfavorable as to make any offered loan unacceptable to a credit-worthy applicant. If the applicant were trying to purchase a property for its market value of $40,000 and a bank only offered a 40 percent-of-value loan, the applicant would face the difficult task of raising $24,000. As a result, the applicant might not be able to purchase the property, and the net effect could be the same as if the bank had refused to lend in the area.

If the property were underappraised (for example, at $20,000 with a market value of $40,000), the size of the loan would be limited. Using this tactic, a lender could offer the potential borrower a loan of only $16,000 using the conventional loan-to-value ratio of 80 percent. Again, the net effect could be to prevent the applicant from purchasing the property. Allegations of underappraisal are frequently made by community organizations concerned with mortgage lending in their neighborhoods. Antiredlining groups also allege that the lenders frequently justify lower appraisals by applying more rigid structural standards or other appraisal criteria (for example, minimum house width, use of asbestos shingles, minimum number of bedrooms and bathrooms, minimum garage size, mixed or inharmonious land uses) to properties in redlined areas. They also say that lenders, through their appraisal staff, presume that certain buildings are economically obsolete, even though a market for them still exists. Another common allegation is that banks stall the appraisal until the purchase-and-sale contract has expired.

✳ For the purposes of this study, redlining is defined as the refusal to lend, or the granting of mortgages with less favorable terms, in certain areas even though the expected yield and risk of loss are the same as they are for mortgages granted in other areas. To implement a redlining tactic, lending institutions or some other entity, such as insurance companies, would have to identify the areas to be redlined. Two of the criteria most frequently alleged to be used to differentiate among neighborhoods for these purposes are age of housing and race. People living in neighborhoods having a significant proportion of old housing stock or black or minority households have indicated that they believe that banks are redlining their neighborhoods.

A multitude of studies by community groups in large cities throughout the United States examining the geographic distribution of loans granted by banking institutions purport to provide support for redlining claims. None of these studies, however, even the most carefully done, provide clear evidence of redlining as we define it.[26] The major difficulty arises from their failure either to recognize or to control statistically for the nonredlining measures banks may legitimately use to make either no or only a few loans in specific geographic areas. These include: the lack of adequate demand for mortgage loans in an area, relatively few credit-worthy applicants, external risks such as widespread vandalism or nearby vacant buildings that greatly threaten the value of the property, and decisions by entities beyond the control of lenders such as real estate brokers and insurance companies.

Most previous studies, especially those by community activist groups, can be criticized as well for their failure to distinguish between neighborhood disinvestment and redlining, a distinction particularly important for policy purposes. It would be fair to say that redlining is at least a contributing factor to disinvestment in those neighborhoods where redlining results in an arbitrary withdrawal of funds. Neighborhood disinvestment, however, can take place in the absence of any redlining by banks. For example, property values may fall in a neighborhood because the housing stock is obsolete (the rooms and apartments may be too small with inadequate open play space for children) and the households' real incomes have increased enough to allow them to buy or rent houses or apartments elsewhere with larger rooms and more open space. If an area is considered very risky (that is, has high foreclosure rates, high rates of fire loss, or large property tax arrearages) and banks are no longer lending there, it is difficult to determine whether their decision to stop lending in the area preceded and precipitated the decline, accelerated an already existing decline, or occurred subsequent to the decline.

Study Outline

This study examines empirically the extent to which mortgage applicants are discriminated against because of their sex, race, marital status, or age or because of the neighborhood (its age, racial composition, or geographic location) in which their property is located. Whenever possible, we examine this issue using individual mortgage applications data. For the analysis, we needed detailed information (1) on the objective factors such as the credit worthiness of individual applicants and the security value of the property that legitimately affect the mortgage lending decision and (2) on the characteristics of the applicant or the property that constitute illegal discrimination. Fortunately, California and New York state laws require state-regulated banks to maintain this detailed information on all mortgage applications.[27] With the exception of the pilot study conducted by the Federal Home Loan Bank, no other comparable data set is available.[28]

The California and New York mortgage application data sets are not identical; both have strengths and weaknesses. The New York recording form includes, for example, marital status, net wealth, and years at present occupation, all of which are omitted from the California form. The New York form records house purchase price and income by ranges; California provides much more precise and detailed information on these variables, including the separate incomes of the applicant and co-applicant where applicable. In addition, the California form provides information on the final terms of the mortgage contract, which, except for the loan-to-value ratio, is not available in New York.

By relying on both data sources, this study can focus on a broader range of issues than would be possible with a single data set. In particular, the New York information makes possible a test of discrimination on the basis of marital status, and the California data set permits an examination of discriminatory behavior in the treatment accorded secondary income, the setting of mortgage terms, and appraisal practices.

In New York, state-regulated lenders are also required to disclose all their own-serviced mortgage activity in each census tract; we used this information to examine risk of loss, flow of mortgage funds, and terms of mortgage credit by census tract. Risk of loss was further examined using data from a survey of the mortgage portfolios of mutual savings banks. This survey was conducted by us at the Joint Center for Urban Studies to gather detailed information on delinquency and foreclosure experience and on the characteristics of the borrower, the property, the neighborhood, the loan, and the loan history since approval.

Two major advantages flow from the use of data from two states. First, a wide variety of lending institutions can be analyzed and compared. The California data cover all state-chartered savings and loan associations in California, whereas the New York data apply to state-chartered commercial banks, savings and loan associations, and mutual savings banks. To the extent possible, the New York data are analyzed separately by type of bank.

Second, the data cover a wide range of economic conditions. The rapid economic growth and booming housing market in California contrast sharply with the situation in New York State. In addition, a wide variety of metropolitan areas can be studied in both states, allowing large areas to be compared with small, and rapidly growing with slowly growing areas. For example, the San Jose metropolitan area is growing more rapidly than the rest of California because of the growth of the high technology firms in the "Silicon Valley." And in New York, the Rochester area's economy is much better off than that of the rest of the state.

An important consequence of the variety of banks and economic conditions covered by the two data sources is the potential generalizability of the results. Results that are consistent across such a wide variety of circumstances will provide a firm foundation for the formulation of national policy.

The following aspects of residential mortgage lending are analyzed:

1. The geographic distribution of actual mortgage delinquencies and foreclosures in New York.

2. The supply of mortgage funds relative to their demand by geographic area in New York.

3. Discrimination in the review of mortgage applications on the basis of the sex, marital status, race, or age of the applicant, location of the property, or the age or racial composition of the neighborhood in California and New York.

4. Discrimination in the setting of credit terms in California and New York.

5. Appraisal practices in California and New York.

Although the numerous factors that affect risk of loss in mortgage lending are considered throughout this book, Chapter 2 gives more detailed attention to these issues using data from New York State, especially information from the Joint Center Mortgage Loan Survey. The ability to predict mortgage losses at the time the loan is granted and the relationship between these losses and the characteristics of the loan, borrower, property, and neighborhood are analyzed. In addition, the extent to which mortgage delinquencies and foreclosures are higher, as lenders claim, in allegedly redlined neighborhoods is examined.

In Chapter 3, the factors that affect mortgage demand and supply by geographic area are examined. Mortgage demand in a given geographic area depends on the demand for housing, the level of turnover in the stock of housing (that is, the frequency with which ownership changes hands), the net asset and income situation of new purchasers, and the terms under which mortgage credit is available. The supply of mortgage funds to a specific geographic area depends on the rate of return (interest rate, maturity, and loan-to-value ratio), which is a function of demand, and the risk of loss on the investment. In Chapter 3, census-tract data on housing transactions, various characteristics of the residents and housing stock, and the level and terms of mortgage lending are used to estimate a model of the quantity of mortgage funds provided by state-regulated lending institutions in New York. Once these market factors have been controlled, the analysis can focus on the effects of property location, neighborhood racial composition, and age of housing in a neighborhood on the quantity of mortgage funds provided to the particular neighborhood.

Chapters 4–8 focus explicitly on the lender's decisions about whether to approve particular mortgage applications and about what terms to set on approved loans. Chapter 4 presents the theoretical underpinnings of the estimated models. Specifically, we use a portfolio choice framework to model lender decisions to approve, modify, or deny mortgage applications and their decisions about interest rates, loan-to-value ratios, maturity periods, downward modifications, and loan fees.

Chapters 5 and 6 present the results for California savings and loan associations. In Chapter 5, the lending decision is analyzed by considering four outcomes to a loan application: approval as applied for, increasing the requested loan amount prior to approval, decreasing the requested loan amount prior to approval, and denial. Chapter 6 contains an analysis of the conditions under which mortgage credit is extended; that is, the interest rate, loan amount, maturity period, and loan fees.

Chapters 7 and 8 present the results for state-regulated lenders in New York State. Chapter 7 is devoted to the analysis of four outcomes to a mortgage application: approval as applied for, modification prior to approval, denial, and withdrawal. Chapter 8 analyzes downward modifications in the requested loan amount. In addition, Chapter 8 contains estimates of a model of mortgage credit terms based on census-tract averages because individual mortgage application data on credit terms are unavailable for New York.

In Chapter 9, appraisal practices are analyzed. In California, information on denied as well as approved mortgage applications is used. In New York, however, information exists only on the appraised values of mortgages that have been granted by mutual savings banks.

The final two chapters summarize the findings and discuss policy recommendations.

2
Default Risk in Mortgage Lending

Sound management practice requires mortgage-lending institutions to evaluate the potential risk inherent in each loan application. When a loan application is judged to have a higher-than-normal likelihood of defaulting in the future, the lending institution may decide to balance this increased risk with a higher interest rate, a shorter term, or a lower loan-to-value ratio. If the risk of default is high enough, the institution may decide not to grant the loan.

Several neighborhood organizations believe that lenders arbitrarily limit the amount of mortgage funds available to borrowers purchasing housing within their neighborhoods; in other words, these neighborhoods are believed to be redlined. Lenders frequently respond that any geographic variation in the availability of mortgage funds is not due to arbitrary lending decisions, but rather is a reflection of actual variations in the risk of loss associated with particular investment opportunities. As a result, it is important to assess the extent to which risk of loss (that is, the likelihood of delinquent mortgage payments or of foreclosure) is positively associated with the neighborhoods that are alleged to be redlined.

Table 2.1 summarizes the delinquency rates by type of loan for the five largest metropolitan areas in New York State. Separate figures are given for the portions of these areas alleged to be redlined. The boundaries of these neighborhoods were developed through conversations with community leaders. According to these figures, the areas alleged to be redlined have an above-average risk of loss for at least some type of loan. In particular, the delinquency rate on conventional mortgages (those lacking government insurance or guarantees) on one- to four-family houses are substantially higher in the redlined neighborhoods than in their metropolitan area, as much as four times higher in Syracuse. However, these delinquency rates do not control for other

Table 2.1
Delinquency rates by location, type of property, and type of loan, 1975

Area	1- to 4-Family Houses		Multifamily Conventional
	Conventional	Federally Assisted	
Albany-Schenectady-Troy			
SMSA	0.0229	0.0538	0.0039
Alleged redlined areas	0.0414	0.1085	0.0156
Buffalo			
SMSA	0.0089	0.0192	0.0015
Alleged redlined areas	0.0166	0.0447	0.0000
New York-Nassau-Suffolk			
Bronx, Kings and Queens counties	0.0371	0.0379	0.0558
Alleged redlined areas	0.0420	0.0360	0.0700
Rochester			
SMSA	0.0325	0.0716	0.0535
Alleged redlined areas	0.1073	0.1216	NA
Syracuse			
SMSA	0.0308	0.0709	0.0047
Alleged redlined areas	0.1299	0.1153	0.0000

Delinquent loans are mortgages whose payments are 60 days or more overdue. The delinquency rate is the dollar value of the unpaid principal of delinquent mortgages divided by the dollar value of the unpaid principal of current and delinquent mortgages

SMSA stands for Standard Metropolitan Statistical Area. It is the county or counties containing the named cities together with some of the adjacent counties.

Source: New York State Banking Dept., Supervisory Procedure G-107, Appendix 8.
NA = not applicable.

factors, such as borrower characteristics, that may explain their variation across neighborhoods.

In this chapter, a model of the relationship between several measures of loan default and the characteristics of the loan, borrower(s), property, and neighborhood is developed and estimated. This statistical analysis of past experience with previously granted loans provides information that lending institutions can use to reduce default rates on their current and future mortgage portfolios. In particular, it should indicate to what extent conditions of the neighborhood as opposed to borrower characteristics and property conditions affect the likelihood and severity of default.

The causes of mortgage default can be grouped into four categories: economic burden of the loan repayments, borrower's equity, market value of the mortgaged property, and personal problems. Default risk should increase as loan repayments become more burdensome to the borrower and decrease as the borrower's equity in the mortgaged property increases. Of course, if the market value of the property falls during the period of the loan, real equity will not necessarily increase as the loan matures. In such an event, default risk should increase because the borrower has little incentive to continue repayment of the loan's principal. Finally, if the borrower suffers severe personal problems, such as job loss, illness, or marital difficulties, during the period of the loan, default risk will likely increase. In developing a predictive model of default risk, it is important to distinguish between those factors for which a lender has relevant information at the time of the decision to lend and other factors that cannot be predicted at that time.

A survey of the mutual savings banks in New York State provides information on the status of mortgage loans in their portfolios as well as ones that have been satisfied by full payment or through foreclosure. Similar information is not available for New York commercial banks and savings and loan associations or California lenders.

Factors Leading to Default

To specify the default models, it is necessary to understand the causes of mortgage default. The mortgage loan survey (MLS) of mutual savings banks provides information on the cause of default for loans that entered foreclosure proceedings.[1] Of the 4,392 loans in the MLS sample, 1,114 entered foreclosure proceedings at least once. As part of the MLS questionnaire, mutual savings banks were asked whether there were any changes in the status of the borrower, the property, or the neighborhood that might have contributed to these loans entering foreclosure. Banks were also asked to describe such changes.

Complete answers to the first question are recorded for 711 of the 1,114 loans entering foreclosure. The distribution of responses is given in Table 2.2. The banks indicated that they knew of no change in borrower, property, or neighborhood status that might have contributed to the initiation of foreclosure proceedings for 299 of the loans. Of the remaining 412 loans, changes in borrower status alone is the

Table 2.2
Factors that might have contributed to foreclosure proceedings: New York State
mutual savings banks

	Incidence	
Factor	Number	%
Borrower status only	269	37.8
Property status only	32	4.5
Neighborhood status only	7	1.0
Borrower and property status, but not neighborhood status	43	6.0
Borrower and neighborhood status, but not property status	3	0.4
Property and neighborhood status, but not borrower status	18	2.5
Borrower, property, and neighborhood status	40	5.6
No change of status listed as contributing to foreclosure proceedings	299	42.1
Total	711	100.0[a]
Incomplete responses	403	NA

NA – not applicable.
a. The sum of the percents does not add to 100.0 because of rounding error.

most frequent (269 cases) reason given for mortgages entering foreclosure. Borrower changes played no role in only 57 cases. Property
changes were the sole reason given for defaults that led to foreclosure
proceedings in 32 cases. However, changes in property status played
a partial role in 101 other cases. Finally, neighborhood changes were
listed as the sole cause of a mortgage entering foreclosure in only 7
cases. Neighborhood changes coupled with borrower or property
changes were a factor in an additional 61 loans.

The specific changes in borrower, property, and neighborhood characteristics (the second question addressed to the lenders) are reported
in Table 2.3. The sum exceeds the number of loans with an indicated
change in circumstances because multiple reasons for the default were
given in several cases, and responses were sometimes given for the
loans that had incomplete responses to the first question.

The major borrower characteristics that lead to foreclosure action
are financial difficulties and marital problems. Change in ownership of

Table 2.3
Specific reasons that might have contributed to foreclosure proceedings: New York State mutual savings banks

Characteristic	Incidence (number)
Borrower	
Financial difficulties (reduction in income, unemployment, bankruptcy)	159
Marital problems or divorce	88
Change in ownership (usually through assumption)	43
Illness or death of borrower or co-borrower	42
Owner moved out and rented property	3
Property	
Property deteriorated or abandoned (poor maintenance, fire, or water damage)	155
Tenant problems	29
Increased operating costs	21
Property tax arrears	15
Rent control	15
Excessive vacancies	4
Inability to sell	2
Neighborhood	
Neighborhood decline	80

the property and illness or death of the borrower or co-borrower also are frequent causes of foreclosure action. Change in ownership usually involved the assumption of responsibility for the mortgage by a third party with the bank's apparent approval, although not all responses were detailed enough to make this clear. In a few cases, the cause of foreclosure is listed as failure to continue payments after the borrower had moved out of the house and rented the property.

The major property characteristic cited as contributing to. foreclosure action is deterioration or abandonment. When described in more detail, deterioration is specifically attributed to poor maintenance practices. Occasionally, fire or water damage is listed as causing deterioration. All but 5 of the other property-related reasons are listed for mortgages on properties located in the greater New York City area. The 5 exceptions are tenant problems in upstate properties.

Multivariate Model of Mortgage Default

Mortgage default may be modeled by either identifying the causes of default or by estimating the probability that a loan would default on the basis of information known at the time of closing.

The first model would include variables for the loan, borrower, property, and neighborhood characteristics at both the time of loan closing and the time of actual default. For example, the impact of such personal problems as job loss or marital problems on default incidence would be measured. Although estimation of this model would benefit loan-servicing policies by enabling bank personnel to spot loans in imminent trouble and devise means of avoiding actual default, such estimation is severely hampered by the need to collect borrower, property, and neighborhood characteristics on both defaulted and non-defaulted loans at the time of sampling.

The second model, designed to estimate the probability that a loan would enter default status solely on the basis of information known at the time of closing, would be most useful to loan officers who process mortgage applications, evaluate the riskiness of individual applications, and decide which applications should be approved. The multi-variate models examined in this chapter are generally of this second type.

A small but growing body of literature exists that studies the relationship between default risk and mortgage characteristics at the time of closing.[2] Nearly all this literature has relied on loan characteristics, such as the maturity and loan-to-value ratio, as determinants of default risk. In most cases, data on some borrower characteristics (income level, occupation status or employment record, age, and number of dependents) have been included as well. Very little of this research has included information on the property or neighborhood. Consequently, little is known about the effects of selected property and neighborhood characteristics on future mortgage defaults. The primary results thus far are that delinquency rates are positively associated with age of property, and when property age is controlled for, these rates are not associated with the racial composition of the neighborhood or with recent changes in that composition.[3]

In formal terms, the model of default risk has the following general specification:

$$P(D) = f(LC, BC, PC, NC), \tag{3.1}$$

where

$P(D)$ = the risk of default,

LC = the loan characteristics at time of closing,

BC = the borrower(s) characteristics at time of closing,

PC = the property characteristics at time of closing,

NC = the neighborhood characteristics at time of closing.

The loan, borrower, property, and neighborhood characteristics provide measures of the economic burden of the loan payments, the level of acquired equity and its rate of growth, and the expectations of the future market values of the mortgaged property. The model captures some of the effects of borrower characteristics related to largely unpredictable personal problems such as job loss, martial problems, or illness and death. It is expected, however, that a large, unexplained random component of default risk will remain in the model because of the incidence of these personal problems.

As the economic burden of loan repayments increases, the probability that the borrower will be unable or unwilling to make the contracted monthly payments increases. The most obvious indicator of economic burden is the ratio of the monthly loan repayment to the borrower's monthly income. Lending institutions are generally careful to grant only those loans whose terms are structured so that this ratio is not unreasonably high at the time the loan is granted. The income per household member and the net wealth of the borrower are also included as measures of economic burden; the larger the value of these variables, the lesser the economic burden.[4] Even so, the borrower's income may decrease in the future or his future expenditures on other items (including property-related expenses) may increase to a point where the monthly installments cannot be paid. For this reason, characteristics of the borrower and the property that could be expected to relate to future income potential and future expense levels are analyzed along with several measures of economic burden.

As the borrower increases his or her equity in the property, the potential loss of wealth from foreclosure proceedings following a serious default increases. The borrower should, therefore, make greater efforts to avoid possible foreclosure action, and the probability of default on the mortgage should decrease as equity increases. The equity in the property is directly related to the size of the down payment, the maturity period, and the age of the loan. Loans with high down payments require the borrower to have more equity unless there are also second mortgages. Loans with longer maturity periods build equity more slowly than those with shorter maturities; the age of the loan relative to its maturity period is used to measure this effect.

If the market value of a mortgaged property falls during the life of the mortgage, the owner's equity may also fall. If the decline in value exceeds the sum of the initial down payment and past principal payments, there may be little incentive for the borrower to continue loan repayments. Unless the market value is expected to increase in the future, the borrower may decide to default on the loan and move elsewhere.

The level and stability of market value bear directly on possible loss should a mortgage become delinquent or enter foreclosure proceedings. The higher the level of the market value relative to the loan amount, the smaller the risk of loss. The larger the uncertainty about any given market value, the greater the risk of loss. At the time of the mortgage application, the lender must predict the level and stability of the subject property's market value over the expected life of the mortgage. Although the expected life of the mortgage is approximately half the maturity period, it is still difficult to predict market value over this period. The lender must rely on information on the age, type and condition of the property and neighborhood to anticipate changes in market value over the life of the mortgage. In particular, trends in population, income and property values in the neighborhood may indicate the value of a mortgage applicant's property in the future. Unfortunately, data on these neighborhood factors was unavailable at the time the loan was made because of the large number of years covered by the MLS sample.[5] However, two measures of neighborhood characteristics have been included: the change in neighborhood population and the change in neighborhood income between 1969 and 1976.

The risk-of-default model may indicate whether property age and the age of housing stock in the surrounding neighborhood are valid indicators of potential risk of loss.

As reported in Table 2.2, personal factors, such as job loss, marital problems, and illness or death, are also important causes of mortgage default. However, it is very difficult to predict these events at the time of the lending decision. A number of variables are included to account for some of these possibilities. The age of the borrower at the time of loan closing is such a variable. Because there is some documented evidence indicating that adults pass through age-specific periods of inner crisis, age intervals have been defined to test whether delinquency risk is associated with these periods of crisis.[6] One period of crisis usually develops between 28 and 33 years of age; another develops between the ages of 40 and 45. Because the model is designed to predict default on the basis of information available at the time of closing, the borrower's age at the time of loan closing, rather than at the time of default, is used to construct the series of age variables. One consequence of using the age at the time of closing may be a low association between risk and the age of the borrower.

In addition, the model includes the borrower's marital status, whether or not the borrower previously owned a house, self-employment status, and the number of wage earners. The latter two variables are included as measures of the likelihood of a future loss of income. The type of structure and the type of loan (conventional, FHA or VA) are included as a control variable.

The sex of the borrower and variables identifying whether or not the property is located in a neighborhood alleged to be redlined are included to test the objectivity of lending decisions.

Estimation of Default Models for One- to Four-Family Houses

The basic default model is estimated using four different measures of mortgage default. The first three measures, which are based on the active mortgage portfolio, are: the probability that loan payments are sixty or more days delinquent, the number of days a loan is delinquent, and the number of times per year a loan is delinquent sixty or more days. The latter two measure the severity of default. The final measure, the probability of foreclosure, is based on inactive mortgages (those that have been paid or foreclosed).

The model results for the probability of delinquency, the severity of default, and the probability of foreclosure are given below for three regions of New York State. These results cover the largest metropolitan area in the state (New York-Nassau-Suffolk), the metropolitan area surrounding the state's capitol (Albany-Schenectady-Troy), and three other metropolitan areas (Buffalo, Rochester, and Syracuse), combined because of limited observations.

Probability of Delinquency

The results for the model of the probability of delinquency are presented in Appendix C. None of the variables perform consistently across the three regions. Since the coefficient of the variable representing areas alleged to be redlined is statistically insignificant in all three equations, the relationship between risk of loss and these areas illustrated in Table 2.1 must be based on other neighborhood factors such as age of housing stock (Albany-Schenectady-Troy model) and property characteristics that are correlated with location (for example, building condition in New York-Nassau-Suffolk and the three combined upstate regions, or age of the building in the Albany-Schenectady-Troy region). Antiredlining organizations also allege that older neighborhoods are arbitrarily denied adequate mortgage funds, and these results suggest that these apparent inadequacies may be the result of a higher risk of loss associated with older neighborhoods (age-of-housing-stock variable) or older buildings. In the Albany-Schenectady-Troy region, mortgages on properties located in a neighborhood with 50 percent of its housing built before 1940 are nearly twice as likely to be delinquent as are those on properties located in a neighborhood of post-1939 houses.

The three measures of economic burden perform inconsistently across regions. The mortgage-payment-to-income ratio has the positive impact on the likelihood of delinquency that it should have and is statistically significant in the New York-Nassau-Suffolk model. However, it is insignificant in the other two regions and has a negative impact on risk in one of them. Larger values of the other two measures of economic burden (income per capita and net wealth) should reduce the risk of default. This only occurs in the Albany-Schenectady-Troy model, and both coefficients are statistically significant at the 10 percent level.

The models contain two measures of equity: down payment and the relative age of the mortgage. Mortgages with larger down payments are less likely to be delinquent than those with smaller down payments in all three regions, but it is statistically significant (10 percent level) in only one (New York-Nassau-Suffolk).

The dummy variables measuring the relative age of the mortgage perform best in the New York-Nassau-Suffolk region. The coefficients are small when the mortgage is new, increase as the loan ages, begin decreasing when the loan's age is about 20 percent of its maturity, and continue to decrease as the loan approaches maturity. The annual increment to equity becomes large only after the mortgage age is equal to approximately 20 percent of the maturity. The highest risk of delinquency occurs when the loan's age is equal to 15–25 percent of the maturity period. For a twenty-year loan, this corresponds to a loan age of three to five years; for a thirty-year loan, the highest risk interval is between four and a half and seven and a half years. The delinquency rate on loans within this time interval is 2.8 percentage points higher than the rate for loans that are at least 50 percent matured. This increase is quite high when compared to an overall delinquency rate in that sample of 2.9 percent. Nearly all the coefficients for the relative-age variables are statistically significant at either the 5 or 10 percent level.

Although the coefficients for the relative-age variables follow a similar pattern in the other two regions, none are statistically significant in the Albany-Schenectady-Troy region and only one is significant in the other region.

Buildings in less than good condition at the time of closing are more likely to be delinquent than are buildings judged to be in good condition in all three regions.[7] The coefficient of this variable is statistically significant in the New York-Nassau-Suffolk and combined upstate region. Buildings in less than good condition are more likely to deteriorate further and decline in market value than are buildings in good condition. Such buildings increase the chance of delinquency by 60 percent: from 2.9 percent to 4.5 percent in the case of an average mortgage in the New York-Nassau-Suffolk region.

The building-age variables give inconsistent results in the three regions. Older buildings (especially 20 to 29 and 40 to 49 years old) are significantly more likely to be delinquent in the Albany-Schenectady-Troy region, but they (especially 10 to 19 and 50 or more years old) are less likely to be delinquent in the New York-Nassau-Suffolk region. In both cases, the effect of building age is substantial, leading to 60–100 percent shifts in the average likelihood of delinquency. The results are mixed in the combined upstate region, and all the coefficients are statistically insignificant.

Personal characteristics of the applicant at the time of closing have little, if any, relationship to the likelihood of delinquency. Marital status, prior home-owning experience, self-employment, and multiple wage earners are not significantly related to risk of loss in any of the three regions. The borrower's age is also generally unrelated to the likelihood of delinquency with two exceptions: older borrowers (over 50 years of age) in the New York-Nassau-Suffolk region are less likely to be delinquent and 30- to 39-year-old borrowers in the combined upstate region are more likely to be delinquent.[8]

Mortgages on two- to four-family houses have a positive and statistically significant effect on the probability of delinquency in the New York-Nassau-Suffolk region; namely, mortgages on these houses are 70 percent more likely to be delinquent than are mortgages on single-family houses. The model results indicate that reliance on the rental income in two- to four-family houses to meet mortgage payments increases the risk of delinquency. This result probably occurs because of the impact of vacancies on rental income. The increased risk may also reflect the impact of nonowner occupancy. Unfortunately, the MLS data do not contain information on whether the mortgaged property is owner occupied.

Federally assisted (FHA and VA) mortgages are more likely to be delinquent than are conventional mortgages in all three regions. In the Albany-Schenectady-Troy and New York-Nassau-Suffolk regions, the effects are large (50–100 percent higher likelihood of delinquency) and statistically significant. An analysis of covariance was performed for the New York-Nassau-Suffolk region to test whether the coefficients of the rest of the variables included in this delinquency model are different for federal (FHA and VA) mortgages and conventional mortgages. The test indicated that the difference in the coefficients is not statistically significant, thus justifying the use of FHA and VA dummy variables rather than separate delinquency models for the two classes of mortgages.

The coefficient of the dummy variable indicating that the borrower is a woman is negative and statistically insignificant in the only region with sufficient variation to include this variable. Finally, the two variables measuring neighborhood changes in the seven years prior to the mortgage loan survey have inconsistent signs across the three regions and are generally statistically insignificant.

Severity of Delinquency
Two measures of the severity of mortgage delinquency are used as dependent variables: the number of days a mortgage was delinquent (duration of delinquency) at the time of MLS sampling, and the number

of times a mortgage has been delinquent sixty days or more during its history divided by the number of years since its closing (frequency of delinquency).[9]

It is important to note the differences underlying the two models of delinquency severity. Factors contributing to delinquency risk that could be single, temporary occurrences may better explain the duration of a specific delinquency than the frequency of delinquencies. Examples are illness and job loss. On the other hand, factors that remain in effect over a lengthy period of time may explain the frequency of delinquency better than the duration of a single delinquency. Examples are most property- and neighborhood-related variables.

Models of estimates of the severity of delinquency are presented in Appendix C for the three regions. These results parallel those for the models of the probability of delinquency with only a few exceptions. The most important difference is that the severity models add support to the bankers' view that mortgages on properties located in neighborhoods alleged to be redlined or containing older buildings are more risky. In the combined upstate region, the frequency of delinquency in neighborhoods alleged to be redlined is 3.69 times its value in other neighborhoods. The age-of-housing-stock variable also indicates that older neighborhoods have substantially more severe delinquencies than newer ones in the New York-Nassau-Suffolk region (frequency model) as well as the Albany-Schenectady-Troy region (duration and probability models).

Both severity models indicate that multiple-earner borrowers have significantly higher risks of loss than single-earner households in the New York-Nassau-Suffolk region. In addition, federally assisted mortgages do not have more severe delinquencies than conventional ones. Finally, prior ownership has a surprisingly positive and significant correlation with the measure of duration of delinquency in the Albany Schenectady-Troy region.

As in the model of the probability of delinquency, almost all of the coefficients of the borrower's age variables are statistically insignificant. When the two severity models are reestimated using borrower's age at the time of sampling, the coefficients provide mixed support for the adult-crisis hypothesis. In the model of delinquency duration for the New York-Nassau-Suffolk region, the coefficients of the adult-crisis periods of 28 to 33 years and of 40 to 45 years are positive and statistically significant at the 6 and 11 percent levels, respectively. All other age coefficients are smaller and statistically insignificant. In the model of delinquency frequency for the same region, the largest positive coefficients are again found in the adult-crisis age periods, but none of these are statistically significant. The signs and statistical significance of the remainining variables are not altered by this reestimation. The results for the other two regions did not yield any statistically significant coefficients for these variables.

Probability of Foreclosure

Models of the probability of foreclosure for mortgages on one- to four-family houses in the three regions are presented in Appendix C. The models are estimated using loans from the inactive files of the mutual savings banks included in the MLS.

Interpretation of a foreclosure model is hampered by the wide range of policies that mortgage lenders may use in foreclosure action. In some instances, the lender may considerably delay foreclosure proceedings in the hope or expectation that mortgage repayments will resume. In other cases, foreclosure action may proceed quite swiftly. Whether action is swift or slow will quite often be related to the value of the property relative to the mortgage's outstanding balance. Although legal fees and lost interest charges are not negligible items, a mortgage lender is unlikely to suffer large monetary losses through foreclosure when the property's value is relatively high. In such instances, a lender may foreclose mortgages that have serious delinquencies as quickly as is legally possible. When the property value is lower than the outstanding balance, the lender may select a strategy of postponing foreclosure proceedings in the hope of working out a settlement or renegotiating the mortgage with the borrower. Each lender may have a different policy regarding the decision to foreclose on a mortgage. In addition, many lenders prefer to partially write down a bad loan than to take a large, immediate foreclosure loss. In this way, the total loss may be spread over several accounting periods. Therefore, foreclosure is not a good indicator of mortgage loss because equally bad losses may be treated differently across banks. A model of the probability of foreclosure thus may indicate differentials in bank policy, as well as those characteristics of the mortgage that are associated with severe default problems.

Another caveat is the impossibility of defining an adequate variable measuring the level of acquired equity in the case of mortgages that were satisfied but not foreclosed. The lack of a measure of acquired equity in the foreclosure model may bias the coefficients of some of the other variables included in the model.

The foreclosure models indicate that risk of loss is positively associated with areas alleged to be redlined in the Albany-Schenectady-Troy region. The coefficient is very significant. The likelihood of foreclosure is more than doubled when the property is located in the neighborhoods alleged to be redlined. Foreclosure is also more likely to occur on properties located in older neighborhoods in the combined upstate region. Mortgages on properties in a neighborhood with 50 percent of its housing built before 1940 are a third more likely to be foreclosed than mortgages on houses in new neighborhoods.

The other variables in the foreclosure models are generally consistent with the results reported for the various delinquency models. Some interesting differences do occur. None of the variables of economic burden have statistically significant coefficients. In the Albany-Schenectady-Troy region, lower-quality buildings are surprisingly less likely to be foreclosed. An adequate explanation cannot be offered.

Married households in the New York-Nassau-Suffolk region are more likely to have their mortgages foreclosed. However, multiple-unit properties are less likely to be foreclosed in this region than are single-family properties.

Estimation of Default Models for Multifamily Buildings

Although the general model of default is applicable to mortgages on multifamily properties, many of the explanatory variables used in the one- to four-family analysis must be redefined or reinterpreted for use in the multifamily default models.

The only measure of economic burden available for multifamily buildings is the ratio of mortgage repayments to the net income derived from the property. Net income is defined as gross rental income less real estate taxes, utilities, and operating and maintenance expenses.

Unlike one- to four-family houses, mortgages on multifamily properties are often of fairly short duration (ten to fifteen years), and repayment schedules may not provide for complete amortization of the loan. Refinancing at regular intervals is common. As a result, a measure of acquired equity, such as the relative maturity variables, cannot be defined for the multifamily model. This is a serious constraint on the specification of the default model for mortgages on multifamily properties.

The MLS includes loan data on the most recent refinancing of the mortgage. In most cases, the mortgage had been refinanced in the absence of any property transaction. As a result, there is no meaningful, consistent measure of down payment. Instead, the difference between the appraised value and the mortgage amount per dwelling unit is used as a measure of equity.

The loan-to-value ratio is another measure of equity employed in the multifamily analysis; it indicates the degree of leveraging and is a common measure of expected loan risk.[10]

The multifamily models use the same measures of expected future property value as the one- to four-family default models.

The MLS contains no information on characteristics of the borrower for most multifamily properties because such properties are usually owned by corporations.

Because there are only a few FHA and VA mortgages on multifamily properties in the MLS sample, they have been excluded from this analysis.

A dummy variable indicating the presence of commercial use in the structure is included in the multifamily default models to test whether the presence of such activity increases or decreases the probability of severity of default. Because the market for storefront commercial space in New York has appeared to decline over the period covered by the MLS mortgages, owners of residential properties containing some commercial space may have experienced difficulty renting such space. If this is true, default risk should be higher on these properties.

Mortgage default risk on multifamily properties should be associated with the level of managerial expertise of those operating the property. It is, of course, very difficult to quantify such expertise. Dummy variables indicating the number of units in the property are included in the default models to test whether larger buildings, which are more likely to have full-time or professional managers, are less likely than smaller buildings to experience high levels of default. The size categories are 5 to 24 units, 25 to 48 units, 49 to 72 units, 73 to 96 units, and more than 96 units. These variables may also capture other effects, such as the sensitivity of the rent roll to vacancies or differences in consumer demand for properties of different sizes.

Variables indicating whether the property is located in an area alleged to be redlined, recent change in neighborhood population per capita, and recent change in neighborhood median income are also included in the multifamily models.

Four models of mortgage default on multifamily properties are presented. The first three are based on a sample of active mortgages from the portfolios of all mutual savings banks with branches in Bronx, Kings, and Queens counties. They measure, respectively, the probability of delinquency, the duration of delinquency, and the frequency of delinquency. The fourth model measures the probability of foreclosure and is based on a sample of mortgages from the banks' inactive files. There are fewer multifamily properties in upstate New York, and as a result, the MLS contains too few to estimate any default relationships there.

The results of the four models are presented in Appendix C. These models also provide weak support for the position that mortgages in the neighborhoods alleged to be redlined are more risky than ones on properties in other locations. The likelihood of foreclosure is significantly higher in these neighborhoods. Although the coefficient of the age-of-housing-stock variable is not significant in any of these four models, it is large, negative, and nearly statistically significant in the model of the probability of delinquency. This indicates that mortgages in older neighborhoods are less risky, a result inconsistent with the contention of mortgage lenders.

Very few of the remaining variables are statistically significant at the 10 or 5 percent level. The variable of economic burden has a positive association with default in all four models, but it is statistically significant only in the probability-of-delinquency equation. The sign of the coefficient of initial equity is inconsistent and is surprisingly positive in the case of statistical significance (probability-of-foreclosure model). The loan-to-value-ratio variable has a positive coefficient in all four models, indicating that higher ratio mortgages are more risky, and is statistically significant in two models (probability of delinquency and delinquency duration). The only other variable with a statistically significant coefficient is building condition in the probability-of-delinquency model. The positive coefficient (in all four models) indicates that mortgages on lower-quality buildings are more likely to enter default.

Summary

The geographic variation in delinquency rates is closely associated with allegations that certain neighborhoods are redlined. As lenders frequently contend, most of the neighborhoods alleged to be redlined have higher-than-average default rates.

The MLS provides information on the perceptions of lenders as to what changes in borrower, property, or neighborhood characteristics may have contributed to defaults involving foreclosure proceedings. Borrower changes are the most frequent response, followed by property and neighborhood changes. Lenders perceive financial difficulties and marital problems as the major sources of borrower-related factors contributing to default. Deterioration of the structure is easily the most frequently cited property-related factor leading to default. Lenders tend to classify all neighborhood-related factors into a category of general decline.

Multivariate models of mortgage default are also estimated for several metropolitan areas in New York State. In general, these models view the probability and severity of mortgage default as a function of the economic burden of the mortgage payments, the amount of equity the borrower has accumulated in the property, the expected future value of the property, and the characteristics of the borrower. For one- to four-family houses and mortgages on multifamily buildings, four models of default are estimated. the probability of delinquency, the duration of delinquency, the frequency of delinquency, and the probability of foreclosure.

In general, the default models indicate that the economic burden, equity, and building condition have important effects on the risk of default. Mortgages with larger economic burdens (higher loan payments relative to income) are more likely to experience a default. Similarly, the larger the initial equity, the less likely the mortgage is to experience default. Although default risk rises during the first years of a mortgage, it begins to decline steadily after approximately the fifth year as acquired equity accumulates. Finally, mortgages on buildings in poor condition are more likely to encounter payment problems during their history than are buildings in good condition.

The default models provide inconsistent evidence concerning the relationship between default risk and the age of the housing stock within a neighborhood. In most of the models, the risk of default is higher in older neighborhoods, and this relationship is statistically significant in at least one model in each of the three regions studied (Albany-Schenectady-Troy, New York-Nassau-Suffolk, and Buffalo-Rochester-Syracuse).

Another debated measure of default risk is the age of the property being mortgaged. In the New York-Nassau-Suffolk region, the age of the property does not have a statistically significant effect on the probability and severity of default with one exception. Mortgages on one- to four-family houses that are 10 to 19 or over 50 years old have a lower probability of delinquency than do mortgages on new houses. On the other hand, new houses in the Albany-Schenectady-Troy region have lower levels of default than older houses. The results are mixed for the other upstate region.

The initial relationship between delinquency rates and property location (that is, higher rates in allegedly redlined neighborhoods) is considerably weaker in the multivariate models. If the multivariate models adequately control for the objective factors determining high risk of default, the crude measure of property location should play a smaller role. In fact, property location is statistically significant in only three of the fifteen models, and in each case the coefficient indicates that risk is higher in allegedly redlined neighborhoods than in other neighborhoods.

In general, the results reported in this chapter are not inconsistent with the lenders' position that apparent mortgage deficiencies in certain neighborhoods are due to the higher risk of loss on loans in those areas. However, the multivariate analysis of default risk suggests that (1) many factors other than location may be responsible for the high delinquency rates that are occurring in these areas, and (2) lenders can develop techniques for evaluating risk of loss using information specific to the property and the applicant without recourse to crude neighborhood-level rules of thumb. The development of such credit evaluation models requires more research, and this chapter provides the foundation for their evolution.[11]

3
Flow of Funds

Criticism of mortgage-lending practices has focused on the amounts of lending in specific neighborhoods. A frequent assertion is that the demand for funds in a neighborhood exceeds the supply. This relationship between demand and supply has become the central issue in the redlining debate. Even though data limitations preclude the estimation of the relationship between supply and demand, a theoretical model is developed in this chapter because most studies of redlining have focused on this relationship. The theoretical model serves to highlight the inadequacies of these other analyses. An alternative model of the quantity of mortgage funds supplied by a subset of lenders can be used to analyze the redlining allegations. This model is estimated for conventional mortgages on one- to four-family houses, federally assisted mortgages on one- to four-family houses, and conventional mortgages on multifamily buildings.

Demand and Supply Model

Information on the flow of mortgage funds is available throughout the country (although in considerably less detail than in New York State) and has been used to support various positions in the redlining debate. However, none of these analyses have employed an appropriate model and estimation technique. In fact, many of these studies merely map the geographic distribution of the flow of mortgage funds. Because these previous studies fail to incorporate all the various factors delineated in the demand and supply model described in this section, their results should receive little weight in policy formation.

Demand for residential mortgage credit depends on the dollar volume of transactions and mortgage prices. More specifically, demand rises as the volume of transactions increases and falls as mortgage prices increase. (Higher interest rates, shorter maturities, and lower loan-to-value ratios are all elements of higher mortgage prices.) Transactions are, in turn, a function of mortgage prices, average turnover rates, income, and changes in income and population. Population changes should reflect the net effect of new construction, mergers, conversions, demolition, and modifications in average household size. Transactions are expected to decline as mortgage prices increase. More transactions should occur in areas that have higher turnover rates and more residential buildings or are experiencing greater changes in income and population.

The supply of mortgage credit depends on mortgage prices, risk of loss on the investment, portfolio factors, and the geographic area serviced by the bank. The supply of mortgage credit depends on mortgage prices, risk of loss on the investment, portfolio factors, and the geographic area serviced by the bank. The supply should increase as mortgage prices increase and decrease when the risk of loss rises. Consideration of risk in portfolio development should increase geographical diversification, but service-area considerations might lead to a geographic concentration of lending near branch offices.

Mortgage price is composed of three elements: interest rate, maturity, and loan-to-value ratio. Each element is a function of the other two, as well as of the risk of loss. Because the system of equations is closed by equating supply and demand, only two of these three price elements need be explicitly modeled. The third price variable is determined by the remaining equations. Because the loan-to-value ratio may depend on the assets and income of the borrower, the loan-to-value ratio also includes the average price of residential buildings, the percentage of neighborhood households with high incomes, and the per capita income.

The mortgage supply and price equations also include the racial composition, age of housing, and geographic location of the neighborhood, in an attempt to provide some insight into mortgage-lending practices as they relate to the redlining debate.

This system of six simultaneous equations is described in Table 3.1. Inspection of each equation shows that all are overidentified; therefore, two-stage least squares could be used to provide consistent estimates of the parameters.[1] The mortgage-demand, mortgage-supply, transactions, and mortgage-stock variables should be deflated by the dollar value of the housing stock (or the number of buildings if mort-

Table 3.1
Flow-of-funds model

Equations

(3.1)	MD	$= f$ (T, INT, MAT, LTV)
(3.2)	MS	$= g$ (INT, MAT, LTV, RISK, STOCK, LOC, OLD, PNW, DPNW)
(3.3)	T	$= h$ (INT, MAT, LTV, HW, MOB, PHI, PCINC, DPCINC, PCWEL, DPCWEL, DPOP)
(3.4)	MAT	$= l$ (INT, LTV, RISK, LOC, OLD, PNW, DPNW)
(3.5)	LTV	$= m$ (INT, MAT, RISK, PHI, PCINC, AVGVAL, LOC, OLD, PNW, DPNW)
(3.6)	MD	$=$ MS

Endogenous Variables

MD = mortgage funds (dollars) demanded in year t for census tract i[a]

MS − mortgage funds (dollars) supplied in year t to census tract i[a]

T = dollar value of transactions in year t and census tract i[a]

INT = average interest rate in year t and census tract i

MAT = average maturity in year t and census tract i

LTV = average loan-to-value ratio in year t and census tract i

Exogenous Variables

LOC = several dummy variables that identify specific neighborhoods

OLD = fraction of buildings built in 1939 or earlier

PNW = percent of population that is nonwhite

DPNW = change in the percent of population that is nonwhite over a recent period of years

RISK = several measures of risk of loss on an investment in census tract i (e.g., incidence of serious fires, property tax delinquencies per building, and mortgage delinquency rates)

STOCK = the stock of residential mortgages in census tract i at the end of year $t - 1$ (four separate measures based on type of financing and structure)[a]

BLDG = number of residential buildings in census tract i

HW = fraction of households that are husband-wife households between 30 and 44 years of age

MOB = measure of average turnover of buildings based on household mobility (per building)

PHI = percent of households with high incomes in census tract i

PCINC = per capita income in census tract i

DPCINC = change in per capita income in census tract i over some recent period

PCWEL = per capita welfare payments in census tract i (RISK also includes this variable)

Table 3.1 (cont.)

DPCWEL	= change in per capita welfare payments in census tract i over some recent period (RISK also includes this variable)
DPOP	= change in the population of census tract i since 1960 divided by the average population over the period (RISK also includes this variable)
AVGVAL	= average selling price of property in census tract i in year t

a. When estimating the equations, these variables are divided by the number of buildings (BLDG) because the dollar value of buildings is not available.

gage-stock variables are not available) in any estimation to ensure that all variables are measured in comparable units.

As shown in Table 3.1, mortgage demand and supply, interest rate, maturity, loan-to-value ratio, and property transactions are endogenous (their values are determined by the model). The remaining variables are exogenous to the model. That property transactions are endogenous is important because this means that mortgage demand is not measured by the actual amount of transactions within a census tract (which is probably affected by the supply of mortgage financing). Rather, mortgage demand is measured by the amount of transactions that would occur in the absence of any artificial constraints on mortgage supply.

Limitations of Available Data

The New York State data on residential mortgage lending are reported in four categories: conventional loans on one- to four-family houses, federally assisted loans on one- to four-family houses, conventional loans on multifamily (over four housing units) buildings, and federally assisted mortgages on multifamily buildings. Outstanding mortgages, new mortgages, foreclosures over the last five years, and current delinquencies are reported in dollars and numbers of loans for each of the four categories. In addition, the average terms (interest rate, maturity, and loan-to-value ratio) of each type of new mortgage are reported.[2]

Table 3.2 summarizes the data on property transactions and the new mortgage loans and outstanding mortgage balances of lenders for one- to four-family and multifamily buildings. Because the average loan-to-

Table 3.2
Number of buildings, property transactions, new mortgage loans, and outstanding mortgage balances by type of structure and county

Building Type by County	Number of Buildings	Property Transactions, 1975[a]		New Mortgages, 1975[b]				Outstanding Mortgage Balances, 1975[b]			
				Conventional		FHA-VA		Conventional		FHA-VA	
		Number	Value (thousands of $)	Number	Value (thousands of $)	Number	Value (thousands of $)	Number	Value (thousands of $)	Number	Value (thousands of $)
1- to 4-family buildings											
Bronx	55,761	2,758	96,581	141	4,944	20	650	4,727	122,514	2,378	76,745
Kings	200,221	9,624	307,366	1,352	48,668	285	9,890	27,580	1,119,695	16,627	276,356
Queens	266,772	11,157	443,977	1,546	53,786	743	24,220	34,959	809,048	29,300	568,708
Multifamily buildings											
Bronx	14,174	1,384	88,033	32	4,123	1	54	2,815	1,321,763	34	25,491
Kings	42,489	2,772	147,802	177	10,598	36	2,049	5,337	1,564,662	1,554	72,024
Queens	14,084	765	145,318	49	9,761	33	1,503	1,479	1,087,358	764	91,873

a. Estimated from computerized assessor's files.
b. Based on lender reports under New York State Banking Department Supervisory Procedure G-107, Appendix 8. Only own-serviced mortgages are reported under this procedure.

value ratio in the sample is 65 percent and institutional lenders (commercial banks, savings banks, and savings and loan associations) hold approximately 70 percent of the nation's mortgage loans,[3] these lenders might be expected to finance approximately 46 percent of the dollar value of transactions. The lenders in the sample supplied only 13.9 percent of the dollar value of transactions in 1975.

According to Table 3.3, reporting lenders in Albany, Erie, and Onondaga counties provided a larger share of the financing for transactions than they did in Bronx, Kings, and Queens counties.[4] It is, however, substantially below the expected figure of 46 percent. In Albany County, the reporting lenders financed 19.9 percent of the dollar value of transactions; in Erie County, they financed 20.6 percent; and in Onondaga County, 25.9 percent.

These discrepancies are partially due to the exclusion of some types of lenders. The data only report the lenders who properly reported their activities to the New York State Banking Department. Several state-regulated lenders are absent because their computerized files on lending information contained too many errors to be processed. Federally regulated commercial banks and savings and loan associations are also excluded because they are not required to comply with the state regulation requiring the disclosure of the detailed lending data.

Nevertheless, the lenders who provided usable information are an important source of new mortgage funds: in 1975, they supplied over $329 million in mortgage monies for 11,150 properties in Albany, Bronx, Erie, Kings, Onondaga, and Queens counties. However, the demand and supply model depicted in Table 3.1 should not be estimated using these incomplete data because a meaningful interpretation of the coefficients of the system of simultaneous equations would not be possible. Other studies of the flow of funds in New York have been based on an even smaller sample of reporting lenders, an important limitation on the results of these studies. The next section describes an alternative model designed to explain the behavior of the reporting banks.

Two other practical constraints on estimating the demand and supply model are the existence of credit rationing when the New York usury ceiling is binding and the relatively small variations in mortgage prices across space during the same year. When credit rationing occurs, demand probably exceeds supply, and Equation 3.6 is probably not satisfied. Therefore, even if complete mortgage-lending data were available, only the supply equation could be estimated.

Table 3.3
Property transactions, new mortgage loans, and outstanding mortgage balances by type of structure for Albany, Erie, and Onondaga counties, 1975

| Building Type by County | Property Transactions, 1975[a] | | New Mortgages, 1975[b] | | | | Outstanding Mortgage Balances, 1975[b] | | | |
| | | | Conventional | | FHA-VA | | Conventional | | FHA-VA | |
	Number	Value (thousands of $)	Number	Value (thousands of $)	Number	Value (thousands of $)	Number	Value (thousands of $)	Number	Value (thousands of $)
1- to 4-family buildings										
Albany	3,171	96,248	697	16,230	143	3,051	10,899	156,027	4,328	66,094
Erie	10,635	333,041	2,167	48,051	1,238	22,907	32,546	459,404	31,440	302,766
Onondaga	7,547	208,611	2,011	49,513	417	8,378	19,332	303,900	14,370	150,561
Multifamily buildings										
Albany	24	16,431	6	3,172	0	0	324	185,395	13	179
Erie	62	34,374	8	4,705	0	0	234	147,725	7	387
Onondaga	44	25,081	8	2,704	0	0	213	71,542	11	1,176

a. Estimated from transactions data provided by Teela Market Surveys.
b. Based on lender reports under New York Banking Department Supervisory Procedure G-107, Appendix 8. Only own-serviced mortgages are reported under this procedure.

The Quantity Model for Bronx, Kings and Queens

Although a demand and supply model cannot be estimated using available data, it is possible to analyze the quantity of mortgage funds provided by reporting lenders. This quantity depends on the mortgage demand in an area, as well as on those factors that normally enter the supply equation. In the absence of complete data on area-specific mortgage demand, the variables that affect demand (see Table 3.1) are used to estimate this alternative model. The signs of these variables for the quantity model should be the same as those for the demand equation. The remaining variables (from the supply equation in Table 3.1) should have the signs predicted for their role in a supply equation. The quantity model is:

$$Q = m \text{ (INT, MAT, LTV, T, RISK, STOCK, OLD, PNW,}$$
$$\text{DPNW)} \qquad (3.7)$$

where Q is the quantity of mortgage funds provided by reporting lenders to a census tract in a given year and the other variables are as defined in Table 3.1. Both Q and STOCK are divided by the number of buildings to ensure consistency in varaible definitions across the equation.[5]

All three mortgage terms (interest rate, maturity, and loan-to-value ratio) are included as variables because lenders may use them to compensate for risk differentials. For example, higher interest rates or shorter maturities may accompany mortgages that have higher risks of loss.

Bronx, Kings, and Queens counties are divided into two parts: neighborhoods that are alleged to be redlined and neighborhoods that have not been alleged to be redlined. The information on allegations of redlining is based on the responses of community organizations and published reports. The model is estimated separately for each neighborhood category.

If comparison of the results indicates that approximately the same model operates in areas that are alleged to be redlined and those that are not, it will be estimated on the pooled sample from both areas with dummy variables identifying each neighborhood. If neighborhoods that are alleged to be redlined have significant positive coefficients in the pooled equation, the model results will be inconsistent with the redlining allegations. On the other hand, if these areas have significant negative coefficients, the results will be ambiguous because there are two plausible explanations: redlining may exist or demand for mortgages may simply be lacking in these areas. The latter explanation cannot be eliminated because complete information on mortgage demand in the three counties is lacking.

If the separate estimates of the quantity model for the two types of areas do not justify a pooled approach, the coefficients from the two estimations should be compared. There are two explanations for the coefficients of the same variable having significantly different signs in allegedly redlined areas and nonredlined areas. First, the risk of loss may be a nonlinear function of the variables. In this case, the variables that measure risk of loss should be more important in the model estimated on the allegedly redlined areas if the properties in these communities are subject to a higher risk of loss than properties in the rest of the city. For example, the number of serious fires per building should have a significantly greater negative sign in the model estimated for the allegedly redlined areas than in the one estimated for the other areas. Second, if the relationship between lending and the risk of loss is linear, the existence of different coefficients in the two types of areas is evidence that the same risk of loss is arbitrarily assigned a different evaluation in one of the areas. If the redlining allegations are correct, the same risk of loss will likely be given greater weight in the neighborhood alleged to be redlined than in other neighborhoods. In this case, the different coefficients are evidence of redlining. These two competing explanations for the same empirical result cannot be distinguished by examination of the relative values of the coefficients.

In addition, the separate estimates of the model can be used to predict the amount of mortgage lending by reporting lenders in both areas. Comparison of these predictions provides valuable information that bears on the redlining debate. If redlining is practiced by the reporting banks, the model estimated for the allegedly redlined areas should predict less lending in all locations than the model estimated for the nonredlined areas. Any other pattern of predictions from the two equations would be at least partially inconsistent with the redlining allegation and, as such, could not be unambiguously interpreted.

In the quantity model (as in the model depicted in Table 3.1), the risk of loss on an investment at any given location is measured indirectly using several variables that capture the likelihood that a specific property is exposed to various risks associated with the general characteristics of the census tract in which it is located. The following characteristics are included in the risk measures: the incidence of housing code violations, vacant buildings, property tax arrearages, and serious fires; mortgage foreclosure and delinquency rates; change in per capita income; per capita welfare payments and change in per capita welfare payments; and population change. Larger values for all these measures, except change in per capita income and population, indicate that the properties in those census tracts are subject to a higher risk of loss, which is a valid explanation for less mortgage lending. Larger values for change in per capita income and population indicate less risk of loss (that is, higher income and greater demand for housing, which is a valid reason for more mortgage lending in these neighborhoods.

In general, these variables are defined to measure the level of risk at some time prior to the year covered by the mortgage-lending data and the change in that measure of risk between the two points in time. Both level and change variables are important because risk is a function of the incidence of a particular characteristic (for example, the incidence of vacant buildings) and the degree of uncertainty about its future level (for example, whether the incidence of vacant buildings has been increasing or decreasing in the last few years).

Estimates for Conventional Mortgages on One- to Four-Family Houses
Estimates of the quantity model for conventional mortgages on one- to four-family houses in Bronx, Kings, and Queens counties are presented in Appendix C. The model has been estimated separately for neighborhoods alleged to be redlined and other neighborhoods. The neighborhoods alleged to be redlined consist of South Bronx, Central Brooklyn, Crown Heights, East Flatbush, Park Slope, and Southeast Queens. The other neighborhoods are all other parts of Bronx, Kings, and Queens counties with the exception of Northeast Kings, which includes Bedford-Stuyvesant, Brownsville, Bushwick, East New York, Greenpoint, and Williamsburg. Northeast Kings is excluded from the analysis because, although it is not alleged to be redlined, many of its neighborhoods have a housing market that nearly everyone agrees needs direct government assistance. Lenders are not expected to lend in Northeast Kings without government assistance because of the high risk of loss.

The equation for the allegedly redlined areas explains 68 percent of the variation in conventional mortgage lending per building on one- to four-family houses; the equation for the other neighborhoods explains only 25 percent of the variation in the same variable. Both equations are highly statistically significant.

In view of the preceding discussion, it is important to determine if a single pooled estimate based on observations from both of the two mutually exclusive locations would be superior to the two separate estimates. The appropriate statistical test compares the pooled estimate with the combined performance of the two separate estimates. On the basis of the resulting statistic, $F(34,682) = 2.28$, the hypothesis that the two equations are the same may be rejected with a less than 1 percent chance of being incorrect.

The results of the separate estimates indicate that conventional mortgage lending on one- to four-family houses (per building) increases with the dollar value of transactions (per building) involving such houses. Although this relationship is statistically significant in both areas, transactions have a larger impact on lending in the allegedly redlined neighborhoods. A change in the transactions variable increases lending by reporting institutions in the allegedly redlined neighborhoods by an amount five times as much as in the other neighborhoods. (The means and standard deviations of the transactions variable are comparable in the two areas.)

The coefficients of several other variables reflect the differences between the two areas. The stock of conventional mortgages on one- to four-family houses has a positive, large, and statistically significant effect on additional lending of the same type in the allegedly redlined neighborhoods but has virtually no effect in the other neighborhoods. In the allegedly redlined neighborhoods, conventional lending on one- to four-family houses is highest in census tracts where the reporting lenders already have similar mortgages. In the other neighborhoods, slightly more conventional mortgages on one- to four-family houses occur in census tracts where the reporting lenders have conventional mortgages on multifamily buildings.

The only other variables that are statistically significant, or nearly so, in both equations are pending housing-code violations per building for one- to four-family buildings in 1972 and the fraction of one- to four-family buildings with fewer pending housing-code violations in 1976 than in 1972. The first variable measures the increase in risk of loss attributable to the poor condition of neighborhood buildings. The second measures an improvement in the condition of neighboring buildings that should reduce the risk of loss. Therefore, the first variable should show a negative relationship with mortgage lending (that is, more pending housing-code violations should lead to less lending) and the second should have a positive relationship with mortgage lending (that is, a decrease in housing-code violations should lead to increased lending). However, this is not the case; they have the opposite relationships.

Examination of the eight other coefficients of housing-code variables in the two equations indicates that only two have the correct sign and are statistically significant. In the allegedly redlined area, lending has increased in census tracts where housing-code violations on multifamily buildings have decreased between 1972 and 1976. In the other neighborhoods lending has declined in census tracts where housing-code violations on one- to four-family houses have increased between 1972 and 1976.

Only one other housing-code-violation variable's coefficient has a sign consistent with the hypothesized relationship between lending and risk of loss, but it is statistically insignificant. Two other coefficients are statistically significant at the 10 percent level, but have signs indicating that lending increases when pending housing-code violations increase.

Most of the housing-code-violation variables have an inconsistent relationship with mortgage lending in both equations. There are two possible explanations. First, the housing code is enforced in a manner that tends to understate the incidence of violations in neighborhoods that contain the lowest-quality housing.[6] Second, the data used to develop these measures probably constitute a weaker measure of violations on one- to four-family buildings than multifamily buildings. In any case, it is more reasonable to conclude that the housing-code-violation variables are poor measures of risk than that lenders prefer to lend in riskier neighborhoods.

Only four of the other risk-of-loss measures are statistically significant in either equation: tax arrearage on one- to four-family buildings in 1972 in the alleged-redlined-neighborhood equation; and per capita welfare payments in 1970, change in per capita welfare payments, and the delinquency rate in the other-neighborhood equation. The relative signs and magnitudes of these coefficients indicate that lenders are more sensitive to the first variable and are less sensitive to the last three variables in the allegedly redlined neighborhoods. Although substantially higher values for the first variable in the allegedly redlined neighborhoods may, in part, explain lenders' greater sensitivity to it, a similar explanation is lacking for the other three variables.

Most of the other risk-of-loss measures (vacant buildings, serious fires) are statistically insignificant. Risk of loss from neighboring buildings may not have been adequately measured because coefficients have signs that are inconsistent with the relationship between risk of loss and lending in each equation and have relative values across equations that are inconsistent with the hypothesis that risk is more important in the allegedly redlined neighborhood.

Only one of the six price coefficients is statistically significant. Although more mortgage funds are provided as the interest rate increases in both locations, the relationship is only statistically significant in the equation for the neighborhoods not alleged to be redlined.[7] It is not clear what signs should be expected in the quantity model because price variables appear in both the supply and demand equations (see Table 3.1). In this case, the supply effect seems to dominate the demand effect. Overinterpretation of the coefficients of the price variables should be avoided, and they may be best viewed as control variables.

Older neighborhoods (as measured by the age of the housing stock in the census tract) receive more mortgages than newer ones in both locations. Although this result contradicts allegations that lenders limit the amount of mortgage funds available to older neighborhoods, both coefficients are statistically insignificant at the 10 percent level.

Conventional mortgage lending on one- to four-family houses declines as the percent of nonwhite residents increases in neighborhoods not alleged to be redlined. The coefficient is large and statistically significant. Mortgage lending per building is 51.4 percent less in a 50 percent nonwhite census tract than in an otherwise equivalent all-white census tract.

On the other hand, lending in the allegedly redlined neighborhoods tends to rise with the percent nonwhite but has a smaller coefficient that is statistically insignificant. However, mortgage lending in the allegedly redlined area is substantially lower in census tracts that have recently undergone racial change, a statistically significant result. A 20 percentage point increase in the nonwhite population during the last four years reduced mortgage lending by $175 per building in the allegedly redlined area compared to the mean value of $293 per building, a 60 percent decline.

The equations have been used to predict the amount of conventional mortgage lending on one- to four-family houses in each of several subareas.[8] If the allegations of redlining are correct, the predictions of mortgage lending based on the alleged-redlined-neighborhood equation should be less than the ones based on the other-neighborhood equation. Table 3.4 summarizes the predicted and actual lending for the reporting banks. Four of the six neighborhoods alleged to be redlined (South Bronx, Crown Heights, East Flatbush, and Southeast Queens) would have had more mortgage lending using the other-neighborhood equation ($11.85 million) than they would have had under their own equation ($6.47 million), or than they actually had ($5.50 million). This result is consistent with the allegation that these four neighborhoods are redlined. However, two other allegedly redlined neighborhoods (Central Brooklyn and Park Slope) received considerably more mortgage funds than they would have received using the other-neighborhood equation ($2.97 million versus $1.59 million). The predicted lending based on the alleged-redlined-neighborhood equation ($2.60 million) is consistent with actual lending in these two neighborhoods.

Furthermore, two of the neighborhoods not alleged to be redlined (South Kings and the rest of Queens County) would receive more mortgage money under the alleged-redlined-neighborhood equation ($90.31 million) than either under their own equation ($84.86 million) or than they actually received ($86.45 million). This result is inconsistent with the redlining allegations. North Bronx and Northeast Kings would receive more funds under the other-neighborhood equation.

A comparison of the predicted amounts of conventional lending derived from the two equations for Central Brooklyn, Park Slope, South Kings, and the rest of Queens indicates that these neighborhoods would receive more funds if they were redlined than if they were not (see the last column in Table 3.4). Because it is highly unlikely that South Kings and the rest of Queens would have received more funds if they were redlined, it is necessary to examine the possibility that some of the allegations are not accurate. If an area that is alleged to be redlined is in fact not redlined, lending in this area would have been incorrectly included in the data base for the alleged-redlined-area equation and might be responsible for the unusual results for South Kings and the rest of Queens. On the basis of a comparison between predicted and actual amounts of mortgage lending, the allegations of redlining in the neighborhoods of Central Brooklyn and Park Slope are probably inaccurate as these neighborhoods are predicted to receive more mortgage funds if they were redlined than if they were not redlined.

Table 3.4
Actual and predicted conventional mortgage lending on 1- to 4-family houses in
Bronx, Kings, and Queens counties, 1975

Locations	Actual (thousands of $)	Predicted from Alleged-Redlined-Area Equation[a] (thousands of $)	Predicted from Other-Areas Equation[b] (thousands of $)	Predicted Lending Ratio[c]
Alleged Redlined Areas				
South Bronx	1,559	1,767	3,184	0.55
Central Brooklyn in Kings	1,121	942	811	1.16
Crown Heights in Kings	313	302	675	0.45
East Flatbush in Kings	1,478	2,296	3,875	0.59
Park Slope in Kings	1,851	1,661	777	2.14
Southeast Queens	2,154	2,100	4,117	0.51
Subtotal	8,476	9,068	13,439	0.67
Other Areas				
North Bronx	3,233	3,885	6,792	0.57
Northeast Kings[d]	3,060	4,182	5,070	0.82
South Kings	40,100	38,047	35,781	1.06
Rest of Queens	46,352	52,265	49,074	1.07
Subtotal	92,745	98,379	96,717	1.02
Total	101,221	107,447	110,156	0.98

a. The first equation (column) in Table C.5, Appendix C (this book).
b. The second equation (column) in Table C.5, Appendix C (this book).
c. This is column 2 divided by column 3.
d. Lending in Northeast Kings has been excluded from both equations in the estimates.

To investigate the possibility of inaccurate allegations, the alleged-redlined-neighborhood equation is re-estimated using a data base that excludes Central Brooklyn and Park Slope. The resulting equation is presented in Appendix C. As before, the hypothesis that this equation is the same for the neighborhoods not alleged to be redlined can be rejected with a less than 5 percent chance of being incorrect, $F(34,658) = 1.64$.

Although the alleged-redlined equation without Central Brooklyn and Park Slope is significantly different from the comparable equation for the neighborhoods not alleged to be redlined, its coefficients are not the same as those when the equation for the allegedly redlined areas includes Central Brooklyn and Park Slope.

For example, in the new equation, the coefficients of the variables for transactions and the stock of conventional mortgages on one- to four-family houses are smaller and no longer statistically significant at the 10-percent level. The interest-rate coefficient is larger and now statistically significant at the 5 percent level. The coefficients of the variables for neighborhood attributes and risk of loss in mortgage lending are more consistent with the a priori hypothesis that areas with higher risks of loss should receive fewer mortgage loans. With Central Brooklyn and Park Slope included, only six of these twenty-two coefficients had signs consistent with this hypothesis, and with them excluded, twelve have consistent signs. In terms of statistical significance, however, there is little change. Both equations have four coefficients that are statistically significant and have signs that are inconsistent with the a priori hypothesis. Only two of the consistent signs are now statistically significant; in the earlier version, only one sign is statistically significant.

According to the new equation, older or largely nonwhite neighborhoods receive fewer mortgages, but the relationships are still not statistically significant at the 10 percent level. The change in the coefficient of the percentage nonwhite variables remains negative but is no longer statistically significant at the 10 percent level.

Table 3.5 shows the amount of mortgage lending predicted by this alternative equation of allegedly redlined areas and the ratios of these amounts to the amounts predicted by the equation for the areas not alleged to be redlined. If we eliminate Central Brooklyn and Park Slope from the data base, all neighborhoods receive less conventional mortgage funds for one- to four-family houses if they are allegedly redlined than if they are not. This suggests that South Bronx, Crown

Table 3.5
Predicted conventional mortgage lending on 1- to 4-family houses in Bronx, Kings, and Queens counties based on an alternative alleged-redlined-area equation, 1975

Locations	Predicted from Modified Alleged-Redined Equation[a] (thousands of $)	Predicted Lending Ratio (Redlined to Other-Areas Equations)[b]
Alleged Redlined Areas		
South Bronx	1,806	0.57
Central Brooklyn in Kings[c]	236	0.29
Crown Heights in Kings	288	0.43
East Flatbush in Kings	1,504	0.39
Park Slope in Kings[c]	479	0.62
Southeast Queens	2,265	0.55
Subtotal	6,578	0.49
Other Areas		
North Bronx	3,297	0.49
Northeast Kings[c]	3,566	0.70
South Kings	23,754	0.66
Rest of Queens	24,923	0.51
Subtotal	62,118	0.56
Total	68,696	0.62

a. Central Brooklyn and Park Slope have been excluded.
b. This is the ratio of the number in the first column of this table to the number in the third column in Table 3.4.
c. Lending in Central Brooklyn, Northeast Kings, and Park Slope is excluded from both equations.

Heights, East Flatbush, and Southeast Queens may be redlined, but Central Brooklyn and Park Slope may not be redlined.

It is important to examine the sensitivity of these predictions to variations in the specification of the equation because many of the proxies for risk of loss have signs that are contrary to reasonable expectations. Consequently, the models were re-estimated with two modifications. First, the six housing-code variables were deleted because they are believed to be the least satisfactory of the risk measures. Second, a measure of the composition of the housing stock (fraction of one- to four-family houses that are single-family) is added because the number of buildings rather than the dollar value had to be used to deflate the dependent variable. All the coefficients that are statistically significant are no less significant under this alternative specification. The predicted lending ratios are also generally consistent with those reported in Tables 3.4 and 3.5.

Estimates for Federally Assisted Mortgages on One- to Four-Family Houses

Estimates of the quantity model for federally assisted mortgages on one- to four-family houses are presented in Appendix C. Federally assisted mortgages are insured or guaranteed by the Federal Housing Administration (FHA), the Farmers Home Administration (FmHA), or the Veterans Administration (VA) and serviced by reporting lenders. As in the case of conventional mortgages, the model is estimated separately for allegedly redlined neighborhoods and other neighborhoods. Both equations explain approximately the same amount (36 to 40 percent) of the variation in federally assisted mortgage lending. However, the two equations are not identical; the hypothesis that the model is the same in both areas can be rejected with a less than 1 percent chance of error, $F(34,316) = 2.88$. The differences between the two equations are highlighted in the following discussion of the statistically significant variables.

Although federally assisted mortgage lending increases significantly with the amount of transactions in both areas, the effect in the allegedly redlined neighborhoods is less than half that in the other neighborhoods—a statistically significant difference.[9] The same dollar volume of transactions per building generates 2.12 times as much federally assisted mortgage lending on one- to four-family houses outside the allegedly redlined neighborhoods than inside them.

Higher loan-to-value ratios on federally assisted mortgages lead to less federally assisted lending in the allegedly redlined neighborhoods but more in the other neighborhoods. Both coefficients are statistically significant. Moreover, the magnitudes of the two coefficients are very different. A 10 percent increase above the mean loan-to-value ratio on federally assisted mortgages would reduce federally assisted lending in the allegedly redlined neighborhoods by 50 percent while increasing it in the other neighborhoods by 12 percent.[10] These loan-to-value ratio coefficients suggest that supply factors dominate in the neighborhoods alleged to be redlined, and demand factors dominate in the other neighborhoods.

The stock of federally assisted mortgages in one- to four-family houses has a positive and statistically significant (10 percent level) relationship with federally assisted lending in both types of neighborhoods. However, the magnitude of the coefficient is over ten times as large in the allegedly redlined neighborhoods.[11] These results indicate that federally assisted mortgage lending is much more geographically concentrated within the allegedly redlined neighborhoods than within the other neighborhoods.

Neighborhood attributes that are related to the risk of loss should play a smaller role in explaining federally assisted mortgage lending than conventional mortgage lending because the federal assistance is designed to encourage more risk taking than mortgage lenders could otherwise prudently accept. A comparison of the results provides some support for this hypothesis. Although nine of the neighborhood risk-related attributes are statistically significant in the conventional mortgage-lending models, only two (tax arrearage and change in welfare payments) are statistically significant in the federally assisted models.

An increase of 1 standard deviation in the tax arrearages on one- to four-family houses would slightly more than double (a 107 percent increase) federally assisted mortgage lending in the allegedly redlined neighborhoods but would increase the same lending in other neighborhoods by less than 1 percent.[12] Although this variable is also statistically significant in the conventional mortgage-lending models, it has the opposite sign. The same increase in tax arrearages would reduce conventional mortgage lending by 83 percent. Therefore, it appears that federal assistance increases mortgage funds in situations that are generally too risky for private mortgage investment.

In neighborhoods that are not alleged to be redlined, federally assisted mortgage lending is larger and conventional mortgage lending is smaller the more positive the change in welfare payments in the immediate neighborhood. The result is consistent with one purpose of federal assistance—providing funds where the level of risk is a deterrent to private investment. However, in the allegedly redlined neighborhoods, the same variable has the opposite sign pattern indicating more conventional lending and less federally assisted lending when the immediate neighborhood has had large increases in welfare payments.

Older areas receive significantly more federally assisted mortgages in neighborhoods that are not alleged to be redlined than do newer areas; a 23 percentage point increase in the amount of housing (for example 55 percent versus 78 percent) built before 1940 would increase federally assisted mortgage lending by 21 percent. In the allegedly redlined neighborhoods, the amount of federally assisted mortgage lending is virtually unaffected by the age of the neighborhood.

Federally assisted mortgage lending is substantially higher in census tracts that have recently undergone a change in racial composition and are located in neighborhoods that are not alleged to be redlined. A 10 percentage point increase in the percent of the population that is nonwhite over a four-year period would increase federally assisted mortgage lending by 46 percent.[13] This association, which is very statistically significant, indicates that a disproportionately high amount of aid from federal mortgage assistance programs has been provided to areas undergoing racial transition. Although the coefficient of the racial change variable in the model of allegedly redlined neighborhoods has approximately the same magnitude, it is not statistically significant.

Although conventional mortgage funds are less available in allegedly redlined neighborhoods underdoing racial change and are less available in nonwhite neighborhoods that are not alleged to be redlined, federally assisted mortgages are not more available in these areas. Instead, federally assisted mortgages are more available in neighborhoods that are not alleged to be redlined but are undergoing racial change.

Geographic differentials in federally assisted mortgage lending are more difficult to interpret than those in conventional lending. Although an increase in conventional lending in a neighborhood is viewed as a positive sign, interpretation of an increase in federally assisted lending is more ambiguous. In the late 1960s, the FHA and VA began to insure housing in older neighborhoods they had previously neglected. Community organizations around the country believe that an unintentional consequence of this activity has been the institutionalization of redlining. FHA- or VA-insured mortgages are virtually risk free from the lender's perspective and may be the only source of financing in neighborhoods where private lenders refuse to grant home mortgages for arbitrary or subjective reasons.[14] It is also claimed that various federal procedures such as fast foreclosure and mortgage assignment contribute to urban decay. In other words, it is alleged that FHA and VA policies encourage lenders to ignore risk of loss and foster neighborhood transition from stable to unstable. These allegations make interpretation of geographic differentials difficult for two reasons. First, an increase in FHA and VA lending in a neighborhood is consistent with: (1) allegations that the neighborhood is redlined, and (2) the hypothesis that loans require federal insurance to compensate for additional risks. Second, if FHA and VA activity were associated with redlining, this association may only occur during neighborhood transition. The results for the change-in-racial-composition variable are consistent with the second hypothesis.

Table 3.6 shows the actual and predicted amounts of federally assisted mortgage lending in each of nine subareas of Bronx, Kings, and Queens counties. Two sets of predictions are presented—one for the estimate of the quantity model based on the neighborhoods alleged to be redlined and one for the estimate based on the other neighborhoods. If the redlining allegations are valid and applicable to federally assisted lending in the same manner applicable to conventional lending, the model estimated for the allegedly redlined neighborhoods should predict a smaller amount of federally assisted lending than the model estimated for the other neighborhoods. However, as shown in Table

Table 3.6
Actual and predicted federally assisted mortgage lending on 1- to 4-family houses in Bronx, Kings, and Queens counties, 1975

Locations	Actual (thousands of $)	Predicted from Alleged-Redlined-Area Equation (thousands of $)	Predicted from Other-Areas Equation (thousands of $)	Predicted Lending Ratios[a]
Alleged Redlined Areas				
South Bronx	231	657	379	1.73
Central Brooklyn and Park Slope	587	629	170	3.70
Crown Heights	419	516	406	1.27
East Flatbush	3,111	3,042	3,417	0.89
Southeast Queens	5,098	5,441	3,691	1.47
Subtotal	9,446	10,285	8,063	1.28
Other Areas				
North Bronx	419	1,794	1,006	1.78
Northeast Kings[b]	1,858	4,413	1,683	2.62
South Kings	3,688	8,939	4,847	1.84
Rest of Queens	16,918	14,371	16,964	0.85
Subtotal	22,883	29,517	24,500	1.20
Total	32,329	39,802	32,563	1.22

a. This is column 2 divided by column 3.
b. Lending in Northeast Kings is excluded from both equations.

3.6, this holds true for only one of the neighborhoods alleged to be redlined (East Flatbush). Other allegedly redlined neighborhoods exhibit a pattern that is consistent with either the allegation that increased FHA and VA lending results from redlining by private lenders or the allegation that increased risk of loss justifies more FHA and VA activity. The equation for allegedly redlined neighborhoods predicts 56 percent more federal assistance in these neighborhoods than does the equation for other neighborhoods.

North Bronx, Northeast Kings, and South Kings are predicted to receive more federally assisted mortgages by the equation for allegedly redlined neighborhoods ($15.1 million) than they are predicted to receive by the equation for other neighborhoods ($7.54 million) or than they actually received ($5.97 million). However, the rest of Queens (that is, exclusive of the southeast corner) is predicted to have more federally assisted mortgages by the equation for other neighborhoods than by the equation for the allegedly redlined neighborhoods.

Since the earlier analysis of conventional mortgage lending suggested that the characterization of Central Brooklyn and Park Slope as redlined may be inaccurate, an alternative equation for allegedly redlined areas was also estimated for federally assisted mortgages. As in the conventional case, this equation was estimated for the allegedly redlined areas other than Central Brooklyn and Park Slope. Unlike conventional lending, the results for federally assisted lending were similar to those based on the alleged redlined area equation that included Central Brooklyn and Park Slope.[15] The only difference is that these two neighborhoods were predicted to receive an even larger amount of federally assisted mortgages.

Table 3.7 compares federally assisted mortgage lending to conventional mortgage lending on one- to four-family houses. The amount of federally assisted lending has been divided by the corresponding amount of conventional lending for each location and for actual and predicted lending. Federally assisted lending is greater than conventional mortgage lending in Crown Heights, East Flatbush, and Southeast Queens but not in other parts of Bronx, Kings, and Queens counties. The ratio of federal to conventional lending is smallest in South Kings. The predicted values, which are based on models that control for differences in risk of loss, yield the same results with one exception. For the alternative equation for allegedly redlined areas, federally assisted lending is also predicted to be greater than conven-

Table 3.7
Comparison of federally assisted with conventional mortgage lending on 1- to 4-family houses in Bronx, Kings, and Queens counties, 1975

Locations	Actual	Predicted from Alleged-Redlined-Area Equation	Predicted from Alternative Alleged-Redlined-Area Equation	Predicted from Other-Areas Equation
	Ratio of Federally Assisted to Conventional Mortgage Lending			
Alleged Redlined Areas				
South Bronx	0.148	0.372	0.338	0.119
Central Brooklyn and Park Slope	0.198	0.242	2.116	0.107
Crown Heights	1.339	1.709	1.663	0.601
East Flatbush	2.105	1.325	2.188	0.882
Southeast Queens	2.367	2.591	2.238	0.897
Other Areas				
North Bronx	0.130	0.462	0.598	0.148
Northeast Kings	0.607	1.055	1.263	0.332
South Kings	0.092	0.235	0.451	0.135
Rest of Queens	0.365	0.275	0.712	0.346

Source: Tables 3.4, 3.5, and 3.6.

tional lending in Central Brooklyn and Park Slope. This prediction is the only major deviation from the ratio of actual lending for any equation or location.

In general, the results summarized in Table 3.7 support the allegation that federally assisted lending is more prevalent in neighborhoods alleged to be redlined than in other neighborhoods. If federally assisted lending is higher in redlined neighborhoods than in other neighborhoods, the actual ratio of federally assisted to conventional lending should be higher in these neighborhoods than the comparable predicted ratio based on the equations for other areas. This holds true for all neighborhoods alleged to be redlined (compare column one to column four). In three neighborhoods (Crown Heights, East Flatbush, and Southeast Queens), the actual ratio is more than twice as large as the predicted ratio; in one (Central Brooklyn-Park Slope), it is nearly twice as large; in another (South Bronx), it is 20 percent larger.

Only one of the neighborhoods not alleged to be redlined (Northeast

Kings) has an actual ratio that is more than 5 percent above the ratio predicted from the equation for other areas. Northeast Kings' actual ratio is more than twice as large as that predicted ratio, a result that suggests federal assistance is provided to housing markets where the risk of loss is substantial. It is important, however, to remember that Northeast Kings is not a homogeneous area; it includes both the seriously troubled housing markets of Bedford-Stuyvesant and Brownsville and the stronger markets of Greenpoint and Williamsburg. In any case, federally assisted lending relative to conventional lending in most of the neighborhoods alleged to be redlined closely resembles that in Northeast Kings, which, on average, is the weakest housing market. Because the housing markets in the allegedly redlined areas, with the exception of South Bronx, are generally stronger than those in Northeast Kings, the similar lending pattern among these different housing markets is surprising.

Estimates for Conventional Multifamily Mortgages

Conventional mortgage lending on multifamily buildings (more than four housing units) is concentrated in an insufficient number of census tracts to allow estimation of two separate equations. Instead, a single equation is estimated with three dummy variables for the type of neighborhood: neighborhoods alleged to be redlined, Northeast Kings, and South Kings. North Bronx and Queens County outside of Southeast Queens are the reference areas for interpreting the coefficients of these neighborhood variables.[16] The coefficient of the allegedly redlined neighborhoods should be negative and statistically significant if, on average, conventional multifamily mortgages are less available in these neighborhoods than in neighborhoods not alleged to be redlined.

This model explains 80 percent of the variation in conventional multifamily mortgage lending. The volume of transactions is the most important variable in this model; conventional multifamily mortgage lending increases by 90 percent when the mean value of the transactions variable is doubled.[17] Four other variables play a lesser, but still important, role in this model.

Conventional multifamily mortgage lending decreases by 59 percent when the maturity is increased by 1 standard deviation (5.92 years above its mean). This result suggests that supply may be a stronger influence than demand.

Conventional lending on multifamily buildings has been significantly less in neighborhoods that experienced an increase in vacant multifamily buildings between 1969 and 1975. An increase equal to the standard deviation of this variable reduces such lending by 42 percent.

Census tracts that have higher mortgage foreclosure or delinquency rates receive smaller amounts of conventional mortgages on multifamily buildings. An increase of 1 standard deviation in the foreclosure rate leads to a 26 percent decrease in conventional multifamily lending. A comparable increase in the delinquency rate leads to a 22 percent decline. Both effects are consistent with rational economic behavior on the part of reporting lenders: decreasing lending in response to higher risk of loss.

The age-of-housing stock, racial-composition, and neighborhood variables are not statistically significantly related to conventional multifamily mortgage lending at even the 10 percent level. The estimated model does not support allegations of redlining on multifamily buildings (see Appendix C).

The Quantity Model for Upstate Metropolitan Areas

Estimates of a model of the flow of funds in Albany, Erie, and Onondaga counties differ from the approaches outlined in the preceding sections in two ways. First, it is not possible to estimate separate equations for the neighborhoods alleged to be redlined and those not so alleged in each county because of the limited number of observations. Therefore, a single equation model is estimated. Second, the number of variables available as proxies for the risk of loss to a property is smaller. The results are presented in Appendix C. All three models explain over 80 percent of the variation in conventional mortgage lending.

Albany County

Only one coefficient is statistically significant in the entire equation. It is the coefficient of the stock of conventional mortgages on one- to four-family houses. An increase of 1 standard deviation in the value of this variable increases mortgage lending per building by 60.5 percent of its mean value. Reporting lenders appear to provide conventional mortgages for houses in tracts where they already have such mortgages.

A variable designed to compare lending in the neighborhoods alleged to be redlined with other neighborhoods could not be used because of the small sample size. The model, however, does not show any significant difference between the city of Albany and the suburbs in the quantity of mortgage funds provided by reporting lenders. All of the alleged redlined neighborhoods are within the city of Albany.

The age of the neighborhood's housing stock and the racial composition of the neighborhood also have no significant effect on the amount of mortgage lending per building.

Erie County

Mortgage lending is significantly higher in census tracts that have more transactions. An increase of 1 standard deviation in the dollar value of transactions per building increases mortgage lending by 27.6 percent.

Mortgage lending is positively associated with maturity, stock of conventional mortgages on one- to four-family houses, and property location in certain neighborhoods. These variables have coefficients that are statistically significant at the 10 percent level. The maturity coefficient indicates that the demand influence dominates the supply influence in this county. An extra five years (approximately equal to 1 standard deviation) in the maturity raises the lending per building by 16.7 percent above its mean. An increase of 1 standard deviation in the stock of conventional mortgages on one- to four-family houses increases lending per building by 62.9 percent of its mean.

The Buffalo neighborhoods of North Buffalo and East Elmwood, Shiller and University, and South Buffalo receive significantly more (46–72 percent) conventional mortgages per building than do the Erie County suburbs. None of the neighborhoods alleged to be redlined receive less mortgage lending than do the Erie County suburbs. If anything, the results suggest they receive slightly more lending, but their coefficients are not statistically significant.

There is only one other statistically significant coefficient. Conventional mortgage lending is significantly lower in census tracts with relatively large amounts of federally assisted mortgages on one- to four-family buildings. An increase of 1 standard deviation in the value of this federally assisted stock variable decreases conventional lending per building by 34.5 percent.

Conventional mortgage lending is not significantly associated with the age of the neighborhood's housing stock or the racial composition of the neighborhood.

Onondaga County

Mortgage lending is positively associated with the amount of trans-actions, the stock of federally assisted mortgages, and population change. It is negatively associated with the delinquency rate. All four coefficients are statistically significant at the 10 percent level.

An increase of 1 standard deviation in dollar volume of transactions increases mortgage lending per building by 9.3 percent.

Census tracts with larger stocks of federally assisted mortgages on one- to four-family houses receive more conventional mortgages on one- to four-family houses. An increase of 1 standard deviation in this federally assisted stock variable increases conventional lending by 30.9 percent.

Census tracts with population increases that are 1 standard deviation above the mean population change receive 42.7 percent more conven-tional lending than census tracts with the mean value of population change.

Areas with high delinquency rates receive significantly less conven-tional mortgages on one- to four-family houses. If the delinquency rate is 1 standard deviation above its mean, conventional mortgage lending will be 23.5 percent below its mean.

Conventional mortgage lending is not significantly associated with the age of the area's housing stock, the racial composition of the area, or the location of the property.

Summary

The geographic distribution of the mortgage funds provided by banks complying with New York's disclosure laws are analyzed. If these lenders practice redlining, as alleged by community organizations, a model of the amount of conventional lending estimated on information from the allegedly redlined areas should predict lending in all locations to be less than estimated predictions from a similar model on infor-mation from areas not alleged to be redlined. At the same time, these results could arise from nonlinearities in the relationship between the amount of mortgage lending and risk of loss.

The model is estimated for conventional and federally assisted lend-ing on one- to four-family houses, and conventional lending on mul-tifamily houses. Interpretation of the results for federally assisted mortgage lending is not as straightforward as those for conventional mortgage lending. Although more conventional lending in a neighborhood is generally considered desirable, many persons assert that more federally assisted lending in a particular neighborhood is sometimes a cause or a result of the arbitrary withdrawal, or redlining, of conventional funds.

In general, the variables used to measure the variation in risk of loss across neighborhoods have coefficients that are not always consistent with expectations that more housing-code violations, property tax arrears, vacant buildings, or serious fires should correspond to less conventional lending. These measures of risk factors are the best available, and, although the results could be improved, the measures are adequate controls for present purposes. For example, they indicate that federally assisted mortgages are less sensitive to these risk factors than conventional mortgages—a result consistent with the public policy that federal assistance should encourage lending in situations that are too risky for private lending.

Mortgage-lending models are estimated for three New York City counties (Bronx, Kings, and Queens) and three counties in upstate New York (Albany, Erie, and Onondaga). In the upstate counties, mortgage lending is not associated with the age or racial composition of the neighborhood; and the only significant relationship between lending and property location indicates that certain portions of the city of Buffalo that are not alleged to be redlined receive more lending than the Erie County suburbs. The remainder of this summary focuses on the results from the more detailed analysis of the New York City counties.

Contrary to the redlining allegation, neighborhoods with older housing receive slightly (although not statistically significantly) more conventional mortgage funds in areas alleged to be redlined, as well as areas not alleged to be redlined.

Conventional mortgage lending is, however, significantly lower in areas that are largely nonwhite and are not alleged to be redlined. A racially stable 50 percent nonwhite neighborhood in such an area receives 48.5 percent fewer conventional mortgage funds than an otherwise similar racially stable all-white neighborhood. Furthermore, conventional lending is dramatically lower in areas that have recently undergone racial transition and are alleged to be redlined. If a neighborhood alleged to be redlined has changed from all-white to 20 percent nonwhite in the last four years, it receives 59.8 percent fewer mortgage funds than a racially stable neighborhood that is alleged to be redlined. These are large and statistically significant differences.

Federally assisted mortgages are less available (although insignificantly) in older neighborhoods that are alleged to be redlined but significantly more available in older neighborhoods that are not alleged to be redlined. These results are inconsistent with the claim that federal assistance primarily occurs in redlined areas. However, the results are consistent with allegations that federal assistance precedes redlining of older neighborhoods but disappears once an area is redlined.

Federally assisted mortgage lending is not significantly related to the percent of nonwhite residents in neighborhoods whether or not they are alleged to be redlined, providing the racial composition is stable. However, neighborhoods that have recently undergone racial transition receive substantial amounts of federally assisted mortgages, especially those neighborhoods that are not alleged to be redlined. For example, a neighborhood that is not alleged to be redlined but has changed from all white to 20 percent nonwhite in the last four years receives over 90 percent more federally assisted mortgage funds than a racially stable neighborhood. Federal programs may be encouraging racial transition. At the same time, these federal programs do not offset the discrimination in conventional lending against nonwhite neighborhoods that are not alleged to be redlined or the racially unstable neighborhoods that are alleged to be redlined.

Geographic differentials in conventional and federally assisted mortgage lending exist for one- to four-family houses. It appears that the community organizations may be incorrect about the existence of redlining in the Central Brooklyn and Park Slope neighborhoods, but they may be correct in their allegations concerning South Bronx, Crown Heights, East Flatbush, and Southeast Queens.

4

Lending Decision Models

The access to mortgage credit of women, minorities, elderly, and those trying to purchase houses in allegedly redlined areas may be limited or restricted through the application process in at least four ways. First, a lender may discourage certain potential borrowers from submitting a formal application for a mortgage. Second, after the borrower has submitted a formal application, the person authorized by the lending institution to estimate the value of, or appraise, the property may differentially and systematically underappraise certain types of properties relative to others. Underappraisal of this type reduces the maximum loan amount below what it would be with nondiscriminatory appraisal. Third, the lender may use its evaluation process to discriminate systematically against certain types of applicants with the result that such applicants face higher probabilities of loan denial or adverse modification than similarly situated applicants who are not discriminated against. Fourth, the lender may arbitrarily impose harsher mortgage terms (for example, higher interest rates, shorter maturity periods, and higher loan fees) on some applicants relative to others. In cases where the potential borrower cannot afford the harsher terms, this practice may have impacts similar to those of outright loan denial.

This chapter develops models of the last two of these ways that lenders may limit access to mortgage credit. Since our data base includes only formal applications for residential mortgages in California and New York, we are unable to examine the first method, prescreening by lenders. This is unfortunate; many allege that prescreening is a widespread method of lender discrimination. To the extent that our results provide evidence of discrimination at the subsequent stages of the lending process, they suggest that discriminatory prescreening may exist as well. The reverse is not true, however; absence of evidence supporting charges of discrimination related to formal applications does not imply a lack of discrimination at the preapplication stage. Appraisal practices are examined in Chapter 9.

The following sections present the general form of the models used in our empirical analysis of both the California and New York data sets. First, we outline a portfolio-choice model of the lending decision. Second, we discuss the decision-to-lend models, models that predict the probabilities of various loan application outcomes such as denial, approval with modification, and approval with no modification. Finally, we present three sets of mortgage-term models: a downward-modification model; a simultaneous model of the interest rate, term-to-maturity, and loan-to-value ratio; and a loan-fee model.

Portfolio-Choice Model

On receiving an application for a mortgage, a lender must decide whether to approve the application as received, approve it with some modification in terms, or turn it down. Lenders may discourage the submission of formal applications from applicants they believe will likely be denied. Applicants may also withdraw their applications prior or subsequent to a lender's decision (Figure 4.1).

A lender's decision on a mortgage application can be viewed as a function of borrower characteristics, the quality of the collateral, and the requested terms as expressed in the following model:

$$P_{ij} = f(B_j, C_j, T_j), \tag{4.1}$$

where

P_{ij} = probability of outcome i (ranging from approval as applied for to denial) on the jth application,

B_j = vector of borrower characteristics, such as income and net wealth,

C_j = vector of property characteristics that describe the quality of the collateral,

T_j = vector of the requested terms of the mortgage.

As noted in Chapter 1, this lending decision should be viewed in the context of portfolio choice.

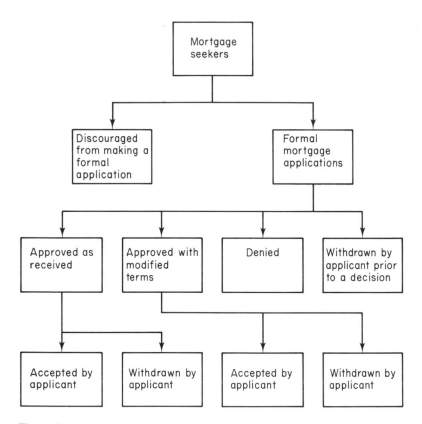

Figure 4.1
Mortgage applications and lender decisions.

Borrower Characteristics

The bank is concerned with the return it will earn on each mortgage loan. For given loan terms, the net income received by the bank in any year t of the loan contract depends on whether the borrower makes the scheduled payments on time. This, in turn, depends on certain characteristics of the borrower such as his or her income in year t. A simple linear relationship between the probability of default in year t (P_t) and borrower characteristics in year t (Y_t) is shown in figure 4.2.[1]

From the perspective of the banker at the time of mortgage application, the characteristics of the borrower in year t are unknown. At best, Y_t is a random variable with a known distribution. Figure 4.3 shows two probability distributions of, for example, household income

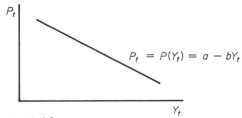

Figure 4.2
Probability of default.

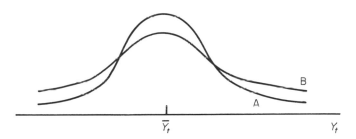

Figure 4.3
Probability distributions of household income.

in year t where household A's income has a smaller variance than household B's income, while expected incomes of the two households are the same.[2]

The banker wants to maximize the return on his or her portfolio, constrained by his or her attitudes toward risk as measured by the variance of the return. The dollar return (R_t) of a mortgage in year t is a random variable with mean, ER_t, and variance, $E(R_t - ER_t)^2$. We can express the expected return as:

$$ER_t = X[1 - P(Y_t)] + X'P(Y_t) \tag{4.2}$$

where

X = return if no default,

X' = return if borrower defaults for all or part of year (net of costs of collecting payments).

Given our linear specification of $P(Y_t)$, it can be shown that ER_t is a linear function of $\overline{Y}_t$ and $E(R_t - ER_t)^2$ is a linear function of $E(Y_t - \overline{Y}_t)^2$.[3] Hence, the expected return on the mortgage in year t and its variance depend on the mean and variance of the household's income in year *t*. The banker will be concerned with the return in each year of the mortgage contract; we will keep the analysis simple, however, by focusing on a single year t.[4]

The preceding discussion implies that the higher the expected value of certain borrower characteristics such as income in year t, the higher the quality (Q) of the loan, while the greater the variance, the lower the quality. Hence, we have:

$$Q = Q(\overline{Y}_t, \text{Var}\, Y_t), \tag{4.3}$$

with

$$\frac{\partial Q}{\partial \overline{Y}_t} > 0 \text{ and}$$

$$\frac{\partial Q}{\partial \text{Var}\, Y_t} < 0.$$

Two issues arise in this context. First, the banker does not know $\overline{Y}_t$ and $\text{Var}\, Y_t$ at the time of the mortgage decision and thus must project them. Second, the way in which $\overline{Y}_t$ and $\text{Var}\, Y_t$ combine to determine quality depends on the banker's attitude toward risk.

Projection of Borrower Characteristics At the time of the lending decision, the banker has information only on the current and past characteristics of the borrower. With this information, the banker might use current values of characteristics such as net wealth or income as proxies for future expected values. The projection of future variances is more difficult; the applicant's previous employment stability represents one crude measure that might be used for this purpose.

The limited information on which to base projections for individual households may induce bankers, in some cases, to simplify their task by categorizing applicants into groups. This allows them to use group projections, for which information may be available, rather than individual projections to determine the quality of an application. To the extent that an applicant household is not typical of the group in which it has been categorized or that the group projections are based on outdated stereotypes, the banker's estimate of the quality of the application will be in error. This use of group projections is discussed further in the section on discrimination variables.

Banker Attitudes toward Risk The functional relationship between $\overline{Y}_t$, $\text{Var}\, Y_t$, and the quality of the application reflects the banker's subjective attitudes toward risk. Figure 4.4 represents two sets of iso-quality contours. Each contour represents a different quality level. Since quality increases with $\overline{Y}$ and decreases with Var$Y$, quality rises with moves in a northwesterly direction. Bank A is more risk averse than bank B in that it is willing to give up more $\overline{Y}$ for a given reduction in Var$Y$ than is the other bank.

The points C and D represent two different households. Although the projected mean income of D is higher than that for C, the projected variance of D is higher, thereby increasing the risk associated with lending to D. For example, household C might represent a white married male engineer; D, a white married male self-employed entre-preneur. Whether D is preferred to C or vice-versa depends on the banker's attitudes toward risk. The more risk-averse banker (bank A in Figure 4.4) prefers C; the more risk-neutral banker (bank B in Figure 4.4), D.

The preceding discussion yields two major implications for our study. First, measures of borrower characteristics (B_j) should, as far as possible, include measures of variance as well as measures of expected value. Second, different types of banks should, as far as possible, be analyzed separately because of their potentially different attitudes toward risk taking.

Customer Relationship One additional, potentially important bor-rower characteristic remains to be mentioned: the borrower's rela-tionship to the lending bank. Because lenders' portfolio-composition decisions may affect their deposits and hence the total size of their investment portfolio, profit maximization may in some instances in-duce banks to give priority in lending decisions to their depositors.

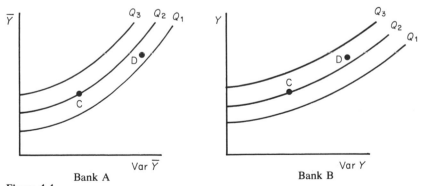

Figure 4.4
Lender attitude toward risk.

This appears to be common practice, for example, in connection with bank loans to business firms during periods of tight credit. In this situation, business loan recipients might be required to maintain a given level of compensating balances on deposit at the lending banks, a practice that lowers the effective cost to the bank of making the loan. Whether this customer relationship is equally important for mortgage lenders is not known. To the extent that it exists at all, preferential mortgage lending based on the depositor relationship is likely to be most prevalent when mortgage funds must be rationed by nonprice means either because of a credit crunch or because of a binding usury law.

Quality of the Collateral
The quality of the collateral can be viewed analogously to the borrower characteristics. The probability that a bank will foreclose in year t is determined by the probability that the borrower will default in year t and by bank policy toward foreclosure. In the event of foreclosure in year t, the return to the bank on the loan depends on the value of the collateral in year t, the outstanding loan balance, and the costs of foreclosure.

Hence, at the time of the mortgage application, the lender must project distributions of the property value for future years of the mortgage contract. The current market value of the property is presumably the best, single measure of the expected value of the property. It does not, however, incorporate fully the variance in the expected value of the property. To the extent that house buyers are concerned about future salability and uncertainty, market values will reflect both market expectations about the future salability of individual properties and the certainty with which those expectations are held. The more uncertain buyers are about the future expected sales price of a property, the more its market value will be discounted. However, market values do not reflect all the risks borne by lenders because mortgagors and mortgagees may have different expectations about the useful life of the property or the future viability of the neighborhood and are likely to discount uncertainties at different rates.

Some of these differences between mortgagors and mortgagees may be reflected in differences between the appraised value and the sales price. For example, appraisers might value properties below the sales price because lenders use a longer time horizon than the purchaser (mortgage applicant) when predicting events that might affect the future value of the property, because lenders attach more weight than the purchaser to the uncertainty associated with housing-market externalities (that is, the effects on the market value of any given property of the conditions of surrounding properties and the neighborhood), or because the lender lacks control over decisions of the purchaser, such as maintenance, that will affect the property's future value. Thus, from the perspective of the lender, the appraised value may be a better proxy than the sales price for the future value of the property.

In addition to appraised value, lenders are likely to pay particular attention to neighborhood factors in determining the quality of the collateral. Measures such as the average income in the neighborhood or the extent of housing-code violations, for example, might be used as proxies for the expected outlook for the neighborhood, whereas the rate of change of income or of population might be used as proxies for the variance associated with that expected outlook. Such measures assume that the greater the past instability, the greater the expected variance in the future.

Hence, as in the case of borrower characteristics, when examining the quality of the collateral (for any given terms of the mortgage, including the loan-to-value ratio), the lender needs to project both the expected future value of the property and the variance of that future value in order to project the expected rate of return and variance of a specific mortgage. One additional complication should be noted. The future value of the property may influence the return to the bank in two ways: (1) directly through its impact on the sales value in the event of foreclosure and (2) indirectly through its impact on borrower decisions. If the value of the property should decline below the outstanding loan amount, the borrower, regardless of his or her ability to make loan payments, may decide to default, thereby hastening foreclosure.

Loan Terms

The final element of the portfolio-choice model is the lender's choice of terms. The decision-to-lend model, as specified in Equation 4.1 includes as independent variables the terms as requested by the borrower. These might include the borrower's requested interest rate (presumably the lowest market rate of interest, consistent with the other terms), maturity period, and the loan-to-value ratio. Holding other factors constant, the higher the interest rate, the greater is the expected return to the lender, while the longer the maturity period or the higher the loan-to-value ratio, the greater the risk associated with the loan.

If, after evaluating a mortgage application, the lender decides that the loan would represent an unacceptable risk in relation to the expected return, the lender can choose either to refuse to grant the loan at all or to modify the terms to bring the return in line with the risk. Raising the interest rate is generally the simplest way of making the terms more favorable to the lender, but in some states may be ruled out by binding usury laws. In addition, lenders may decrease the loan amount below the requested amount, thereby decreasing the loan-to-value ratio. Variations in the maturity period of the loan are more difficult to interpret. On the one hand, shortening the maturity period would appear to reduce the riskiness of the investment to the bank since short-term events are more predictable than long-term events. On the other hand, the shorter maturity may increase the risk, other factors held constant, by increasing the size of the monthly payments in relation to income.

In summary, a complete model of the outcome of a nondiscriminatory lending decision process would include:

1. Current or past characteristics of the applicant representing both the expected level and the variance of future characteristics (for example, current income, current net wealth, employment history, and credit history).
2. Characteristics representing the applicant's relationship to the lending bank (for example, whether the applicant is a depositor at the bank).
3. Characteristics of the property and its neighborhood representing the expected value of the property and variance of its value (for example, appraised value, neighborhood income, change in neighborhood income, population, change in population, average housing prices).
4. Requested terms (for example, interest rate, loan-to-appraised-value ratio, and maturity period).

Although the variables are listed separately in the above summary, their potential interaction should be noted. For example, borrower income interacts with the requested terms as a determinant of the quality of the application. The question is whether household income will be sufficient to permit the household to make the required monthly payments which are determined jointly by the interest rate, loan amount, and the maturity period.

These portfolio choice considerations apply to all aspects of the decision-to-lend process.[5] This process can be divided into two parts. First, for all applications the lender must decide whether to grant the loan as requested, to grant it after modifying the loan amount, or to deny it. Second, for all approved loans, the lender must set the terms of the mortgage contract. In the next section, we focus on the first stage of the process.

Decision Model

Using data from individual mortgage applications on the borrower characteristics and quality of collateral variables listed above and on the outcome of the decision process (that is, deny, accept, or modify), models of the first stage of the lending decision can be estimated. Two major types of models are available for this purpose: linear and S-shaped models. Although easier and cheaper to estimate than S-shaped models, linear models have three major drawbacks: first, the predicted probabilities may fall outside the zero-to-one range reasonable for probabilities; second, each variable is constrained to have a constant marginal impact on the probability that a certain action will be taken; and third, linear models do not simultaneously account for the possibility of more than two outcomes. The first two points are illustrated by the line labeled "linear" in Figure 4.5 in which the probability of denial is depicted as a function of the requested loan-to-value ratio.

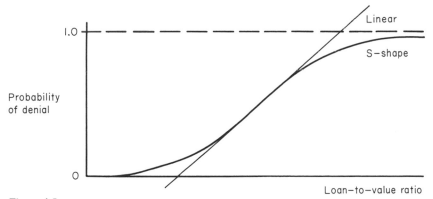

Figure 4.5
S-shaped versus linear model.

An appropriately specified S-shaped curve allows the probability to approach zero and one asymptotically, and allows an independent variable's marginal impact on the probability of an outcome to vary with the probability of that outcome. For example, a given increase in the requested loan-to-value ratio has a smaller impact on the probability of denial for low or high denial probabilities than for intermediate probabilities.

The specific technique used in this study involves estimating S-shaped curves using multinomial logit analysis. By estimating the logarithm of the odds rather than the probability directly, the logit model has an S-shaped form that remains within the zero-to-one bounds of probability.

In addition, this technique allows the simultaneous consideration of more than two outcomes. If there are four outcomes, three independent equations can be estimated within the constraint that the sum of the probabilities of all four outcomes must be one. Therefore, one outcome becomes the reference point for calculating the odds. More specifically,

$$\ln \left(\frac{P_i}{P_1} \right) = \beta X \qquad \text{for } i = 2, 3, 4 \tag{4.4}$$

and

$$\sum_{i=1}^{4} P_i = 1 \tag{4.5}$$

where P_i is the probability of the ith outcome, X is a vector of explanatory variables, and β is a vector of parameters. All four choices are tied together simultaneously through P_1 and Equation 4.5. Ideally, the vector X should include all the variables discussed above in the context of the portfolio-choice model. In other words, X would include borrower characteristics, property and neighborhood characteristics, and requested terms.

Discrimination
As discussed in Chapter 1, prejudicial attitudes of bankers or standard operating procedures designed to reduce costs or to simplify the evaluation of applications may lead lenders to make mortgage lending decisions that discriminate illegally against some borrowers. To ascertain whether discrimination on the basis of sex, marital status, age, or property location exists at the first stage of the lending process, we

can add variables measuring those characteristics to the multinomial logit model and test for their statistical significance.

The nature of statistical hypothesis testing makes it difficult to prove that discrimination exists. If the discrimination variables are not statistically significant, it can be inferred that discrimination is not a factor, provided that the discrimination variables are correctly specified and that they are not correlated with any relevant variables excluded because of inadequate information. If the discrimination variables are statistically significant, on the other hand, we can only state that the results are consistent with the existence of discriminatory behavior. The extent to which a result is interpreted as support for the hypothesis of discrimination depends on the completeness of the rest of the model; that is, on how well the model controls for the nondiscriminatory factors that enter into the decision to lend.

Sex To test for discrimination by mortgage lenders on the basis of the sex of the applicant or applicants, we first define the following three categories of applications:

1. Female only: no male applicant
2. Male-female: one male applicant and one female applicant
3. Male only: no female applicant

Categories 1 and 3 include both individual and joint applications (the joint applicant is often referred to as the co-applicant) while category 2, by definition, includes only joint applications.

The simplest form of sex discrimination could be examined by adding to the portfolio-choice model variables for two of these three categories, using the excluded category as a base, or reference point. In other words, two variables might be added, one denoting whether the application is female only and the other male only. The coefficients of these two variables in the probability-of-denial equation would then measure the impact of an all-female or all-male application on the probability of denial compared to the more traditional male-female application, controlling for other relevant factors.

Testing for discrimination on the basis of sex is complicated by the fact that lenders, to the extent they discriminate, may not discriminate equally against all members of a particular sex. For example, consider the finding of a statistically insignificant coefficient on the female-only variable in the probability of denial equation. On the one hand, this may reflect a true absence of discrimination against female applicants; on the other hand, it may also be consistent with discrimination against some female applicants, such as those of childbearing age, but not against others. To test this more subtle hypothesis, the model would need to be respecified with two female sex variables, one denoting that at least one of the female applicants is of childbearing age and the other that none of the female applicants is of childbearing age.

The allegations relating to sex discrimination outlined in Chapter 1 indicate the desirability of working with a more detailed breakdown that takes account of whether or not the female applicant is in the childbearing-age range or is employed. The distinction between working and nonworking female applicants reflects the allegation that bankers may discriminate against applications where part of the income comes from an allegedly unreliable source, the earnings of the working woman. The breakdown between women of childbearing and nonchildbearing age captures the potential distinction made by bankers between those women for whom the threat of pregnancy increases the probability that they will leave the labor force or will incur additional expenses and those for whom little threat is present.

To implement this disaggregated model, one type of applicant would again be excluded from the model and used as the base, and separate variables would be defined for all remaining types of applicants. In general, we exclude the type of applicant least likely to be discriminated against; in this case, it is the joint application from a male-female couple with the woman beyond childbearing age. The employment status of women applicants is treated differently in New York than in California. In New York, we know only whether the female applicant works; in California we know the actual income earned by all applicants. Therefore, in New York the working status of women is analyzed by adding this factor to the description of the types of applicants; the base would then be a joint application from a male-female couple with a nonworking woman beyond childbearing age. The feasibility of this approach in any particular data set depends on the number of observations from the various types of applicants; in many cases data limitations may require types of applications to be consolidated.

The allegation of income discounting can be tested more explicitly in California where information on the separate incomes of the applicant and the co-applicant is available. With such data, models can be specified that allow explicitly for differential treatment of the income of the primary and secondary workers. In addition, these models can be used to test the hypothesis that lenders treat the income of the secondary worker differently for female workers than for male workers.

Marital Status   The basic application categories relating to marital status are constructed as follows:

1. unmarried: at least one applicant unmarried, none separated
2. separated: at least one applicant separated
3. married: No applicant unmarried or separated

An unmarried applicant is one who is either single (never married), divorced, or widowed. As with sex discrimination, the simplest test for marital discrimination involves including in the portfolio-choice model variables representing two of the three categories; the category married is the logical choice as a base since applications by married couples represent the traditional type of mortgage application.

Again, such a simple specification may be inadequate to detect discrimination on the basis of marital status where such discrimination interacts with discrimination of other types. As a related point, this simple specification does not permit a test of the hypothesis that unmarried women are discriminated against and unmarried men are not. Hence, the final model specifications interact the marital-status categories with sex of the applicant, and where data are adequate, with the age of the female applicant. Marital-status data are available only for New York.

Race of Applicant   The allegations of discriminatory lending on the basis of race are tested by including separate variables for each minority racial category sufficiently represented in the particular sample. In some samples, black and other minorities are the only feasible categories; in others, the "other minorities" category can be subdivided into Hispanics and Asians.[6] The nonminority category, used as the base, includes all those applicants for which no applicant is a member of a racial minority.

Age of Applicant   Applicants are grouped into one of the following five age categories to test for age-based discrimination.

1. under 25 years
2. 25 to 34 years
3. 35 to 44 years
4. 45 to 54 years
5. 55 or more years

The middle-age group (35 to 44) has been selected to serve as the base because applicants in that group are least likely to be discriminated against.

Property Location or Neighborhood Factors   Redlining allegations are examined in two ways. First, the geographic area containing the property is identified through dummy variables. In the New York and a few of the California metropolitan areas, we are able to test local allegations that certain neighborhoods are redlined by lenders. In the other metropolitan areas, we are only able to compare lending decisions in the central city to those in the surrounding suburbs. In all cases, a suburban area is the base for comparison.

Second, neighborhood characteristics such as the racial composition or the age of the neighborhood are included to test for discrimination against largely minority or very old neighborhoods. It should be noted that the results for the age of the neighborhood measure are likely to be ambiguous because of its correlation with objective measures of the risk of loss (such as the condition of the property) that may have been excluded. Although this is likely to be the case in the New York models, the California models include the age of the specific property. Therefore, the measure for the age of the neighborhood (fraction of housing built before 1940) probably provides a reasonably clear test of discrimination against old neighborhoods in California. At the same time, the exact meaning of the coefficients of the building-age variables is ambiguous; they could reflect risk factors such as building condition or discrimination against old buildings.

Models of Mortgage Terms

Whether or not illegal discrimination exists at the loan decision stage, institutional lenders may discriminate in setting mortgage terms. This section describes three models relating to terms: (1) a model of downward adjustments of loan amounts for modified loans, (2) a complete model of mortgage terms for all approved loans, and (3) a model of loan fees. With the exception of the model of loan fees, the portfolio-choice considerations outlined at the beginning of this chapter are applicable.

Modified Loan Amount
The decision-to-lend model predicts the probabilities of a range of outcomes, one of which involves modifying the loan amount. The

discrimination variables in the modification equation are hard to interpret, however, because some applicants may be more aggressive than
others in seeking large loans, and the equation does not distinguish
between large and small modifications. To supplement the modification model, we restrict the sample to loans that are modified downward
and estimate a model of the dollar amount of modification. Defining
MODOWN as the requested amount minus the granted amount (a
positive number), the model can be expressed as follows:

MODOWN = f(REQLOAN, RISK, DISC),   (4.6)

where

REQLOAN = the requested loan amount,

RISK = the risk of the loan as measured by a vector of financial
characteristics of the borrower and the property, given
the requested terms,[7]

DISC = a vector of discrimination variables.

The higher the requested loan, all other factors held constant, the
larger the dollar amount of the modification is likely to be. Risk factors
enter positively since the higher the risk associated with the requested
terms, the greater the incentive for the lender to reduce the risk by
reducing the size of the loan. Finally, a finding of a positive sign on
one or more of the discrimination variables would be consistent with
the hypothesis of discriminatory behavior. For example, a positive
sign on the variable representing applicants over fifty-four years old
would imply that, among those applicants whose applications are modified downward, old people on average experience larger modifications
ceteris paribus than the 34- to 45-year-old reference group. Provided
the other variables included in the equation adequately control for the
risk of loss, such a finding can be interpreted as discriminatory behavior by lenders rather than as a reflection of excessive loan demands
by that age group.

Since this model has very few data requirements beyond those
needed to estimate the decision-to-lend models, it can be estimated in
any New York or California metropolitan area with a sufficient number
of downward-modified applications. The specific variables included as
measures of risk or discriminatory behavior will vary across the two
states and across metropolitan areas.

Interest Rate, Maturity Period, and Loan-to-Value Ratio

Having decided to grant mortgage credit, the lending bank must set the terms of the mortgage contract, including the interest rate, maturity, and loan-to-value ratio. The final terms reflect the interaction of borrower and lender preferences, objective measures of risk, and possibly discriminatory behavior by the lending institution. Both lenders and borrowers may be willing to make trade-offs among the three terms. For example, a lender may offset a high loan-to-value ratio with an above average interest rate, and similarly, a borrower may prefer the combination of a high interest rate and a long maturity period to that of a low interest rate and a short maturity. Hence, a complete model of mortgage terms should incorporate the simultaneous determination of the three variables. Moreover, testing for discriminatory behavior requires structural rather than reduced form equations. This follows because the relevant question with respect to interest rates, for example, is not whether similarly-situated blacks and whites are charged the same interest rate in general, but whether they are charged the same interest rate for comparable loans.

The following three equations represent a complete structural model of the jointly determined mortgage terms.

$$INT = f(LTOAV, \quad MAT, \quad INT_m, \quad VRM, \quad REQLOAN, \\ RISK, DISC), \tag{4.7}$$

$$MAT = h(INT, LTOAV, REQMAT, RISK, DISC), \tag{4.8}$$

$$LTOAV = g(INT, MAT, RLTOAV, RISK, DISC), \tag{4.9}$$

where

INT = the contract interest rate,

MAT = the maturity period,

$LTOAV$ = the ratio of the granted loan amount to the appraised value of the property,

INT_m = the market rate of interest,

VRM = one if the mortgage is a variable rate mortgage and zero otherwise,

$REQLOAN$ = the requested loan amount,

$RISK$ = risk as measured by a vector of financial characteristics of the borrower and the property,

DISC = a vector of discrimination variables,

REQMAT = the requested maturity period,

RLTOAV = the ratio of the requested loan amount to the appraised value of the property.

In addition to the three jointly determined endogenous variables (INT, MAT, LTOAV), the model includes specific determinants of the interest rate (INT_m, and VRM), measures of borrower preference (REQMAT in the MAT equation and RLTOAV in the LTOAV equation), measures of the riskiness of the loan to the bank as measured by the financial characteristics of the borrower and property (RISK in all equations plus REQLOAN in the INT equation) and discrimination variables (DISC).

Controlling for maturity period (MAT) and loan-to-value ratio (LTOAV) and in the absence of discriminatory lending behavior, the contract interest rate (INT) on an approved loan is expected to be higher the higher the market rate of interest, to be lower on variable rate loans than fixed rate loans provided interest rates are expected to continue to rise, and to be higher the greater the riskiness of the loan to the bank. Inclusion of the requested loan amount accounts for the fact that large loans are riskier than small loans. Provided returns on small loans are not perfectly correlated, the lender reduces risk by spreading available funds among a large number of borrowers. Discriminatory lending behavior with respect to contract interest rates can be examined by testing for the statistical significance of each of a vector of variables representing categories of race, sex, marital status, age, location of property, and age and racial composition of the neighborhood. A finding of higher interest rates for any one of these categories would be consistent with the hypothesis of discriminatory behavior towards the persons represented by that category.

The logic of the maturity equation is similar to that of the interest rate equation. From the lender's perspective, higher risk legitimately requires harsher terms, in this case shorter maturities. Since discriminatory motives would also lead bankers to impose harsher terms, a finding of shorter maturities associated with any one of the suspect categories would be consistent with the hypothesis of discriminatory behavior, provided the equation was properly specified.

In contrast to interest rates, however, where borrowers unambiguously prefer lower interest rates (controlling for the other mortgage terms), different borrowers may prefer different maturities depending on their stage in the life cycle, their expected patterns of future income, and the size of their requested loan. Ideally, the borrower's requested maturity should be included explicitly in the maturity equation as indicated in Equation 4.8. To the extent that data limitations prevent this preference variable from being correctly measured, the discrimination variables must be interpreted cautiously. For example, if the preference of older people for shorter maturities is not fully captured in the preference variable, a statistical finding that older applicants end up with shorter maturity loans than younger applicants does not necessarily imply that lenders discriminate against old people. On the other hand, even with an imperfectly specified variable for borrower preferences, a finding that black applicants are given shorter maturity loans on average than similarly situated white applicants might legitimately be interpreted as indicating discriminatory lending behavior unless a convincing case can be made that the maturity preferences of blacks differ significantly from those of similarly situated whites.

Differing wealth positions and other factors may lead borrowers to prefer different loan-to-value ratios. These borrower preferences are represented by the requested loan-to-appraised-value (RLTOAV) variable in the loan-to-value equation. Since RLTOAV data are readily available, improper specification presents less of a problem in this equation than in the maturity equation. As in the other two equations, higher risk as measured by the financial characteristics of the borrower and the property legitimately leads the lender to impose harsher terms, in this case lower loan-to-value ratios. Discriminatory behavior, to the extent it exists, also leads to lower loan-to-value ratios.

Equations 4.7 to 4.9 can be estimated only for the California data because of the absence of information on mortgage contract terms in the New York data set. Separate data have been estimated for 1977 and 1978 in four California metropolitan areas. It should be noted that the presence of a binding usury law in New York State during the study period would make Equation 4.7 largely irrelevant in any case.

Loan-Fees Model
Mortgage lenders may also discriminate by charging some applicants higher loan fees than others simply because of their sex, marital status, race, or age; the location of their property; or the age or racial com-

position of the neighborhood. Since loan fees must be fully paid when the mortgage contract is signed, high loan fees increase the immediate financial burden on these borrowers and, in some cases, may keep them from proceeding with the planned house purchase.

Information on loan fees is unavailable for the New York banks; hence, the model outlined here specifically reflects the type of loan fees used by California savings and loan associations. Included in the total loan fees are the average costs to the bank of making the loan, generally assessed as a percentage of the loan amount; appraisal, inspection, and other fees for services; and charges for title insurance, credit report, and other services related to making loans that are not usually performed by savings and loan associations to the extent that such charges exceed standard or billed costs for the services. To examine discriminatory behavior in the setting of these loan fees, we can estimate the following model for approved loans:

LOANFEE $= f$(LOANAMT, PROP, NEIGH, DISC),   (4.10)

where

LOANFEE $=$ the amount of the loan fee,

LOANAMT $=$ the amount of the loan,

PROP $=$ a vector of property characteristics (including appraised value, size of property, and building age),

NEIGH $=$ a vector of neighborhood characteristics (including level and change variables),

DISC $-$ a vector of discrimination variables.

Since the basic fee is determined as a percentage of the size of the loan, loan amount (LOANAMT) is expected to be an important explanatory variable. Property characteristics (PROP), such as the property's appraised value, physical size, and age, represent the property specific factors that might influence the cost to the bank of making the loan and, hence, the size of the fee charged. The neighborhood variables (NEIGH) represent those neighborhood characteristics that might influence the bank's costs and that can legitimately be passed on to the borrowers in the form of higher fees.

It should be noted that variables representing the financial characteristics of the borrower are not included in the model. This exclusion reflects our view that loan fees are not part of the general portfolio-choice model; more specifically, the purpose of loan fees is to recover the legitimate costs of processing loan applications rather than to offset the risk of the loan to the lender.

The discrimination variables, most of which are dichotomous dummy variables, have straightforward interpretations; statistically significant positive coefficients are consistent with the hypothesis that lenders discriminate against certain types of applicants by setting loan fees higher than warranted by the size of the loan and the characteristics of the property.

Conclusion

We have described two general approaches for analyzing the criteria used by lenders in processing mortgage applications:

1. lender action on the application (approve, modify, or deny)

2. credit terms for approved and modified applications, including a model of the amount by which requested loan amounts are reduced; a simultaneous three-equation model of the interest rate, maturity, and loan-to-value ratio; and a model of loan fees

We have endeavored to specify these models properly in this chapter. As we move into the following chapters that contain empirical estimates of the models, data limitations sometimes prevent us from fully implementing the proper specification. For example, a measure of market interest rates is unavailable for use in the equation for interest rates in California.

5
Decision to Lend
in California

The evaluation of applications for loans on specific properties to distinguish the different risks of loss among them represents a major part of the residential lending process. In general, lenders approve those applications having lower risks of loss, provided there are enough funds in the portfolio for this type of investment; other applications are rejected. (Although this description of the lending process indicates sequential steps, the actual process is interactive. For example, if most of its residential mortgage applications have high risks of loss, a bank may decide to reduce that portion of its portfolio available for residential mortgages). When receiving an application for a mortgage, a lender must decide whether to approve the application as received, approve it with some modification in terms, or turn it down. Lenders may discourage the submission of formal applications from applicants who, they believe, will likely be denied. Applicants may also withdraw their applications prior or subsequent to a lender's decision.

In Chapter 4, a lender's decision on a mortgage application was viewed as a function of the credit worthiness of the borrower, the quality of the collateral, and the requested terms of the mortgage. In this chapter, we report estimates of this decision-to-lend model for California.

Data Base

All state-regulated savings and loan associations in California must maintain detailed data on mortgage applicants. The state's department of savings and loan prescribes the form of the information through its Loan Register Report. The report form contains the following information: total family income, income of applicant and co-applicant, purchase price of subject property, whether the subject property will be owner occupied, sex of the applicant and co-applicant, race or national origin of applicant and joint applicant, age of the applicant and joint applicant, type of loan, requested loan amount, appraised value, type of structure, living area, year built, number of residential units in the building, action taken by lender, granted loan amount, interest rate and maturity period for granted loans, loan fees and discounts, whether the interest rate is variable, and the census tract in which the property is located.

Four types of lender action on mortgage applications are identifiable on the Loan Register Reports: approved as applied for, approved with a loan amount less than requested, approved with a loan amount larger than requested, and denied. There is no information on withdrawals by the applicant. Cases where the lenders offered a loan amount less than requested and the applicant rejected it are not separately identified. It is presumed that these have been treated as denials.

The lack of information on applicants who were discouraged from making a written application could create a methodological problem for this study. Under the California regulations, each state-regulated savings and loan association is required to prepare a Loan Register Report for all written applications for mortgages on residential properties. It appears, however, that this regulation does not clearly delineate the circumstances under which a written application is required. However, the regulation may act to minimize the practice of informal screening, although the opposite effect, obviously, is also possible. As long as there are an adequate number of modified approvals and denials among the written applications, the explanation for these actions should reflect the reasons for discouraging written applications. For example, if the analysis of denials indicates the existence of racial discrimination, discrimination is also a likely factor in deciding which applicants should be discouraged from applying. A lender is unlikely to discriminate against formal applicants but not against informal ones. However, if the statistical analysis does not indicate the existence of discrimination, it is still possible that lenders use a different set of criteria, including sex or race, in their informal screening of applicants.

This study analyzes applications for conventional mortgages to finance the purchase of single-family houses for owner occupancy during 1977 and 1978 in sixteen metropolitan areas. The loan register data are supplemented by 1970 census data and income and household estimates from income tax returns matched to each response by census tract number. In some areas (Anaheim-Santa Ana-Garden Grove, Sacramento, San Diego, San Jose, and Stockton metropolitan areas, and City of Los Angeles), additional information from local surveys was added to the Loan Register data.

Model Description

In general, four outcomes of the lending behavior of California savings and loan associations can be studied: approved as applied for, approved with a loan amount less than requested (modified down), approved with a loan amount larger than requested (modified up), and denied. The lender's decision depends on the credit worthiness of the borrower, the quality of the collateral, and the requested terms of the mortgage. Various measures of financial and neighborhood characteristics are used to capture the influence of these factors.

The financial characteristics are the requested loan amount in relation to annual income and the ratio of the requested loan amount to the appraised value of the property. We experimented with several specifications of the effect of household income on lender decisions including income as a continuous variable, several income categories with dummy variables, requested-loan-to-income ratio, several categories of the requested-loan-to-income ratio with dummy variables, and a variable equal to the positive values of the requested-loan-to-income ratio minus 2.5 and zero when this difference is negative. Since the last variable captured the effect of income better than any other, the equations containing it are reported here. Risk of loss to the lender and, hence, the probability of adverse action, should rise as the amount of the requested loan rises relative to either income or appraised value. Ideally, these two financial measures should be supplemented by measures representing the stability of the applicant's income, his or her credit history, or his or her net wealth. Unfortunately, the California data set does not include any of this information. In addition, no information is available on the applicant's relationship with the lending bank.[1]

Neighborhood characteristics are included to control for risk of loss in the value of property resulting from housing market externalities. Although it would be ideal to include direct measures of these externalities such as whether the subject property is adjacent to a vacant building, this is generally impossible because the requisite information is unavailable. Therefore, neighborhood conditions are proxied by measures of the income of residents, change in income and population, and in a few areas sales price, change in sales price, and vacancy rates. Risk of loss should be lower in neighborhoods with a larger proportion of high-income residents. In general, neighborhoods with larger increases in average income and population should have rising property values and less risk of loss in value. High vacancy rates should signal a larger risk of loss.

The measures of neighborhood characteristics are calculated for the census tracts containing the subject property. This is true for the fraction of households with high income (FHI) in all metropolitan areas using 1970 census data with four exceptions. FHI for the Anaheim-Santa Ana-Garden Grove, Sacramento, San Diego, and San Jose metropolitan areas is calculated by census tract from a special census in 1975. Other supplemental variables from local surveys, such as sales price, vacancy rate, and more recent income and population data are also calculated by census tract. (See Table 5.1). A major source of current data on income and population is federal income tax returns, which have been summarized by ZIP code for nearly all the metropolitan areas under study. Aggregation by ZIP code is less desirable than by census tract because it includes a larger geographic area and, as a result, is a less accurate measure of the condition of the market in the immediate neighborhood surrounding the property.

The California model only includes one requested term (loan-to-appraised-value ratio) because information on interest rate and maturity period are only available for granted loans.

Two of the four lender actions have clear meaning: approved as applied for and denial. The other two (modification down and modification up) are somewhat ambiguous. One of the four must be selected as a reference against which to compare the other three. Since it is important that this reference action have a clear meaning in relation to all other actions, the job falls to applications that are approved as applied for (that is, approval with the loan-to-appraised value ratio and loan amount requested by the borrower).

The likelihood of a lender deciding to deny an application for a conventional mortgage loan should increase as an applicant's requested-loan-to-income ratio increases and as the quality of the collateral decreases (for example, as the requested loan-to-appraised-value ratio increases). Differences in the risk of loss associated with the borrower and the property may be offset, to some extent, by modifications in the terms of the mortgage (interest rate, maturity, and

Table 5.1
Geographic aggregation and year of observation for the neighborhood characteristics

Study Area[a]	FHI	Other Income Variables	Population Change	Sales-Price Variables	Vacancy Rate
Anaheim-Santa Ana-Garden Grove	CT75	CT75	CT7075	NA	NA
Bakersfield	CT70	ZIP7576	ZIP7076	NA	NA
Fresno	CT70	ZIP7576	ZIP7076	NA	NA
Los Angeles-Long Beach	CT70	ZIP7576	ZIP7076	NA	NA
Los Angeles City	CT70	ZIP7576	ZIP7076	CT7377	NA
Modesto	CT70	NA	NA	NA	NA
Oxnard Ventura	CT70	ZIP7576	ZIP7076	NA	NA
Sacramento	CT75	CT75	CT7075	NA	NA
Salinas-Monterey	CT70	ZIP7576	ZIP7076	NA	NA
San Bernardino-Riverside-Ontario	CT70	ZIP7576	ZIP7076	NA	NA
San Diego	CT75	ZIP7576 CT75	ZIP7076	NA	NA
San Francisco-Oakland	CT70	ZIP7576	ZIP7076	NA	NA
San Jose	CT75	ZIP7576	ZIP7076	NA	CT76
Santa Barbara	CT70	ZIP7576	ZIP7076	NA	NA
Santa Rosa	CT70	ZIP7576	ZIP7076	NA	NA
Stockton	CT75	NA	CT7075	CT7677	CT7075
Vallejo-Napa	CT70	ZIP7576	ZIP7076	NA	NA

CT indicates census tract; ZIP indicates ZIP Code Area. The numbers following CT and ZIP are the last two digits of the year(s) of observation. Complete definitions are given in Appendix A. NA indicates that the data was not available.
a. Metropolitan area in all areas except the City of Los Angeles.

down payment). Unfortunately, the only information on modification is change in the requested loan amount.

It is more difficult to relate each of the independent variables to a lender's decision to modify the terms. For example, downward modification could be the result of an applicant's request because of a desire to maximize equity or revised estimates of the amount of household funds that can be allocated to purchasing a house.

To ascertain whether discrimination on the basis of sex, race, marital status or age of the applicant, or on the basis of property location exists in mortgage lending, variables along the lines discussed in Chapter 4 are also included in the models. One of the distinct advantages of the California over the New York data is that the incomes of the applicant and co-applicant are reported separately, which permits analysis of discriminatory treatment of secondary income. The variables measuring the racial composition of the neighborhood are calculated for census tracts in the case of the fraction black and the fraction Spanish in all study areas.[2] The fraction Asian is calculated for ZIP Code areas. These racial composition variables are based on 1970 data with the following exceptions: Sacramento and San Jose (all three by census tract for 1976); and Stockton (reduced to two census-tract measures for 1975).

Sample Characteristics
The samples have been limited to applications for conventional mortgages on single-family residences intended to be owner occupied. Applications for federally assisted mortgages have been excluded because the involvement of a third party, the government, substantially affects the decision-making process, and the Loan Register does not identify the decision maker. In addition, there are not enough observations to analyze separately such applications. Multifamily and non-owner-occupied properties are excluded because the Loan Register contains insufficient information to control for the effect of investment income as a factor in the lending process. Applications that indicated they were for refinancing or for home improvement loans have also been excluded because they do not involve a property transaction and the Loan Register generally lacks the information necessary to analyze these decisions. Again, only a small percentage of the forms were affected. The final sample sizes (after eliminating forms with critical nonresponses) are summarized in Table 5.2. Multinomial logit models are estimated for every metropolitan area in each year.

Table 5.2
Number of observations by metropolitan area and year: California savings and loan associations

Study Area[a]	1977	1978
Anaheim-Santa Ana-Garden Grove	16,672	12,542
Bakersfield	1,722	1,646
Fresno	3,173	2,850
Los Angeles-Long Beach	38,398	34,792
Los Angeles City	14,060	13,662
Modesto	1,885	1,558
Oxnard-Ventura	4,631	3,970
Sacramento	5,163	4,884
Salinas-Monterey	1,860	1,530
San Bernardino-Riverside-Ontario	2,606	2,038
San Diego	7,628	7,508
San Francisco-Oakland	24,766	21,608
San Jose	9,887	7,691
Santa Barbara	1,401	1,254
Santa Rosa	3,419	3,307
Stockton	2,432	2,381
Vallejo-Napa	1,884	1,866

a. Metropolitan area in all cases except the City of Los Angeles.

Results

The multinomial logit estimates of lender behavior are reported in Appendix B. (Complete variable definitions are presented in Appendix A.) The following discussion presents the implications of these results for a typical application and key variations in its characteristics.

We have defined the typical application as having a requested loan amount that is less than 2.5 times the applicant household's annual income (82 to 96 percent of all applications). The typical application is also from an all-white household (68 to 93 percent of all applications), an applicant between the ages of 35 and 44 (22 to 29 percent of all applications), a male-female couple with the female applicant beyond childbearing age (22 to 35 percent of all applications), and with no secondary income (83 to 86 percent of all applications). These characteristics were selected because they describe a household which is least likely to be the target of discrimination, if any exists. Therefore, they do not always represent a plurality of all applications. The

Table 5.3
Mean values of continuous variables by California metropolitan area, 1977

Metropolitan Area	RLTOINC	RLTOAV	FHI	INC1976	DINC7675
Anaheim-Santa Ana-Garden Grove	0.071	0.76	0.61[a]	18.14[b]	NA
Bakersfield	0.013	0.81	0.26	14.10	0.91
Fresno	0.036	0.80	0.20	13.14	0.88
Los Angeles-Long Beach	0.061	0.78	0.31	14.42	1.10
Modesto	0.016	0.79	0.17	NA	NA
Oxnard-Ventura	0.059	0.76	0.31	14.63	1.07
Sacramento	0.032	0.78	0.42[a]	13.43[b]	NA
Salinas-Monterey	0.086	0.78	0.20	12.84	0.83
San Bernardino-Riverside-Ontario	0.030	0.79	0.23	13.01	1.23
San Diego	0.080	0.79	0.39[a]	18.82[b]	0.98
San Francisco-Oakland	0.072	0.77	0.33	15.59	1.09
San Jose[d]	0.073	0.76	0.50[a]	15.44	1.12
Santa Barbara	0.138	0.74	0.24	10.90	0.77
Santa Rosa	0.048	0.76	0.17	NA	NA
Stockton[e]	0.014	0.78	0.23[a]	NA	NA
Vallejo-Napa	0.040	0.78	0.22	NA	NA

a. These data in these metropolitan areas are based on a 1975 survey instead of the 1970 census.
b. This data is based on a 1975 survey with census-tract detail instead of the 1976 ZIP Code values from the IRS files.
c. This data is based on a 1975 or 1976 survey and the 1970 census with census-tract values instead of the 1975 IRS and 1970 census information with ZIP Code area values.

age of applicant and the age of the woman are selected to compare childbearing to nonchildbearing women.

The typical application is also defined as having the average values of all the continuous variables for applications in the metropolitan area being studied: requested-loan-to-appraised-value ratio, fraction high-income households, income and population change, age of neighborhood, and racial composition of neighborhood. These values are summarized in Table 5.3. In addition, the building is assumed to be new (8 to 38 percent of all applications), and the property is located in a suburb.

The treatment accorded applications with characteristics different than the typical application are compared to the treatment received by the typical application. The treatment is measured by the probability of a given decision such as denial or downward modification.[3]

Table 5.3 (continued)

DINC7570	DHH7675	DHH7570	PRE1940	FBLACK	FSPANISH	FASIAN
4.85ᶜ	NA	5.74ᶜ	0.06	0.01	0.0 9	0.01
3.43	0.86	2.65	0.11	0.06	0.09	0.01
2.64	−0.16	3.55	0.14	0.01	0.13	0.02
1.62	−0.15	1.87	0.15	0.04	0.12	0.02
NA	NA	NA	0.19	0.003	0.07	NA
1.09	1.30	10.36	0.06	0.02	0.13	0.02
2.12ᶜ	NA	1.62ᶜ	0.13	0.02	0.03	0.03
2.98	0.39	1.91	0.16	0.06	0.14	0.04
2.36	1.42	2.28	0.13	0.03	0.11	0.01
5.31	0.99	3.17	0.10	0.02	0.09	0.01
2.19	0.56	2.07	0.21	0.06	0.10	0.03
2.28	1.34	8.72	0.08	0.02	0.09	0.04
2.11	0.13	−2.48	0.16	0.02	0.13	0.01
NA	NA	NA	0.22	0.004	0.05	NA
NA	NA	1.25	0.15	0.02	[←— 0.04 —→]	
NA	NA	NA	0.17	0.05	0.07	NA

d. Mean value of the fraction of dwelling units vacant is 0.052 for San Jose.
e. The mean values of additional variables for Stockton are: average sales price (1977) = 43.32 (thousands of dollars); average change in sales price (1977–1976) = 7.8 (thousands of dollars); fraction vacant 1975 = 0.047; change in percent vacant (1975–1970) = 0.87.

In general, we report comparisons in terms of the ratio of the probability of a given decision for an application with certain characteristics to the probability of that decision for the typical application. The probabilities of each decision for the typical application are presented in Tables 5.4 and 5.5 for 1977 and 1978, respectively. They vary considerably across metropolitan areas. It is for this reason that ratios must be used to compare the differential impact of discrimination measures on outcomes across areas.

Since the denial of an application is clearly an adverse decision, the following discussion focuses on these results. Although downward modification has a somewhat ambiguous meaning, the measures of discrimination are unlikely to be strongly correlated with the types of applicants who revise their requested loan amounts downward. Therefore, downward-modification results are summarized but should be interpreted cautiously as evidence of adverse action.

Table 5.4
Probability of various outcomes for the typical application in California, 1977 (percent)

Study Area[a]	Denial	Modification	
		Down	Up
Anaheim-Santa Ana-Garden Grove	1.49	2.94	4.13
Bakersfield	0.87	[◄——— 3.99 ———►]	
Fresno	4.41	2.00	1.16
Los Angeles-Long Beach	3.57	4.36	6.37
Los Angeles City	2.47	6.19	4.84
Modesto	3.57	[◄——— 0.42 ———►]	
Oxnard-Ventura	2.39	1.83	0.85
Sacramento	2.56	3.17	1.13
Salinas-Monterey	2.91	[◄——— 4.89 ———►]	
San Bernardino-Riverside-Ontario	0.54	2.42	0.85
San Diego	2.35	3.68	4.45
San Francisco-Oakland	2.54	5.54	0.88
San Jose	1.75	2.62	1.18
Santa Barbara	2.81	[◄——— 5.14 ———►]	
Santa Rosa	0.94	0.83	0.77
Stockton	1.71	[◄——— 1.76 ———►]	
Vallejo-Napa	1.74	0.54	2.56

a. Metropolitan area in all cases except the City of Los Angeles.

Financial Characteristics

The financial characteristics serve the purpose of controlling for the risk of loss associated with the credit worthiness of the applicant, the value of the property, and the requested loan terms. These variables have the expected relationship to lender behavior and are highly significant across equations. Table 5.6 presents denial ratios for the typical application with variations in its financial characteristics that should make it more likely to be denied. As a result, we expect all the ratios in the table to be greater than one, as most of them are; only one is less than one (Santa Barbara in 1977).

The requested-loan-to-appraised-value ratio (RLTOAV) is the most consistent variable; it has a positive coefficient in all the denial and downward-modification equations, and a negative coefficient in all the upward-modification equations. All but one of the coefficients are large and very significant; the exception is the denial equation for the Sali-

Table 5.5
Probability of various outcomes for the typical application in California, 1978 (percent)

Study Area[a]	Denial	Modification	
		Down	Up
Anaheim-Santa Ana-Garden Grove	3.34	4.11	3.02
Bakersfield	1.83	[←——— 4.49 ———→]	
Fresno	6.06	3.91	1.35
Los Angeles-Long Beach	3.34	7.22	2.58
Los Angeles City	3.03	7.01	2.27
Modesto	2.94	[←——— 4.62 ———→]	
Oxnard-Ventura	1.90	5.49	2.34
Sacramento	2.72	4./4	1.60
Salinas-Monterey	12.04	[←——— 4.50 ———→]	
San Bernardino-Riverside-Ontario	1.16	3.01	2.12
San Diego	2.11	5.19	3.34
San Francisco-Oakland	3.53	4.06	3.14
San Jose	2.37	2.45	3.00
Santa Barbara	2.53	[←——— 3.05 ———→]	
Santa Rosa	3.03	0.81	1.61
Stockton	2.01	[←——— 0.50 ———→]	
Vallejo-Napa	1.01	1.90	0.76

a. Metropolitan area in all cases except the City of Los Angeles.

nas-Monterey metropolitan area in 1978. These results indicate that an application is more likely to be denied or modified down, and less likely to be modified up, the higher is the requested loan amount relative to the appraised value of the property.

The coefficients of the requested-loan-to-income ratio variable (RLTOINC) indicate that applications are more likely to be denied or modified down the more this ratio exceeds 2.5. The RLTOINC coefficients are statistically significant at the 5 percent or less level in all the modified-down equations and all but five of the denial equations. In one of the five denial equations, the coefficient is statistically significant at the 10 percent level. It is not statistically significant at the 10 percent or less level in the 1977 equations for the Modesto, San Diego, Santa Barbara, and Stockton metropolitan areas.

At least one of these two financial control variables (RLTOAV and RLTOINC) has a large and statistically significant impact on the lend-

Table 5.6
Denial ratios for several different applications relative to the typical applicant (TA) in California, 1977 and 1978

Study Areas[a]	TA with higher RLTOINC (+1)		TA with higher RLTOAV (+0.1)	
	1977	1978	1977	1978
Anaheim-Santa Ana-Garden Grove	2.36**	2.26**	1.98**	1.52**
Bakersfield	4.27**	7.39**	1.74**	2.37**
Fresno	1.56**	2.00**	1.55**	1.27**
Los Angeles-Long Beach	2.46**	2.03**	1.77**	1.62**
Los Angeles City	1.97**	1.72**	1.75**	1.79**
Modesto	1.88	1.92**	1.39**	1.60**
Oxnard-Ventura	2.64**	3.20**	2.03**	1.77**
Sacramento	2.28**	4.09**	2.43**	2.17**
Salinas-Monterey	1.60**	2.05**	1.93**	1.12
San Bernardino-Riverside-Ontario	5.77**	3.31**	1.58**	3.03**
San Diego	1.33	1.86**	1.49**	1.63**
San Francisco-Oakland	2.17**	2.58**	1.66**	1.85**
San Jose	2.59**	2.20**	1.97**	2.11**
Santa Barbara	0.97	2.86**	2.69**	1.81**
Santa Rosa	2.60**	2.79**	1.93**	2.79**
Stockton	1.30	4.03**	2.01**	2.13**
Vallejo-Napa	3.98**	2.06*	3.34**	2.96**

The ratio is equal to the probability that an application with the indicated characteristics will be denied divided by the probability that the typical application (TA) will be denied. A single asterisk (*) indicates that the coefficient of RLTOINC or RLTOAV is statistically significant at the 5–10 percent level. Two asterisks (**) indicate that it is significant at the 5 percent or less level.
a. Metropolitan area in all cases except the City of Los Angeles.

ing decision in the direction predicted by the theoretical discussion in Chapter 4 in each metropolitan area for each year. In fact, both variables are statistically significant with the expected signs in all but one of the models where the data is sufficient to separate downward and upward modifications; the San Diego metropolitan area for 1977 is the exception.

Neighborhood Characteristics

The neighborhood characteristics have been included to control for the effect of housing-market externalities on the future value of the property securing the loan. The coefficients of these variables are not consistent across metropolitan areas and are sometimes inconsistent across time within the same metropolitan area. The average income and the change in income over a recent year in an area containing the property have the most consistent coefficients. The average income has the expected negative relationship with the likelihood of denial in fifteen of twenty-six cases. All but two of the negative relationships are statistically significant (5 percent level), but only three of the positive relationships are statistically significant.

Contrary to expectations, the change in income between 1975 and 1976 is positively related to the likelihood of denial in nineteen of twenty-two cases and statistically significant in thirteen of them. Two of the three negative relationships are statistically significant. This suggests that any recent change in property values, even if it is an increase, is viewed by lenders as an indication of higher risk of loss.

The variable representing the fraction of households with high income in the census tract generally has the expected negative relationship to the likelihood of denial (nineteen out of thirty-four cases). Only eight of these negative coefficients are statistically significant, and six of the positive ones are significant (10 percent level).

The income change between 1970 and 1975 and change in households between 1975 and 1976 for the area containing the property have coefficients that are positive approximately as often as they are negative. Coefficients of either sign are equally likely to be statistically significant for these two variables.

The coefficient of the change in households between 1970 and 1975, however, is negative more often (seventeen out of twenty-six cases) than it is positive. In addition, nine of the negative coefficients and only four of the positive ones are significant (10 percent level). The negative coefficients indicate that mortgage applications are more likely to be denied if they are secured by properties located in areas that have experienced a decline in population over a period of five years. Population changes over a shorter time period have no consistent relationship to the likelihood of denial.

In a few metropolitan areas, we were able to include additional measures of neighborhood characteristics. The average sales price was positively related to the chance of denial in three of the four cases where it was available; two of these were statistically significant. The change in sales price had statistically significant coefficients in all four cases, but they were positive equally as often as they were negative.

The vacancy rate also had mixed results. It had an expected positive relationship with the likelihood of denial in two of four cases, and one of these positive coefficients was the only statistically significant one among the four. In the Stockton metropolitan area, we also had a measure of the change in the vacancy rate. In both years, the variable indicated that application denial was more likely if the property was located in a neighborhood that had a rising vacancy rate. One of the coefficients was statistically significant at the 5 percent level.

At least one of the neighborhood characteristic variables has a statistically significant (5 percent level) coefficient with the expected relationship to the likelihood of denial for each year in all the large metropolitan areas: Anaheim-Santa Ana-Garden Grove, Los Angeles-Long Beach, Sacramento, San Diego, San Francisco-Oakland, and San Jose. The performance is more mixed for the smaller metropolitan areas; some have a significant expected relationship in only one year and others in neither year. In the Modesto, Santa Rosa, and Vallejo-Napa metropolitan areas, we had only one neighborhood characteristic (FHI) because none of the more recent sources of data (for example, geocoded information from the Internal Revenue Service) provided information for these areas.

Sex

The denial and downward-modification ratios for seventeen study areas in each of two years are presented in Tables 5.7 to 5.10. Four types of applications are compared to the typical application: male-female applications with the woman of childbearing age and the applicant between twenty-five and thirty-four years of age (MFCB25–34); female-only applications with no woman of childbearing age (FONLYNCB); female-only applications with at least one woman of

Table 5.7
Denial ratios by sex for the typical California application, 1977

Study Area[a]	MFNCB[b]	MFCB and 25–34	FONLYNCB	FONLYCB and 25–34	MONLY
Anaheim-Santa Ana-Garden Grove	1.00	1.30*	1.25	1.50	1.23
Bakersfield	1.00	1.14[c]	0.00**	0.48	0.19**
Fresno	1.00	1.21	0.55	0.83	1.07
Los Angeles-Long Beach	1.00	0.61**	0.62**	0.72**	0.69**
Los Angeles City	1.00	0.97	1.10	0.84	0.89
Modesto	1.00	0.42**	0.40	0.91	1.14
Oxnard-Ventura	1.00	0.59*	1.50	0.30	0.76
Sacramento	1.00	1.16	0.71	0.79	0.90
Salinas-Monterey	1.00	1.20	1.15	1.47	0.95
San Bernardino-Riverside-Ontario	1.00	1.01[c]	1.11	0.00**	1.73
San Diego	1.00	0.92[d]	2.43**	1.03	1.96**
San Francisco-Oakland	1.00	1.05[c]	1.08	0.85	1.18
San Jose	1.00	0.56**	0.56**	0.42**	0.64**
Santa Barbara	1.00	1.90[e]	1.06	1.15[c]	0.89
Santa Rosa	1.00	1.38	0.59	1.39	1.09
Stockton	1.00	0.37[d]	0.71	1.06[d]	1.00
Vallejo-Napa	1.00	0.22**	0.07**	0.14	0.41*

The ratio is equal to the probability that an application with the indicated characteristics will be denied divided by the probability that the typical application will be denied. A single asterisk (*) indicates that the numerator of the ratio is statistically significantly different from the denominator at the 5–10 percent level. Two asterisks (**) indicate that the difference is significant at the 5 percent or less level.

a. Metropolitan area in all cases except the City of Los Angeles.

b. This is the typical application described in the text. It is the base for calculating the denial ratios. The other applications involve variations from the typical one in one or more characteristics. See Table 5.4 for the probability of denial for the typical application in each area.

c. Since the ratio for MFCB or FONLYCB for the 35- to 44-year-old age range of the typical application is less than one, it is the 25- to 34-year-old age coefficient that makes the ratio in the table greater than one. The MFCB or FONLYCB coefficient is not statistically significant at the 10 percent or less level.

d. Since the ratio for MFCB or FONLYCB for the 35- to 44-year-old age range of the typical application is greater than one, it is the 25- to 34-year-old age coefficient that makes the ratio in the table less than, or closer to, one. The MFCB or FONLYCB coefficient, however, is not statistically significant at the 10 percent or less level.

e. Same situation as note (c) except the MFCB or FONLYCB ratio for the 35 to 44 age range of the typical application was slightly larger than one.

Table 5.8
Denial ratios by sex for the typical California application, 1978

Study Area[a]	MFNCB[b]	MFCB and 25–34	FONLYNCB	FONLYCB and 25–34	MONLY
Anaheim-Santa Ana-Garden Grove	1.00	1.24	1.34	0.86	1.00
Bakersfield	1.00	1.61	1.05	0.80[c]	0.35*
Fresno	1.00	1.21	1.08	0.83	0.77
Los Angeles-Long Beach	1.00	0.76**	0.84	0.55**	1.08
Los Angeles City	1.00	0.92	0.87	0.39**	1.20*
Modesto	1.00	1.35**	0.45	1.79*	0.68
Oxnard-Ventura	1.00	0.77**	1.26	1.40	1.00
Sacramento	1.00	0.89[d]	1.17	1.08*	1.66**
Salinas-Monterey	1.00	0.89[c]	0.86	0.93[c]	0.88
San Bernardino-Riverside-Ontario	1.00	0.82[d]	2.95*	2.00*	1.53
San Diego	1.00	1.12	1.36	1.61	1.23
San Francisco-Oakland	1.00	0.72**	0.92	0.77*	0.95
San Jose	1.00	0.82[c]	0.69	0.46*	0.96
Santa Barbara	1.00	0.92	2.47*	1.07[e]	0.71
Santa Rosa	1.00	0.63**	0.39**	0.41**	0.58**
Stockton	1.00	1.21	2.65*	0.99	0.96
Vallejo-Napa	1.00	1.76	2.38	0.00**	1.78

The ratio is equal to the probability that an application with the indicated characteristics will be denied divided by the probability that the typical application will be denied. A single asterisk (*) indicates that the numerator of the ratio is statistically significantly different from the denominator at the 5–10 percent level. Two asterisks (**) indicate that the difference is significant at the 5 percent or less level.

a. Metropolitan area in all cases except the City of Los Angeles.

b. This is the typical application described in the text. It is the base for calculating the denial ratios. The other applications involve variations from the typical one in one or more characteristics. See Table 5.5 for the probability of denial for the typical application in each area.

c. See note d, Table 5.7, for explanation.

d. Same situation as in note d to Table 5.7 except the MFCB or FONLYCB coefficient is statistically significant at the 10 percent or less level.

e. See note c, Table 5.7, for explanation.

Table 5.9
Downward-modification ratios by sex for the typical California application, 1977

Study Area[a]	MFNCB[b]	MFCB and 25–34	FONLYNCB	FONLYCB and 25–34	MONLY
Anaheim-Santa Ana-Garden Grove	1.00	0.84[c]	1.02	0.92[c]	1.24
Fresno	1.00	0.81	0.35**	0.41	1.27
Los Angeles-Long Beach	1.00	0.89**	0.97	0.90	0.83**
Los Angeles City	1.00	0.60**	0.73**	0.52**	0.94
Oxnard-Ventura	1.00	0.71	1.19	0.21**	0.70
Sacramento	1.00	0.82[c]	0.92	0.43*	1.09
San Bernardino-Riverside-Ontario	1.00	0.45	1.39	0.42	0.82
San Diego	1.00	0.89	1.00	0.99	0.78
San Francisco-Oakland	1.00	0.67*	0.54**	0.49**	0.67**
San Jose	1.00	0.51**	0.94	0.39**	0.74**
Santa Rosa	1.00	1.42[d]	2.49**	2.15	0.79
Vallejo-Napa	1.00	1.56	3.46	1.20	2.92**

The ratio is equal to the probability that an application with the indicated characteristics will be modified downward divided by the probability that the typical application will be modified downward. A single asterisk (*) indicates that the numerator of the ratio is statistically significantly different from the denominator at the 5–10 percent level. Two asterisks (**) indicate that the difference is significant at the 5 percent or less level.
a. Metropolitan area in all cases except the City of Los Angeles.
b. This is the typical application described in the text. It is the base for calculating the downward-modification ratios. The other applications involve variations from the typical one in one or more characteristics. See Table 5.4 for the probability of downward modification for the typical application in each area.
c. See note d, Table 5.7, for explanation.
d. See note c, Table 5.7, for explanation.

Table 5.10
Downward-modification ratios by sex for the typical California application, 1978

Study Area[a]	MFNCB[b]	MFCB and 25–34	FONLYNCB	FONLYCB and 25–34	MONLY
Anaheim-Santa Ana-Garden Grove	1.00	0.82	0.90	0.57	0.80*
Fresno	1.00	0.71[c]	0.99	0.91[c]	1.00
Los Angeles-Long Beach	1.00	0.63**	0.87	0.62**	0.82**
Los Angeles City	1.00	0.66**	0.76**	0.39**	0.73**
Oxnard-Ventura	1.00	0.71	0.93	0.49	0.76
Sacramento	1.00	0.71**	0.71	0.64	0.85
San Bernardino-Riverside-Ontario	1.00	0.94	0.56	0.52	0.60*
San Diego	1.00	0.73[c]	0.71	0.46	0.87
San Francisco-Oakland	1.00	0.55**	0.63**	0.48**	0.77**
San Jose	1.00	1.03	0.90	0.70	0.83
Santa Rosa	1.00	1.35*	2.81**	0.78	2.35**
Vallejo-Napa	1.00	0.22**	1.50	0.32	0.57

The ratio is equal to the probability that an application with the indicated characteristics will be modified downward divided by the probability that the typical application will be modified downward. A single asterisk (*) indicates that the numerator of the ratio is statistically significantly different from the denominator at the 5–10 percent level. Two asterisks (**) indicate that the difference is significant at the 5 percent or less level.
a. Metropolitan area in all cases except the City of Los Angeles.
b. This is the typical application described in the text. It is the base for calculating the downward-modification ratios. The other applications involve variations from the typical one in one or more characteristics. See Table 5.5 for the probability of downward modification for the typical application in each area.
c. See note d, Table 5.7, for explanation.

childbearing age and the applicant between twenty-five and thirty-four years of age (FONLYCB25–34); and male-only applications (MONLY). Each of these four household types resembles the typical application in all other characteristics.

In the case of households with women of childbearing age, we altered the age of the applicant to make it consistent with having a woman of childbearing age. This was more critical in the case of the female-only than in the male-female applications because the applicant in the latter household is usually the male and he is three to four years older on average than the female. As a result, it would not be unreasonable to illustrate a male-female typical application with a woman of childbearing age (MFCB); however, this household type occurs less frequently than the MFCB25–34 one. One consequence of combining sex and age coefficients for two household types (MFCB25–34 and FONLYCB25–34) is that their denial and downward-modification ratios depend on both factors. When the age coefficient materially alters the ratio, additional footnotes have been used to alert the reader. Any reader wishing to examine additional sex and age interactions can do so with the help of the denial and downward-modification ratios for applications from households of different ages, which are discussed in a later section.

When the denial ratio is greater than one, the evidence is consistent with allegations of discrimination against that household type. According to Tables 5.7 and 5.8, denial ratios less than one occur more frequently than denial ratios greater than one for each of the four household types. In addition, more of the ratios less than one are based on statistically significant coefficients than are the ratios greater than one.

The tables of denial ratios indicate that male-female applications with a woman of childbearing age and an applicant between twenty-five and thirty-four (MFCB25–34) are statistically significantly more likely to be denied in the Anaheim-Santa Ana-Garden Grove (1977) and Modesto (1978) metropolitan areas than an otherwise similar application.[4] The ratios are 1.30 and 1.35, respectively. Older, male-female households with a woman of childbearing age (MFCB) are significantly more likely to be denied in the Sacramento (1978) and San Bernardino-Riverside-Ontario (1978) metropolitan areas, with ratios of 1.48 and 1.12, respectively.[5]

Female-only applications with no women of childbearing age (FON-LYNCB) are more than twice as likely to be denied than the typical application in San Bernardino-Riverside-Ontario (1978), San Diego (1977), Santa Barbara (1978), and Stockton (1978) metropolitan areas; all four coefficients are statistically significant. The denial ratios for the first three of these four study areas are also greater than one in the other year, but the underlying coefficients are not statistically significant for that year.

Female-only applications with at least one woman of childbearing age and an applicant between twenty-five and thirty-four years of age (FONLYCB25–34) are statistically significantly more likely to be denied in the Modesto (1978), Sacramento (1978), and San Bernardino-

Riverside-Ontario (1978) metropolitan areas. The denial ratios of 1.79, 1.08 and 2.00, respectively, indicate relatively large differentials in two of the three study areas.

The tables also indicate that male-only households (MONLY) have a significantly harder time having their application approved than the typical application in the City of Los Angeles (1978) and the Sacramento (1978) and San Diego (1977) metropolitan areas. The chance of denial is 20–96 percent more likely for male-only applications than the typical application in these three study areas in the indicated years. The San Diego MONLY denial ratio is also greater than one in 1978 but the underlying coefficient is not statistically significant.

The downward-modification results are even more inconsistent with sex discrimination allegations than are the denial results. Only 18 of the 96 downward-modification ratios (Tables 5.9 and 5.10) are greater than one compared to 57 of the 136 denial ratios. Furthermore, only 5 of the downward-modification ratios in excess of one are based on statistically significant sex coefficients.

Four of these five occur in the Santa Rosa metropolitan area. Female-only applications with no woman of childbearing age (FONLYNCB) are more than twice as likely to be modified downward than the typical application in 1977 and 1978. Male-female applications with a woman of childbearing age and an applicant between twenty-five and thirty-four years of age (MFCB25–34) and male-only applications are 1.35 and 2.35 times as likely to be modified downward as the typical application in 1978.

The fifth downward-modification ratio that is significantly above one occurs in the Vallejo-Napa metropolitan area in 1978. Male-only applications are nearly three times as likely to be modified downward as the typical application.

Many allegations of sex discrimination assert that lenders discount secondary income, especially when the wage earner is female. Denial and downward-modification ratios for two-worker households by sex are compared to the one-worker typical application in Tables 5.11 to 5.14. Each worker contributes 50 percent of the household income. In general, these results indicate that income from a second worker is favored in the lender decision process. Perhaps two sources of income reduce the variance of income and, hence, the credit risk. Most of the denial and downward-modification ratios are less than one.

When the sex of the applicant is examined, two types of applications have denial ratios greater than one more often than less than one.

Table 5.11
Denial ratios for applications with 50% secondary income by sex relative to the typical application, 1977

Study Area[a]	MFNCB	MFCB and 25–34	FONLYNCB	FONLYCB and 25–34	MONLY
Anaheim-Santa Ana-Garden Grove	1.34**	0.99	1.66**	1.03	0.44**
Bakersfield	0.66	0.58	0.00[b]	0.25	0.12[b]
Fresno	1.41	1.04	0.78	0.90	1.21
Los Angeles-Long Beach	0.60**	0.55[b]	0.37**	0.63[b]	0.81
City of Los Angeles	0.66	0.63**	0.71	0.54**	0.81
Modesto	0.81	0.33[b]	0.32	0.73	2.27*
Oxnard-Ventura	1.29	0.96	1.95	0.49	0.86
Sacramento	1.02	0.76*	0.72	0.51*	0.64*
Salinas-Monterey	1.32	0.68*	1.48	0.82*	0,56*
San Bernardino-Riverside-Ontario	1.05	1.59	1.17	0.00[b]	3.36*
San Diego	1.02	1.44*	2.47[b]	1.61*	2.16[b]
San Francisco-Oakland	1.33	0.65**	1.42	0.52**	0.84**
San Jose	0.61	0.55[b]	0.34[b]	0.40[b]	0.53[b]
Santa Barbara	2.43**	0.95	2.50**	0.57	0.15**
Santa Rosa	1.80	0.90	1.04	0.92	1.68
Stockton	1.48	0.34[b]	1.06	0.98	0.60
Vallejo-Napa	0.23**	0.38[b]	0.02[b]	0.24	0.58[b]

The ratio is equal to the probability than an application with the indicated characteristics will be denied divided by the probability that the typical application will be denied. A single asterisk (*) indicates that the underlying secondary-income coefficients that account for the difference between the numerator and the denominator of the ratio are statistically significant at the 5–10 percent level. Two asterisks (**) indicate that said coefficients are significant at the 5 percent or less level. The typical application is described in the text. It has no secondary income and is the base for calculating the denial ratios. The other applications involve variations from the typical one in one or more characteristics. See Table 5.4 for the probability of denial for the typical application in each area.
a. Metropolitan area in all cases except the City of Los Angeles.
b. The substantial difference of this ratio from 1.00 is largely due to statistically significant sex or age coefficients and not the coefficients of the secondary-income variables. However, if one or more asterisks appear with a b, the secondary-income coefficients are also statistically significant. See Tables 5.7 to 5.10 and 5.15 to 5.18 for a summary of the sex and age results.

Table 5.12
Denial ratios for applications with 50% secondary income by sex relative to the typical applications, 1978

Study Area[a]	MFNCB	MFCB and 25–34	FONLYNCB	FONLYCB and 25–34	MONLY
Anaheim-Santa Ana-Garden Grove	1.44*	0.55**	1.91*	0.38**	1.11
Bakersfield	1.56	0.62**	1.65	0.31**	0.62
Fresno	1.17	0.68	1.26	0.49	0.34*
Los Angeles-Long Beach	0.71**	0.54**	0.60**	0.39**	0.81**
City of Los Angeles	0.78*	0.55**	0.67*	0.23**[b]	1.07
Modesto	1.23	0.57	0.53	0.76	0.39
Oxnard-Ventura	1.69	0.68[b]	2.16	1.21	1.13
Sacramento	1.14	1.07	1.34	1.29	1.81[b]
Salinas-Monterey	1.09	0.51**	0.93	0.54**	1.07
San Bernardino-Riverside-Ontario	1.17	1.03	3.42[b]	2.56[b]	0.36**
San Diego	1.44*	0.99	1.96*	1.42	1.12
San Francisco-Oakland	0.93	0.64[b]	1.05	0.59[b]	0.99
San Jose	0.57**	0.57**[b]	0.39**	0.32**[b]	0.99
Santa Barbara	1.26	0.53	3.07[b]	0.61	0.73
Santa Rosa	0.61*	0.67[b]	0.24*[b]	0.44[b]	0.71[b]
Stockton	0.49	0.72	1.33[b]	0.59	0.92
Vallejo-Napa	1.36	0.56	2.83	0.00[b]	1.20

The ratio is equal to the probability that an application with the indicated characteristics will be denied divided by the probability that the typical application will be denied. A single asterisk (*) indicates that the underlying secondary-income coefficients that account for the difference between the numerator and denominator of the ratio are statistically significant at the 5–10 percent level. Two asterisks (**) indicate that they are significant at the 5 percent or less level. The typical application is described in the text. It has no secondary income and is the base for calculating the denial ratios. The other applications involve variations from the typical one in one or more characteristics. See Table 5.5 for the probability of denial for the typical application in each area.
a. Metropolitan area in all cases except the City of Los Angeles.
b. See note b, Table 5.11.

Table 5.13

Downward-modification ratios for applications with 50% secondary income by sex relative to the typical application, 1977

Study Area[a]	MFNCB	MFCB and 25–34	FONLYNCB	FONLYCB and 25–34	MONLY
Anaheim-Santa Ana-Garden Grove	1.38**	0.58*	1.40**	0.63*	1.09
Fresno	0.84	0.59	0.30[b]	0.29	0.74
Los Angeles-Long Beach	0.95	0.79	0.92	0.81	0.78
City of Los Angeles	0.65**	0.48**	0.47**	0.40**	0.74**
Oxnard-Ventura	0.92	0.79	1.09	0.23[b]	1.06
Sacramento	0.79	0.41**	0.73	0.21**[b]	1.23
San Bernardino-Riverside-Ontario	0.74	0.23*	1.04	0.21*	2.50*
San Diego	1.28	0.41**	1.27	0.46**	0.91
San Francisco-Oakland	0.64**	0.37**[b]	0.34**[b]	0.27**[b]	0.51**[b]
San Jose	0.74	0.52[b]	0.70	0.39[b]	0.64[b]
Santa Rosa	1.50*	0.80**	3.68*[b]	1.23[b]	1.94**
Vallejo-Napa	1.34	2.80	4.58	2.15	7.19**[b]

The ratio is equal to the probability that an application with the indicated characteristics will be downward modified divided by the probability that the typical application will be downward modified. A single asterisk (*) indicates that the underlying secondary-income coefficients that account for the difference between the numerator and denominator of the ratio are statistically significant at the 5–10 percent level. Two asterisks (**) indicate that they are significant at the 5 percent or less level. The typical application is described in the text. It has no secondary income and is the base for calculating the downward-modification ratios. The other applications involve variations from the typical one in one or more characteristics. See Table 5.4 for the probability of downward modification for the typical application in each area.

a. Metropolitan area in all cases except the City of Los Angeles.

b. See note b, Table 5.11.

Table 5.14
Downward-modification ratios for applications with 50% secondary income by sex
relative to the typical application, 1978

Study Area[a]	MFNCB	MFCB and 25–34	FONLYNCB	FONLYCB and 25–34	MONLY
Anaheim-Santa Ana-Garden Grove	0.84	0.52**	0.76	0.36**	0.52**
Fresno	1.61	0.81[b]	1.59*	1.05	1.64*
Los Angeles-Long Beach	0.66**	0.58[b]	0.57**	0.57[b]	0.78[b]
City of Los Angeles	0.62**	0.40**[b]	0.47**	0.23**[b]	0.58**[b]
Oxnard-Ventura	0.50	0.35**[b]	0.47	0.24**[b]	0.66
Sacramento	0.73*	0.91	0.51	0.82	0.63
San Bernardino-Riverside-Ontario	0.51*	0.44*	0.28*	0.25*	0.15**
San Diego	0.82	0.54**[b]	0.58	0.34**[b]	0.58**
San Francisco-Oakland	0.80*	0.48[b]	0.49*[b]	0.42[b]	0.79
San Jose	1.41**	0.46**	1.26**	0.31**	0.68
Santa Rosa	0.90	1.51[b]	2.52[b]	0.88	1.75[b]
Vallejo-Napa	0.45	1.06	0.60	1.51	0.00**

The ratio is equal to the probability that an application with the indicated characteristics will be downward modified divided by the probability that the typical application will be downward modified. A single asterisk (*) indicates that the underlying secondary-income coefficients that account for the difference between the numerator and denominator of the ratio are statistically significant at the 5–10 percent level. Two asterisks (**) indicate that they are significant at the 5 percent or less level. The typical application is described in the text. It has no secondary income and is the base for calculating the downward-modification ratios. The other applications involve variations from the typical one in one or more characteristics. See Table 5.5 for the probability of downward modification for the typical application in each area.
a. Metropolitan area in all cases except the City of Los Angeles.
b. See note b, Table 5.11.

These are applications from male-female and female-only households provided there are no women of childbearing age (MFNCB and FON-LYNCB, respectively). However, very few of the secondary-income coefficients responsible for these ratios in excess of one are statisti cally significant at the 10 percent level. The following paragraphs summarize the cases of those ratios larger than one that are based on statistically significant secondary-income coefficients.

Male-female applicants with no woman of childbearing age (MFNCB) with two equal incomes are 1.34 to 2.43 times as likely to be denied than are typical applicants with no secondary income in the Anaheim-Santa Ana-Garden Grove (1977 and 1978), San Diego (1978), and Santa Barbara (1977) metropolitan areas.[6] These types of appli cants are also 1.38 to 1.50 times as likely to receive downward modi fications than the typical applicant with only one worker in the Anaheim-Santa Ana-Garden Grove (1977), San Jose (1978), and Santa Rosa (1977) metropolitan areas. Female-only households with no women of childbearing age (FONLYNCB) receive essentially the same treatment as MFNCB applicants in these metropolitan areas and the Fresno (1978) metropolitan area.

Applications from households with women of childbearing age, whether male-female or female only, who have two workers earning equal incomes are approximately 1.50 times as likely to be denied than the typical application with only one worker in only one metropolitan area: San Diego (1977).

Male-only applications with two workers earning equal income are more than twice as likely to be denied than the typical application with only one worker in the Modesto (1977) and San Bernardino-Riverside-Ontario (1977) metropolitan areas. These applicants are also 1.64 to 7.19 times as likely to be downward modified in the Fresno (1978), San Bernardino-Riverside-Ontario (1977), Santa Rosa (1977), and Val-lejo-Napa (1977) metropolitan areas.

Age of Applicant
The denial and downward-modification ratios for applicants of various ages are presented in Tables 5.15 to 5.18. The denial ratios indicate that the typical applicant who is 35 to 44 years old is the most likely to be denied; nearly all the denial ratios for the other four age cate gories (under 25, 25 to 34, 45 to 54, and over 54) are less than one. In addition, nearly half the ratios below one are statistically significant.

The downward-modification ratios are substantially below one for

Table 5.15
Denial ratios by age of the applicant for typical applications, 1977

Study Area[a]	ALT25	A25–34	A35–44[b]	A45–54	AGE55
Anaheim-Santa Ana-Garden Grove	0.85	1.12	1.00	0.83	0.87
Bakersfield	0.90	1.40	1.00	1.04	1.83
Fresno	0.87	1.05	1.00	0.81	1.14
Los Angeles-Long Beach	0.61**	1.08	1.00	0.68**	0.66**
City of Los Angeles	0.75	1.01	1.00	0.61**	0.56**
Modesto	0.60	0.74	1.00	0.50**	0.23**
Oxnard-Ventura	0.69	0.83	1.00	0.49**	0.17**
Sacramento	1.03	1.02	1.00	1.30	1.38
Salinas-Monterey	0.40*	1.12	1.00	0.76	0.41*
San Bernardino-Riverside-Ontario	0.74	1.18	1.00	0.98	0.55
San Diego	0.72	0.89	1.00	0.87	0.88
San Francisco-Oakland	0.63**	1.09	1.00	0.89	0.81
San Jose	1.04	0.92	1.00	0.63**	0.21**
Santa Barbara	0.80	1.87*	1.00	0.66	0.76
Santa Rosa	0.99	1.05	1.00	1.74*	1.04
Stockton	0.19**	0.26**	1.00	0.31**	0.34*
Vallejo-Napa	1.85	0.46**	1.00	0.53	1.41

The ratio is equal to the probability that an application with the indicated characteristics will be denied divided by the probability that the typical application will be denied. A single asterisk (*) indicates that the numerator of the ratio is statistically significantly different from the denominator at the 5–10 percent level. Two asterisks (**) indicate that the difference is significant at the 5 percent or less level.
a. Metropolitan area in all cases except the City of Los Angeles.
b. This is the typical application described in the text. It is the base for calculating the denial ratios. The other applications involve variations from the typical one in one or more characteristics. See Table 5.4 for the probability of denial for the typical application in each area.

Table 5.16
Denial ratios by age of the applicant for typical applications, 1978

Study Area[a]	ALT25	A25–34	A35–44[b]	A45–54	AGE55
Anaheim-Santa Ana-Garden Grove	0.80	1.15*	1.00	0.89	0.72**
Bakersfield	0.70	0.76	1.00	1.04	0.78
Fresno	0.95	0.76*	1.00	0.92	0.85
Los Angeles-Long Beach	0.69**	0.88**	1.00	0.89**	0.80**
City of Los Angeles	0.94	0.90**	1.00	0.85*	1.00
Modesto	0.80	0.62*	1.00	1.09	1.75
Oxnard-Ventura	1.56	1.12	1.00	1.05	0.57**
Sacramento	0.83	0.60**	1.00	1.28	1.05
Salinas-Monterey	0.67	0.71	1.00	0.55**	0.79
San Bernardino-Riverside-Ontario	0.80	0.73	1.00	1.37	1.89
San Diego	0.93	1.10	1.00	1.43**	0.94
San Francisco Oakland	0.78*	0.87**	1.00	1.02	0.79*
San Jose	0.89	0.78**	1.00	0.66**	0.83
Santa Barbara	0.71	1.06	1.00	0.53	1.03
Santa Rosa	0.84	1.06	1.00	1.18	0.64*
Stockton	0.37*	1.15	1.00	0.75	0.45*
Vallejo-Napa	0.22**	0.86	1.00	1.06	0.00**

The ratio is equal to the probability that an application with the indicated characteristics will be denied divided by the probability that the typical application will be denied. A single asterisk (*) indicates that the numerator of the ratio is statistically significantly different from the denominator at the 5–10 percent level. Two asterisks (**) indicate that the difference is significant at the 5 percent or less level.
a. Metropolitan area in all cases except the City of Los Angeles.
b. This is the typical application described in the text. It is the base for calculating the denial ratios. The other applications involve variations from the typical one in one or more characteristics. See Table 5.5 for the probability of denial for the typical application in each area.

Table 5.17
Downward-modification ratios by age of applicant for typical applications, 1977

Study Area[a]	ALT25	A25–34	A35–44[b]	A45–54	AGE55
Anaheim-Santa Ana-Garden Grove	0.43**	0.69**	1.00	0.96	1.18
Fresno	0.54*	0.82	1.00	0.34**	1.05
Los Angeles-Long Beach	0.90	0.96	1.00	1.41**	1.40**
City of Los Angeles	0.90	0.78**	1.00	1.08	1.18
Oxnard-Ventura	0.47**	0.86	1.00	1.13	0.81
Sacramento	0.51*	0.80*	1.00	0.92	0.99
San Bernardino-Riverside-Ontario	0.88	0.52**	1.00	0.88	1.53
San Diego	0.91	0.99	1.00	1.30	1.15
San Francisco-Oakland	0.79	0.73**	1.00	0.90	0.94
San Jose	1.04	0.78**	1.00	1.01	0.80
Santa Rosa	0.91	1.72**	1.00	0.49*	1.63
Vallejo-Napa	0.33*	0.70	1.00	1.00	3.63**

The ratio is equal to the probability that an application with the indicated characteristics will be downward modified divided by the probability that the typical application will be downward modified. A single asterisk (*) indicates that the numerator of the ratio is statistically significantly different from the denominator at the 5–10 percent level. Two asterisks (**) indicate that the difference is significant at the 5 percent or less level.
a. Metropolitan area in all cases except the City of Los Angeles.
b. This is the typical application described in the text. It is the base for calculating the downward-modification ratios. The other applications involve variations from the typical one in one or more characteristics. See Table 5.4 for the probability of downward modification for the typical application in each area.

the youngest applicants (under 25) and above one for the oldest applicants (over 54). This is the only identifiable pattern in the downward-modification results. It indicates that applicants over 54 years of age are more likely to receive downward modifications in their requested loan amount than are applications from similarly situated persons between 35 and 44, and that the reverse is true for applications from persons under 25.

Race
Tables 5.19 to 5.22 present denial and downward-modification ratios for typical applications from different racial groups that are otherwise similar. The denial ratios provide strong and consistent evidence that members of minority groups receive unfavorable treatment from California savings and loan associations. The clearest case of discriminatory treatment exists for blacks. Applications from blacks are 1.54

Table 5.18
Downward-modification ratios by age of applicant for typical applications, 1978

Study Area[a]	ALT25	A25–34	A35–44[b]	A45–54	AGE55
Anaheim-Santa Ana-Garden Grove	0.49**	0.82**	1.00	0.70**	1.23
Fresno	0.59*	0.61**	1.00	0.98	1.00
Los Angeles-Long Beach	0.73**	0.78**	1.00	0.96	1.06
City of Los Angeles	0.77*	0.78**	1.00	0.86*	0.94
Oxnard Ventura	0.52*	0.73*	1.00	0.85	1.16
Sacramento	0.59**	0.94	1.00	1.01	1.00
San Bernardino-Riverside-Ontario	1.01	1.12	1.00	1.63*	0.96
San Diego	0.72*	0.67	1.00	1.19	1.17
San Francisco-Oakland	0.54**	0.80**	1.00	1.14	1.05
San Jose	0.74	0.97	1.00	0.95	1.00
Santa Rosa	0.62	0.75	1.00	1.30	1.17
Vallejo-Napa	0.00**	1.28	1.00	2.31**	2.91**

The ratio is equal to the probability that an application with the indicated characteristics will be downward modified divided by the probability that the typical application will be downward modified. A single asterisk (*) indicates that the numerator of the ratio is statistically significantly different from the denominator at the 5–10 percent level. Two asterisks (**) indicate that the difference is significant at the 5 percent or less level.
a. Metropolitan area in all cases except the City of Los Angeles.
b. This is the typical application described in the text. It is the base for calculating the downward-modification ratios. The other applications involve variations from the typical one in one or more characteristics. See Table 5.5 for the probability of downward modification for the typical application in each area.

to 7.82 times as likely to be denied than applications from similarly situated whites. This pattern of ratios greater than one holds for all the metropolitan areas in nearly every year. The only exceptions are in the Anaheim-Santa Ana-Garden Grove (1977), Santa Rosa (1978), and Stockton (1978) metropolitan areas. These large differentials in the treatment of black applicants are generally statistically significant; twenty-four of the twenty-seven denial ratios in excess of one are significant at the ten percent one-tail level. In two metropolitan areas (Modesto and Santa Barbara), black and other minority applicants had to be grouped together because of limited observations. In these cases, as well, the combined coefficient is greater than one in all four samples and highly significant in two.

The denial ratio evidence is also consistent with allegations that mortgage lenders discriminate against Spanish and other minority ap-

Table 5.19
Denial ratios by race of applicant for typical applications, 1977

Study Area[a]	White[b]	Black	Spanish	Asian	Other Minority
Anaheim-Santa Ana-Garden Grove	1.00	0.00**	1.20	1.15	1.31
Bakersfield	1.00	7.82**	2.14[c]	5.75**	5.95**
Fresno	1.00	3.13**	1.62*	1.38	2.39**
Los Angeles-Long Beach	1.00	1.54**	1.16*	0.83	1.31[c]
City of Los Angeles	1.00	2.77**	1.08	0.85	1.75*
Modesto	1.00	[d]	1.08	[e]	2.88**
Oxnard-Ventura	1.00	2.04	1.50	0.64	1.35
Sacramento	1.00	2.03[c]	1.29	1.19	1.70
Salinas-Monterey	1.00	2.70*	1.89*	0.28*	1.94*
San Bernardino-Riverside-Ontario	1.00	2.72[c]	0.85	0.73	0.71
San Diego	1.00	2.47**	1.01	0.87	0.83
San Francisco-Oakland	1.00	1.56**	1.01	0.98	1.37*
San Jose	1.00	4.16**	1.71**	1.64**	1.21
Santa Barbara	1.00	[d]	1.54	0.00**	2.12
Santa Rosa	1.00	1.76	1.39	3.13*	2.00
Stockton	1.00	7.29**	2.52*	2.44	1.81
Vallejo-Napa	1.00	4.92**	1.58	2.69[c]	2.09

The ratio is equal to the probability that an application with the indicated characteristics will be denied divided by the probability that the typical application will be denied. A single asterisk (*) indicates that the numerator of the ratio is statistically significantly different from the denominator at the 5–10 percent level. Two asterisks (**) indicate that the difference is significant at the 5 percent or less level.
a. Metropolitan area in all cases except the City of Los Angeles.
b. This is the typical application described in the text. It is the base for calculating the denial ratios. The other applications involve variations from the typical one in one or more characteristics. See Table 5.4 for the probability of denial for the typical application in each area.
c. The numerator is statistically significantly larger than the denominator at the 10 percent one-tail level.
d. Grouped together with other minorities because of the limited number of observations on this type of household.
e. Grouped together with whites due to the limited number of observations.

Table 5.20
Denial ratios by race of applicant for typical applications, 1978

Study Area[a]	White[b]	Black	Spanish	Asian	Other Minority
Anaheim-Santa Ana-Garden Grove	1.00	2.37**	1.29[c]	0.75*	1.29
Bakersfield	1.00	4.15**	0.47*	1.31	0.00**
Fresno	1.00	1.81[c]	1.28	0.76	1.51
Los Angeles-Long Beach	1.00	1.69**	1.04	0.79**	1.50**
City of Los Angeles	1.00	2.12**	1.28**	1.11	1.57*
Modesto	1.00	[d]	1.27	[e]	1.40
Oxnard-Ventura	1.00	1.34	1.60*	0.97	1.51
Sacramento	1.00	3.44**	1.66*	0.97	2.11**
Salinas-Monterey	1.00	2.12**	1.69**	1.25	2.46**
San Bernardino-Riverside-Ontario	1.00	4.27**	1.54[c]	0.75	0.43
San Diego	1.00	1.95*	1.05	1.32	1.21
San Francisco-Oakland	1.00	1.59**	1.29**	1.16[c]	1.19
San Jose	1.00	2.67**	1.22	0.76	1.79*
Santa Barbara	1.00	[d]	1.12	0.95	3.60**
Santa Rosa	1.00	0.67	0.69	0.49	0.00**
Stockton	1.00	0.38	0.78	0.50	0.40
Vallejo-Napa	1.00	2.65[c]	2.20	1.35	0.00**

The ratio is equal to the probability that an application with the indicated characteristics will be denied divided by the probability that the typical application will be denied. A single asterisk (*) indicates that the numerator of the ratio is statistically significantly different from the denominator at the 5–10 percent level. Two asterisks (**) indicate that the difference is significant at the 5 percent or less level.
a. Metropolitan area in all cases except the City of Los Angeles.
b. This is the typical application described in the text. It is the base for calculating the denial ratios. The other applications involve variations from the typical one in one or more characteristics. See Table 5.5 for the probability of denial for the typical application in each area.
c. See note c, to Table 5.19.
d. See note d, to Table 5.19.
e. See note e, to Table 5.19.

Table 5.21
Downward-modification ratios by race of applicant for typical applications, 1977

Study Area[a]	White[b]	Black	Spanish	Asian	Other Minority
Anaheim-Santa Ana-Garden Grove	1.00	0.95	0.82	1.25	1.15
Fresno	1.00	0.45	0.81	0.88	1.67
Los Angeles-Long Beach	1.00	0.74**	0.98	1.06	1.05
City of Los Angeles	1.00	0.40**	1.19[c]	0.94	1.19
Oxnard-Ventura	1.00	1.32	1.08	1.14	1.76
Sacramento	1.00	0.00**	0.80	0.79	1.53
San Bernardino-Riverside-Ontario	1.00	0.39	1.02	1.36	0.00**
San Diego	1.00	0.59	1.65**	0.63	0.61
San Francisco-Oakland	1.00	0.78	1.10	1.05	0.75*
San Jose	1.00	1.15	1.15	0.97	0.76
Santa Rosa	1.00	1.44	0.79	0.00**	1.61
Vallejo-Napa	1.00	2.23	2.11	2.07	1.53

The ratio is equal to the probability that an application with the indicated characteristics will be downward modified divided by the probability that the typical application will be modified downward. A single asterisk (*) indicates that the numerator of the ratio is statistically significantly different from the denominator at the 5–10 percent level. Two asterisks (**) indicate that the difference is significant at the 5 percent or less level.
a. Metropolitan area in all cases except the City of Los Angeles.
b. This is the typical application described in the text. It is the base for calculating the downward-modification ratios. The other applications involve variations from the typical one in one or more characteristics. See Table 5.4 for the probability of downward modification for the typical application in each area.
c. See note c, Table 5.19.

plicants: thirty of the thirty-four denial ratios for Spanish applicants and twenty-seven of the thirty-four for other minority applicants are greater than one. Approximately half of these ratios in excess of one are statistically significant at the 10 percent two-tail level; three more are significant at the 10 percent one-tail level. Spanish applicants are as much as 2.5 times as likely to be denied than similarly situated white applicants; other minorities are as much as 5.9 times as likely to be denied.

Applications from Asians receive more favorable treatment than similarly situated white applicants as often as they receive less favorable treatment. Since very few of these differentials are statistically significant at the two-tail 10 percent level, it appears that similarly situated Asian and white applicants receive equal treatment with re-

Table 5.22
Downward-modification ratios by race of applicant for typical applications, 1978

Study Area[a]	White[b]	Black	Spanish	Asian	Other Minority
Anaheim-Santa Ana-Garden Grove	1.00	0.53	1.11	0.91	0.87
Fresno	1.00	0.77	1.18	0.47	0.86
Los Angeles-Long Beach	1.00	0.69**	1.07	1.05	1.07
City of Los Angeles	1.00	0.87	1.04	1.05	1.12
Oxnard-Ventura	1.00	0.89	1.16	1.46	0.98
Sacramento	1.00	1.29	1.28	1.16	1.00
San Bernardino-Riverside-Ontario	1.00	3.30**	1.08	2.00[c]	2.38[c]
San Diego	1.00	1.01	1.11	1.23	0.86
San Francisco-Oakland	1.00	0.93	0.84	0.96	0.84
San Jose	1.00	1.09	0.61*	0.72	0.76
Santa Rosa	1.00	0.98	0.74	3.22**	1.17
Vallejo-Napa	1.00	3.71**	0.57	2.09[c]	1.17

The ratio is equal to the probability that an application with the indicated characteristics will be downward modified divided by the probability that the typical application will be modified downward. A single asterisk (*) indicates that the numerator of the ratio is statistically significantly different from the denominator at the 5–10 percent level. Two asterisks (**) indicate that the difference is significant at the 5 percent or less level.
a. Metropolitan area in all cases except the City of Los Angeles.
b. This is the typical application described in the text. It is the base for calculating the downward-modification ratios. The other applications involve variations from the typical one in one or more characteristics. See Table 5.5 for the probability of downward modification for the typical application in each area.
c. See note c, Table 5.19.

gard to a decision to deny an application. The only results consistent with discrimination against Asian applicants occur in the Bakersfield (1977), San Francisco-Oakland (1978), San Jose (1977), and Santa Rosa (1977) metropolitan areas.

The downward-modification ratios in Tables 5.21 and 5.22 are greater than one approximately as frequently as they are less than one for all races. In addition, very few of these differentials are statistically significant. Therefore, there is little evidence that minorities are discriminated against in the decision to modify downward a requested loan amount. The statistically significant exceptions are: black applicants in the San Bernardino-Riverside-Ontario (1978) and Vallejo-Napa (1978) metropolitan areas; Spanish applicants in the City of Los Angeles (1977) and the San Diego (1977) metropolitan area; Asian applicants in the San Bernardino-Riverside-Ontario (1978), Santa Rosa (1978), and Vallejo-Napa (1978) metropolitan areas; and other minorities in the San Bernardino-Riverside-Ontario (1978) metropolitan area.

Redlining

Three types of redlining allegations have been analyzed: specific neighborhoods that community-based or other organizations have alleged to be redlined, older neighborhoods, and largely minority neighborhoods.

Property Location   Information containing allegations that specific neighborhoods are redlined by mortgage lenders was available to us for Los Angeles County and the cities of Oakland and Sacramento. In addition to examining these specific allegations, we also compared lending practices in the central cities to those in the surrounding suburbs because of general allegations that lenders favor the suburbs over the older central cities.

The denial and downward-modification ratios for Los Angeles neighborhoods are presented in Table 5.23. In general, the results are inconsistent with allegations that the twelve neighborhoods are redlined. There are, however, some important and statistically significant exceptions. The denial and modification ratios are greater than one for the Long Beach-Southwest and San Pedro neighborhoods in both years, with three of the four denial ratios being based on statistically significant (10 percent one-tail level) differentials between these neighborhoods and the Los Angeles County suburbs. In addition, the denial ratios are consistent with redlining allegations and are based on statistically significant differentials in the East Los Angeles-Boyle Heights-Echo Park (1978) and Pomona (1977) neighborhoods. Similarly, the downward-modification ratios support redlining allegations for the Covina-Azusa (1977), Pacoima-San Fernando (1977 and 1978), and Venice-Santa Monica (1978) neighborhoods. However, the downward-modification ratios for the portion of the City of Los Angeles that is not alleged to be redlined are also consistent with redlining in both years. Therefore, the redlining results are mixed for Los Angeles County. The Los Angeles City model has essentially the same results except that the South Central Los Angeles denial ratio for 1977 and downward-modification ratio for 1978 and the East Los Angeles-Boyle Heights-Echo Park downward-modification ratio, although still greater than one, are based on statistically significant differentials relative to

Table 5.23
Denial and downward-modification ratios by property location: Los Angeles-Long Beach SMSA

Neighborhood	Denial		Downward Modification	
	1977	1978	1977	1978
Allegedly red-lined neighborhoods[a]				
Compton	0.00**	1.04	2.88	1.80
Covina-Azusa	0.00**	1.08	2.62**	0.07**
East L.A.-Boyle Heights-Echo Park	0.57	1.61**	0.77	1.10
Highland Park	1.39	1.30	0.18**	0.30**
Long Beach-Southwest	2.48[b]	1.56[b]	1.19	1.94
Pacoima-San Fernando	0.59	0.97	2.46**	1.58**
Pasadena-North Central	1.17	1.15	1.50	0.64
Pomona	1.99[b]	1.38	0.82	0.92
San Pedro	1.47	2.00**	1.52	1.23
South Central L.A.	1.17	0.86	0.61**	1.19
Venice-Santa Monica	1.24	1.09	0.54	2.47**
West Covina	1.07	0.54	3.82	1.17
Other areas				
Rest of the City of Long Beach	0.96	0.68**	0.84	0.58**
Rest of the City of Los Angeles	1.04	0.93	1.30**	1.09**
Rest of Los Angeles County[c]	1.00	1.00	1.00	1.00

The ratio is equal to the probability that an application with the indicated characteristics will be denied or modified divided by the probability that the typical application will be denied or modified. A single asterisk (*) indicates that the numerator of the ratio is statistically significantly different from the denominator at the 5–10 percent level. Two asterisks (**) indicate that the difference is significant at the 5 percent or less level.
SMSA is the abbreviation for Standard Metropolitan Statistical Area as defined by the U.S. Bureau of the Census.
a. The redlining allegations are derived from *Where the Money Is: Mortgage Lending, Los Angeles County* (Los Angeles: The Center for New Corporate Priorities, 1975). This report is reprinted in *Hearings on the Home Mortgage Disclosure Act of 1975*, U.S. Senate, Committee on Banking, Housing and Urban Affairs, 94th Cong., 1st sess., May 5–8, 1975.
b. The numerator is statistically significantly larger than the denominator at the 10 percent one-tail level.
c. This is the typical application described in the text. It is the base for calculating the denial or modification ratios. The other applications involve variations from the typical

Table 5.24

Denial and downward-modification ratios by property location: Sacramento SMSA

Neighborhood	Denial		Downward Modification	
	1977	1978	1977	1978
Allegedly redlined neighborhood[a]				
Old Sacramento	0.69	0.28**	1.03	0.46
Other areas				
Rest of Sacramento City	0.76*	0.40**	0.69**	0.66**
Rest of the Sacramento SMSA[b]	1.00	1.00	1.00	1.00

The ratio is equal to the probability that an application with the indicated characteristics will be denied or modified divided by the probability that the typical application will be denied or modified. A single asterisk (*) indicates that the numerator of the ratio is statistically significantly different from the denominator at the 5–10 percent level. Two asterisks (**) indicate that the difference is significant at the 5 percent or less level.

SMSA is the abbreviation for Standard Metropolitan Statistical Area as defined by the U.S. Bureau of the Census.

a. The redlining allegation is derived from Dennis Dingemans, *Residential Mortgage Lending Patterns: A Case Study of Sacramento in 1976* (Davis, California: University of California Institute of Governmental Affairs, 1978).

b. This is the typical application described in the text. It is the base for calculating the denial or modification ratios. The other applications involve variations from the typical one in one or more characteristics. See Tables 5.4 and 5.5 for the probability of denial or modification for the typical application in each area-year.

the rest of the City of Los Angeles instead of suburban Los Angeles County.[7]

The denial and modification ratios by property location in the Sacramento and San Francisco-Oakland metropolitan areas are presented in Tables 5.24 and 5.25. There is no evidence that applications for mortgages on properties in the two neighborhoods alleged to be redlined have a statistically significantly higher chance of denial or downward modification than similar applications on suburban properties.

Central city denial and downward-modification ratios for the typical application are presented in Table 5.26. Only six of these ratios indicate that either denial or downward modification is statistically significantly more likely for mortgage applications on central-city properties than for similar applications on suburban properties. These central

one in one or more characteristics. See Tables 5.4 and 5.5 for the probability of denial or modification for the typical application in area-year. The term "area-year" refers to the results for a study area in a specific year.

Table 5.25
Denial and downward-modification ratios by property location: San Francisco-Oakland SMSA

Neighborhoods	Denial		Downward Modification	
	1977	1978	1977	1978
Allegedly redlined neighborhood[a]				
Central Oakland	0.85	0.65*	0.48**	1.37
Other areas				
Alameda City	0.38**	0.88	0.62	0.93
Berkeley	0.97	1.13	0.24**	1.34
East Oakland	0.57**	0.84	0.46**	1.25
West Oakland	0.80	0.77	0.00**	0.64
Rest of Alameda County	1.00	0.86	0.47**	0.90
Contra Costa County	0.80**	0.72**	0.64**	0.93
Marin County	0.90	0.96	0.76**	1.68**
San Francisco	0.81*	0.56**	1.07	0.86*
San Mateo County[b]	1.00	1.00	1.00	1.00

The ratio is equal to the probability that an application with the indicated characteristics will be denied or modified divided by the probability that the typical application will be denied or modified. A single asterisk (*) indicates that the numerator of the ratio is statistically significantly different from the denominator at the 5–10 percent level. Two asterisks (**) indicate that the difference is significant at the 5 percent or less level.
SMSA is the abbreviation for Standard Metropolitan Statistical Area as defined by the U.S. Bureau of the Census.
a. The redlining allegation is derived from William M. Frej, "Discriminatory Lending Practices in Oakland," in *Hearings on the Home Mortgage Disclosure Act of* 1975, U.S. Senate, Committee on Banking, Housing and Urban Affairs, 94th Cong., 1st sess., May 5–8, 1975.
b. This is the typical application described in the text. It is the base for calculating the denial or modification ratios. The other applications involve variations from the typical one in one or more characteristics. See Tables 5.4 and 5.5 for the probability of denial or modification for the typical application in each area-year.

Table 5.26
Denial and downward-modification ratios for the typical application in the central city(s) relative to the suburbs

Metropolitan Area		Denial 1977	Denial 1978	Downward Modification 1977	Downward Modification 1978
Anaheim-Santa Ana-	A[a]	0.64*	0.90	1.15	0.60**
Garden Grove	B	0.84	1.42**	1.04	0.93
	C	0.51**	0.79	0.55**	0.61**
Bakersfield		2.21**	1.23	NA	NA
Fresno		0.63**	0.79*	1.06	0.91
Modesto		0.52**	0.49**	NA	NA
Oxnard-Ventura	A	0.78	0.76	0.62	0.55
	B	0.65	1.68*	0.97	1.47*
Salinas-Monterey	A	0.40**	0.86	NA	NA
	B	3.13**	0.21**	NA	NA
San Bernardino-	A	0.53	0.14**	0.20**	1.72
Riverside-Ontario	B	0.78	0.17**	0.38**	0.30**
	C	2.45	0.80	0.59	0.84
San Diego		1.02	0.76**	0.77**	0.80**
San Jose		0.67**	1.53**	1.14	0.89
Santa Barbara		1.09	0.51	NA	NA
Santa Rosa		1.03	1.15	0.69	0.84
Stockton		0.30**	1.16	NA	NA
Vallejo-Napa	A	1.04	1.10	1.60	0.67
	B	0.82	0.71	0.79	0.68

The ratio is equal to the probability that an application with the indicated characteristics will be denied or modified divided by the probability that the typical application will be denied or modified. A single asterisk (*) indicates that the numerator of the ratio is statistically significantly different from the denominator at the 5–10 percent level. Two asterisks (**) indicate that the difference is significant at the 5 percent or less level. The typical application is described in the text. It is the base for calculating the denial or modification ratios. The other applications involve variations from the typical one in one or more characteristics. See Tables 5.4 and 5.5 for the probability of denial or modification for the typical application in each area-year.

a. The three letters refer to the metropolitan areas with more than one central city. In these cases, A refers to the first city in the name of the metropolitan area, B to the second, and C to the third.

cities are: Santa Ana (1978 denial ratio), Bakersfield (1977 denial ratio), Ventura (1978 denial and downward-modification ratios), Monterey (1977 denial ratio), and San Jose (1978 denial ratio). At the same time, there are twenty-one ratios indicating that applications on central-city properties receive statistically significantly more favorable treatment than similar applications on suburban properties.

Age of Neighborhood The allegation that older neighborhoods are redlined is one of the most difficult to analyze because the age of the neighborhood may have high spurious correlations with objective measures of risk of loss arising from housing market externalities such as adjacent vacant buildings. We have attempted to control these objective factors through the variables for neighborhood characteristics. This approach is reasonably successful and evidence of multicollinearity is absent, probably in part because of the large sample sizes. Another problem confronting the age of neighborhood analysis is the possibility of a spurious correlation with the condition of the building being used as security for the loan. Including the age of the specific building should remove this. We have done this in California with no evidence of a remaining multicollinearity problem.[8] The inclusion of the age of the building variables strengthens the interpretation of the age-of-neighborhood variable (PRE1940) as a redlining measure. However, it is important to emphasize that the building-age results cannot be interpreted as a measure of the extent to which old buildings may be discriminated against because the building age results are probably strongly correlated with the remaining economic life of the building.

The denial and downward-modification ratios for typical applications on buildings of various ages are presented in Tables 5.27 to 5.30. These results illustrate the importance of including these variables. Applications for mortgages on older buildings (over thirty years) are much more likely to be denied than similar applications on new buildings. It is also interesting that applications on buildings that are one to nine years old are significantly less likely to be denied than similar applications on new buildings. The downward-modification ratios indicate a similar but weaker pattern.

The denial and downward-modification ratios for applications on properties located in older neighborhoods are presented in Table 5.31. The reader should note that an older neighborhood has been taken as one with an additional 10 percentage points of housing built before 1940 (PRE1940) above the value of PRE1940 for an average neighborhood. Applications on properties in older neighborhoods are more

Table 5.27
Denial ratios by building age for typical applications, 1977

Study Area[a]	New[b]	BA1–9	BA10–19	BA20–29	BA30–39	BA40–49	BAGE50
Anaheim-Santa Ana-Garden Grove	1.00	0.82**	0.91	1.34**	2.54**	2.23**	4.40**
Bakersfield	1.00	1.63	0.96	0.93	3.57**	0.00**	11.61**
Fresno	1.00	0.66**	0.76	1.06	1.38	1.49	2.36**
Los Angeles-Long Beach	1.00	0.50**	0.74**	0.57**	0.79**	0.85**	1.04
City of Los Angeles	1.00	0.53**	0.67**	0.63**	1.02	1.15	1.26
Modesto	1.00	0.83	1.53	2.45**	1.44	1.99	6.14**
Oxnard-Ventura	1.00	0.53**	0.49**	0.77	1.62	0.94	2.57
Sacramento	1.00	0.66**	0.71**	0.84	2.31**	1.60	1.86
Salinas-Monterey	1.00	0.83	0.52**	1.38	1.52	1.29	2.77
San Bernardino-Riverside-Ontario	1.00	2.26**	2.74**	2.31**	4.31**	15.10**	10.13**
San Diego	1.00	0.48**	0.51**	0.53**	0.63	1.03	0.56
San Francisco-Oakland	1.00	0.63**	0.84*	0.80**	0.98	0.84	1.05
San Jose	1.00	1.21	1.11	2.04**	2.17**	2.39**	4.55**
Santa Barbara	1.00	0.44*	0.64	0.57	0.66	0.40	0.16**
Santa Rosa	1.00	0.75	1.21	1.62	1.12	3.59**	3.81**
Stockton	1.00	0.68	1.73	1.66	2.06	2.66	0.00**
Vallejo-Napa	1.00	0.58	1.29	1.26	0.76	4.15**	0.00**

The ratio is equal to the probability that an application with the indicated characteristics will be denied divided by the probability that the typical application will be denied. A single asterisk (*) indicates that the numerator of the ratio is statistically significantly different from the denominator at the 5–10 percent level. Two asterisks (**) indicate that the difference is significant at the 5 percent or less level.
a. Metropolitan area in all cases except the City of Los Angeles.
b. This is the typical application described in the text. It is the base for calculating the denial ratios. The other applications involve variations from the typical one in one or more characteristics. See Table 5.4 for the probability of denial for the typical application in each area.

Table 5.28
Denial ratios by building age for typical applications, 1978

Study Area[a]	New or 1 Year Old[b]	BA2–10	BA11–20	BA21–30	BA31–40	BA41–50	BAGE51
Anaheim-Santa Ana-Garden Grove	1.00	0.61**	0.85*	0.80	1.66	1.77*	1.01
Bakersfield	1.00	0.80	0.97	0.91	1.26	1.73	1.14
Fresno	1.00	0.81	0.78	0.86	1.04	0.83	0.66
Los Angeles-Long Beach	1.00	1.08	1.12	1.17**	1.24**	1.44**	1.77**
City of Los Angeles	1.00	0.92	0.78*	1.07	1.20	1.28**	1.32**
Modesto	1.00	1.33	2.20**	2.41**	3.61**	2.10*	0.00**
Oxnard-Ventura	1.00	0.83	1.21	1.64	1.24	2.54	4.04**
Sacramento	1.00	0.63**	0.94	1.13	1.45	2.00**	3.02**
Salinas-Monterey	1.00	0.51**	0.54**	0.84	0.42**	1.20	0.68
San Bernardino-Riverside-Ontario	1.00	0.78	1.45	1.31	5.96**	14.09**	4.29*
San Diego	1.00	1.32**	1.32	1.13	2.25**	1.65*	2.32**
San Francisco-Oakland	1.00	0.82**	0.85**	0.81**	0.91	1.14	1.50**
San Jose	1.00	1.08	1.30*	0.95	0.95	1.51	1.16
Santa Barbara	1.00	1.65	1.29	1.09	4.17**	3.21**	6.28**
Santa Rosa	1.00	1.03	1.20	1.65**	2.90**	4.41**	4.20**
Stockton	1.00	0.53**	1.65	1.01	0.58	0.32*	0.67
Vallejo-Napa	1.00	0.53	0.38*	1.03	0.96	0.49	1.02

The ratio is equal to the probability that an application with the indicated characteristics will be denied divided by the probability that the typical application will be denied. A single asterisk (*) indicates that the numerator of the ratio is statistically significantly different from the denominator at the 5–10 percent level. Two asterisks (**) indicate that the difference is significant at the 5 percent or less level.
a. Metropolitan area in all cases except the City of Los Angeles.
b. This is the typical application described in the text. It is the base for calculating the denial ratios. The other applications involve variations from the typical one in one or more characteristics. See Table 5.5 for the probability of denial for the typical application in each area.

Table 5.29
Downward-modification ratios by building age for typical applications, 1977

Study Areas[a]	New[b]	BA1–9	BA10–19	BA20–29	BA30–39	BA40–49	BAGE50
Anaheim-Santa Ana-Garden Grove	1.00	0.84**	0.76**	0.76*	0.10**	0.41**	0.89
Fresno	1.00	1.26	1.07	1.48	1.15	2.29*	3.76**
Los Angeles-Long Beach	1.00	0.66**	0.53**	0.43**	0.60**	0.61**	0.65**
City of Los Angeles	1.00	0.83*	0.67**	0.55**	0.67**	0.65**	0.95
Oxnard-Ventura	1.00	1.20	1.13	1.42	3.62**	2.09	0.00**
Sacramento	1.00	0.95	0.89	1.12	1.41	1.10	0.99
San Bernardino-Riverside-Ontario	1.00	0.88	1.25	0.87	1.91	0.80	2.25
San Diego	1.00	0.71**	0.55**	0.59**	0.60*	0.95	1.19
San Francisco-Oakland	1.00	0.93	0.75**	0.67**	0.83	0.89	0.93
San Jose	1.00	1.07	0.96	0.79	1.13	1.51	1.73
Santa Rosa	1.00	1.07	1.76*	1.47	1.36	1.46	1.01
Vallejo-Napa	1.00	0.60*	0.89	0.68	0.91	0.23*	1.17

The ratio is equal to the probability that an application with the indicated characteristics will be modified downward divided by the probability that the typical application will be modified downward. A single asterisk (*) indicates that the numerator of the ratio is statistically significantly different from the denominator at the 5–10 percent level. Two asterisks (**) indicate that the difference is significant at the 5 percent or less level.

a. Metropolitan area in all cases except the City of Los Angeles.

b. This is the typical application described in the text. It is the base for calculating the downward-modification ratios. The other applications involve variations from the typical one in one or more characteristics. See Table 5.4 for the probability of downward modification for the typical application in each area.

Table 5.30
Downward-modification ratios by building age for typical applications, 1978

Study Area[a]	New or 1 Year Old[b]	EA2-10	BA11-20	BA21-30	BA31-40	BA41-50	BAGE51
Anaheim-Santa Ana-Garden Grove	1.00	0.93	0.86	1.15	1.07	1.55	1.87
Fresno	1.00	0.82	0.54**	0.82	0.62	0.91	0.97
Los Angeles-Long Beach	1.00	0.69**	0.67**	0.62**	0.67**	0.61**	0.70**
City of Los Angeles	1.00	0.94	0.92	0.63**	0.78**	0.87	0.76**
Oxnard-Ventura	1.00	0.68**	0.65**	0.98	1.25	0.74	1.78
Sacramento	1.00	0.94	1.03	1.19	0.83	0.80	1.47
San Bernardino-Riverside-Ontario	1.00	0.99	1.30	1.41	3.54**	1.20	1.52
San Diego	1.00	0.87*	0.78*	1.08	1.71**	1.67**	1.34
San Francisco-Oakland	1.00	0.79**	0.79**	0.91	0.84*	1.26*	1.18
San Jose	1.00	0.82*	1.05	1.15	0.65	1.80	0.88
Santa Rosa	1.00	2.09**	2.99**	1.89*	2.64**	3.79**	0.58
Vallejo-Napa	1.00	1.34	1.09	0.51	1.06	1.52	2.50

The ratio is equal to the probability that an application with the indicated characteristics will be modified downward divided by the probability that the typical application will be modified downward. A single asterisk (*) indicates that the numerator of the ratio is statistically significantly different from the denominator at the 5–10 percent level. Two asterisks (**) indicate that the difference is significant at the 5 percent or less level.

a. Metropolitan area in all cases except the City of Los Angeles.
b. This is the typical application described in the text. It is the base for calculating the downward-modification ratios. The other applications involve variations from the typical one in one or more characteristics. See Table 5.5 for the probability of downward modification for the typical application in each area.

Table 5.31
Denial and downward-modification ratios for typical applications in older (+0.10
added to PRE1940) neighborhoods

Study Area[a]	Denial		Downward Modification	
	1977	1978	1977	1978
Anaheim-Santa Ana-Garden Grove	1.12**	1.18**	1.20**	0.95
Bakersfield	1.13	1.33**	NA	NA
Fresno	1.09**	1.15**	0.98	1.03
Los Angeles-Long Beach	0.92**	1.01	1.08**	1.05**
City of Los Angeles	0.89**	1.02	1.00	0.97**
Modesto	0.99	0.88*	NA	NA
Oxnard-Ventura	1.01	0.92	0.76**	0.96
Sacramento	0.99	1.05	1.01	0.99
Salinas-Monterey	0.99	0.93	NA	NA
San Bernardino-Riverside-Ontario	0.69**	0.78**	0.89	0.73**
San Diego	0.99	1.00	1.00	0.98
San Francisco-Oakland	1.01	1.04**	1.01	0.97*
San Jose	1.09**	1.23**	1.04	0.92
Santa Barbara	1.18	0.92	NA	NA
Santa Rosa	0.93	1.03	0.97	0.93
Stockton	1.15	1.09	NA	NA
Vallejo-Napa	1.10	1.07	1.20**	1.04

The ratio is equal to the probability that an application with the indicated characteristics
will be denied or modified divided by the probability that the typical application will be
denied or modified. A single asterisk (*) indicates that the numerator of the ratio is
statistically significantly different from the denominator at the 5–10 percent level. Two
asterisks (**) indicate that the difference is significant at the 5 percent or less level. The
typical application is described in the text. It has each area's mean value of PRE1940
and is the base for calculating the denial or modification ratios. The other applications
involve variations from the typical one in one or more characteristics. See Tables 5.4
and 5.5 for the probability of denial or modification for the typical application in each
area. See Table 5.3 for the mean values of PRE1940.
a. Metropolitan area in all cases except the City of Los Angeles.

likely to be denied than similar applications on properties in newer neighborhoods in twenty of the thirty-four cases, and the differential is statistically significant in eight of these twenty cases. According to these results, an additional 10 percentage points in the PRE1940 variable increases the chances of denial by 9–33 percent. The significant increases occur in the following metropolitan areas: Anaheim-Santa Ana-Garden Grove (1977 and 1978), Bakersfield (1978), Fresno (1977 and 1978), San Francisco-Oakland (1978), and San Jose (1977 and 1978).

The downward modification ratios show a more mixed pattern. Older neighborhoods are about as likely to receive favorable as unfavorable treatment with regard to a decision to modify a requested loan amount downward. There are four cases of statistically significant adverse treatment of older neighborhoods through downward modification: Anaheim-Santa Ana-Garden Grove (1977), Los Angeles-Long Beach (1977 and 1978), and Vallejo-Napa (1977).

Racial Composition of Neighborhood   The effect of the racial composition of the neighborhood is illustrated by comparing the likelihood of denial and downward modification for typical applications in a neighborhood with a relatively high concentration of a minority population to the respective likelihood in a neighborhood with an average value of the racial composition variables. The relatively high value used in these simulations is the maximum value in the sample minus 2 standard deviations, providing the result is greater than the mean. The mean and simulation values are summarized in Table 5.32. The denial and downward-modification ratios by racial composition of the neighborhood are presented in Tables 5.33 to 5.36. The results vary by race, year, and metropolitan area. Applications on properties located in black or Spanish neighborhoods have higher chances of denial or downward modification than similar applications in neighborhoods with mean values of minorities in several metropolitan areas. The following paragraphs describe the statistically significant (10 percent level) two-tail differentials.

Mortgage applications are more likely to be denied in black neighborhoods than in largely white neighborhoods in the Los Angeles-Long Beach (1978), Modesto (1977), Oxnard-Ventura (1977), Salinas-Monterey (1977), San Diego (1977 and 1978), and San Jose (1977) metropolitan areas. Applications in black neighborhoods are more

Table 5.32
Values of racial composition variables used in the simulations reported in tables 5.33–5.36

Study Area[a]	FBLACK		FSPANISH		FASIAN	
	M	S	M	S	M	S
Anaheim-Santa Ana-Garden Grove	0.01	0.36	0.09	0.46	b	b
Bakersfield	0.06	0.73	0.09	0.48	b	b
Fresno	0.01	0.83	0.13	0.27	b	b
Los Angeles-Long Beach	0.04	0.76	0.12	0.76	0.02	0.14
City of Los Angeles	0.06	0.68	0.11	0.67	0.02	0.14
Modesto	0.003	0.20	0.07	0.34	c	c
Oxnard-Ventura	0.02	0.15	0.13	0.67	b	b
Sacramento	0.02	0.50	0.03	0.29	0.03	0.25
Salinas-Monterey	0.06	0.33	0.14	0.44	b	b
San Bernardino-Riverside-Ontario	0.03	0.62	0.11	0.74	b	b
San Diego	0.02	0.71	0.09	0.54	0.01	0.05
San Francisco-Oakland	0.06	0.75	0.10	0.75	0.03	0.49
San Jose	0.02	0.15	0.09	0.51	0.04	0.24
Santa Barbara	0.02	0.08	0.13	0.25	b	b
Santa Rosa	b	b	0.05	0.09	c	c
Stockton	0.02	0.37	[0.04	0.22 ————————→]		
Vallejo-Napa	0.05	0.74	0.07	0.12	c	c

M = the mean value and S = the value used for the simulations reported in Tables 5.33 to 5.36. The S values are equal to the maximum value in the sample minus 2 standard deviations.
a. Metropolitan area in all cases except the City of Los Angeles.
b. Maximum value minus 2 standard deviations is less than the mean value.
c. Data unavailable.

Table 5.33
Denial ratios by racial composition of neighborhood for typical applications (TA), 1977

Study Area[a]	TA[b]	FBLACK	FSPANISH	FASIAN
Anaheim-Santa Ana-Garden Grove	1.00	3.38	0.62**	c
Bakersfield	1.00	2.45	0.15*	c
Fresno	1.00	0.93	1.02	c
Los Angeles-Long Beach	1.00	0.52**	1.27	1.70**
City of Los Angeles	1.00	0.34**	1.26	0.98
Modesto	1.00	4.45*	6.13**	d
Oxnard-Ventura	1.00	8.63**	0.06**	c
Sacramento	1.00	0.61	1.34	2.33**
Salinas-Monterey	1.00	2.41**	1.41	c
San Bernardino-Riverside-Ontario	1.00	5.61	1.90	c
San Diego	1.00	2.61*	1.33	0.88
San Francisco-Oakland	1.00	0.73*	0.50**	0.08**
San Jose	1.00	2.88**	2.74**	0.26**
Santa Barbara	1.00	0.90	1.36**	c
Santa Rosa	1.00	c	1.63**	d
Stockton	1.00	0.20	[←———— 6.66** ————→]	
Vallejo-Napa	1.00	1.13	1.00	d

See table 5.32 for the values of FBLACK, FSPANISH, and FASIAN. The ratio is equal to the probability that an application with the indicated characteristics will be denied divided by the probability that the typical application will be denied. A single asterisk (*) indicates that the numerator of the ratio is statistically significantly different from the denominator at the 5–10 percent level. Two asterisks (**) indicate that the difference is significant at the 5 percent or less level.
a. Metropolitan area in all cases except the City of Los Angeles.
b. This is the typical application described in the text. It is the base for calculating the denial ratios. The other applications involve variations from the typical one in one or more characteristics. See Table 5.4 for the probability of denial for the typical application in each area.
c. Maximum value minus 2 standard deviations is less than the mean value.
d. Data unavailable.

Table 5.34
Denial ratios by racial composition of neighborhood for typical applications (TA), 1978

Study Area[a]	TA[b]	FBLACK	FSPANISH	FASIAN
Anaheim-Santa Ana-Garden Grove	1.00	1.36	0.55**	c
Bakersfield	1.00	0.72	2.43**	c
Fresno	1.00	0.35	0.88	c
Los Angeles-Long Beach	1.00	1.18*	1.02	1.00
City of Los Angeles	1.00	1.09	0.93	0.79**
Modesto	1.00	1.63	0.74	d
Oxnard-Ventura	1.00	0.25	4.82	c
Sacramento	1.00	2.23	0.27**	2.09**
Salinas-Monterey	1.00	0.85	0.46*	c
San Bernardino-Riverside-Ontario	1.00	0.33	3.13**	c
San Diego	1.00	1.11*	1.00	0.87
San Francisco-Oakland	1.00	1.19	1.34	0.19**
San Jose	1.00	0.60**	1.30*	0.42**
Santa Barbara	1.00	0.81	0.93	c
Santa Rosa	1.00	c	1.27**	d
Stockton	1.00	1.19	[← 1.94 ⎯⎯⎯⎯⎯→]	
Vallejo-Napa	1.00	0.31	0.99	d

See table 5.32 for the values of FBLACK, FSPANISH, and FASIAN. The ratio is equal to the probability that an application with the indicated characteristics will be denied divided by the probability that the typical application will be denied. A single asterisk (*) indicates that the numerator of the ratio is statistically significantly different from the denominator at the 5–10 percent level. Two asterisks (**) indicate that the difference is significant at the 5 percent or less level.
a. Metropolitan area in all cases except the City of Los Angeles.
b. This is the typical application described in the text. It is the base for calculating the denial ratios. The other applications involve variations from the typical one in one or more characteristics. See Table 5.5 for the probability of denial for the typical application in each area.
c. Maximum value minus 2 standard deviations is less than the mean value.
d. Data unavailable.

Table 5.35
Downward-modification ratios by racial composition of neighborhood for typical
applications (TA), 1977

Study Area[a]	TA[b]	FBLACK	FSPANISH	FASIAN
Anaheim-Santa Ana-Garden Grove	1.00	0.65	0.83	c
Fresno	1.00	0.00**	1.25**	c
Los Angeles-Long Beach	1.00	1.37**	1.27**	1.12
City of Los Angeles	1.00	1.80**	0.96	0.43**
Oxnard-Ventura	1.00	0.11**	2.15	c
Sacramento	1.00	1.63	0.04**	0.98
San Bernardino-Riverside-Ontario	1.00	1.13	2.18	c
San Diego	1.00	1.11	0.28**	1.17
San Francisco-Oakland	1.00	0.81	0.58**	0.27**
San Jose	1.00	0.51**	1.00	0.54
Santa Rosa	1.00	c	0.87	d
Vallejo-Napa	1.00	0.08	0.84	d

See table 5.32 for the values of FBLACK, FSPANISH, and FASIAN. The ratio is
equal to the probability that an application with the indicated characteristics will be
modified downward divided by the probability that the typical application will be modified downward. A single asterisk (*) indicates that the numerator of the ratio is statistically significantly different than the denominator at the 5–10 percent level. Two
asterisks (**) indicate that the difference is significant at the 5 percent or less level.
a. Metropolitan area in all cases except the City of Los Angeles.
b. This is the typical application described in the text. It is the base for calculating the
downward-modification ratios. The other applications involve variations from the typical
one in one or more characteristics. See Table 5.4 for the probability of downward
modification for the typical application in each area.
c. Maximum value minus 2 standard deviations is less than the mean value.
d. Data unavailable.

likely to be modified downward in the Los Angeles-Long Beach (1977)
and San Francisco-Oakland (1978) metropolitan areas.

Spanish neighborhoods receive adverse treatment in the decision to
deny a mortgage application in the Bakersfield (1978), Modesto (1977),
San Bernardino-Riverside-Ontario (1978), San Jose (1977 and 1978),
Santa Barbara (1977), and Santa Rosa (1977 and 1978) metropolitan
areas. In the Stockton metropolitan area, applications in other minority neighborhoods, which includes Spanish households, are more likely
to be denied in 1977. Downward modifications are also more likely in
Spanish neighborhoods in the Fresno (1977), Los Angeles-Long Beach
(1977), San Jose (1978), and Vallejo-Napa (1978) metropolitan areas.

Applications on properties in Asian neighborhoods are more likely
to be denied than those in white neighborhoods in the Los Angeles-
Long Beach (1977) and Sacramento (1977 and 1978) metropolitan

Table 5.36
Downward-modification ratios by racial composition of neighborhood for typical
applications (TA), 1978

Study Area[a]	TA[b]	FBLACK	FSPANISH	FASIAN
Anaheim-Santa Ana-Garden Grove	1.00	1.04	1.11	[c]
Fresno	1.00	0.94	0.60*	[c]
Los Angeles-Long Beach	1.00	0.99	0.90	1.16*
City of Los Angeles	1.00	0.89	0.62**	0.80**
Oxnard-Ventura	1.00	0.04	1.30	[c]
Sacramento	1.00	0.51	0.78	1.11
San Bernardino-Riverside-Ontario	1.00	2.60	0.57	[c]
San Diego	1.00	1.09	0.77**	1.12
San Francisco-Oakland	1.00	1.38**	0.75	1.49
San Jose	1.00	0.87	1.70**	1.01
Santa Rosa	1.00	[c]	1.07	[d]
Vallejo-Napa	1.00	0.25	1.32**	[d]

See table 5.32 for the values of FBLACK, FSPANISH, and FASIAN. The ratio is
equal to the probability that an application with the indicated characteristics will be
modified downward divided by the probability that the typical application will be modified downward. A single asterisk (*) indicates that the numerator of the ratio is statistically significantly different from the denominator at the 5–10 percent level. Two
asterisks (**) indicate that the difference is significant at the 5 percent or less level.
a. Metropolitan area in all cases except the City of Los Angeles.
b. This is the typical application described in the text. It is the base for calculating the
downward-modification ratios. The other applications involve variations from the typical
one in one or more characteristics. See Table 5.5 for the probability of downward
modification for the typical application in each area.
c. Maximum value minus 2 standard deviations is less than the mean value.
d. Data unavailable.

areas. Downward modifications are more likely in the Asian neighborhoods of the Los Angeles-Long Beach (1978) metropolitan area.

Summary

The decisions of California savings and loan associations on applications for conventional mortgages on single-family houses being purchased for owner occupany are analyzed using a multivariate statistical
technique known as the multinomial logit. In general, four possible
outcomes are considered simultaneously: approved as applied for,
approved after increasing the requested loan amount, approved after
decreasing the requested loan amount, and denial. A lender's decision
is viewed as a function of the financial characteristics of the borrower,
the loan, and the property, and housing market externalities that may

affect the future value of the property. Lending in sixteen metropolitan areas is analyzed for 1977 and 1978. The race, sex, and age of the applicant and the location of the property are also included to determine whether they affect mortgage-lending decisions after controlling for objective factors.

Objective factors such as the ratios of requested loan amount to income and to appraised value play a major role in mortgage lending. The vast majority of decisions are based on these criteria. However, there is some strong evidence that certain types of applicants are arbitrarily discriminated against by California savings and loan associations. We interpret a significantly higher chance of denial or downward modification as evidence of discrimination. The following paragraphs summarize our findings on discrimination.

Sex

There is little evidence of sex discrimination. Households are divided into five categories on the basis of the sex of the applicants: male-female nonchildbearing, male-female childbearing, female only non-childbearing, female only childbearing, and male only. The last four types are compared to the first, which is viewed as least likely to be a target of discrimination. There is evidence consistent with the allegation that each of these four are discriminated against in at least one metropolitan area. However, there is no consistent pattern across metropolitan areas or time. There is no evidence of discrimination in the denial or downward-modification decisions on the basis of sex in the Bakersfield, Oxnard-Ventura, Salinas-Monterey, and San Francisco-Oakland metropolitan areas. The only evidence of sex discrmination in the Fresno metropolitan area is that the income of a second worker in male-only or female-only nonchildbearing households is discounted. In general, income from a second worker is accorded a premium in the lending process.

Male-female childbearing households receive less favorable treatment than similar male-female nonchildbearing households in the Anaheim-Santa Ana-Garden Grove (1977) and Modesto (1978) metropolitan areas. Female-only childbearing households receive less favorable treatment from lenders in Modesto (1978), Sacramento (1978), and San Bernardino-Riverside-Ontario (1978), and Santa Rosa (1978). The income from a second worker in either type of childbearing household is discounted in only one area: San Diego (1977).

Female-only nonchildbearing households receive adverse treatment in the San Bernardino-Riverside-Ontario (1978), San Diego (1977), Santa Barbara (1978), Santa Rosa (1978), and Stockton (1978) metropolitan areas. In addition, the income from a second worker in this household type is discounted in the Anaheim-Santa Ana-Garden Grove (1977 and 1978), San Diego (1978), San Jose (1978), Santa Barbara (1977), and Santa Rosa (1977) metropolitan areas.

Applications from male-only households are more likely to be denied or modified downward in Los Angeles City (1978) and the Sacramento (1978), San Diego (1977), and Vallejo-Napa (1977) metropolitan areas. In addition, the income of second workers is discounted for male-only households in the Fresno (1978), Modesto (1977), San Bernardino-Riverside-Ontario (1977), Santa Rosa (1977), and Vallejo-Napa (1977) metropolitian areas.

Age
Contrary to allegations of discrimination against older applicants, those between thirty-five and forty-four years old are more likely to be denied than older or younger applicants. However, older applicants are substantially more likely to be modified downward than the younger applicants.

Race
The evidence of racial discrimination is strong and consistent across metropolitan areas and time. Applications from blacks are 1.54 to 7.82 times as likely to be denied than those from similarly situated whites. Spanish and other minority (excluding Asians) are also heavily discriminated against. Spanish applicants are as much as 2.5 times as likely to be denied than similarly situated whites; other minorities are as much as 5.9 times as likely to be denied. Applications from Asians receive more favorable treatment than similarly situated whites as often as they receive less favorable treatment. However, there is little evidence that minorities are discriminated against in the decision to modify a requested loan amount downward prior to approval.

Redlining
Three types of redlining have been analyzed: specific neighborhoods that have been alleged to be redlined, older neighborhoods, and largely minority neighborhoods.

Information containing allegations that specific neighborhoods are redlined was available to us for Los Angeles County and the cities of Oakland and Sacramento. The results do not support the redlining allegations for Oakland and Sacramento and are mixed for Los Angeles County. The denial results for at least one year are consistent with allegations that the neighborhoods of Long Beach-Southwest, San Pedro, East Los Angeles-Boyle Heights-Echo Park, and Pomona are redlined. The downward-modification results are also consistent with the allegations that the Covina-Azusa, Pacoima-San Fernando, and Venice-Santa Monica neighborhoods are redlined. The evidence does not support the redlining allegations for the Compton, Highland Park, Pasadena-North Central, South Central Los Angeles, and West Covina neighborhoods, but is occasionally consistent with a redlining hypothesis in areas that are not alleged to be redlined.

A comparison of lending practices on central-city properties to those on suburban properties indicated that the central-city properties generally received more favorable treatment than the suburban ones.

Applications on older buildings are much more likely to be denied than similar applications on new buildings, but these results do not necessarily indicate that older buildings are being arbitrarily denied mortgages because the age variable is probably serving as a measure of the remaining economic life of the building. It is important to include the building age measure because it ensures that the variable for the age of the neighborhood is not a proxy for the economic life of the building.

Applications on properties located in older neighborhoods are more likely to be denied with significant differentials in the Anaheim-Santa Ana-Garden Grove, Bakersfield, Fresno, San Francisco-Oakland, and San Jose metropolitan areas. Older neighborhoods, however, are about as likely to receive favorable as unfavorable treatment in a decision to modify the requested loan amount downward prior to approval.

Applications for mortgages in black or Spanish neighborhoods have higher chances of denial or downward modification than similar applications in neighborhoods with average concentrations of minorities. The significant differentials between predominantly black and large white neighborhoods occur in the Los Angeles-Long Beach, Modesto, Oxnard-Ventura, Salinas-Monterey, San Diego, San Francisco-Oakland, and San Jose metropolitan areas. The significant Spanish differentials occur in the Bakersfield, Fresno, Los Angeles-Long Beach,

Modesto, San Bernardino-Riverside-Ontario, San Jose, Santa Barbara, Santa Rosa, Stockton, and Vallejo-Napa metropolitan areas.

In addition, applications on properties in Asian neighborhoods receive adverse treatment in the Los Angeles-Long Beach and Sacramento metropolitan areas.

6
Mortgage Credit Terms in California

The availability of mortgages is not the only element of mortgage transactions on which the discrimination debate focuses; representatives of women's groups, minority groups, and community organizations allege that lenders discriminate against certain types of applications by charging higher interest rates and granting mortgages with shorter terms and lower loan-to-value ratios than warranted by the objective characteristics of the applications. Although less direct than outright mortgage denial, discrimination of this form can have equally serious implications for potential borrowers.

We examine discriminatory behavior with respect to the setting of mortgage terms using data for four California metropolitan areas: Fresno, Los Angeles-Long Beach, San Francisco-Oakland, and San Jose. The large number of mortgage loans granted in both Los Angeles-Long Beach and San Francisco-Oakland make them obvious choices for analysis; large sample sizes assure adequate numbers of applications from the groups of primary interest for this study. Fresno is included as representative of a relatively small metropolitan area for which sufficient data are available for all parts of the terms analysis. In addition, its location in the Central Valley contributes to the generalizability of the results. Finally, San Jose represents a medium-sized metropolitian area undergoing rapid economic growth. For each metropolitan area, separate models were estimated for 1977 and 1978.

This chapter is divided into three sections. The first section presents the results of the interest rate, maturity period, and loan-to-value analysis—analysis that is limited to California because of the absence of the necessary data in New York. The second section focuses on the pattern of downward modification, the results of which can be compared across states since similar models have been estimated for metropolitan areas in New York. The final section deals with the fees lenders charge applicants for processing loan applications. Again, the analysis is limited to California because of the absence of data on loan fees in New York.

Interest Rate, Maturity, and Loan-to-value Ratio

Chapter 4 summarizes our basic approach to modeling the contract interest rate, loan-to-value ratio, and maturity period for all approved mortgages. Starting from the recognition that the three terms are simultaneously determined, each term is modeled as a function of the other two terms and relevant risk, preference, and potential discrimination variables. We begin our analysis of the results with a more detailed discussion of the equation specifications, paying particular attention to the identification problem. We then present the results, focusing primarily, but not exclusively, on the findings on interest rates.

Two estimation strategies are possible in the context of simultaneously determined variables. On the one hand, structural equations that explicitly model the simultaneity among the endogenous variables can be estimated directly using the technique of two-stage least squares, provided the equations are identified. On the other, structural equations can be simplified to reduced-form equations by substituting for the endogenous variables, leaving the complete set of exogenous variables as the only explanatory variables in each of the individual equations. The two strategies yield identical estimates of the structural parameters in exactly identified systems. In underidentified systems, however, only the latter strategy is feasible, and no structural parameters can be derived; in overidentified systems, the reduced form approach leads to multiple estimates of the structural parameters.

Unless they can be used to calculate the structural parameters, reduced form coefficients are inadequate for testing the extent of discriminatory behavior in the setting of mortgage terms. This is illustrated by the following example. Suppose that the reduced form equations imply that, controlling for the other exogenous explanatory factors, black mortgage applicants are charged higher interest rates than white applicants. By itself, this appears to suggest that lenders discriminate against such applicants. But if it is also true that black borrowers are given larger loans in relation to appraised value than similarly situated whites, the interest-rate finding would be difficult to interpret. In this case, the issue is whether the interest rate charged black borrowers is sufficiently above that charged white borrowers to offset the fact that interest rates associated with high loan-to-value ratios are generally above those charged on loans with low loan-to-value ratios. The relevant question is not whether similarly situated blacks and whites are charged the same interest rate in general, but whether they are charged the same interest rate for comparable types of loans as measured by the loan-to-appraised value and the maturity period.

The preceding discussion emphasizes the importance of estimating structural parameters. Equations 4.7 to 4.9 represent one such three-equation structural model of mortgage terms. The technique of two-stage least squares could, in principle, be used to obtain consistent estimates of the parameters because each of the equations is either exactly identified or overidentified.[1] In particular, the interest-rate equation is exactly identified because two variables, the requested maturity (REQMAT) and the requested loan-to-appraised value (RLTOAV), are excluded from the equation; the maturity equation is overidentified because the market rate of interest (INT_m), whether or not the mortgage is a variable rate mortgage (VRM), the requested loan amount (REQLOAN), and the requested loan-to-appraised value (RLTOAV) are excluded; and the loan-to-value equation is overidentified because the two interest-rate variables, the requested loan amount and the requested maturity are all excluded.

Unfortunately, data limitations prevent us from estimating the three equation model exactly as specified. First, we do not know the market interest rate because we have no information on the timing of the mortgage contract.[2] Absence of this information is unfortunate; rising mortgage rates during the study period suggest that a substantial proportion of the variance of interest rates on individual mortgage contracts during any one year could be explained by a variable representing the month of the contract acting as a proxy for the market interest rate. It should be noted, however, that the exclusion of such a variable from the equation does not necessarily bias the remaining coefficients; it would bias the coefficient of another variable only if that variable were correlated with the excluded variable. Since we have no reason to believe that such correlations are present, especially with respect to any of the discrimination variables, the potential bias is likely to be minimal. Moreover, the exclusion of INT_m does not alter the conclusion that all three equations either exactly identified or overidentified.

The absence of information related to the borrower's requested maturity (REQMAT) presents a more serious data problem. In this case, we cannot simply leave the variable out of the equation; doing so might bias the coefficients of certain discrimination variables in the maturity equation and would keep the interest-rate equation from being identified. Unfortunately, no proxies for REQMAT that would identify the interest rate equation are available in our data set; all possible proxies, such as age of applicant or size of requested loan, are already included in the interest-rate equation.

Thus, we have a dilemma. On the one hand we believe structural equations are needed to test for discriminatory lending behavior. This makes it undesirable to estimate reduced form parameters unless they can be used to calculate the structural parameters. On the other hand, data limitations prevent us from identifying the important interest rate equations. We have chosen to deal with this problem by respecifying the model. Specifically, we treat the maturity period as exogenous to the interest-rate and loan-to-appraised-value decision. In other words, we impose the restriction that the coefficients of INT and LTOAV in Equation 4.8 are equal to zero. Although we cannot adequately test this assumption, we believe it can be defended in the light of the following plausible two-step decision-making process. First, the lender determines the appropriate maturity period based on the characteristics of the borrower and the property to be mortgaged, the borrower's requested maturity, and legal limits on the maturity period. In many cases, the maximum maturity period will be granted. By affecting the borrower's monthly payments, the maturity period then affects the lender's joint decision on the interest-rate and loan-to-value ratio.[3]

These statistical considerations yield the following revised model:

$$INT = f(LTOAV, MAT, VRM, REQLOAN, RISK, DISC) \qquad (6.1)$$

$$MAT = h(REQLOAN, RLTOAV, RISK, DISC) \qquad (6.2)$$

$$LTOAV = g(INT, MAT, RLTOAV, RISK, DISC) \qquad (6.3)$$

The maturity equation now includes REQLOAN and RLTOAV as proxies for the requested maturity. Since the larger the amount requested by the borrower, either absolutely or relative to appraised value, the greater his or her incentive is to spread the loan over a longer time period, we expect both additional variables to have positive impacts, *ceteris paribus*, on the maturity granted by the lender.

To obtain consistent estimates of the structural parameters, we use single-equation estimating methods, namely two-stage least squares for Equations 6.1 and 6.3 and ordinary least squares for Equation 6.2. The limited number of identifying variables and the likelihood that the correlations of the errors across equations are low assures that single-equation methods make use of most of the available information.[4] The results for the four metropolitan areas (eight samples in total) are reported in Appendix B. (Complete variable definitions are presented in Appendix A.)

Like the California decision-to-lend model (see Chapter 5), risk (RISK) is measured by a vector of financial characteristics of the borrower and the property, a vector of neighborhood characteristics, and a vector of building age dummies. The discrimination variables (DISC) also replicate exactly those used in the decision-to-lend models. They include variables for the sex, race, or age of the applicant or applicants; secondary income by itself and interacted with the sex of the secondary earner; racial composition and age of the neighborhood; and location of the property.

Control Variables

Endogenous Variables   In most cases, the other two mortgage credit terms emerge as statistically significant explanatory variables in the interest-rate and loan-to-value ratio equations. The direction of impact is consistent across samples and can be summarized as follows:

$$INT \text{ (percent)} = f(LTOAV, MAT \ldots)$$
$$\qquad\qquad\qquad\quad + \qquad -$$

$$LTOAV \text{ (years)} = g(INT, MAT \ldots)$$
$$\qquad\qquad\qquad\quad - \text{ or } 0 \quad +$$

As indicated by the + sign under LTOAV in the interest-rate equation, the results imply that lenders offset the higher risk associated with higher loan-to-value ratios with higher interest rates. The interest-rate impact of a 10 percentage point increase in the loan-to-value ratio (for example, from 70 to 80 percent) ranges from one- to six-tenths of a percentage point across samples (for example, an interest rate of 9 percent for a loan equal to 70 percent of the appraised value would be increased to as much as 9.6 percent for a loan amounting to 80 percent of appraised value). These results are statistically significant at the five percent level in all samples except San Jose in 1977 which has a positive but insignificant coefficient.

The negative impact of MAT on the contract interest rate suggests that lenders view longer maturity loans as less risky than shorter maturity loans, *ceteris paribus*. The additional risk involved in tying money up for long periods appears to be more than offset by the reduction in the monthly payments resulting from longer maturities. This negative relationship is found in 7 of the 8 samples and is statistically significant in six.

Lender attention to the size of the borrower's monthly payment also explains the maturity period and interest rate signs in the loan-to-apprasied value equation. Higher interest rates and shorter maturities both raise the borrower's monthly payment, and, according to the equations induce the lender to reduce the size of the loan. The interest rate variable is negative and statistically significant in four of the eight samples. In the two samples in which the coefficient is positive, it is small and statistically insignificant. Maturity period enters the equation positively in all eight samples and is highly significant in seven. For those seven samples, a five year increase in the maturity of the loan induces lenders to increase the loan as a percentage of appraised value by an average of three quarters of a percentage point.

Financial Characteristics   The requested loan and requested loan-to-appraised value variables have significant positive impacts, as expected, in the relevant equations for almost all samples.[5] The results imply that lenders increase interest rates by 0.01 to 0.02 percentage points per $10,000 increase in the requested loan, presumably in response to the higher risk associated with larger loans.

As noted above, we included REQLOAN and RLTOAV in the maturity equation as determinants of the unobserved requested maturity variable. As predicted, larger requested loans, both absolutely and in relation to appraised values, consistently lead to longer maturity loans. Finally, the requested-loan-to-value ratio is a primary determinant of the actual loan-to-value ratio. The point estimates indicate that a 10 percentage point difference in the requested-loan-to-value ratio leads to a 9.6 percentage point difference in the final loan-to-value ratio.

Requested loan-to-income (RLTOINC), which takes on the value 0 for ratios below 2.5 and the value of the ratio itself minus 2.5 above 2.5, exerts its strongest and most consistent impact in the loan-to-value equations. All eight samples provide strong evidence that lenders respond to loan requests that are large in relation to applicant income by reducing the loan-to-value ratio. This behavior reflects the lender's rational attempt to assure that borrowers will be able to meet the monthly mortgage payments as determined by the size of the loan, its term to maturity, and the contract interest rate.

Somewhat surprisingly, higher requested loans in relation to income lead to significantly higher interest rates in only three of the eight samples. In three other samples the impact is small and insignificant, while in two samples (San Francisco-Oakland, 1978 and Los Angeles-Long Beach, 1978), above average requested loans in relation to income lead to lower interest rates. In addition, the requested loan-to-income ratio plays almost no role in the maturity equations.[6]

If borrowers and lenders expect mortgage rates to rise, variable rate mortgages should have lower contract interest rates than conventional mortgages. The empirical results are consistent with this expectation in Los Angeles and Fresno where interest rates are lower on variable rate mortgages by 0.01 and 0.19 percentage points. Contrary to our expectations, the 1977 results for both the San Francisco-Oakland and San Jose areas indicate higher interest rates for these non-conventional mortgages and the 1978 results are insignificant.

Neighborhood Characteristics   Variables representing both the level and rate of change of neighborhood characteristics control for neighborhood factors that might legitimately influence the lender's evaluation of the risk of a particular mortgage loan. The most consistent patterns emerge for the level variables. Mortgages on properties in neighborhoods with above-average income and/or with above-average proportions of high income households are charged lower interest rates in all metropolitan areas other than Fresno in both years. In some cases, longer maturities are also granted in these high income areas.

The effects on mortgage terms of the neighborhood-change variables are less consistent. The clearest patterns appear for the 1977 Los Angeles-Long Beach and San Francisco-Oakland metropolitan areas where all statistically significant coefficients are negative. These results support the view that mortgages on properties in neighborhoods with above average growth in income or households or both are less risky than those in neighborhoods experiencing relative decline. This pattern generally holds in the 1978 equations for these two areas as well, but somewhat less consistently. No pattern emerges for the San Jose and Fresno samples.

The San Jose equations also include a measure of the vacancy rate in the census tract in which the property is located. The 1978 interest rate equation supports the view that lenders view neighborhoods with high vacancy rates as riskier than those with low vacancy rates.

Building Age Building age is a statistically significant determinant of mortgage terms in all of the metropolitan areas under investigation. Table 6.1 summarizes the effects of building age on interest rates. Each entry shows the predicted difference between the interest rate charged on a building with the indicated age and that charged on a new building. The results are striking: lenders charge the lowest interest rates on loans for either new houses (in 4 samples) or 1- to 9-year-old houses (in 4 samples). In all cases these interest rates are significantly below those charged for loans on older houses.

To put the table entries into perspective, consider the entry for houses greater than 50 years old for the Los Angeles-Long Beach area (1978). This indicates that, controlling for other factors including the other mortgage terms, interest rates on loans for houses built fifty or more years before 1978 exceed those on houses built during 1978 by 0.10 percentage point. Using a base interest rate of 9 percent and a maturity period of 30 years, the 0.10 percent higher interest rate translates into an additional payment of $35 per year required on a loan of $40,000 and $52 per year on a loan of $60,000. Similarly, purchasers of 1- to 9-year-old houses in Fresno during 1978 benefitted from interest rates significantly below those charged purchasers of either brand new or older houses. Using the same base interest rate and maturity assumptions, the −0.16 coefficient for the Fresno 1978 sample implies that these borrowers on average pay $56 less per year on a $40,000 loan and $83 less per year on a $60,000 loan than what comparable purchasers of new homes pay and at least this much less than what purchasers of houses more than 40 years old pay. Hence, we conclude that borrowers mortgaging older houses pay significantly higher interest rates and bear substantially larger annual costs than those mortgaging new or recently built houses.

The interpretation of these findings is problematic. On the one hand, lenders may claim that a property's age represents risk factors (for example, building condition) that may legitimately be considered in evaluating loans. According to this interpretation the findings imply that lenders consider mortgages on older buildings to be substantially riskier than those on new buildings. On the other hand, to the extent that risk is not related to building age, the findings suggest that lenders

Table 6.1
Impact of building age on interest rates for conventional mortgages on owner-occupied single family houses in four California metropolitan areas, 1977 and 1978

Building Age (years)	Fresno		Los Angeles-Long Beach		San Francisco-Oakland		San Jose	
	1977	1978	1977	1978	1977	1978	1977	1978
New (base)	—	—	—	—	—	—	—	—
BA1–9	−0.09**	−0.16**	0.05**	−0.02**	0.04**	−0.02**	0.02**	0.02
BA10–19	−0.04**	−0.10**	0.03**	0.08**	0.04**	0.03**	0.02**	0.04**
BA20–29	−0.03	−0.09**	0.03**	0.08**	0.05**	0.05**	0.05**	0.05**
BA30–39	0.03	−0.00	0.09**	0.07**	0.06**	0.06**	0.04**	0.08**
BA40–49	0.02	0.01	0.09**	0.07**	0.08**	0.08**	0.04**	0.13**
BAGE50	0.04	0.08	0.11**	0.10**	0.09**	0.07**	0.07**	0.10**

Each entry shows the predicted difference between the interest rate charged on an application with the indicated characteristics and that charged on an application with the base characteristics. A single asterisk (*) indicates that the relevant difference is statistically significant at the 5–10 percent level (2-tailed test). Two asterisks (**) indicate that the difference is significant at the 5 percent level or less.

in California discriminate against the purchasers of old buildings by imposing harsher terms than otherwise warranted. Since building age is probably a reasonable proxy for the remaining economic life of the building, the discrimination interpretation is at best a weak explanation.

We find a comparable pattern for the impact of building age on the maturity of the loan. In all study areas, mortgages on houses more than 30 years old have shorter maturities than those on new or relatively new houses.

The results for the loan-to-value ratio are less clear cut. In six samples, building age has little impact on loan-to-value ratios. In Los Angeles-Long Beach (1977) and San Jose (1978), however, the evidence suggests that loan-to-value ratios are higher for mortgages on older homes than for those on recently built houses. Thus, on the one hand, lenders in these areas may facilitate purchases of old houses by offering larger loans in relation to appraised value, the effect of which is to reduce the required downpayment. On the other hand, the evidence clearly implies that lenders in all areas discourage such purchases by charging interest rates that are higher than otherwise warranted. These higher interest rates reflect both the direct and indirect impacts of building age. The direct effects have already been shown in Table 6.1. The indirect effects reflect the fact that the shorter maturities in all areas and higher loan-to-value rations in some areas given on loans for old houses also lead to higher interest rates.

Discrimination Results
In this section, we focus primarily, but not exclusively, on the interest rate results. A statistically significant positive coefficient on a discrimination variable in an interest rate equation unambiguously implies adverse treatment. In the maturity equations, by contrast, the coefficients of the discrimination variables may reflect borrower preference for different maturity periods as well as differential treatment by the lender. Where patterns emerge in the maturity and loan-to-value equations, they will be noted. As noted above, however, whether adverse treatment is equivalent to discriminatory lending behavior depends on how well we have controlled for the factors correlated with the prohibited criteria that lenders may legitimately consider. Hence, evidence of adverse treatment is consistent with, but does not prove, the hypothesis that lenders discriminate on the basis of the prohibited characteristic.

To summarize the results, we show the predicted difference in interest rate associated with the difference between the indicated category, for example, black applicant(s) or applicants under age twenty-five, and the base category, white applicant(s) or applicants between thirty-five and forty-four. Asterisks are used to indicate the statistical significance of the difference. By making assumptions about the maturity period, the size of the loan, and the interest rate on a base application, each of the differences in interest rates can be translated into an impact on the borrower's yearly mortgage payments. For example, starting with a mortgage rate of 9 percent and a 30-year maturity period, a difference of 0.125 percent translates into 11¢ per $100 of the mortgage contract. Hence, a $40,000 mortgage would cost $44 more per year and a $60,000 mortgage would cost $66 more per year.

Sex   The basic sex discrimination results are reported in Table 6.2. Two clear patterns emerge. First, lenders in three of the four metropolitan areas apparently treated female-only applicants adversely during 1977 but not 1978. The table shows that interest rates charged female-only applications in 1977 by lenders in all areas other than Fresno exceeded those charged otherwise similar male-female applications where the woman is beyond childbearing age by 0.02 to 0.04 percentage points. Moreover, lenders apparently treated female-only applications in which there was no woman of childbearing age slightly more adversely than those in which at least one woman was of childbearing age.

The second pattern involves possible discrimination against male-only applications. In all areas except Fresno where male-only applications were favored in 1977, lenders charged male-only borrowers interest rates that were from 0.01 to 0.03 percentage points higher than those charged otherwise similar male-female borrowers with the woman beyond childbearing age. In contrast to the results for females, however, lenders in the two largest metropolitan areas continued to charge male-only applications differentially high interest rates in 1978. The LTOAV equations show that the same groups of lenders who charged male-only applications higher interest rates (controlling for the other mortgage terms) favored them with higher loan-to-value ratios.

Finally, we should note that lenders in Los Angeles-Long Beach charged lower interest rates for loans to male-female couples with a

Table 6.2
Impact of sex on interest rates for conventional mortgages on owner-occupied single family houses in four California metropolitan areas, 1977 and 1978

Sex of Applicant	Fresno		Los Angeles-Long Beach		San Francisco-Oakland		San Jose	
	1977	1978	1977	1978	1977	1978	1977	1978
MFNCB (base)	—	—	—	—	—	—	—	—
MFCB25–34[a]	-0.02	0.02	-0.01**	-0.02**	0.01	-0.01	-0.01	0.00
FONLYCB25–34[a]	-0.01	0.05	0.02**	0.01	0.03**	0.01	0.02*	0.02
FONLYNCB	-0.02	-0.00	0.03**	0.01	0.03**	-0.00	0.04**	-0.00
MONLY	-0.07**	0.02	0.01**	0.02**	0.02**	0.03**	0.02**	-0.01

Each entry shows the predicted difference between the interest rate charged on an application with the indicated characteristics and that charged on an application with the base characteristics. A single asterisk (*) indicates that the relevant difference is statistically significant at the 5–10 percent level (2-tailed test). Two asterisks (**) indicate that the difference is significant at the 5 percent level or less.
a. These coefficients reflect the effects of both sex and age. See Table 6.5 for the difference between interest rates charged on loans to applicants between 25 and 34 and those charged to applicants between 35 and 44.

woman of childbearing age than to those of the base category in which the woman is assumed to be beyond childbearing age. This result, when combined with the previously mentioned results for female-only applications, suggests that, contrary to common allegations relating to the probability of having children, younger women receive more favorable treatment than older women.

In addition to testing for outright discrimination based on the sex of the applicant, we tested for discrimination based on differential treatment of secondary income. Table 6.3 indicates that lenders in Los Angeles-Long Beach, San Francisco-Oakland, and San Jose (1977) treat income from secondary earners, especially that earned by men, differently from that of primary earnings. The first line of numbers indicates the extent by which interest rates on loans to homebuyers in which a male secondary earner contributes fifty percent of total income exceeds those on similar applications from single-earner households. For example, in San Jose (1977), an all male household in which the secondary (male) earner contributes fifty percent of total income is charged an interest rate 0.05 percentage points above that charged an all male household with a single earner.[7] Although the table reports differential interest rates for a fifty percent contribution, it should be noted that the statistical significance holds for any contribution rate.

The entries in the two lines of Table 6.3 for female secondary earners indicate that lenders discount secondary income less when it is earned by a woman, especially one beyond childbearing age, than when it is earned by a man. In particular, in 4 of the 5 cases where there is statistically significant evidence that lenders discount secondary income earned by men, lenders apparently do little or no discounting of secondary income earned by women over thirty-five. Income of female secondary earners under thirty-five appears to be discounted in 1977 in Los Angeles-Long Beach and San Francisco-Oakland. Thus, the evidence supports the hypothesis that lenders in three California metropolitan areas discount the income of secondary workers, at least in some cases. This adverse differential treatment of secondary income is greatest for income earned by men, next largest for income earned by women of childbearing age, and least (or non-existent) for income earned by women over childbearing age.

Race   We study the treatment of four groups of racial minorities and compare them with the treatment of white applicants. The equations provide substantial evidence that members of minority groups are

Table 6.3
Impact of secondary income by sex on interest rates for conventional mortgages on owner-occupied single family houses in four California metropolitan areas, 1977 and 1978

Secondary Income	Fresno		Los Angeles-Long Beach		San Francisco-Oakland		San Jose	
	1977	1978	1977	1978	1977	1978	1977	1978
No secondary earner (base)	—	—	—	—	—	—	—	—
Male secondary earner	0.01	0.01	0.02**	0.04**	0.03**	0.02**	0.05**	0.01
Female childbearing secondary earner	0.00	0.02	0.02**	0.02	0.02*	0.01	0.02	−0.02
Female nonchildbearing secondary earner	−0.02	0.03	0.00	0.01	0.01	0.03*	0.01	0.02

Each entry shows the predicted difference between the interest rate charged on an application for which 50 percent of the total income is earned by the indicated secondary earner and that charged on a similar application with a single earner. One asterisk (*) indicates that the differential in the indicated category is based on a coefficient that is statistically significant at the 5–10 percent level. Two asterisks (**) indicate significance at the 5 percent level or less.

charged higher interest rates than similarly situated whites. Table 6.4 indicates that most of the interest rate differentials for minorities in the three major categories—blacks, Spanish people, and Asians—are positive and statistically significant.[8] Lenders in all four metropolitan areas charge members of these minority groups interest rates that average 0.01 to 0.06 percentage points higher than those charged similarly-situated white applicants for comparable loans. The only exception to this pattern is in San Jose where lenders apparently treat Asians the same way they treat white applicants.

Turning briefly to the equations for the other mortgage terms, we find that lenders in Los Angeles-Long Beach, San Francisco-Oakland and Fresno give shorter maturity loans to Spanish and Asian applicants; and that the results for blacks are mixed. In addition, lenders in Los Angeles-Long Beach and San Francisco-Oakland tend to grant larger loans in relation to appraised value to minority borrowers than to otherwise similar white borrowers. This result for loan-to-value ratios may reflect the relatively low wealth of many minority borrowers. These shorter maturities (for Spanish and Asian borrowers) and higher loan-to-value ratios (for members of all three minority groups) increase further the interest rates paid by minority borrowers.

Age   Although the law prohibits discriminatory lending based on the age of the applicant, allegations persist that lenders treat both very young applicants and old applicants adversely. Support for the allegation relating to young borrowers is found in Table 6.5. In five of the eight samples, lenders treat applicants under twenty-five adversely by charging them interest rates that average 0.02 to 0.04 percentage points above those charged similarly situated applicants between the ages of thirty-five and forty-four. Only the Fresno (1978) results are consistent with the allegation that lenders charge higher interest rates to older borrowers, however. Indeed, lenders in San Francisco-Oakland (1978) apparently favor 45 to 54-year-old applicants.

Not surprisingly, the maturity equations provide evidence that applicants over forty-five end up with shorter maturities, especially in Los Angeles-Long Beach, San Francisco-Oakland, and San Jose (1977), than applicants between thirty-five and forty-four. This result cannot be interpreted as evidence of discriminatory behavior based on age because the outcome may reflect a preference of older applicants for shorter maturities. This alternative explanation cannot be ruled

Table 6.4

Impact of race on interest rates for conventional mortgages on owner-occupied single family houses in four California Metropolitan areas, 1977 and 1978

Race of Applicant	Fresno		Los Angeles-Long Beach		San Francisco-Oakland		San Jose	
	1977	1978	1977	1978	1977	1978	1977	1978
White (base)	—	—	—	—	—	—	—	—
Black	0.04	0.06	0.05**	0.05**	0.02**	0.04**	0.05**	0.01
Spanish	0.06**	−0.00	0.03**	0.04**	0.02**	0.02**	0.02**	0.02
Asian	0.02	0.03	0.01**	0.02**	0.02**	0.02**	−0.00	−0.00
Other minority	0.00	0.06	0.00	0.01	0.00	0.02	0.02*	0.02

Each entry shows the predicted difference between the interest rate charged on an application with the indicated characteristics and that charged on an application with the base characteristics. A single asterisk (*) indicates that the relevant difference is statistically significant at the 5–10 percent level (2-tailed test). Two asterisks (**) indicate that the difference is significant at the 5 percent level or less.

Table 6.5
Impact of age of applicant on interest rates for conventional mortgages on owner-occupied single family houses in four California metropolitan areas, 1977 and 1978

Age of Applicant	Fresno		Los-Angeles-Long Beach		San Francisco-Oakland		San Jose	
	1977	1978	1977	1978	1977	1978	1977	1978
<25	0.04**	0.02	0.02**	0.01	0.02**	0.00	0.03**	0.03*
25–34	0.01	0.01	0.00	−0.00	0.01*	−0.00	0.00	0.00
35–44 (base)	—	—	—	—	—	—	—	—
45–54	0.01	0.06**	−0.00	0.00	−0.00	−0.02**	0.00	−0.00
>54	0.01	0.03	−0.01	0.00	0.01	−0.00	−0.00	0.01

Each entry shows the predicted difference between the interest rate charged on an application with the indicated characteristics and that charged on an application with the base characteristics. A single asterisk (*) indicates that the relevant difference is statistically significant at the 5–10 percent level (2-tailed test). Two asterisks (**) indicate that the difference is significant at the 5 percent level or less.

out since data limitations keep us from controlling adequately for the borrower's preferences with respect to maturity length.

In the loan-to-value equations, we find support for the hypothesis that lenders in all areas other than Fresno grant loans that are smaller in relation to appraised value to applicants over 45 than to those between thirty-five and forty-four.[9]

Redlining   Table 6.6 summarizes the evidence pertaining to allegations that lenders impose harsher terms on applications from older neighborhoods or from neighborhoods with above average proportions of minorities. Each entry in the first row of the table represents the predicted impact on the interest rate of an increase of 0.10 in the fraction of housing built before 1940 (PRE1940) in the census tract in which the property is located. The entries in the next three rows show the impact associated with an increase in the fraction of a particular minority (FBLACK, FSPANISH, FASIAN) in the census tract (or zip code area for the Asian fraction) in which the property is located from the average level to a sample specific "high" level.[10]

The results contradict allegations by community groups that lenders impose harsher terms in older neighborhoods, *ceteris paribus*. In all eight samples, loans on houses in neighborhoods with above average proportions of old houses are found to have interest rates that are statistically significantly lower than those on houses in neighborhoods with average proportions of old housing. The appearance that lenders are discriminating on the basis of neighborhood age probably comes from their behavior with respect to building age; as noted above, the evidence suggests that lenders consistently charge higher interest rates on older buildings than on new and that the differential increases with the age of the building.

In contrast to the findings on neighborhood age, the results generally support the hypothesis that lenders impose harsher terms on applications from black and Spanish neighborhoods than on applications from average neighborhoods. Interest rates on loans in highly Spanish neighborhoods exceed those on loans in neighborhoods with average proportions of Spanish people in all study areas other than Los Angeles-Long Beach. The adverse treatment is substantial, particularly in San Francisco-Oakland where the differentials are 0.12 and 0.09 percentage points.

In contrast to the evidence that Los Angeles-Long Beach lenders apparently favored Spanish neighborhoods in 1978, the evidence sug-

Table 6.6
Impact of neighborhood age and racial composition on interest rates for conventional mortgages on owner-occupied single family houses in four California metropolitan areas, 1977 and 1978

Neighborhood Type	Fresno		Los Angeles-Long Beach		San Francisco-Oakland		San Jose	
	1977	1978	1977	1978	1977	1978	1977	1978
PRE1940 (increase to average +0.10)	-0.01**	-0.02**	-0.01**	-0.01**	-0.004**	-0.01**	-0.01**	-0.01**
FBLACK (increase to "high")	0.00	-0.07	0.07**	0.05**	0.13**	-0.00	0.08**	-0.08**
FSPANISH (increase to "high")	0.03**	0.03**	0.01	-0.04**	0.12**	0.09**	0.06**	0.06**
FASIAN (increase to "high")	0.00	0.00	-0.03	-0.03**	-0.12**	-0.04	-0.00	-0.00

Each entry shows the impact on the contract interest rate of increasing each neighborhood variable from its average value to the amount indicated. "High" values of the racial composition variables vary across samples; they are calculated as the maximum value in the sample minus two standard deviations. See Table 5.32 for representative values. A single asterisk (*) indicates that the relevant difference is statistically significant at the 5–10 percent level (2-tailed test). Two asterisks (**) indicate the difference is significant at the 5 percent level or less.

gests that they treated black neighborhoods adversely in both years by charging interest rates 0.05 to 0.07 percentage points higher than otherwise warranted. Black neighborhoods in San Francisco-Oakland and San Jose also received adverse treatment, but apparently only during 1977. Indeed, San Jose leaders apparently favored black neighborhoods during 1978.[11]

The maturity equations provide additional evidence of lending practices that work to the disadvantage of Spanish and black neighborhoods. In many of the samples (but excluding both San Jose samples), there is statistically significant evidence that home buyers in black and Spanish neighborhoods are granted shorter maturity loans than comparable buyers in average neighborhoods.

Unlike black and Spanish neighborhoods, neighborhoods with high proportions of Asians tend to be favored. In some cases (for example, San Francisco-Oakland in 1977 and Los Angeles-Long Beach in 1978), loans on properties in these neighborhoods have lower contract interest rates and in others (for example Los Angeles 1977 and 1978 and San Jose 1977), longer maturities.

We have sufficient information to examine explicit allegations of redlining in certain neighborhoods of the Los Angeles-Long Beach and San Francisco-Oakland areas.[12] By comparing interest rates in these neighborhoods with those in a reference suburban area, we can determine whether the evidence supports the redlining allegations. The results for Los Angeles-Long Beach are reported in Table 6.7 and for San Francisco-Oakland in Table 6.8. It should be remembered that these results reflect the effects on the interest rate of location after controlling for all other variables in the equation including the race of the individual and the racial composition of the neighborhood. Hence, an insignificant coefficient does not necessarily imply that buyers of homes in the neighborhoods receive treatment comparable to that of the typical home buyer. Instead, it implies that geographic location *per se* has no influence on the interest rate independent of the other variables.

Of the twelve areas delineated as neighborhoods alleged to be redlined in the Los Angeles-Long Beach metropolitan area, statistically significant findings in support of the redlining hypothesis emerge for three areas in 1977. Location alone raises interest rates by 0.09, 0.06 and 0.05 percentage points in Pomona, San Pedro, and West Covina. While 1977 interest rates in some of the other neighborhoods alleged

Table 6.7
Impact of location on interest rates for conventional mortgages on owner-occupied single family houses in Los Angeles-Long Beach, 1977 and 1978

Neighborhood	1977	1978
Allegedly redlined neighborhoods		
Compton	−0.05	0.12*
Covina-Azusa	0.01	−0.31**
East Los Angeles- Boyle Heights-Echo Park	0.02	0.04
Highland Park	−0.04*	0.03
Long Beach-Southwest	0.04	−0.33**
Pacoima-San Fernando	−0.01	−0.00
Pasadena North Central	0.01	−0.12**
Pomona	0.09**	0.01
San Pedro	0.06**	−0.18**
South Central Los Angeles	−0.01	0.03
Venice-Santa Monica	0.02	−0.04
West Covina	0.08**	0.03
Other neighborhoods		
Rest of the City of Long Beach	0.01	−0.05**
Rest of the City of Los Angeles	−0.02**	−0.03**
Rest of Los Angeles County (base)	—	—

Each entry shows the predicted difference between the interest rate charged on a mortgage loan in the specified location and that charged on a loan in the reference area. A single asterisk (*) indicates that the relevant difference is statistically significant at the 5–10 percent level (2-tailed test). Two asterisks (**) indicate that the difference is significant at the 5 percent level or less.

to be redlined were lower than those charged in the suburban part of Los Angeles County, the favorable treatment is statistically significant only in Highland Park.

The picture changes in the 1978 equations. During this year, only Compton shows evidence of being redlined, while four other areas alleged to be redlined benefit from substantially lower interest rates. These results provide weak support for the hypothesis that geographic redlining in Los Angeles-Long Beach was less prevalent in 1978 than in 1977.

In San Francisco-Oakland, only one area has been identified as allegedly redlined: Central Oakland. As shown in Table 6.8, the results are consistent with the redlining hypothesis in 1977 but not 1978.

Table 6.8
Impact of location on interest rates for conventional mortgages on owner-occupied single family houses in San Francisco-Oakland, 1977 and 1978

Neighborhood	1977	1978
Allegedly redlined neighborhood		
Central Oakland	0.07**	−0.03
Other neighborhoods		
Alameda City	0.00	0.07**
Berkeley	0.01	0.03
East Oakland	0.04**	0.00
West Oakland	−0.05	0.02
Rest of Alameda County	0.01	−0.04
Contra Costa County	0.05**	0.03**
Marin County	0.02**	0.01
San Francisco County	0.00	0.01
San Mateo County (base)	—	—

Each entry shows the predicted difference between the interest rate charged on a mortgage loan in the specified location and that charged on a loan in the reference area. A single asterisk (*) indicates that the relevant difference is statistically significant at the 5–10 percent level (2-tailed test). Two asterisks (**) indicate that the difference is significant at the 5 percent level or less.

Downward Modifications

This section analyzes the differences between requested and granted loan amounts for those applications subject to downward modifications. The specific question addressed here is whether some borrowers experience larger downward modifications than others solely because of membership in groups not legally allowed to be considered by banks in their decision-making process. Large downward modifications of loan amounts may yield effects similar to those of loan denial; the applicant may not be able to proceed with the house purchase because he or she cannot raise the additional down payment necessitated by the bank's decision not to lend the requested amount.

Control Variables

The general form of the model used to test for discriminatory behavior in connection with the determination of loan amounts is discussed in Chapter 4. The equations estimated for California model the downward modification (MODOWN, defined as the requested loan minus the granted loan) as a function of the requested loan amount (REQLOAN); the requested-loan-to-appraised-value ratio (RLTOAV); the requested-loan-to-income ratio (RLTOINC); a vector of variables representing the age of the property; a vector of neighborhood characteristics, including level and change variables; and a vector of discrimination variables, including sex, race, and age of applicants, division of income between the applicant and co-applicant, and the age and racial composition of the neighborhood. This model is estimated only for those applications which received loan amounts below that requested.

Additional financial characteristics of the borrower such as the income, net wealth, and employment stability variables included in the New York MODOWN equations are excluded from the California equations for the following reasons: net wealth and employment stability data are not available in the California data set and preliminary analysis for California indicated that income is relevant only in relation to the size of the requested loan. The California MODOWN equations differ from the New York equations as well by the inclusion of the building-age dummy variables, data not available for New York. To the extent that building age correctly indicates a building's condition, these variables measure objective factors influencing the risk of the loan to the bank; to the extent that building age is imperfectly correlated with the building's remaining useful life, however, these variables might be capturing discrimination against older buildings.

The estimated equations for the eight separate samples (two years for each SMSA) are reported in Appendix B. All equations are linear and were estimated using ordinary least squares. Sample size ranges from a low of 110 in Fresno to a high of 1,519 in Los Angeles-Long Beach. A small number of observations in the 1977 Fresno sample, combined with a large unexplained variation, lead to the conclusion that the 1977 Fresno equation explains a statistically insignificant proportion of the variation in the dependent variable. The other seven equations explain statistically significant proportions of the variation, with the proportions averaging about 25–30 percent.

Size of the requested loan (REQLOAN) and requested loan to income (RLTOINC) are the key control variables. The requested loan amount acts as a scale variable; for any given degree of loan risk as measured by the other control variables, the dollar amount of the modification depends on the size of the loan. The requested-loan-to-income ratio is the bank's primary predictor of the borrower's ability to make timely payments in the future. Beyond a certain point (in the empirical specification, this point is 2.5 times income), the larger the requested loan is in relation to income, the greater is the downward modification needed to bring the actual loan amount in line with borrower income. Both variables have positive impacts on the magnitude of the downward modification, as predicted, and are statistically significant in all eight equations.

The coefficients of requested loan to appraised value (RLTOAV) are less consistent across equations: in three equations they are statistically significant and positive as expected; in three they are positive but not significant; and in two they are negative. The booming California housing market during the study period may partially explain these results; during a period of rising house values, firmly held expectations that housing prices will continue to rise may make loan-to-value ratios a secondary concern for bankers in relation to their primary concern that the borrower have sufficient income to make the monthly payments.

Most of the other control variables have little explanatory power. In a few equations, one or more of the neighborhood variables are significant, but no clear pattern emerges. Some of the building-age variables are statistically significant in the Los Angeles-Long Beach and San Jose equations; in both cases the evidence suggests that applications on old buildings are subject to smaller downward modifications than those on new buildings.

Discrimination Results
The finding of a positive coefficient on a discrimination variable indicates that applicants who are members of the group in question (for example, women, old people, blacks, Spanish, or home buyers in allegedly redlined neighborhoods) experience larger loan reductions than comparable applicants from the baseline groups. Larger loan reductions translate directly into larger than anticipated down payments unless the borrower turns to a more expensive second mortgage. In some cases, larger loan reductions may keep the applicant from purchasing the home at all and, thus, may be an indirect way for the bank to deny the loan. Provided the control variables in the MODOWN equations adequately represent the legitimate factors affecting the size of downward modifications, we can interpret statistically significant positive coefficients on any of the discrimination variables as support for the hypothesis of discriminatory behavior.

For each of the eight samples, we have calculated the expected downward modification for a baseline application. This baseline application represents the type that bankers would be least likely to discriminate against: the applicants are a white, male-female couple; the woman is beyond childbearing age; all the income is earned by the primary worker; the applicant is between thirty-five and forty-four; and the property is in the suburbs.[13] With respect to all other characteristics, the baseline application takes on average values for the particular MODOWN sample involved. In connection with each type of potential discrimination, the predicted downward modification for an application that differs from the baseline application in the discrimination dimension only is reported and compared to the baseline downward modification for that sample. In this way, similarly situated applicants can be compared and the magnitude of the discriminatory differentials can be put into perspective.

Sex   The results by sex are reported in Table 6.9. Each entry represents the predicted amount by which savings and loan associations in each of the eight samples reduce loans for downward-modified applications differing from baseline applications only in terms of sex. The numbers in parentheses represent the ratio of the predicted MODOWN for the given sex type to the type included in the base. For example, the second entry in the second column of Table 6.9 indicates that savings and loan associations in Los Angeles-Long Beach reduce the actual loan below the requested loan on average by $7,819 for a downward-modified application that differs from the base only in that the woman is of childbearing age. The 0.83 in parentheses indicates that this predicted loan reduction is 83 percent of the predicted loan reduction for the base application. The absence of asterisks with this entry indicates that the difference between this and the baseline MODOWN is statistically insignificant. In general, a single asterisk means that the difference is significant at the 5–10 percent level; two asterisks indicate the 5 percent level using a two-tailed test.

Table 6.9 provides almost no evidence of adverse differential treatment based on the sex of the applicants. Four of the five statistically significant effects imply favorable rather than adverse treatment. Moreover, the signs of the other coefficients are inconsistent across equations, indicating no clear pattern of lender behavior.

The one significant finding consistent with discriminatory behavior relates to savings and loan associations in Fresno (1978); lenders in

Table 6.9
Downward modifications (dollar amounts and ratios) by sex for baseline applications in four California metropolitan areas

Sex of Applicant	Fresno	Los Angeles-Long Beach	San Francisco-Oakland	San Jose
1977				
MFNCB (base)	4,603 (1.00)	9,438 (1.00)	7,486 (1.00)	10,434 (1.00)
MFCB25–34[a]	4,101 (0.89)	7,819 (0.83)	7,212 (0.96)	5,423** (0.52)
FONLYCB25–34[b]	↑ 4,682 (1.02)	8,222 (0.87)	4,468 (0.60)	↑ 4,864** (0.47)
FONLYNCB	↓	9,095 (0.96)	7,011 (0.94)	↓
MONLY	5,427 (1.18)	8,842 (0.93)	6,803 (0.91)	6,358** (0.61)
1978				
MFNCB (base)	3,173 (1.00)	11,017 (1.00)	9,679 (1.00)	4,727 (1.00)
MFCB25–34[a]	6,257* (1.97)	8,836 (0.80)	8,148 (0.84)	8,994 (1.90)
FONLYCB25–34[a]	↑ 3,121 (0.98)	9,106 (0.82)	7,558 (0.78)	↑ 6,272 (1.33)
FONLYNCB	↓	11,533 (1.05)	7,552 (0.78)	↓
MONLY	3,178 (1.00)	7,999 (0.73)	7,497** (0.77)	7,000 (1.48)

The entries in the table represent the predicted downward modification (in dollars) for an application similar to the base application in all ways other than the characteristic listed. Numbers in parentheses represent the ratio of the downward modification for an application with the indicated characteristics to the downward modification for the baseline application. See text for definition of the baseline application. A single asterisk (*) indicates that the numerator of the ratio is statistically significantly different from the denominator at the 5–10 percent level (using a 2-tailed test). Two asterisks (**) indicate that the difference is significant at the 5 or less percent level.
a. These estimates reflect the effects of both sex and age in that the age of the applicant is reduced to the 25–34 age category. See Table 6.11 for the separate effects of age.

this area appear to reduce loans for male-female couples in which the woman is of childbearing age (and the applicant is between twenty-five and thirty-four) by almost twice the amount they reduce loans for baseline applications, controlling for all other factors.[14] Since this requires an additional down payment of $3,136, the financial impact on the borrower is substantial.

Lenders might also discriminate by counting secondary income less than primary income when evaluating mortgage applications and deciding what size loan to grant. We can examine this allegation by looking at the impact of the proportion of income earned by the secondary earner on the size of the downward modification. By interacting the proportion of income earned by the secondary earner with the presence of a female secondary earner of childbearing age and with the presence of a female secondary earner beyond childbearing age, we can test the further allegation that bankers treat secondary income earned by females differently from that earned by males.

The results for the four SMSAs examined here do not support the hypothesis that bankers count secondary income less than primary income. Most of the relevant coefficients are statistically insignificant, and a few imply favorable treatment of secondary income. The Fresno 1978 sample provides the exception to this general pattern. The higher the proportion of income from a female secondary earner beyond childbearing age in that sample, the larger is the predicted downward modification.

Race The findings with respect to differential treatment based on race, summarized in Table 6.10, fail to support the hypothesis of discriminatory behavior. Most of the ratios are less than one, implying that, if anything, lenders modify loans downward by less for members of racial minorities than for similarly situated whites; furthermore, none of the four ratios greater than one is derived from a statistically significant coefficient.

Age Turning now to the results by age, we find evidence that savings and loan associations reduce loan amounts by more for applicants over forty-five than for otherwise comparable younger applicants (see Table 6.11). The findings are strongest for Los Angeles-Long Beach (1977 and 1978) and San Francisco-Oakland (1977 and 1978), where applicants in both the forty-five to fifty-four and the over fifty-four age groups experienced larger downward modifications than similarly situated applicants between the ages of thirty-five and forty-four. This

Table 6.10
Downward modifications (dollar amounts and ratios) by race for baseline applications in four California metropolitan areas

Race of Applicant	Fresno	Los Angeles-Long Beach	San Francisco-Oakland	San Jose
	1977			
White (base)	4,603	9,438	7,486	10,434
	(1.00)	(1.00)	(1.00)	(1.00)
Black	3,224[a]	12,222	4,771	8,098[a]
	(0.70)	(1.29)	(0.63)	(0.78)
Spanish	5,306	8,722	5,660	10,081
	(1.15)	(0.92)	(0.76)	(0.96)
Asian	—	8,400	6,176	—
		(0.89)	(0.83)	
Other minority	—	9,593	5,426	—
		(1.02)	(0.72)	
	1978			
White (base)	3,173	11,017	9,679	4,727
	(1.00)	(1.00)	(1.00)	(1.00)
Black	959[a]	8,090*	7,103**	7,187[a]
	(0.30)	(0.73)	(0.73)	(1.52)
Spanish	3,012	9,686*	8,450	7,778
	(0.94)	(0.87)	(0.87)	(1.65)
Asian	—	10,153	7,779**	—
		(0.92)	(0.80)	
Other minority	—	7,647*	9,634	—
		(0.69)	(0.99)	

The entries in the table represent the predicted downward modification (in dollars) for an application similar to the base application in all ways other than the characteristic listed. Numbers in parentheses represent the ratio of the downward modification for an application with the indicated characteristics to the downward modification for the baseline application. See text for definition of the baseline application. A single asterisk (*) indicates that the numerator of the ratio is statistically significantly different from the denominator at the 5–10 percent level (using a 2-tailed test). Two asterisks (**) indicate that the difference is significant at the 5 percent or less level.
a. Includes other minorities; Asians are grouped with whites in the base.

Table 6.11
Downward modifications (dollar amounts and ratios) by age for baseline applications in four California metropolitan areas

Age of Applicant	Fresno	Los Angeles-Long Beach	San Francisco-Oakland	San Jose
1977				
<25	3,224	7,925	6,594	7,989
	(0.70)	(0.84)	(0.88)	(0.76)
A25–34	3,961	8,761	7,444	9,618
	(0.86)	(0.93)	(0.99)	(0.92)
A35–44 (base)	4,603	9,438	7,486	10,434
	(1.00)	(1.00)	(1.00)	(1.00)
A45–54	4,456	10,923*	10,276**	10,753
	(0.97)	(1.16)	(1.37)	(1.03)
>54	4,710	12,496**	9,678*	9,989
	(1.02)	(1.32)	(1.29)	(0.95)
1978				
<. 25	6,233	9,795	8,927	6,014
	(1.96)	(0.89)	(0.92)	(1.27)
25–34	5,566*	10,432	9,689	6,224
	(1.75)	(0.94)	(1.00)	(1.32)
35–44 (base)	3,173	11,017	9,679	4,727
	(1 00)	(1.00)	(1.00)	(1.00)
45–54	8,361**	12,363*	11,533**	6,415
	(2.63)	(1.12)	(1.19)	(1.36)
>54	4,388	11,781	9,762	8,752
	(1.38)	(1.07)	(1.01)	(1.85)

The entries in the table represent the predicted downward modification (in dollars) for an application similar to the base application in all ways other than the characteristic listed. Numbers in parentheses represent the ratio of the downward modification for an application with the indicated characteristics to the downward modification for the baseline application. See text for definition of the baseline application. A single asterisk (*) indicates that the numerator of the ratio is statistically significantly different from the denominator at the 5–10 percent level (using a 2-tailed test). Two asterisks (**) indicate that the difference is significant at the 5 percent or less level.

conclusion is based on statistically significant coefficients in six of the eight cases involved. The predicted downward modifications for applicants in these age groups are substantial in absolute amount, ranging from $9,678 for applicants over fifty-four in the San Francisco-Oakland area during 1977 to $12,496 for applicants over fifty-four in the Los Angeles-Long Beach area during the same year. The predicted amounts for these two age groups exceed the modification amounts experienced by 35- to 44-year-old applicants by up to 37 percent.

In the two smaller metropolitan areas, the results are mixed, especially for the 1977 data. The 1978 results for both Fresno and San Jose, however, indicate a clear, although not generally statistically significant, pattern of larger than warranted downward modifications for applicants over forty-five. In addition, applicants between the ages of twenty-five and thirty-four applying for mortgages in Fresno during 1978 also appear to experience larger downward modifications than 35- to 44-year-old applicants.

Redlining   Table 6.12 summarizes the evidence relating to allegations that bankers treat applications from older neighborhoods or neighborhoods with high proportions of minorities differently from those from other neighborhoods. Each entry in the first row of the table represents the predicted change in the downward modification associated with an increase of 0.10 in the fraction of housing built before 1940 in the census tract in which the property is located. The entries in the next three rows show the change in the downward modification associated with an increase in the fraction of a particular minority, say Spanish, in the census tract (or zip-code area for Asians) in which the property is located from the average level to a sample-specific "high" level.[15] The results for the Los Angeles-Long Beach and San Francisco-Oakland metropolitan areas provide limited support for these allegations; the results for the Fresno and San Jose metropolitan areas provide no support.

Downward modifications increase with the proportion of old housing in both the San Francisco-Oakland and Los Angeles-Long Beach areas during both years, although the positive coefficients are statistically significant in only two of the four samples. In addition, savings and loan associations in the San Francisco-Oakland area appear to treat applications from tracts with higher than average proportions of blacks adversely; savings and loan associations in the Los Angeles-Long Beach area do the same with respect to applications from tracts with

Table 6.12
Changes in downward modifications (dollar amounts) associated with changes in the age and racial composition of the neighborhood

Neighborhood Type	Fresno		Los Angeles-Long Beach		San Francisco-Oakland		San Jose	
	1977	1978	1977	1978	1977	1978	1977	1978
PRE1940 (increase to average +0.10)	195	−355	386*	212	249	554**	−709	1,352
FBLACK (increase to "high")	17,376	−3,596	−3,895*	6,512	3,343*	4,567	−4,687	−7,460
FSPANISH (increase to "high")	−563	843	3,693**	1,865	−4,785	−4,495	416	3,560
FASIAN (increase to "high")	−163	−442	539	−1,525	−11,510	621	1,796	8,640

The entries in the table represent the change in the downward modifications associated with an increase in the neighborhood-age or racial-composition variable from its average level to the indicated level. "High" levels for the racial-composition variables are sample specific. See Table 5.32 for representative values. A single asterisk (*) indicates that the numerator of the ratio is statistically significantly different from the denominator at the 5–10 percent level (using a 2-tailed test). Two asterisks (**) indicate that the difference is significant at the 5 percent or less level.

higher than average proportions of Spanish. Again, only two of the four coefficients on which these conclusions are based are statistically significant.

Finally, we examine the hypothesis of differential downward modifications in neighborhoods alleged to be redlined in the Los Angeles-Long Beach metropolitan area. Only for this area are the sample sizes sufficiently large to examine this redlining issue. Even here, however, data limitations force us to aggregate all the areas alleged to be redlined into one category. Results from the interest-rate equation (and the lender action models in Chapter 5) suggest that such aggregation is undesirable. Interest rates relative to the reference suburban area varied substantially across the twelve neighborhoods alleged to be redlined. In any case, the results reported in Table 6.13 provide no support for the hypothesis that savings and loan associations in Los Angeles-Long Beach reduce loan amounts by more in areas alleged to be redlined than in other areas.

Loan Fees

The final component of mortgage terms that can be analyzed with the California data are the fees that savings and loan associations charge for making mortgage loans. As developed more fully in chapter 4, we expect loan fees to be a function of the loan amount, property characteristics, and neighborhood characteristics. In addition, we include

Table 6.13
Downward modifications (dollar amounts and ratios) by location for baseline applications in Los Angeles-Long Beach, 1977 and 1978

Property Location	1977	1978
Suburbs (base)	9,438	11,017
	(1.00)	(1.00)
Areas alleged to be redlined	8,298	11,160
	(0.88)	(1.01)
Rest of City of Los Angeles	8,674	11,836
	(0.92)	(1.07)
Rest of Long Beach	8,625	8,943
	(0.91)	(0.81)

The entries represent the predicted downward modification (in dollars) for an application similar to the base application in all ways other than the characteristic listed. Numbers in parentheses represent the ratio of the downward modification for an application with the indicated characteristics to the downward modification for the baseline application. See text for definition of the baseline application.

variables to test for the existence of discrimination. Implicit in this general model is the view that lenders should set loan fees to cover the administrative costs of making the loan rather than to adjust for the riskiness of the loan. Since borrower income affects the riskiness of the loan (controlling for loan amount) but not the administrative costs, it is not included as an explanatory control variable.

The eight estimated equations are reported in Appendix B. All equations are linear, are estimated using ordinary least squares, and cover all approved loans for which complete data exist. The equations explain from 50 to 75 percent of the variation in the dependent variable.

Control Variables

Reflecting the fact that the basic loan fee is assessed as a fraction of the loan amount, the loan amount exerts a strong and statistically significant positive impact on the size of the loan fee across all eight equations. The coefficients imply that loan fees average slightly over 1 percent of the loan amount.

The property specific characteristics included in the loan fee equations are the property's appraised value, its size (measured in thousands of interior square feet), and its age (represented by a vector of dummy variables). These variables control for the factors that might affect the appraisal, inspection, escrow, and title insurance costs that associations may legitimately include in loan fees to offset the costs of processing loans.

Appraised value (AV) enters significantly and negatively in all equations other than those for Los Angeles-Long Beach, presumably reflecting economies of scale in the appraisal process. For unknown reasons, higher appraised values are associated with higher loan fees, controlling for all other factors, in the two Los Angeles samples. Economies of scale in the appraisal or inspection process also explain the negative signs of the four statistically significant coefficients of the building-age variable (SPACE).

Building-age variables enter most consistently and significantly in the Los Angeles-Long Beach and San Francisco-Oakland equations, as shown in Table 6.14. The table entries show the difference between the predicted loan fee for a house of the given age compared to a new house, controlling for other factors.

In the San Francisco-Oakland area, loan fees generally increase systematically with building age; in Los Angeles, loan fees are higher on average for all older houses relative to new, but the differential is

Table 6.14
Impact of building age on loan fees for four California metropolitan areas, 1977 and 1978

Building Age (number of years before 1977 that house was built)	Fresno		Los Angeles-Long Beach		San Francisco-Oakland		San Jose	
	1977	1978	1977	1978	1977	1978	1977	1978
New (base)[a]	—	—	—	—	—	—	—	—
BA1-9	7	-9	19**	20**	30**	8	67**	15**
BA10-19	0	-7	8*	14**	33**	21**	73**	8
BA20-29	-4	-1	9**	22**	38**	35**	77**	4
BA30-39	-62**	-8	14**	29**	38**	38**	58**	8
BA40-49	-93**	-4	21**	40**	46**	44**	47**	2
BAGE50	-90**	1	18**	44**	45**	60**	67**	-40*

Each entry shows the predicted difference between the loan fee charged on an application with the indicated characteristics and that charged on an application with the base characteristics. A single asterisk (*) indicates that the relevant difference is statistically significant at the 5–10 percent level (using a 2-tailed test). Two asterisks (**) indicate that the difference is significant at the 5 percent or less level.
a. Because of a programming error in the 1978 estimates, building age in the 1978 samples is measured relative to new and 1-year-old buildings, and the other variables are: BA2–10, BA11–20, BA21–30, BA31–40, BA41–50, and BAGE51.

lowest for 10 to 19-year-old houses. In the San Jose area, the results are mixed. During 1977, applications on houses built before 1977 are charged higher loan fees than applications on new houses, but the fees exhibit no other pattern with respect to age of house. During 1978, applications on houses built in 1977 or 1978 have larger fees than those on the oldest houses. In the Fresno metropolitan area, savings and loan associations charged significantly and substantially lower loan fees during 1977 on mortgage applications for houses more than thirty years old than for new houses. Unfortunately, the determination of whether differential loan process costs justify the difference in loan fees associated with building age is beyond the scope of this study.

The loan-fee models include as control variables the same neighborhood variables that were included in the California lender action models, but for different reasons. Here the variables are intended to control for any legitimate costs of processing loans, whereas in the lender action models, they control for the riskiness of the loan. The variables include change-in-income variables (DINC7675 and DINC7570) and change in number of households variables (DHH7675 and DHH7570); 1976 average income (INC1976); the fraction of households with high income (FHI); and in San Jose, the vacancy rate (FVACANTSJ).

Many of the income-change and household-change variables are statistically significant, but the signs vary across equations, making them hard to interpret and explain. The level variables yield more consistent results. Whenever either 1976 average income or the fraction of high income households is statistically significant, its coefficient is negative. We conclude that in the Los Angeles-Long Beach, San Francisco-Oakland, and San Jose (1978 only) metropolitan areas, borrowers receiving mortgages for houses in higher-income areas are charged lower loan fees, *ceteris paribus,* than comparable borrowers in lower-income areas.

Discrimination Results
The finding of a statistically significant positive coefficient on a discrimination variable indicates that applicants who are members of the group in question (for example, women, old people, blacks, or home buyers in allegedly redlined neighborhoods) are charged higher loan fees than otherwise comparable applicants. We interpret results of this sort as evidence of discriminatory behavior. This interpretation is straightforward provided the control variables in the loan-fee equations

adequately represent the factors affecting the costs of processing loans. Even when a relevant factor is left out of the equation, however, higher loan fees associated with a discrimination variable may still indicate discriminatory behavior. This is true provided the variable that is left out and the discrimination variable are not positively correlated.

For each of the eight samples, we have calculated the expected loan fee for a baseline application. This baseline application represents the type that bankers would be least likely to discriminate against and is defined analogously to baseline applications in the MODOWN section: the applicants are a white, male-female couple, the woman is beyond childbearing age, the applicant is between thirty-five and forty-four, and the property is located in the suburbs.[16] With respect to all other characteristics, the baseline application takes on average values for the particular LOANFEE sample involved. In connection with each type of potential discrimination, the predicted loan fee for an approved application that differs from the baseline application in the discrimination dimension only is reported and compared to the loan fee for the baseline application for that sample. In this way, similarly situated applicants can be compared and the magnitude of the discriminatory differential put into perspective.

Sex   The results by sex of the application are reported in Table 6.15. Each entry represents the predicted loan fee for applications differing from baseline applications only in terms of the sex of the applicants. The numbers in parentheses represent the ratio of the predicted loan fee for the sex type to the type included in the base. The asterisks, as in previous tables, indicate the statistical significance of the relevant coefficients.

Starting with the clearest pattern of statistically insignificant results, we conclude that female-only applications in which no applicant is below thirty-four (FONLYNCB) are charged loan fees no higher on average than those charged baseline applications. In other words, the results contradict allegations that banks discriminate against women in this age group by imposing excessive financial burdens in the form of high loan fees.

The results for female-only applications where the applicant is between twenty-five and thirty-four years old (FONLYCB) are mixed. Of the four statistically significant coefficients, two indicate higher loan fees and two indicate lower loan fees than those for baseline

Table 6.15
Loan fees (dollar amounts and ratios) by sex for baseline applications in four California metropolitan areas

Sex of Applicant	Fresno	Los Angeles-Long Beach	San Francisco-Oakland	San Jose
	1977			
MFNCB (base)	620	695	678	690
	(1.00)	(1.00)	(1.00)	(1.00)
MFCB25–34[a]	608*	703**	686*	687
	(0.98)	(1.01)	(1.01)	(1.00)
FONLYCB25–34[a]	590*	707*	689*	687
	(0.95)	(1.02)	(1.02)	(1.00)
FONLYNCB	630	695	684	679
	(1.02)	(1.00)	(1.01)	(0.98)
MONLY	658**	704**	680	686
	(1.06)	(1.01)	(1.00)	(0.99)
	1978			
MFNCB (base)	720	843	823	873
	(1.00)	(1.00)	(1.00)	(1.00)
MFCB25–34[a]	723	847	827	865*
	(1.00)	(1.00)	(1.00)	(0.99)
FONLYCB25–34[a]	741	851	826	864*
	(1.03)	(1.01)	(1.00)	(0.99)
FONLYNCB	718	840	820	859
	(0.99)	(0.99)	(0.99)	(0.98)
MONLY	733	848	837**	894**
	(1.02)	(1.01)	(1.02)	(1.02)

The entries in the table represent the predicted loan fee (in dollars) for an application similar to the baseline application in all ways other than the characteristic listed. Numbers in parentheses represent the ratio of the loan fee for an application with the indicated characteristics to the loan fee for the baseline application. See text for definition of the baseline application. A single asterisk (*) indicates that the numerator of the ratio is statistically significantly different from the denominator at the 5–10 percent level (using a 2-tailed test). Two asterisks (**) indicate that the difference is significant at the 5 percent or less level.
a. These estimates reflect the effects of both sex and age in that the age of the applicant is reduced to the 25–34 category. See Table 6.17 for the separate effects of age.

applications. Moreover, the ratios above one are relatively small; in the Los Angeles-Long Beach (1977) and San Francisco-Oakland (1977) metropolitan areas, loan fees for approved applications of this type exceed those for baseline applications by 2 percent. A similar pattern emerges for male-female applications that differ from the base only in that the woman is of childbearing age and the applicant is between twenty-five and thirty-four (MFCB 25–34). Again the magnitudes are small and the signs are mixed.

The only consistent pattern of higher loan fees is found for male-only applications (MONLY). In each of the four SMSAs, one of the two samples yields a positive loan-fee differential for male-only applications relative to the base that is statistictically significant at the 5 percent level. The differential ranges from 1 percent of the loan fee in Los Angeles-Long Beach (1977) to 6 percent of the fee in Fresno (1977).

Race   The findings with respect to differential treatment based on race, summarized in Table 6.16, provide substantial support for the hypothesis of discriminatory behavior. Black applicants are charged higher loan fees than similarly situated whites in the Fresno (1978), Los Angeles-Long Beach (1977 and 1978), San Francisco-Oakland (1978) and San Jose (1977) metropolitan areas.[17] All the coefficients on which these results are based are statistically significant at the 5 percent level. The magnitudes of the differentials are relatively large, ranging from 3 percent of the baseline loan fee in Los Angeles-Long Beach (1977) to 16 percent in Fresno (1978).

Spanish applicants face statistically significantly higher loan fees in the Los Angeles-Long Beach (1977 and 1978), San Francisco-Oakland (1977), and San Jose (1977) metropolitan areas. Moreover, all eight loan fee ratios exceed one for Spanish applicants. Finally, Asians experience higher loan fees than similarly situated whites in Los Angeles-Long Beach (1977 and 1978) and San Jose (1977). The magnitudes of the statistically significant differentials for Spanish and Asians range from 1 percent to 3 percent.

Age   The results by age of the applicant, summarized in Table 6.17, suggest that savings and loan associations in the Los Angeles-Long Beach, San Francisco-Oakland, and San Jose metropolitan areas charge higher loan fees on average on approved loans to applicants under twenty-five than to similarly situated older applicants. Five of the six coefficients on which this conclusion is based are statistically

Table 6.16
Loan fees (dollar amounts and ratios) by race for baseline applications in four California metropolitan areas

Race of Applicant	Fresno	Los Angeles-Long Beach	San Francisco-Oakland	San Jose
1977				
White (base)	620	695	678	690
	(1.00)	(1.00)	(1.00)	(1.00)
Black	591	719**	685	739**
	(0.95)	(1.03)	(1.01)	(1.07)
Spanish	630	709**	691**	711**
	(1.02)	(1.02)	(1.02)	(1.03)
Asian	612	704**	680	704*
	(0.99)	(1.01)	(1.00)	(1.02)
Other minority	608	698	680	654**
	(0.98)	(1.00)	(1.00)	(0.94)
1978				
White (base)	720	843	823	873
	(1.00)	(1.00)	(1.00)	(1.00)
Black	832**	888**	857**	910
	(1.16)	(1.05)	(1.04)	(1.04)
Spanish	728	869**	832	891
	(1.01)	(1.03)	(1.01)	(1.02)
Asian	740	870**	825	866
	(1.03)	(1.03)	(1.00)	(0.99)
Other minority	742	855	825	871
	(1.03)	(1.01)	(1.00)	(1.00)

The entries in this table represent the predicted loan fee (in dollars) for an application similar to the baseline application in all ways other than the characteristic listed. Numbers in parentheses represent the ratio of the loan fee for an application with the indicated characteristics to the loan fee for the baseline application. See text for definition of the baseline application. A single asterisk (*) indicates that the numerator of the ratio is statistically significantly different from the denominator at the 5–10 percent level (using a 2-tailed test). Two asterisks (**) indicate that the difference is significant at the 5 percent or less level.

Table 6.17
Loan fees (dollar amounts and ratios) by age of applicant for baseline applications in four California metropolitan areas

Age of Applicant	Fresno	Los Angeles-Long Beach	San Francisco-Oakland	San Jose
1977				
ALT25	582**	707**	695**	711**
	(0.94)	(1.02)	(1.02)	(1.03)
A25–34	585**	695	686**	693
	(0.94)	(1.00)	(1.01)	(1.00)
A35–44 (base)	620	695	678	690
	(1.00)	(1.00)	(1.00)	(1.00)
A45–54	610	691	678	689
	(0.98)	(0.99)	(1.00)	(1.00)
AGE55	598	695	688*	680
	(0.97)	(1.00)	(1.01)	(0.99)
1978				
ALT25	727	863**	839**	878
	(1.01)	(1.02)	(1.02)	(1.01)
A25–34	720	841	829	856**
	(1.00)	(1.00)	(1.01)	(0.98)
A35–44 (base)	720	843	823	873
	(1.00)	(1.00)	(1.00)	(1.00)
A45–54	730	846	824	863
	(1.01)	(1.00)	(1.00)	(0.98)
AGE55	725	838	815	868
	(1.01)	(0.99)	(0.99)	(0.99)

The entries represent the predicted loan fee (in dollars) for an application similar to the baseline application in all ways other than the characteristic listed. Numbers in parentheses represent the ratio of the loan fee for an application with the indicated characteristics to the loan fee for the baseline application. See text for definition of the baseline application. A single asterisk (*) indicates that the numerator of the ratio is statistically significantly different from the denominator at the 5–10 percent level (using a 2-tailed test). Two asterisks (**) indicate that the difference is significant at the 5 percent or less level.

significant at the 5 percent level. The average differential is 2–3 percent of the loan fee for the baseline applicant, which amounts to less than $20 in most cases.

Redlining Finally, we examine allegations that lenders treat applications from older neighborhoods or from neighborhoods with a high proportion of minorities differently than applications from neighborhoods characterized by average proportions of old housing or racial minorities. To do so, we calculate the differences in loan fees associated with specific differences in the values of the neighborhood variables under investigation. These loan-fee differentials are reported in Table 6.18. For the variable representing the fraction of old houses (PRE1940), we report for all samples the change in loan fees associated with a 0.10 increase in the fraction of houses built before 1940. Since the meaning of a "highly" black, Spanish, or Asian neighborhood varies across metropolitan areas, however, the underlying change in the value of each racial-composition variable differs across samples.[18] The table entries for each racial-composition variable should be interpreted as the difference between the loan fee lenders would charge for a property in a neighborhood with an average proportion of the particular minority group and that charged for a property in a neighborhood with a "high" proportion of that minority.

In three of the four areas, the results contradict the hypothesis that lenders discriminate against older neighborhoods by charging higher loan fees. Only in San Jose (1977) is a higher proportion of old housing associated with a statistically significant positive impact on loan fees.

With respect to the racial composition of the neighborhood, the results are somewhat mixed. Eleven of the twenty-four coefficients are negative; these indicate that, if anything, lenders favor neighborhoods with high proportions of minorities. On the other hand, the evidence strongly supports the hypothesis that lenders charge higher loan fees on properties in neighborhoods with high proportions of blacks in the Los Angeles-Long Beach (1977 and 1978) and San Jose (1978) areas and with high proportions of all three minority groups in the San Francisco-Oakland area. The magnitudes of the differentials are large, especially in San Francisco-Oakland where loan fees in highly Spanish neighborhoods might average $93 more and in highly Asian neighborhoods $88 more than those in neighborhoods with average proportions of minorities.

Using available information defining which geographic areas are

Table 6.18
Changes in loan fees (dollar amounts) associated with changes in the age and racial composition of the neighborhood in four California metropolitan areas, 1977 and 1978

Neighborhood Type	Fresno		Los Angeles-Long Beach		San Francisco-Oakland		San Jose	
	1977	1978	1977	1978	1977	1978	1977	1978
PRE1940 (increase to average +0.10)	1	−3	−6**	−7**	−2	−6	4*	4
FBLACK (increase to "high")	−66	−81*	32**	27**	38**	13	−19	50**
FSPANISH (increase to "high")	15	6	−3	13	−10	93**	45**	−24
FASIAN (increase to "high")	−37	−8	−1*	−9	88**	40*	10	−7

The entries represent the change in loan fees associated with an increase in the neighborhood-age or racial-composition variable from its average level to the indicated level. "High" levels for the racial-composition variables are sample specific. See Table 5.32 for representative values. A single asterisk (*) indicates that the numerator of the ratio is statistically significantly different from the denominator at the 5–10 percent level (using a 2-tailed test). Two asterisks (**) indicate that the difference is significant at the 5 percent or less level.

alleged to be redlined in the Los Angeles-Long Beach and San Francisco-Oakland areas, we can examine directly the hypothesis that loan fees are higher in allegedly redlined areas than elsewhere in these metropolitan areas.[19] The results are reported in Table 6.19 for Los Angeles-Long Beach and Table 6.20 for San Francisco-Oakland. The table entries show the predicted difference between the loan fee on a house in the specified area and the loan fee in the reference suburban location.

In Los Angeles-Long Beach, we find that loan fees are higher than those in the suburban area in some allegedly redlined areas and lower in others. The most striking evidence of adverse treatment is found for Covina-Azusa-West Covina, where loan fees are predicted to be $156 higher in 1977 and $223 higher in 1978, and in Pomona, where loan fees are $163 higher in 1977 and $116 higher in 1978. All four of

Table 6.19
Impact of geographic location on loan fees in the Los Angeles-Long Beach metropolitan area, 1977 and 1978

Neighborhoods	1977	1978
Allegedly redlined neighborhoods		
Compton	72	−0
Covina-Azusa-West Covina	156**	223**
East Los Angeles-Boyle Heights-Echo Park	4	17
Highland Park	16	43**
Long Beach-Southwest	22	20
Pacoima-San Fernando	−18*	−44**
Pasadena-North Central	−9	−7
Pomona	163**	116**
San Pedro	26	−36
South Central Los Angeles	−26**	29**
Venice-Santa Monica	−36*	−81**
Other neighborhoods		
Rest of the City of Long Beach	−1	−0
Rest of the City of Los Angeles	−22**	−31
Rest of Los Angeles County (base)	—	—

The entries represent the predicted difference between the loan fee for a house in the specified area and the loan fee for a house in the reference suburban location. A single asterisk (*) indicates that the difference is statistically significant at the 5–10 percent level (using a 2-tailed test). Two asterisks (**) indicate that the difference is significant at the 5 percent or less level.

Table 6.20
Impact of geographic location on loan fees in the San Francisco-Oakland metropolitan area, 1977 and 1978

Neighborhoods	1977	1978
Allegedly redlined neighborhood		
Central Oakland	5	12
Other neighborhoods		
Alameda City	−7	12
Berkeley	−32**	−30**
East Oakland	−3	17**
West Oakland	−5	56**
Rest of Alameda County	23**	12**
Contra Costa County	29**	29**
Marin County	24**	20**
San Francisco County	−5	−8
San Mateo County (base)	—	—

The entries represent the predicted difference between the loan fee for a house in the specified area and the loan fee for a house in the reference suburban location. A single asterisk (*) indicates that the difference is statistically significant at the 5–10 percent level (using a two-tailed test). Two asterisks (**) indicate that the difference is statistically significant at the 5 percent or less level.

the coefficients on which these predictions are based are highly statistically significant. Evidence of statistically significant higher loan fees is also found for Highland Park (1978) and South Central Los Angeles (1978), but the magnitudes are much smaller and the effects are less consistent across the two years. It should be noted that the negative loan-fee differences found in many of the allegedly redlined areas are consistent with the conclusion that loan fees in the city tend, on average, to be lower than those in the suburbs. Support for this view comes from the finding that loan fees on mortgage loans to purchasers of houses in the areas of Los Angeles City not alleged to be redlined are lower than those in the suburban reference area.

In San Francisco-Oakland, we have more limited information about redlining allegations; Central Oakland is the only area that our source identifies as an allegedly redlined area. Although the direction of impact is consistent with the hypothesis of adverse treatment for borrowers in this area, the magnitudes are small and the relevant coefficients statistically insignificant. Hence, for San Francisco-Oakland, we reject the hypothesis of adverse differential treatment for this allegedly redlined area.

Summary

To supplement the decision-to-lend model presented in Chapter 5, this chapter analyzes the terms of the mortgage contract. Using data on loans approved by state-chartered savings and loan associations for four metropolitan areas in California (Fresno, Los Angeles-Long Beach, San Francisco-Oakland, and San Jose), we estimate three sets of mortgage-term models. First, we estimate a three-equation model of the interest rate, maturity period, and loan-to-value ratio. The control variables include proxies for borrower preferences, objective measures of risk to the lender, and discrimination variables. Second, we estimate a model of the amount by which lenders modify loan amounts below requested loan amounts for those applications approved after being modified downward. Although these downward modifications are implicit in the loan-to-value equations, we estimate them separately as well so that the results can be compared to those for New York State where only the downward-modification model can be estimated. Finally, loan fees are modeled as a function of the loan amount, those property and neighborhood factors that might legitimately influence loan fees, and discrimination variables.

After controlling for the nondiscriminatory factors influencing mortgage terms, factors that in most cases play major roles, we find substantial evidence that certain types of applicants against whom discrimination is legally prohibited face harsher mortgage terms than those faced by other applicants. Hence, we conclude that in the setting of mortgage terms, California savings and loan associations pursue policies that in many cases have undesirable discriminatory impacts. The following paragraphs summarize our findings on each possible basis of discrimination examined in this chapter. In interpreting the magnitudes of the adverse differential impacts reported for the various groups, the reader should bear in mind that they represent predicted averages only.

Sex

Two patterns emerge with respect to discrimination based on sex: male-only applicants often face harsher terms than similarly situated male-female applicants and female-only applicant(s) received more adverse treatment in 1977 than in 1978. The adverse treatment of men is surprising in light of the focus on women of sex-related allegations of adverse treatment. The evidence supports the conclusion that lenders charge higher interest rates to male-only than to male-female applicants in all areas except Fresno. Moreover, lenders in these same areas apparently discount the income of male secondary earners and charge higher interest rates on loans to households with a male secondary earner than on those to comparable households with a single earner. Finally, male-only applications tend to be charged higher loan fees than otherwise warranted. In each of the four areas, one of the two samples yields a positive loan-fee differential for male-only applications relative to the reference group that is statistically significant at the five percent level. The differential ranges from one percent of the loan fee in Los Angeles-Long Beach (1977) to six percent of the loan fee in Fresno (1977).

Adverse differential treatment of male-only applicants appears to be restricted to interest rates and loan fees. In general, the loan-to-value equations do not support the conclusion that male-only applicants receive lower loans in relation to appraised value than other borrowers and the downward modification equations provide no evidence of excessive downward adjustments of the requested loan amount.

Female applicants received worse treatment in 1977 than in 1978. Lenders on all areas other than Fresno charged female-only applicants in 1977 interest rates that exceeded those charged comparable male-female applicants by 0.02 to 0.04 percentage points. Lenders in Los Angeles-Long Beach and San Francisco-Oakland charged these applicants above average loan fees as well. No evidence of similar adverse treatment is found in 1978. While we find some evidence that lenders discount secondary income earned by women, especially that earned by women under thirty-five, the impact on interest rates is less for female than for male secondary earners.

Race

The interest-rate equations provide substantial evidence that members of minority groups are charged higher interest rates than similarly situated whites. The clearest pattern emerges in Los Angeles-Long Beach and San Francisco-Oakland where interest rates on loans to black, Spanish, and Asian borrowers range from 0.01 to 0.05 percentage points above those charged to comparable white borrowers during both years. Higher interest rates are charged black and Spanish borrowers in San Jose (1977) and Spanish borrowers in Fresno (1977). In many cases minority borrowers also receive shorter maturity loans than their white counterparts.

Adverse treatment of racial minorities also clearly emerges from the loan-fee equations. The evidence suggests that lenders in all four areas charge blacks higher loan fees; that lenders in Los Angeles-Long Beach, San Francisco-Oakland, and San Jose charge Spanish applicants higher fees; and that lenders in Los Angeles-Long Beach and San Jose charge Asians higher loan fees.

Both the loan-to-value equations and the downward-modification equations imply that, if anything, minorities are given larger rather than smaller loans in relation to appraised value or to the requested loan amount.

Age

We find evidence of adverse treatment against members of two separate age groups. First, young applicants (those under twenty-five) apparently are charged higher loan fees than similarly situated older applicants. In addition, young applicants in five of the eight samples pay interest rates that average 0.02 to 0.04 percentage points higher than those paid by similarly situated applicants between the ages of thirty-five and forty-four.

Both the loan-to-value equations and the downward-modification equations support the view that in the larger metropolitan areas, lenders grant smaller loans in relation to appraised value or to the requested loan amount to older applicants (those over 44) than to those in the thirty-five to forty-four age group. In general, however, these older applicants do not pay higher interest rates and loan fees.

Redlining

We examine allegations that California savings and loan associations impose harsher terms in mortgage contracts on properties located in neighborhoods with larger than average proportions of old housing or higher than average proportions of minorities, and in neighborhoods alleged to be redlined.

With respect to the age of the neighborhood, as measured by the proportion of houses built before 1940, we find only limited evidence of adverse treatment. In San Jose (1977), loan fees are higher in older neighborhoods, and in two of the four San Francisco-Oakland and Los Angeles-Long Beach samples, lenders modify loans downward by statistically significant amounts more in older neighborhoods than in new neighborhoods. Both with respect to interest rates and loan fees, however, substantial evidence supports the hypothesis that lenders set harsher mortgage on old buildings relative to new. The magnitudes of the differentials related to building age are large and, in many cases, highly statistically significant. These differentials should not be interpreted as evidence of discriminatory behavior, however, since building age may be serving as a proxy for building condition and, hence, risk to the lender.

In contrast to the age-of-neighborhood finding, the results generally support the hypothesis that lenders charge higher interest rates on applications from "highly" Spanish or black neighborhoods than on applications from average neighborhoods. In the Fresno, San Francisco-Oakland and San Jose metropolitan areas, interest rates on loans to "highly" Spanish neighborhoods are substantially and statistically significantly higher than those on loans in neighborhoods with average minority populations. Black neighborhoods receive adverse treatment in Los Angeles-Long Beach (1977 and 1978), San Francisco-Oakland (1977) and San Jose (1977). In addition, lenders appear to charge higher loan fees on properties in neighborhoods with high proportions of blacks in Los Angeles-Long Beach (1977 and 1978) and San Jose (1978) and with high proportions of all three minority groups in San Francisco-Oakland. Finally, there is limited support for the view that downward modifications are larger in minority neighborhoods.

The results with respect to pure redlining are mixed. Allegations that lenders impose harsher terms on loans for properties in allegedly redlined neighborhoods are supported in only a few of these neighborhoods in Los Angeles-Long Beach. In particular, the Los Angeles-Long Beach neighborhoods of Compton, Pomona, San Pedro and West Covina pay higher interest rates and Covina-Azusa-West Covina and Pomona pay higher loan fees. Some evidence of adverse terms is also found for the allegedly redlined Central Oakland area of San Francisco-Oakland, but only for 1977.

7
Decision to Lend in New York

The evaluation of applications for loans on specific properties for the purpose of distinguishing the different risks of loss among the applications represents a major part of the residential-lending process. In Chapter 4, a lender's decision on a mortgage application was viewed as a function of the credit worthiness of the borrower, the quality of the collateral, and the requested terms of the mortgage. In Chapter 5, we reported estimates of this decision-to-lend model for California savings and loan associations. In this chapter, we report estimates of this model for several types of lenders in New York State.

Data Base

All state-regulated lenders in New York State are required to maintain detailed data on applicants for mortgages on one- to- four-family houses. The state's banking department prescribes the form of the information through its Equal Housing Opportunity Lender (EHOL) form. The form contains the following information: gross annual income of the applicant, years at present occupation (separate answers for applicant and joint applicant), amount of outstanding debts, monthly debt payments, purchase price of subject property, whether the subject property will be owner occupied, race or national origin of applicant and joint applicant, age of the applicant and joint applicant, type of loan, exact dollar amount of the requested loan, requested loan-to-appraised-value ratio, action taken by lender, modified loan amount and modified loan-to-value ratio in case of approval with modified terms, reasons for the decision, and the census tract in which property is located. Since April 1977, the EHOL form has also recorded the sex and marital status of the applicant and joint applicant.

Many of these items have categorical responses; for example, income is reported as being within one of five possible ranges.

Four types of lender action on mortgage applications are identified on the EHOL forms: approved as applied for, approved after modifications, denied, and withdrawn by the applicant. In many cases, lenders indicated that a modified approval was rejected by the applicant by checking both the modified and withdrawal responses on the form. We were only able to separately analyze rejected modifications in one case: mutual savings banks in the New York and Nassau-Suffolk metropolitan areas.

The lack of information on applicants who were discouraged from making a written application could create a methodological problem for this study. Under the New York State Banking Department's Supervisory Procedure G-107, every banking organization is required to maintain an EHOL form on all written applications. Unfortunately, this regulation does not clearly delineate the circumstances under which a written application is required. However, the regulation may act to minimize the practice of informal screening, although the opposite effect, obviously, is also possible. As long as there are an adequate number of modified approvals, denials, and withdrawals within the formal applications, the explanations for these three actions should reflect the bases for discouraging formal applications. For example, if the analysis of denials indicates the existence of racial discrimination, discrimination is also a likely factor in deciding which applicants should be discouraged from applying. A lender is unlikely to discriminate against formal applicants and not against informal ones. However, if the statistical analysis does not indicate the existence of discrimination, it is still possible that lenders use a different set of criteria, including sex or race, in their informal screening of applicants.

For this study, EHOL forms were gathered for mortgage applications at state-regulated commercial banks, mutual savings banks, and savings and loan associations with branches in the five largest metropolitian areas: Albany-Schenectady-Troy, Buffalo, New York-Nassau-Suffolk, Rochester, and Syracuse.[1] The applications at commercial banks and savings and loan associations were made between May 1977 and October 1978, and as a result, they contain sex and marital status information. The applications at mutual savings banks were filed between May 1976 and October 1977. Since sex and marital status were not required by the EHOL form that was in force during most of the period covered by the mutual savings bank data, we were able to analyze these factors only in one metropolitan area. In the New York-Nassau-Suffolk area the number of applications using the newer EHOL form are sufficient to analyze discrimination on the basis of sex and marital status.

The EHOL forms are supplemented by 1970 census data matched to each EHOL response using the census-tract number provided on the forms, and the National Planning Data Corporation's census-tract estimates of 1977 population and 1976 income.

Model Description

In general, four outcomes of the lending behavior of New York banks can be studied: approved as applied for, approved with modifications, denied, and withdrawn. The primary form of modification in our samples is an alteration of the loan amount generally, but not always, below the requested amount. Other modifications include adjustment of the maturity period. The lender's decision depends on the credit worthiness of the borrower, the quality of the collateral, and the requested terms of the mortgage. Various measures of financial and neighborhood characteristics are used to capture the influence of these factors. The financial characteristics are income, net wealth, years at present occupation, requested loan amount in relation to annual income, and the ratio of the requested loan amount to the appraised value of the property. The risk of loss should decline as the income and net wealth of a household increase. Years at present occupation is included in the belief that it will serve as an indicator of the stability of an applicant's credit worthiness; the applicant's income and other measures of credit worthiness should be more stable (have smaller variance) as the years of experience increase.[2] Risk should rise as the amount of requested loan rises relative to income or appraised value. Although experimentation with different measures of the effect of income in California showed that the ratio of requested loan amount to income performed the best, the categorical responses of the New York data prevent replication of the variable used in California. Instead, the New York models include several dummy variables that represent various income categories and one dummy variable that crudely indicates whether the loan amount is more than two times annual income.[3]

Neighborhood characteristics are included to control for risk of loss in the value of property resulting from housing market externalities. Although it would be ideal to include direct measures of these externalities such as whether the subject property is adjacent to a vacant building, this is generally impossible because the requisite information is unavailable. Therefore, neighborhood conditions are proxied by measures of the income of residents, change in income and population, and mortgage foreclosure and delinquency rates. These variables are calculated for the census tract containing the subject property. Risk of loss should be lower in neighborhoods with more higher-income residents and higher in those with higher average foreclosure and delinquency rates. In general, neighborhoods with larger increases in average income and population should have rising property values and less risk of loss in value.

The New York model only includes one requested term (loan-to-appraised-value ratio) because the forms do not provide information on interest rate and maturity period. The interest rate, however, is unlikely to vary much across neighborhoods because the credit market was very tight during the period being analyzed. The low maximum rate permitted by the New York State usury law applied to nearly all the mortgages covered by the EHOL forms.

Two of the four lender actions have clear meaning: approved as applied for and denial. The other two (modification and withdrawl) are somewhat ambiguous. One of the four must be selected as the reference to which the other three will be compared. Since it is important that this reference action have a clear meaning in relation to all other actions, the job falls to applications that are approved as applied for (that is, approved with the terms requested by the borrower).

The likelihood of a lender deciding to deny an application for a conventional mortgage loan should decrease as an applicant's income and wealth increases. The probability of denial should increase as the quality of the collateral decreases (that is, as the loan-to-appraised-value ratio increases). Differences in the risk of loss associated with the borrower and the subject property may be offset, to some extent, by modifications in the terms of the mortgage (interest rate, maturity, and down payment).

It is more difficult, however, to relate each of the independent variables to a lender's decision to modify the terms. For example, although it would be natural to expect the probability of modification to increase as income decreases, applications from higher-income households trying to maximize their leverage might produce the opposite effect. They may apply for mortgage amounts in excess of what their income justifies in order to secure the largest possible mortgage.

Modifications can be subdivided, as in California, into downward and upward movements in the requested loan amount. In New York, however, nearly all the modifications are downward and separate analysis of upward modifications is not possible. It should be remembered, however, that if such a division were analyzable, the downward category would not be a clear one of adverse action. A downward modification could be the result of an applicant's request because of a desire to maximize equity in the house or revised plans as to the amount of household funds that can be allocated to this function.

Unlike California, New York modifications can be subdivided into ones that were accepted and ones that were subsequently withdrawn. This division is analyzable in one case (mutual savings banks in the New York-Nassau-Suffolk area). As a result, it is possible to examine Regulation B's definition of adverse action (denials or modifications unacceptable to the applicant). However, it is important to recognize that modifications which have not been accepted by the applicant are not necessarily adverse actions. The bank may have treated the applicant similarly to other similarly situated applicants at that bank, but the applicant may have received a better offer elsewhere or the sale may have fallen through. When modification is used in the following pages, it includes those withdrawn by the applicant as well as those accepted by the applicant.

The relationship between the independent variables and the applicant's decision to withdraw prior to bank action is even more ambiguous. The application could be withdrawn for a variety of reasons. For example, the lender may have suggested that the application will not be successful or the applicant may have succeeded in obtaining financing from another institution.

To ascertain whether discrimination on the basis of sex, race, marital status, or age of the applicant, or on the basis of property location, exists in mortgage lending, variables along the lines discussed in Chapter 4 are also included in the models.

Sample Characteristics

Versions of the preceding model have been estimated for different types of banks in several metropolitan areas. Small sample sizes limited the ability to look at each type of bank in all five metropolitan areas. All three bank types can be separately analyzed only in the New York-Nassau-Suffolk metropolitan areas. Commercial banks and mutual savings banks can be analyzed in the Buffalo area; mutual savings banks and savings and loan associations, in the Rochester area; and mutual savings banks, in the Albany-Schenectady-Troy and in the Syracuse metropolitan areas. Commercial banks in three upstate areas (Albany-Schenectady-Troy, Rochester, and Syracuse) can be analyzed only if the areas are combined. Although there is some savings and loan association activity in Buffalo and Syracuse, the sample is too small to analyze.

The samples have been limited to applications for conventional mortgages on properties intended to be owner occupied. Applications for federally assisted mortgages have been excluded because the involvement of a third party, the government, substantially affects the decision-making process, and the EHOL forms do not identify which actor was making the decision. In any case, there are not enough observations to separately analyze such applications at commercial banks or savings and loan associations.[4] Applications on properties not to be owner occupied are excluded because most rental properties are not covered by the EHOL forms; as a result, 0.8 to 5.6 percent of the observations are excluded depending on the type of bank and the metropolitan area. Applications that indicated they were for refinancing (written comment to this effect or nonresponse to the purchase price question) have also been excluded because they do not involve a property transaction and the form lacks the information necessary to analyze these decisions. Again, only a small percentage of the forms were affected. The final sample sizes (after eliminating forms with nonresponses to questions critical to the analysis) are summarized in Table 7.1.

Results

Our multinomial logit estimates of lender behavior for six bank and metropolitan area combinations are reported in Appendix C. (Complete variable definitions are presented in Appendix A.)

Table 7.1
Number of observations by bank type and metropolitan area, New York State

Bank Type and Metropolitan Area	Number
Albany-Schenectady-Troy SMSA	
Mutual savings banks	6,173
Albany-Schenectady-Troy, Rochester, and Syracuse SMSAs	
Commercial banks	2,586
Buffalo SMSA	
Commercial banks	1,434
Mutual savings banks	7,408
New York and Nassau-Suffolk SMSAs	
Commercial banks	4,919

Mutual savings banks
  Large sample without sex and
  marital status
	18,696

Small sample with sex and marital status	4,131
Savings and loan associations	2,170
Rochester SMSA	
Mutual savings banks	3,047
Savings and loan associations	1,304
Syracuse SMSA	
Mutual savings banks	2,695

The following discussion presents the implications of our results for a typical application and key variations in its characteristics. We have defined the typical application as one from a household with an annual income in the $15,001 to $25,000 range, very good net wealth (that is, reported assets were two or more categories above reported debts), and a wage earner with more than five years in his or her present occupation. These characteristics are typical in the sense that a plurality of applicants possessed these characteristics in all but two cases.[5] Applicants with income between $15,000 and $25,000 (INC15–25) ranges from 23–57 percent; with very good net wealth (VGNW), from 68–92 percent; and with more than five years experience (OCCGT5), from 59–70 percent.

Furthermore, the typical application is from an all-white household

(84–96 percent of all applications), an applicant between the ages of thirty-five and forty-four (23–28 percent of all applications), a male-female couple with the female applicant beyond childbearing age (over thirty-four years old) and not working (5–9 percent of all applications), and married persons (79–86 percent of all applications). These characteristics were selected because they describe a household that is least likely to be the target of discrimination, if any exists. Therefore, they do not always represent a plurality of all applications. The major exceptions to the plurality rule are age of applicant and the age and work status of the woman. The selection of these characteristics results from a desire to compare working to nonworking women and childbearing to nonchildbearing women.

Our typical applicant is also defined by the average values of all the continuous variables for applications to that type of bank in the metropolitan area being studied: requested-loan-to-appraised-value ratio, fraction high-income households, income and population change, foreclosure and delinquency rates, age of neighborhood, and racial composition of neighborhood. These values are summarized in Table 7.2. In addition, requested loan amount is assumed to be less than two times annual income (96–98 percent of all applications), and the property is assumed to be located in a suburb.

The treatment accorded applications with different characteristics than the typical application is compared to the treatment received by the typical application. The treatment is measured by the probability of a given decision such as denial or modification. These probabilities can be calculated from the logit estimates.[6]

In general, we report comparisons in terms of the ratio of the probability of a given decision for an application with certain characteristics to the probability of that decision for the typical application. The probabilities of each decision for the typical application are presented in Table 7.3. They vary considerably by type of bank and across metropolitan areas. It is for this reason that ratios must be used to compare the differential impact of discrimination measures on outcomes across banks and areas.

Since the denial of an application is clearly an adverse decision, the following discussion focuses on these results. Although modification has a somewhat ambiguous meaning, it is clearer than the meaning of a withdrawn application. Therefore, the modification results are summarized and discussed below, but the withdrawal results are only

Table 7.2
Mean values of continuous variables by bank type and metropolitan area

Bank Type and Metropolitan Area	RLTOAV	FH	DINC	DPOP	FORRATE	DELRATE	PRE1940	FBLACK
Albany-Schenectady-Troy SMSA								
Mutual savings banks	0.80	0.25	4.58	1.97	0.17	2.16	0.47	0.008
Albany-Schenectady-Troy, Rochester, and Syracuse SMSAs								
Commercial banks	0.69	0.30	4.96	2.14	0.52	2.60	0.43	0.007
Buffalo SMSA								
Commercial banks	0.68	0.26	5.08	1.82	0.04	0.51	0.39	0.009
Mutual savings banks	0.73	0.25	4.81	1.80	0.39	0.97	0.39	0.011
New York and Nassau-Suffolk SMSAs								
Commercial banks	0.69	0.43	5.76	1.73	0.49	2.73	0.39	0.028
Mutual savings banks	0.71	0.37	5.89	1.71	0.97	2.67	0.43	0.038
Savings and loan associations	0.69	0.34	5.70	2.51	1.69	3.09	0.42	0.037
Rochester SMSA								
Mutual savings banks	0.70	0.38	5.66	2.53	0.12	2.99	0.36	0.008
Savings and loan associations	0.73	0.34	5.45	2.48	0.08	2.25	0.42	0.008
Syracuse SMSA								
Mutual savings banks	0.77	0.22	4.96	2.43	4.43	7.88	0.40	0.004

Table 7.3
Probability of various outcomes for typical application, New York State (percent)

Bank Type and Metropolitan Area	Denial	Modification	Withdrawal
Albany-Schenectady-Troy SMSA			
Mutual savings banks	5.03	3.88	3.06
Albany-Schenectady-Troy, Rochester, and Syracuse SMSAs			
Commercial banks	3.08	5.78	1.29
Buffalo SMSA			
Commercial banks	4.74	2.66	2.49
Mutual savings banks	6.49	4.56	3.80
New York and Nassau-Suffolk SMSAs			
Commercial banks	9.12	14.42	8.04
Mutual savings banks	6.83	17.39	4.81
Savings and loan associations	4.38	0.53	0.66
Rochester SMSA			
Mutual savings banks	2.81	4.14	3.21
Savings and loan associations	3.55	0.68	0.97
Syracuse SMSA			
Mutual savings banks	4.71	3.23	2.96

discussed when the equations indicate withdrawal to be more likely for a group that is potentially discriminated against.

Financial Characteristics

The financial characteristics serve the purpose of controlling for the risk of loss associated with the credit worthiness of the applicant, the value of the property, and the requested loan terms. In general these variables have the expected relationship to lender behavior and are highly significant. Table 7.4 presents denial ratios for the typical application and variations in its characteristics that should make it more likely to be denied. As a result, the ratios in all but the first column should be greater than one; there are only nine exceptions out of the fifty ratios.

The requested-loan-to-appraised-value ratio is the most consistent variable; it has a positive coefficient in all the denial equations. All but one of these coefficients are large and very significant; the exception occurs for mutual savings banks in Rochester.[7] The coefficients

Table 7.4
Denial ratios for several different applicants relative to the typical applicant (TA)

Bank Type and Metropolitan Area	TA[a]	TA with less income (INC10–15)	TA with less net wealth (GNW)	TA with less experience (OCCLT3)	TA with requested loan > 2 times income	TA with higher RLTOAV (+0.10)
Albany-Schenectady-Troy SMSA						
Mutual savings banks	1.00	1.50**	1.42**	1.05	1.63**	1.27**
Albany-Schnectady-Troy, Rochester, and Syracuse SMSAs						
Commercial banks	1.00	2.41**	1.79**	1.19	0.23**	1.43**
Buffalo SMSA						
Commercial banks	1.00	19.08**	1.13	1.11	0.92	5.29**
Mutual savings banks	1.00	1.46**	1.28**	1.13	1.52**	1.12**
New York and Nassau-Suffolk SMSAs						
Commercial banks	1.00	1.54**	0.96	1.52**	1.66*	1.06**
Mutual savings banks	1.00	1.25**	1.43**	1.37**	1.57*	1.37**
Savings and loan associations	1.00	1.13	1.34**	1.18	3.07*	1.14**
Rochester SMSA						
Mutual savings banks	1.00	1.72*	1.92	1.29	0.00	1.10
Savings and loan associations	1.00	1.17**	1.51**	1.34	3.28**	1.30**
Syracuse SMSA						
Mutual savings banks	1.00	1.00[b]	1.08	1.03	1.34	1.16**

The mutual savings bank estimates are derived from 1976–1977 applications data; other estimates are based on 1977–1978 mortgage applications. The ratio is equal to the probability that an application with indicated characteristics will be denied divided by the probability that the typical application will be denied. A single asterisk (*) indicates that the coefficients used to estimate the numerator and denominator are statistically significant at the 5–10 percent level. Two asterisks (**) indicate they are significant at the 5 percent or less level.

a. This is the typical application described in the text. It is the base for calculating the denial ratios. The other applications involve variations from the typical one in one or more characteristics. See Table 7.3 for the probability of denial for the typical application in each bank type-area.

b. Although there is no statistically significant difference between applicants with $15,001 to $25,000 in annual income and applicants with $10,001 to $15,000 incomes, applicants with lower incomes (under $10,001) are statistically significantly (5 percent level) more likely to be denied than higher-income applicants.

in the modification and withdrawal equations closely follow the same pattern. This positive coefficient indicates that an application is more likely to be denied, modified, or withdrawn the higher the requested loan amount relative to the appraised value of the property.

The income coefficients indicate that the likelihood of denial increases by a statistically significant amount as income decreases except for savings and loan associations in the New York and Nassau-Suffolk metropolitan areas. The mixed signs in the income coefficients of the modification and withdrawal equations is probably due to the ambiguity of these decisions. As a result, the denial equations contain the best information on the performance of the risk measures.

When requested loan amount exceeds two times income, the likelihood of denial should increase. This is the situation in seven cases (six of them statistically significant at the 10 percent level); the three exceptions are commercial banks in the combined upstate area (the only statistically significant exception) and the Buffalo metropolitan area, and mutual savings banks in the Rochester metropolitan area.

Applications are more likely to be denied the smaller the applicant's net wealth with one exception: commercial banks in the New York-Nassau-Suffolk metropolitan area. In six of the nine cases with the expected negative relationship between the likelihood of denial and net wealth, the coefficients are statistically significant at the 5 percent level.

Although the coefficients for the variables representing years at present occupation (reported in Table 7.4) indicate that less experience increases the likelihood of denial in all ten bank type-areas, they are only significant in two (commercial and mutual savings bank in the New York-Nassau-Suffolk metropolitan area).

Neighborhood Characteristics
The neighborhood characteristics have been included to control for the effect of housing market externalities on the future value of the property securing the loan. The coefficients of these variables are not consistent across metropolitan areas. The fraction of households with high income (FHI) and the change in income (DINC) in the census tract containing the property are the most consistent. For example, FHI and DINC have the expected negative relationship with the likelihood of denial in all but three and two cases, respectively. However, these negative relationships are statistically significant (5 percent level) in only three bank type-areas for FHI and two for DINC, and the

positive relationship is statistically significant for each variable in one bank type-area (savings and loan associations in the New York-Nassau-Suffolk area for FHI and commercial banks in the combined upstate areas for DINC).

Contrary to expectations, the change in population is positively related to the likelihood of denial in most of the bank type-areas and significant in two of them. This may reflect the effect of past instability on future uncertainty. One of the three negative relationships is statistically significant.

The coefficients of the two direct measures of the risk of loss on mortgages in the census tract (the foreclosure and delinquency rates) are the most disappointing. The results indicate that the likelihood of denial decreases more often than it increases when the foreclosure rate rises—a result that is statistically significant (5 percent level) in two bank type-areas and contrary to our expectations. It is probably a reflection of foreclosure policies rather than differentials in the risk of loss. Foreclosure policies vary across lenders, even within the same bank type, and frequently exhibit a lender's reluctance to show large losses through the foreclosure route. Consequently, the foreclosure rate may not accurately reflect the risk of loss in lending. The delinquency rate is not subject to the vagaries of bank policy and its coefficients show that the likelihood of denial increases more often than it decreases when the delinquency rate rises. And three of these coefficients are statistically significant at the 5 percent level. However, the delinquency rate coefficient for savings and loan associations in the New York-Nassau-Suffolk area is significantly negative (smaller chance of denial as delinquency rate rises) at the 5 percent level.

Fortunately, at least one of the neighborhood characteristics has a statistically significant (5 percent level) coefficient with the expected relationship to the likelihood of denial in all but two bank type-areas. In one of the bank type-areas (mutual savings banks in the Buffalo area) none of the variables representing neighborhood characteristics have significant coefficients. Also, the savings and loan associations in the New York-Nassau-Suffolk area have three statistically significant neighborhood coefficients in the denial equation that are inconsistent with the risk hypothesis. Commercial banks in the combined upstate area and mutual savings banks in the Albany-Schenectady-Troy metropolitan area have statistically significant coefficients in the denial equation that are consistent and inconsistent with the risk hypothesis.

Sex and Marital Status

Each equation contains nine variables that measure sex and marital status differences across applications. In combination, these coefficients define thirteen different types of applications that are used to illustrate the results. Their denial and modification ratios are presented in Tables 7.5 and 7.6.

The results for the denial equations are inconsistent with the hypothesis that married childbearing women who work (MFCBW) are discriminated against. Although these households have a greater chance of denial than the typical applicant (MFNCBNW) in four of the six bank type-areas, none of these differences are statistically significant at the 10 percent level. Married male-female households with a nonworking childbearing woman (MFCBNW) are also treated much the same as the typical applicant. There is, however, some evidence that male-female households with a working female beyond childbearing age (MFNCBW), regardless of marital status, are discriminated against by Buffalo commercial banks who are approximately twice as likely to deny their applications than those from otherwise identical typical applicants. This differential is statistically significant at the 10 percent level. On the other hand, savings and loan associations in the New York-Nassau-Suffolk area treat these appliants (MFNCBW) more favorably (half the denial rate of the typical application), this differential being statistically significant at the 5 percent level.

New York-Nassau-Suffolk commercial banks and Rochester savings and loan associations discriminate against unmarried or separated male-female couples regardless of the age or work status of the women. These applicants are 1.36 to 1.73 times as likely to be denied than the otherwise identical typical applicant by New York-Nassau-Suffolk commercial banks, and 3.32 to 4.18 times as likely to be denied by the Rochester savings and loan associations.

Unmarried or separated female applicants are not significantly more or less likely to be denied than the typical applicant in any of the bank type-areas, whether or not the woman is in the childbearing years.

Some applications contained responses indicating that the applicant(s) were married but either all female (FONLY) or all male (MONLY). We were surprised by these responses. Some may be from persons not legally separated who are married but choose to live apart from their spouses. In addition, the spouse could be away from the household for various other reasons such as serving a jail sentence or

Table 7.5
Denial ratios by sex and marital status for a typical application, New York State

Sex and Marital Status	AST-ROCH-SYR COM	BUF COM	NYNS COM	MSB	SLA	ROCH SLA
Married						
MFNCBNW[a]	1.00	1.00	1.00	1.00	1.00	1.00
MFNCBW	1.65	2.26*	1.06	1.24	0.54**	0.93
MFCBNW (25–34)	0.58[b]	1.48	0.84	0.70	0.49	1.11
MFCBW (25–34)	0.45[b]	1.01[b]	0.83	0.78[b]	0.50	1.20
FONLY (25–34)	0.35[b]	5.04**	0.47	2.06**	0.90[b]	0.00**
MONLY	1.44	3.04*	1.16	2.54**	1.04	2.03**
Unmarried or Separated						
MFNCBNW	1.52	0.84	1.65*	1.29	0.98	3.58**
MFNCBW	2.45	1.91*	1.73*	1.58	0.52**	3.32**
MFCBNW (25–34)	0.86[b]	1.24	1.40*	0.92[b]	0.48	3.88**
MFCBW (25–34)	0.68[b]	0.85[b]	1.36*	1.01[b]	0.49	4.18**
FONLYNCB	0.74	1.62	1.00	1.47	0.41	0.54
FONLYCB (25–34)	0.55[b]	0.33	1.04	1.05[b]	0.18	0.46
MONLY	2.22	1.68**	1.41**	1.99**	1.18	1.88**

The mutual savings bank estimates are derived from 1976–1977 applications data; other estimates are based on 1977–1978 mortgage applications. The ratio is equal to the probability that an application with the indicated characteristics will be denied divided by the probability that the typical application will be denied. A single asterisk (*) indicates that the numerator of the ratio is statistically significantly different from the denominator at the 5–10 percent level. Two asterisks (**) indicate that the difference is significant at the 5 percent or less level. Bank type abbreviations are: COM = commercial banks; MSB = mutual savings banks; SLA = savings and loan associations. Metropolitan area abbreviations are: AST = Albany-Schenectady-Troy; BUF = Buffalo; NYNS = New York-Nassau-Suffolk; RCCH = Rochester; SYR = Syracuse.

a. This is the typical application described in the text. It is the base for calculating the denial ratios. The other applications involve variations from the typical one in one or more characteristics. See Table 7.3 for the probability of denial for the typical application in each bank type-area.

b. Since the ratio for MFCB or FONLYCB for the 35- to 44-year-old age range of the typical application is greater than one, it is the 25- to 34-year-old age range coefficient that makes the ratio in the table less than, or closer to, one. The MFCB or FONLYCB coefficient is not statistically significant at the 10 percent or less level.

Table 7.6
Modification ratios by sex and marital status for a typical application, New York State

Sex and Marital Status	AST-ROCH-SYR COM	BUF COM	NYNS COM	MSB	SLA	ROCH SLA
Married						
MFNCBNW[a]	1.00	1.00	1.00	1.00	1.00	1.00
MFNCBW	0.45**	0.31**	0.98	0.83	3.61**	0.32**
MFCBNW (25–34)	0.31**	0.56	0.93	0.72	2.92**	3.74
MFCBW (25–34)	0.39*	0.21**	0.86	0.50**	2.07**	2.01[b]
FONLY (25–34)	0.00**	0.00**	1.42	0.99	0.00**	3.17
MONLY	0.61	2.49**	0.92	0.78	4.94**	1.38
Unmarried or separated						
MFNCBNW	0.56	1.10	0.64**	0.96	1.46	1.06
MFNCBW	0.25**	0.34**	0.63**	0.78	5.27**	0.34**
MFCBNW (25–34)	0.18**	0.61	0.60**	0.69	4.27**	3.91
MFCBW (25–34)	0.22*	0.23**	0.55**	0.48**	3.03**	2.09[b]
FONLYNCB	1.00	0.67	0.97	0.80	5.21**	0.71
FONLYCB (25–34)	0.12**	0.00**	0.80	0.67	1.36	1.71
MONLY	0.75	0.26**	1.09	0.82	2.77[c]	1.21

The mutual savings bank estimates are derived from 1976–1977 applications data; other estimates are based on 1977–1978 mortgage applications. The ratio is equal to the probability that an application with the indicated characteristics will be modified divided by the probability that the typical application will be modified. A single asterisk (*) indicates that the numerator of the ratio is statistically significantly different from the denominator at the 5–10 percent level. Two asterisks (**) indicate that the difference is significant at the 5 percent or less level. Abbreviations are defined in Table 7.5.
a. This is the typical application described in the text. It is the base for calculating the modification ratios. The other applications involve variations from the typical one in one or more characteristics. See Table 7.3 for the probability of modification for the typical application in each bank type-area.
b. Since the ratio for MFCB or FONLYCB for the 35- to 44-year-old range is less than one, it is the 25- to 34-year-old age coefficient that makes the ratio in the table greater than one. The MFCB or FONLYCB coefficient is not statistically significant at the 10 percent or less level.
c. This ratio is greater than one because of the influence of the male-only component and not the marital status.

being hospitalized on a long-term basis. However, the large number of male-only married households (approximately 10 percent of each sample) leads us to suspect that many of these applications involve husbands buying property in their individual names rather than jointly with their wives. Since the actual household status of these applicants is not clear, we decided to estimate coefficients for these categories to see if they receive differential treatment. The female-only married applicants are much more likely to be denied than the typical applicant at Buffalo commercial banks and New York area mutual savings banks; the ratios of 5.04 and 2.06, respectively, are both statistically significant at the 5 percent level. Rochester savings and loan associations, however, almost never deny female-only married applicants in our sample.

The only denial relationships consistent across all six bank type-areas are for male-only households; regardless of marital status male-only applicants are more likely to be denied. Three of the six denial ratios for male-only married households range in value from 2.03 to 3.04 and are statistically significant at the 5 or 10 percent level; these occur for applications at the Buffalo commercial banks, New York area mutual savings banks, and Rochester savings and loan associations. In the case of male-only unmarried or separated applicants, it is the sex and not the marital status that accounts for the increased likelihood of denial except in the case of New York-Nassau-Suffolk commercial banks.

The modification ratios summarized in Table 7.6 show that modification of an application from one of the thirteen household types is seldom more likely than modification of the otherwise identical typical application. Applications at New York-Nassau-Suffolk savings and loan associations are a major exception; aside from married female-only households, modification is much more (1.36 to 5.21 times) likely for the other household types in Table 7.6 than for the typical applicant. Nearly all these ratios (fifth column of Table 7.6) are statistically significant at the 5 percent level. Male-only married applicants at Buffalo commercial banks are the only other households that are significantly more likely to be modified than the otherwise identical typical applicant. A surprising result is the extent to which many household types are significantly less likely to be modified than the comparable typical applicant.

The withdrawal equations have only two statistically significant coefficients that are consistent with discrimination on the basis of the household types depicted in Table 7.6. Married female-only applicants at mutual savings banks in the New York-Nassau-Suffolk area have a withdrawal ratio of 2.19, which is statistically significant at the 10 percent level. Unmarried or separated male-only applicants at commercial banks in the combined upstate sample also have above average chances of withdrawal.

Race

Table 7.7 presents ratios of the probability of denial for various racial groups relative to the probability of denial for the typical applicant who is white. A denial ratio greater than one indicates that members of that racial group are more likely to be denied than the otherwise identical typical (white) applicant. Applications from blacks are more likely to be denied than those from similarly situated whites in all but one of the ten bank type-areas. The exception occurs at commercial banks in the combined upstate areas, but the difference is not statistically significant at the 10 percent level. Although blacks are more likely to be denied than whites at commercial banks in the Buffalo and New York-Nassau-Suffolk areas, these differences are not statistically significant at the 10 percent level. Hence, we conclude that commercial banks appear to accord black and white applicants approximately equal treatment.

In contrast to the commercial banks, mutual savings banks are significantly more likely to deny a black applicant than a similarly situated white in four of five metropolitan areas. These differentials are large and statistically significant; the denial ratios range from 1.58 in the New York-Nassau-Suffolk area to 3.61 in the Rochester metropolitan area. Although blacks are also more likely to be denied than whites by mutual savings banks in the Albany-Schenectady-Troy metropolitan area, the difference is not statistically significant at the 10 percent level.

The evidence from the denial equation is also consistent with discrimination against black applicants by savings and loan associations. The New York-Nassau-Suffolk associations are 3.15 times as likely to deny a black applicant than a similarly situated white; in Rochester, the denial rate is 2.64. These ratios are statistically significant at the 5 and 10 percent levels, respectively.

There is less evidence of discrimination against Hispanics and other minorities from the denial equations. Hispanics are significantly more likely to be denied than similarly situated whites in only one bank

Table 7.7
Denial ratios by race of applicant for typical applications

Bank Type and Metropolitan Area	White[a]	Black	Hispanic	Other Minority
Albany-Schenectady-Troy SMSA				
Mutual savings banks	1.00	1.44	[←——— 1.19 ———→]	
Albany-Schenectady-Troy, Rochester, and Syracuse SMSAs				
Commercial banks	1.00	0.82	[←——— 0.35* ———→]	
Buffalo SMSA				
Commercial banks	1.00	1.74	[←———0.54 ———→]	
Mutual savings banks	1.00	2.06**	[←———0.87 ———→]	
New York and Nassau-Suffolk SMSAs				
Commercial banks	1.00	1.18	1.07	1.35*
Mutual savings banks	1.00	1.58**	1.90**	1.35
Savings and loan associations	1.00	3.15**	1.78	0.76
Rochester SMSA				
Mutual savings banks	1.00	3.61**	[←———1.41 ———→]	
Savings and loan associations	1.00	2.64*	1.01	0.74
Syracuse SMSA				
Mutual savings banks	1.00	2.56*	[←——— 1.04 ———→]	

The mutual savings bank estimates are derived from 1976–1977 applications data; other estimates are based on 1977–1978 mortgage applications. The ratio is equal to the probability that an application with the indicated characteristics will be denied divided by the probability that the typical application will be denied. A single asterisk (*) indicates that the numerator of the ratio is statistically significantly different from the denominator at the 5–10 percent level. Two asterisks (**) indicate that the difference is significant at the 5 percent or less level.

a. This is the typical application described in the text. It is the base for calculating the denial ratios. The other applications involve variations from the typical one in one or more characteristics. See Table 7.3 for the probability of denial for the typical application in each bank type-area.

type-area; mutual savings banks in the New York-Nassau-Suffolk area have a denial ratio of 1.90. New York-Nassau-Suffolk commercial banks are significantly more likely to deny other minorities (largely Asians) than the typical white applicant by a ratio of 1.35. However, commercial banks in the combined upstate area favor Hispanics and other minorities over similar white applicants by a statistically significant margin; the denial ratio is 0.35.

The results from the modification equations are summarized in Table 7.8. Although most of the modification ratios exceed one, very few of the racial differentials are statistically significant at the 10 percent level. Black applicants are significantly more likely to be modified than whites at the two types of thrift institutions in the New York-Nassau-Suffolk area; the modification ratio is 1.39 at mutual savings banks and 1.54 at savings and loan associations. Hispanic applicants are also significantly more likely to have their loan requests modified than similarly situated white applicants at the New York-Nassau-Suffolk savings and loan associations, but are significantly less likely to have them modified at the Rochester associations. Hispanics and other minorities are significantly more likely to be modified than whites in the Buffalo metropolitan area; commercial banks have a modification ratio of 4.23 and mutual savings banks have one of 1.80.

The modification decision can be subdivided into modified terms that were accepted by the applicant and modified terms that were followed by the applicant's withdrawal. In the New York-Nassau-Suffolk area, we have a sufficiently large sample of mortgage applications at mutual savings banks to analyze the effect of this refined picture of bank decisions on the racial coefficients if the sex and martial status variables are deleted. The various denial and modification ratios for typical applications are summarized in Table 7.9. These results show that the probability of modification-withdrawal is more likely than modification-acceptance for all three minorities (blacks, Hispanics, and others), but the differential is statistically significant only for Hispanics. All three minorities are significantly more likely to be denied than the typical white applicant, and denial probabilities exceed both modification probabilities. On the basis of this analysis it is clear that separate treatment of the two types of modification may uncover additional differential treatment. In addition, it would be incorrect to group denials and modification-withdrawals together as a single measure of adverse action because differential treatment occurring with regard to one of these decisions could be dampened by equal

Table 7.8
Modification ratios by race of applicant for typical applications, New York State

Bank Type and Metropolitan Area	White[a]	Black	Hispanic	Other Minority
Albany-Schenectady-Troy SMSA				
Mutual savings banks	1.00	0.71	[←——— 1.38 ———→]	
Albany-Schenectady-Troy, Rochester, and Syracuse SMSAs				
Commercial banks	1.00	1.51	[←——— 1.31 ———→]	
Buffalo SMSA				
Commercial banks	1.00	2.82	[←——— 4.23* ———→]	
Mutual savings banks	1.00	1.19	[←——— 1.80** ———→]	
New York and Nassau-Suffolk SMSAs				
Commercial banks	1.00	0.77	0.73	1.17
Mutual savings banks	1.00	1.39**	1.07	1.06
Savings and loan associations	1.00	1.54**	2.20**	1.34
Rochester SMSA				
Mutual savings banks	1.00	0.61	[←——— 0.78 ———→]	
Savings and loan associations	1.00	1.20	0.00**	1.24
Syracuse SMSA				
Mutual savings banks	1.00	0.01	[←——— 1.01 ———→]	

The mutual savings bank estimates are derived from 1976–1977 applications; other estimates are based on 1977–1978 mortgage applications. The ratio is equal to the probability that an application with the indicated characteristics will be modified divided by the probability that the typical application will be modified. A single asterisk (*) indicates that the numerator of the ratio is statistically significantly different from the denominator at the 5–10 percent level. Two asterisks (**) indicate that the difference is significant at the 5 percent or less level.

a. This is the typical application described in the text. It is the base for calculating the modification ratios. The other applications involve variations from the typical one in one or more characteristics. See Table 7.3 for the probability of modification for the typical application in each bank type-area.

Table 7.9
Denial, modification-withdrawal, and modification-acceptance ratios by race of applicant for mutual savings banks (large sample) in the New York-Nassau-Suffolk metropolitan areas, 1976–1977

Type of Decision	White[a]	Black	Hispanic	Other Minority
Denial	1.00	1.56**	1.55**	1.59**
Modification-withdrawal	1.00	1.15	1.42**	1.17
Modification-acceptance	1.00	1.06	0.87	0.88
Withdrawal	1.00	1.22	1.05	4.03

The ratio is equal to the probability that an application with the indicated characteristics will be denied, modified, or withdrawn, divided by the probability that the typical application will be denied, modified, or withdrawn, respectively. A single asterisk (*) indicates that the numerator of the ratio is statistically significantly different from the denominator at the 5–10 percent level. Two asterisks (**) indicate that the difference is statistically significant at the 5 percent or less level.
a. This is the typical application described in the text. It is the base for calculating the denial, modification or withdrawal ratios. The other applications involve variations from the typical one in one or more characteristics. The probabilities of denial, modification-withdrawal, modification-acceptance, or withdrawal for the typical application are 9.15, 3.42, 11.12, and 3.74 percent, respectively. Note that the typical application in this table has no identifiable sex or marital-status characteristics.

treatment with respect to the other one. For example, the significantly unfavorable denial ratios for black applicants might not have shown up as strongly if denials and modification-withdrawals had been grouped together.

We have very detailed information on housing code violations, vacant buildings, property tax delinquency, and serious fires for each census tract in Bronx, Kings (Brooklyn), and Queens counties. Since we have enough observations from mutual savings banks, we estimated a decision model for just these three counties to take advantage of these finer measures of housing market externalities. The results indicate that blacks, Hispanics, and other minorities are all significantly (5 percent level) more likely to be denied and to be modified than similar white applicants. This is an indication of even more discrimination against minority applicants by these banks than the results reported in Tables 7.7, 7.8, or 7.9.

Several of the race coefficients in the withdrawal equations are also consistent with discrimination against minorities. In particular, applications from blacks at commercial banks in the New York-Nassau-Suffolk area and at savings and loan associations in the New York-Nassau-Suffolk and Rochester metropolitan areas are significantly more likely to be withdrawn than those from similarly situated white applicants. The withdrawal ratios are 1.50, 2.75, and 14.75, respectively. In addition, other minorities are more likely to withdraw their applications at Rochester mutual savings banks and savings and loan associations than are similarly situated whites. The withdrawal ratios are 2.73 and 5.75, respectively.

Age

Denial ratios for several age intervals in each bank type-area are presented in Table 7.10. Applicants under thirty-five years tend to be less likely candidates for denial than the typical applicant who is thirty-five to forty-four years old. Nine of the twelve denial ratios for ages under thirty-five are less than 1 and six are based on differences statistically significant at the 5 percent level. The denial ratios for applicants over forty-four years are more mixed; three ratios are significantly less than 1, and two are significantly greater than 1. Applicants between forty-four and fifty-five years of age are more likely to be denied than 35 to 44-year-old typical applicants by savings and loan associations in the New York-Nassau-Suffolk and Rochester metropolitan areas.

The results from the denial equations suggest that younger (under thirty-five) applicants are somewhat less likely to be denied than older applicants (over forty-four) at commercial banks in the combined upstate area and at savings and loan associations. However, Buffalo and the combined upstate commercial banks and New York-Nassau-Suffolk mutual savings banks are most likely to deny 35-to 44-year-old applicants. New York-Nassau-Suffolk commercial banks seem to deny applications equally regardless of the applicant's age.

Modification ratios are summarized in Table 7.11. These results vary markedly by metropolitan area. Commercial banks in the combined upstate area and in the New York-Nassau-Suffolk area are significantly less likely to modify the applications of young applicants (under thirty-five), whereas the Buffalo commercial banks are most likely to modify the applications of young applicants. New York-Nassau-Suffolk savings and loan associations are most likely to modify the application of the typical applicant (thirty-five to forty-four), whereas the same type of bank in Rochester is least likely to modify this application. Mutual savings banks in New York-Nassau-Suffolk are significantly less likely to modify the loan requests of 45- to 54-year-old applicants than they are to modify those of similarly situated 35- to 44-year-old applicants.

Table 7.10
Denial ratios by age of applicant for typical applications, New York State

Bank Type and Metropolitan Area	<25	25–34	35–44[a]	45–54	>54
Albany-Schenectady-Troy, Rochester, and Syracuse SMSAs					
Commercial banks	0.49**	0.35**	1.00	0.85	0.56
Buffalo SMSA					
Commercial banks	0.59	0.67**	1.00	0.59*	0.52*
New York and Nassau-Suffolk SMSAs					
Commercial banks	1.10	0.94	1.00	1.03	1.07
Mutual savings banks	0.65**	0.74**	1.00	0.78**	0.75
Savings and loan associations	0.99	0.62**	1.00	1.64*	1.00
Rochester SMSA					
Savings and loan associations	1.10	1.11	1.00	1.71*	1.18

The mutual savings bank estimates are derived from 1976–1977 applications data; other estimates are based on 1977–1978 mortgage applications. The ratio is equal to the probability that an application with the indicated characteristics will be denied divided by the probability that the typical application will be denied. A single asterisk (*) indicates that the numerator of the ratio is statistically significantly different from the denominator at the 5–10 percent level. Two asterisks (**) indicate that the difference is significant at the 5 percent or less level.

a. This is the typical application described in the text. It is the base for calculating the denial ratios. The other applications involve variations from the typical one in one or more characteristics. See Table 7.3 for the probability of denial for the typical application in each bank type-area.

Table 7.11
Modification ratios by age of applicant for typical applications, New York State

Bank Type and Metropolitan Area	<25	25–34	35–44[a]	45–54	>54
Albany-Schenectady-Troy, Rochester, and Syracuse SMSAs					
Commercial banks	0.39**	0.60**	1.00	0.79	1.36
Buffalo SMSA					
Commercial banks	3.12**	0.64	1.00	0.78	0.00**
New York and Nassau-Suffolk SMSAs					
Commercial banks	0.91	0.91	1.00	1.24**	1.18
Mutual savings banks	1.13	0.94	1.00	0.81**	1.13
Savings and loan associations	0.67	0.54**	1.00	0.62**	0.78
Rochester SMSA					
Savings and loan associations	1.95	2.61**	1.00	4.60**	6.57**

The mutual savings bank estimates are derived from 1976–1977 applications data; other estimates are based on 1977–1978 mortgage applications. The ratio is equal to the probability that an application with the indicated characteristics will be modified divided by the probability that the typical application will be modified. A single asterisk (*) indicates that the numerator of the ratio is statistically significantly different from the denominator at the 5–10 percent level. Two asterisks (**) indicate that the difference is significant at the 5 percent or less level.
a. This is the typical application described in the text. It is the base for calculating the modification ratios. The other applications involve variations from the typical one in one or more characteristics. See Table 7.3 for the probability of modification for the typical application in each bank type-area.

The withdrawal equation for Buffalo commercial banks is the only one that indicates that applications from any age group are significantly more likely to be withdrawn than those from 35 to 44 year olds. Withdrawal ratios at these banks for applicants in the 25 to 34 and 45 to 54 year-old age groups are 1.82 and 1.85, respectively.

Redlining
Three types of redlining allegations have been analyzed: specific neighborhoods that community groups have alleged to be redlined, older neighborhoods, and largely nonwhite neighborhoods.

Property Location   Denial and modification ratios for typical applications from a variety of property locations in each of five metropolitan areas are summarized in Tables 7.12 to 7.17. The role of property

Table 7.12
Denial and modification ratios by property location for mutual savings banks in the Albany-Schenectady-Troy metropolitan area, 1976–1977

Property Location	Denial	Modification
Allegedly redlined neighborhoods:		
City of Albany		
Arbor Hill and South End	2.40	5.05
Hudson-Park	12.51**	1.55
West Hill	1.06	1.20
City of Schenectady		
Central State Street	0.51	1.04
Hamilton Hill	1.61	0.01
City of Troy		
Central South	0.50	0.85
Hillside	10.97**	0.62
North Central and 567	0.99	1.03
Other neighborhoods:		
Rest of the City of Albany	1.01	0.60*
Rest of the City of Schenectady	1.24	0.72
Rest of the City of Troy	0.52**	1.50
Rest of Albany County	1.13	1.12
Rest of Schenectady County	1.23	1.16
Rensselaer County outside the City of Troy	0.76	1.51*
Saratoga County[a]	1.00	1.00

The ratio is equal to the probability that an application with the indicated characteristics will be denied or modified divided by the probability that the typical application will be denied or modified. A single asterisk (*) indicates that the numerator of the ratio is statistically significantly different from the denominator at the 5–10 percent level. Two asterisks (**) indicate that the difference is significant at the 5 percent or less level.
a. This is the typical application described in the text. It is the base for calculating the denial or modification ratios. The other applications involve variations from the typical one in one or more characteristics. See Table 7.3 for the probability of denial or modification for the typical application in each bank type-area.

Table 7.13

Denial and modification ratios by property location in the Buffalo metropolitan area

Property Location	Commercial Banks		Mutual Savings Banks	
	Denial	Modification	Denial	Modification
Allegedly redlined neighborhoods:				
City of Buffalo				
Black Rock	↑	↑	0.69	1.13
Center City	0.45	0.00**	1.24	3.59*
Filmore-Leroy			0.63	1.90
Industrial	↓	↓	1.76	0.99
West Elmwood	0.99	0.00**	0.41**	1.44
West Side	1.77	4.19	0.80	0.82
Other neighborhoods:				
City of Buffalo				
Broadway	↑	↑	0.36**	0.42*
Shiller	0.86	1.04	0.15**	0.55
University	↓	↓	0.43**	0.44**
East Elmwood	↑	↑	0.56	0.37
South Buffalo	0.73	0.16	0.67**	0.87
North Buffalo	0.78	0.37	0.34**	0.65*
City of Niagara Falls	0.60	3.49*	1.06	1.00
Rest of Niagara County	1.23	3.21**	0.89	1.17
City of Lackawanna	↑ 1.00 ↓	↑ 1.00 ↓	0.87	0.83
Rest of Erie County[a]			1.00	1.00

The mutual savings bank estimates are derived from 1976–1977 applications data; other estimates are based on 1977–1978 mortgage applications. The ratio is equal to the probability that an application with the indicated characteristics will be denied or modified divided by the probability that the typical application will be denied or modified. A single asterisk (*) indicates that the numerator of the ratio is statistically significantly different from the denominator at the 5–10 percent level. Two asterisks (**) indicate that the difference is significant at the 5 percent or less level.

a. This is the typical application described in the text. It is the base for calculating the denial or modification ratios. The other applications involve variations from the typical one in one or more characteristics. See Table 7.3 for the probability of denial or modification for the typical application in each bank type-area.

Table 7.14
Denial ratios by property location for the New York-Nassau-Suffolk metropolitan areas

Property Location	Commercial Banks	Mutual Savings Banks		Savings and Loan Associations
		Small Sample	Large Sample	
Allegedly redlined neighborhoods				
South Bronx	1.41	1.26	1.07	—
Central Brooklyn	↑ 2.34**	↑ 0.52	0.82	—
Fort Greene	↓	↓	2.35**	—
Park Slope	1.25	0.44	0.69	—
Crown Heights	↑	↑ 0.66	1.16	—
East Flatbush	2.00	↓	0.82	—
Southeast Queens	↓	1.86	1.65**	—
All of the above	—	—	—	0.37
Other neighborhoods				
North Bronx	1.09	0.83	0.85	0.57
Northeast Kings	2.16**	0.59	1.40**	0.65
South Kings	1.66**	1.11	1.03	0.09**
Rest of Queens	1.57**	1.32	0.96	0.18**
Nassau	0.95	1.24	0.87**	0.21**
New York (Manhattan)	1.32*	0.41	1.31	—
Richmond	0.60	0.59**	0.54**	0.00**
Rockland	1.04	0.32**	1.36**	1.02
Westchester	0.94	0.62**	0.46**	1.54*
Suffolk[a]	1.00	1.00	1.00	1.00

The mutual savings bank estimates are derived from 1976–1977 applications data; other estimates are based on 1977–1978 mortgage applications. The ratio is equal to the probability that an application with the indicated characteristics will be denied divided by the probability that the typical application will be denied. A single asterisk (*) indicates that the numerator of the ratio is statistically significantly different from the denominator at the 5–10 percent level. Two asterisks (**) indicate that the difference is significant at the 5 percent or less level.

a. This is the typical application described in the text. It is the base for calculating the denial ratios. The other applications involve variations from the typical one in one or more characteristics. See Table 7.3 for the probability of denial for the typical application in each bank type-area (Table 7.9, footnote a, for the mutual savings bank large sample).

Table 7.15
Modification ratios by property location for the New York-Nassau-Suffolk
metropolitan area

Property Location	Commercial Banks	Mutual Savings Banks Small Sample	Large Sample[a]	Savings and Loan Associations
Allegedly redlined neighborhoods				
South Bronx	1.08	0.46	1.76	—
Central Brooklyn	↑ 0.45 ↓	↑ 1.42 ↓	2.21**	—
Fort Greene			5.23**	—
Park Slope	0.74	1.41	5.77**	—
Crown Heights	↑ 0.92 ↓	↑ 1.56 ↓	3.18**	—
East Flatbush			3.79**	—
Southeast Queens	↓	1.46	1.38	—
All of the above	—	—	—	2.59
Other neighborhoods				
North Bronx	0.86	0.68	2.01**	3.49*
Northeast Kings	2.35**	1.89**	3.09**	2.60
South Kings	1.33*	1.21	1.84**	3.11**
Rest of Queens	0.65**	0.95	1.29**	3.09**
Nassau	0.95	0.91	1.03	4.90**
New York (Manhattan)	0.83	1.38	1.35	—
Richmond	1.23	0.63**	0.35**	4.86**
Rockland	0.99	0.59**	0.37**	4.88**
Westchester	0.87	0.39**	0.35**	1.84
Suffolk[b]	1.00	1.00	1.00	1.00

The mutual savings bank estimates are derived from 1976–1977 applications data; other
estimates are based on 1977–1978 mortgage applications. The ratio is equal to the
probability that an application with the indicated characteristics will be modified divided
by the probability that the typical application will be modified. A single asterisk (*)
indicates that the numerator of the ratio is statistically significantly different from the
denominator at the 5–10 percent level. Two asterisks (**) indicate that the difference
is significant at the 5 percent or less level.
a. For the mutual savings banks' large sample, this column contains ratios for the action
of modification followed by withdrawal.
b. This is the typical application described in the text. It is the base for calculating the
modification ratios. The other applications involve variations from the typical one in
one or more characteristics. See Table 7.3 for the probability of modification for the
typical application in each bank type-area (Table 7.9, footnote a, for the mutual savings
bank large sample).

Table 7.16
Denial and modification ratios by property location for the Rochester metropolitan area

Property Location	Mutual Savings Banks		Savings and Loan Associations	
	Denial	Modification	Denial	Modification
Allegedly redlined neighborhoods				
Dutchtown	1.40	1.06	0.00**	0.00**
ZIP Code Area 14621 and 16th Ward	0.26	0.62	3.48*	0.00**
Other neighborhoods				
Edgerton-Brown Square-Cornhill-Park-Oxford	1.12	1.42		
South Wedge and Swillberg	0.00	0.00	1.99	7.17**
Rest of the Primary Target Area	0.45	0.76	1.00	3.02
Ward 19	0.32	0.00	0.31	2.03
Rest of City of Rochester	0.68	0.94	2.64	1.58
Livingston, Orleans, and Wayne Counties	0.00	1.32	4.19	7.51**
Monroe County outside City of Rochester[a]	1.00	1.00	1.00	1.00

The mutual savings bank estimates are derived from 1976–1977 applications data; other estimates are based on 1977–1978 mortgage applications. The ratio is equal to the probability that an application with the indicated characteristics will be denied or modified divided by the probability that the typical application will be denied or modified. A single asterisk (*) indicates that the numerator of the ratio is statistically significantly different from the denominator at the 5–10 percent level. Two asterisks (**) indicate that the difference is significant at the 5 percent or less level.
a. This is the typical application described in the text. It is the base for calculating the denial or modification ratios. The other applications involve variations from the typical one in one or more characteristics. See Table 7.3 for the probability of denial or modification for the typical application in each bank type-area.

Table 7.17
Denial and modification ratios by property location for mutual savings banks in the Syracuse metropolitan area, 1976–1977

Property Location	Denial	Modification
Allegedly redlined neighborhoods		
Brighton	0.00	0.00
Near northeast (part)	0.00	0.00
Other neighborhoods		
Rest of community development area	1.94	0.00
Rest of City of Syracuse	0.79	0.25**
Oswego County	1.60*	0.81
Madison County	1.44	0.89
Onondaga County outside City of Syracuse	1.00	1.00

The ratio is equal to the probability that an application with the indicated characteristics will be denied or modified divided by the probability that the typical application will be denied or modified. A single asterisk (*) indicates that the numerator of the ratio is statistically significantly different from the denominator at the 5–10 percent level. Two asterisks (**) indicate that the difference is significant at the 5 percent or less level.
a. This is the typical application described in the text. It is the base for calculating the denial or modification ratios. The other applications involve variations from the typical one in one or more characteristics. See Table 7.3 for the probability of denial or modification for the typical application in each bank type-area.

location in mortgage lending decisions differs among the five metropolitan areas and the types of lender.

In general, the denial ratios provide little evidence consistent with allegations that specified neighborhoods are redlined. The results, however, are consistent with redlining in six cases. New York-Nassau-Suffolk commercial banks are significantly more likely to deny applications on properties in the combined neighborhood of Central Brooklyn and Fort Greene than a similar application on a Suffolk County property; the denial ratio is 2.34 (Table 7.14). Although the other allegedly redlined neighborhoods in the New York-Nassau-Suffolk area have denial ratios greater than one at commercial banks, only the Central Brooklyn-Fort Greene one is statistically significant at the 10 percent level.[8] It should be noted that applications on properties in other parts of New York City (Northeast Kings, South Kings, the rest of Queens, and Manhattan) are significantly more likely to be denied by commercial banks than a similar application on a Suffolk county property.

Mutual savings banks are significantly more likely to deny applications on properties located in the Hudson-Park neighborhood of Albany and the Hillside neighborhood of the city of Troy than they are similar applications on suburban Saratoga County properties; the denial ratios are 12.51 and 10.97, respectively (Table 7.12). No other neighborhoods in the Albany-Schenectady-Troy metropolitan area have denial ratios from mutual savings banks that are significantly greater than one.

New York-Nassau-Suffolk mutual savings banks treat applications on properties located in Fort Greene in Brooklyn and Southeast Queens less favorably than similar applications on Suffolk County properties.[9] The denial ratios are 2.35 and 1.65, respectively, and both are based on statistically significant (5 percent level) differentials (Table 7.14). However, one of the suburban counties (Rockland) also has a denial ratio from mutual savings banks that is significantly above one. Applications on Northeast Kings properties are also significantly more likely to be denied than those on suburban Suffolk County properties, but this result is expected because of the area's generally weak housing market. However, the property location coefficients in the New York-Nassau-Suffolk mutual savings bank sample change magnitudes and signs between the sample including sex and marital status and the sample without these variables.[10]

Applications at Rochester savings and loan associations are more likely to be denied if the property is located in ZIP Code Area 14621 or the 16th Ward than if it is located in suburban Monroe County (Table 7.16). The denial ratio of 3.48 is statistically significant at the 10 percent level. Although some Rochester areas that are not alleged to be redlined also had denial ratios in excess of one, none of them are statistically significant at the 10 percent level.

Mutual savings banks are the only lenders with modification ratios greater than one for allegedly redlined neighborhoods. These occur in the Buffalo and New York-Nassau-Suffolk metropolitan areas. In Buffalo, applications on Center City properties are 3.59 times as likely to be modified as similar applications on suburban Erie County properties. This is the only Buffalo modification ratio in excess of one that is based on a statistically significant (10 percent level) differential. In the New York-Nassau-Suffolk area, applications on properties in New York City, whether or not they are in allegedly redlined neighborhoods, are more likely to be modified than similar applications on Suffolk County properties.

Withdrawal ratios in excess of one occur in a few cases with statistical significance. They exceed one for the allegedly redlined neighborhoods of Central Brooklyn and Park Slope at commercial banks in the New York-Nassau-Suffolk area, but they also exceed one for other areas not alleged to be redlined (for example, Nassau and Westchester counties). Savings and loan associations in the same metropolitan area have withdrawal ratios above one for the neighborhoods alleged to be redlined as well as Rockland and Westchester counties. These inconsistent sets of coefficients from the withdrawal equations offer little support for the redlining allegations.

Neighborhood Characteristics   Denial and modification ratios by the age and racial composition of the neighborhood are summarized in Tables 7.18 and 7.19.

Applications are statistically significantly more likely to be denied in older neighborhoods in four bank type-areas: commercial banks in the combined upstate area, mutual savings banks in the Buffalo and Rochester metropolitan areas, and savings and loan associations in the New York-Nassau-Suffolk area.[11] Although the results are consistent with allegations that lenders avoid old neighborhoods, they may be the result of a spurious correlation between the age of the neighborhood and the condition of the specific property. Unlike California, we were unable to separate these two factors because the age of the building is not provided on the New York EHOL forms. Therefore, caution should be exercised in interpreting these and other age-of-neighborhood results in New York.

All but one of the modification ratios for age of neighborhood exceed one in Table 7.19, indicating that applications on properties in older neighborhoods are more likely to be modified than ones in newer neighborhoods.[12] Seven of the differentials are statistically significant at the 5 percent level. These results are also consistent with the allegation that lenders redline older neighborhoods but they must not be taken out of context. The caveat presented in the preceding discussion of denial ratios also applies here and is even strengthened because some of the modifications may be maturity-period reductions to compensate for the shorter remaining economic lives of older buildings.

Applications on properties in neighborhoods with higher percentages

Table 7.18
Denial ratios by age and racial composition of neighborhood, New York State

Bank Type and Metropolitan Area	Typical Applicant (TA)[a]	TA in Older Neighborhood (+0.10)	TA in a 50% Nonwhite Neighborhood
Albany-Schenectady-Troy SMSA			
Mutual savings banks	1.00	1.01	0.00[b]
Albany-Schenectady-Troy, Rochester, and Syracuse SMSAs			
Commercial banks	1.00	1.08**	0.20
Buffalo SMSA			
Commercial banks	1.00	1.02	0.50
Mutual savings banks	1.00	1.12**	0.92
New York and Nassau-Suffolk SMSAs			
Commercial banks	1.00	1.00	1.33*
Mutual savings banks	1.00	1.00	0.93
Savings and loan associations	1.00	1.11**	1.49
Rochester SMSA			
Mutual savings banks	1.00	1.17**	0.55
Savings and loan associations	1.00	1.06	4.25[c]
Syracuse SMSA			
Mutual savings banks	1.00	0.99	1.67

The mutual savings bank estimates are derived from 1976–1977 applications data; other estimates are based on 1977–1978 mortgage applications. The ratio is equal to the probability that an application with the indicated characteristics will be denied divided by the probability that the typical application will be denied. A single asterisk (*) indicates that the numerator of the ratio is statistically significantly different from the denominator at the 5–10 percent level. Two asterisks (**) indicate that the difference is significant at the 5 percent or less level.
a. This is the typical application described in the text. It is the base for calculating the denial ratios. The other applications involve variations from the typical one in one or more characteristics. See Table 7.3 for the probability of denial for the typical application in each bank type-area.
b. This ratio is so small because nearly all the applications at mutual savings banks on properties in 50 percent nonwhite neighborhoods in the Albany-Schenectady-Troy metropolitan area are withdrawn.
c. This ratio is high because nearly none of the applications at this bank type-area in 50 percent nonwhite neighborhoods are likely to be withdrawn.

Table 7.19

Modification ratios by age and racial composition of neighborhood, New York State

Bank Type and Metropolitan Area	Typical Applicant (TA)[a]	TA in Older Neighborhood (+0.10)	TA in a 50% Nonwhite Neighborhood
Albany-Schenectady-Troy SMSA			
Mutual savings banks	1.00	1.11**	0.01[b]
Albany-Schenectady-Troy, Rochester, and Syracuse SMSAs			
Commercial banks	1.00	0.99	9.42
Buffalo SMSA			
Commercial banks	1.00	1.19**	0.65
Mutual savings banks	1.00	1.10**	0.42
New York and Nassau-Suffolk SMSAs			
Commercial banks	1.00	1.05**	1.14
Mutual savings banks	1.00	1.13**	0.76
Savings and loan associations	1.00	1.06**	0.83
Rochester SMSA			
Mutual savings banks	1.00	1.03	0.46*
Savings and loan associations	1.00	1.02	5.77[c]
Syracuse SMSA			
Mutual savings banks	1.00	1.17**	0.09

The mutual savings bank estimates are derived from 1976–1977 applications data; other estimates are based on 1977–1978 mortgage applications. The ratio is equal to the probability that an application with the indicated characteristics will be modified divided by the probability that the typical application will be modified. A single asterisk (*) indicates that the numerator of the ratio is statistically significantly different from the denominator at the 5–10 percent level. Two asterisks (**) indicate that the difference is significant at the 5 percent or less level.

a. This is the typical application described in the text. It is the base for calculating the modification ratios. The other applications involve variations from the typical one in one or more characteristics. See Table 7.3 for the probability of modification for the typical application in each bank type-area.

b. This ratio is so small because nearly all the applications at mutual savings banks on properties in 50 percent nonwhite neighborhoods in the Albany-Schenectady-Troy metropolitan area are withdrawn.

c. This ratio is high because nearly none of the applications at this bank type-area in 50 percent nonwhite neighborhoods are likely to be withdrawn.

of nonwhite population are significantly more likely to be denied than similar applications in nearly all-white neighborhoods in only one bank type-area: commercial banks in the New York-Nassau-Suffolk metropolitan area. This result is consistent with the redlining allegation. Only one modification ratio is statistically significant, but it indicates that Rochester mutual savings banks favor largely nonwhite neighborhoods.[13]

Withdrawals are significantly more likely to occur in older neighborhoods at commercial banks in the combined upstate area and mutual savings banks in the Albany-Schenectady-Troy metropolitan area.[14] The withdrawal ratios are 1.18 and 1.09, respectively. Applications on properties in majority nonwhite neighborhoods are significantly more likely to be withdrawn than similar ones in nearly all-white neighborhoods in the mutual savings banks in the Albany-Schenectady-Troy and Rochester metropolitan area. The ratios are 32.42 and 6.65, respectively.

Summary

In this chapter, decisions on applications for conventional mortgages on owner-occupied one- to four-family houses in five metropolitan areas of New York State are analyzed. The five areas are: Albany-Schenectady-Troy, Buffalo, New York-Nassau-Suffolk, Rochester, and Syracuse. In general, four possible outcomes are considered: approval as applied for, approval after modification, denial, and withdrawal.

We view a lender's decision as a function of the financial characteristics of the borrower, requested terms of the loan, and collateral value of the property. Information on the neighborhood surrounding the property, including measures of change over time, are used to reflect the risk of loss associated with a particular property because of the condition of neighborhood properties. Most of these neighborhood measures are based on the Census of Population and Housing. However, detailed information on housing code violations, vacant buildings, property tax delinquency, and serious fires is available for each census tract in Bronx, Kings, and Queens counties. The sex, marital status, age, and race of the applicant; the location of the property; and the age and racial composition of the neighborhood are also included to determine whether they affect mortgage-lending decisions after controlling for the other factors. Community organizations and residents identified the neighborhoods that they believed were redlined by lending institutions.

As in California, objective factors play a central role in New York lender decisions on mortgage applications. The likelihood that an application will be denied decreases as income and net wealth increase and the requested-loan-to-appraised-value ratio decreases, and when the requested loan to income ratio decreases below two. At least one proxy for the risk associated with the condition of neighboring buildings is significant in each denial equation. High requested-loan-to-appraised-value ratios are also major contributors to explaining the modification of a mortgage application prior to approval and the withdrawal of an application.

Only two of the lender actions are clear in their meaning: approval as applied for and denial. Modification is ambiguous because, on the one hand, the modification could be a reduction in maturity period to reflect the economic life of the building or a decrease in loan amount to reflect an applicant's desire to invest more equity, and on the other, the modification may represent an adverse action. Withdrawals are even more ambiguous because they could be the result of lender discouragement or applicant success at another lending institution. For these reasons, the analysis of discrimination gives more weight to the denial results than to the modification or withdrawal results where approval as applied for serves as the reference point.

Sex and Marital Status

The evidence supports the view that female-only households or male-female households with working women, especially with women in the childbearing age, experience some discrimination in lending decisions, but that instances of such discrimination are limited. Married female-only applicants are more than twice as likely to be denied by Buffalo commercial banks and New York-Nassau-Suffolk mutual savings banks than married male-female applicants with a nonworking woman beyond the childbearing age. Male-female applicants with working women beyond childbearing age (married, unmarried, or separated) are twice as likely to be denied than similar households with a nonworking woman by Buffalo commercial banks.

In contrast to the limited evidence of discrimination against female-only or male-female households, we find substantial evidence of adverse treatment of male-only households. These households, whether married, unmarried, or separated, are over twice as likely to be denied than similarly situated married male-female households with nonworking women beyond childbearing age at Buffalo commercial banks, New York-Nassau-Suffolk mutual savings banks and Rochester savings and loan associations. In addition, the New York-Nassau-Suffolk commercial banks are more likely to deny applications from unmarried or separated male-only households than those of married male-female applicants with a nonworking woman past the childbearing age. These same banks and the Rochester savings and loan associations also are from 1.44 to 3.82 times as likely to deny the applications of married or separated male-female households, regardless of the work status or childbearing age of the woman.

The modification results suggest that New York-Nassau-Suffolk savings and loan associations are very likely to modify male-female applications, regardless of marital status, providing the woman is either working or in the childbearing years. Married male-only applicants are also very likely to be modified by these lenders.

Race

Considerable evidence supports the allegation that black applicants are denied much more frequently than similarly situated white applicants. Black applicants at mutual savings banks and savings and loan associations are 1.58 to 3.61 times as likely to be denied than similar white applicants. Only one of the seven ratios for lenders of these two types are not statististically significant—that for mutual savings banks in the Albany-Schenectady-Troy metropolitan area. The statistically significant differentials occur for the following lenders: mutual savings banks in Buffalo, New York-Nassau-Suffolk, Rochester, and Syracuse; and savings and loan associations in New York-Nassau-Suffolk and Rochester.

Although two of the three commercial bank ratios indicate black applicants are more likely to be denied, none of these are statistically significant. New York-Nassau-Suffolk commercial banks, however, are significantly more likely to deny other minority (neither black nor Hispanic) applicants than similarly situated white applicants.

New York-Nassau-Suffolk mutual savings banks are also significantly more (nearly twice as) likely to deny Hispanic applicants than similarly situated white applicants.

The modification results indicate that blacks are more likely to be modified by mutual savings banks and savings and loan associations in the New York-Nassau-Suffolk area. The latter are also more likely to modify applications from Hispanics. Commercial and mutual savings banks in Buffalo are more likely to modify applications from other minorities (nonblack).

Age

The evidence suggests that young applicants are less likely to be denied than older ones, but this pattern is statistically significant in only two cases: savings and loan associations in the New York-Nassau-Suffolk and Rochester metropolitan areas. Applicants under thirty-five and over forty-four years old are less likely to be denied than those thirty-five to forty-four years old at Buffalo commercial banks and New York-Nassau-Suffolk mutual savings banks. Applicants under thirty-five are also less likely to be denied than older ones by commercial banks in the combined upstate area (Albany-Schenectady-Troy, Rochester, and Syracuse metropolitan areas).

The modification results are mixed. Younger applicants are less likely to be modified by commercial banks in the combined upstate area and the New York-Nassau-Suffolk metropolitan area, while they are more likely to be modified by Buffalo commercial banks, New York-Nassau-Suffolk mutual savings bank, and Rochester savings and loan associations.

Redlining

We have evaluated a large number of community-based allegations that lenders have redlined a particular neighborhood. The denial results are consistent with the allegations in only six cases. Commercial banks in New York-Nassau-Suffolk are more likely to deny applications on Central Brooklyn-Fort Greene properties than similar applications on suburban Suffolk County properties. Mutual savings banks in the New York-Nassau-Suffolk area are more likely to deny applications on Fort Greene and Southeast Queens properties. The mutual savings banks in the Albany-Schenectady-Troy area are also more likely to deny applications on Hudson-Park (Albany) or Hillside (Troy) properties than similar ones on suburban Saratoga County properties. Finally, Rochester savings and loan associations are more likely to deny applications on properties in ZIP Code Area 14621 or the 16th Ward than similar ones on suburban Monroe County properties.

The modification results are consistent with redlining allegations in only one Buffalo neighborhood (Center City) where mutual savings banks are more likely to modify the application than a similar one on a suburban Erie County property. Although mutual savings banks in the New York-Nassau-Suffolk area are more likely to modify applications on properties in several allegedly redlined neighborhoods than applications on Suffolk County properties, these banks are also more likely to modify applications in several neighborhoods that are not alleged to be redlined.

Community organizations have also alleged that older or nonwhite neighborhoods are redlined by mortgage lenders. The denial results are consistent with the age-of-neighborhood allegations in four instances: commercial banks in the combined upstate area, mutual savings banks in the Buffalo and Rochester metropolitan areas, and savings and loan associations in the New York-Nassau-Suffolk area. It is important to avoid overinterpreting these results because, unlike our California analysis, we were unable to control for the age of the building. Modification was even more closely tied to the age of neighborhood, with more modifications in older neighborhoods. However, the same caveat applies with added strength because the modification could have been a maturity-period reduction to reflect the remaining economic life of the building.

Only one type of lender (commercial banks in New York-Nassau-Suffolk) had significantly higher denial probabilities in largely nonwhite neighborhoods than for similar applications in all white ones.

8
**Mortage Credit Terms
in New York**

Differential credit terms are another mechanism that lenders may use
to discriminate against women, minorities, and neighborhoods. We
examine discrimination with respect to the setting of mortgage terms
using two different data sources in New York. The first approach
parallels the California analysis of downward modification in the requested loan amount and is based on the New York mortgage applications data. The second approach uses information on the average
terms of new mortgages in each census tract in three New York City
counties to analyze the simultaneous determination of interest rate,
maturity period, and loan-to-value ratio.

Downward Modifications

This section analyzes the pattern of downward modification of loan
amounts by bank type in those New York metropolitan areas for which
sufficient data are available. The analysis covers commercial banks,
mutual savings banks, and savings and loan associations in the New
York-Nassau-Suffolk metropolitan area; savings and loan associations
in the Rochester area; and commercial banks in the Albany-Schenectady-Troy, Rochester, and Syracuse metropolitan areas. By focusing
on the difference between the requested and the granted loan amount
for those applications with downward modifications, this chapter sup-
plements the analysis of modification probabilities discussed in Chapter
7. The models in this chapter represent the only analysis of final
mortgage terms that can be performed with the New York data on
mortgage applications, since interest-rate and years-to-maturity data
are not available.[1]
   The specific question addressed here is whether some borrowers
experience larger downward modifications than others solely because

of membership in groups not legally allowed to be considered by banks in their decision-making process. Large downward modifications of loan amounts may yield effects similar to those of loan denial; the applicant may not be able to proceed with the house purchase because he or she cannot raise the additional down payment necessitated by the bank's decision not to lend the requested amount.

The model used to test for discriminatory bank behavior of this type must adequately control for the factors that banks may legitimately use to determine the size of the downward modification. The control factors included in the modification models reported here are essentially the same as those in the decision-to-lend models of the previous chapter; the only addition is a variable for the size of the requested loan.

In the following sections, we first briefly discuss the performance of the overall equations, focusing on the role of the control variables. We then report the equation implications for the hypothesis of discriminatory lending on the basis of sex and marital status, race, age, and property location. The results support the view that banks in the New York-Nassau-Suffolk metropolitan area discriminate on the basis of age and provide weak support for the hypothesis of discrimination against female applicants.

Control Variables

The estimated equations take the following form:

MODOWN = f (REQLOAN, RLTOAV, BORR, NEIGH, DISC),

where

MODOWN = requested loan amount less granted loan amount,

REQLOAN = requested loan amount,

RLTOAV = the requested loan amount as a fraction of the appraised value,

BORR = a vector of borrower characteristics (including income, net wealth, employment history, and requested loan amount in excess of two times income),

NEIGH = a vector of neighborhood characteristics (including level and change variables),

DISC = a vector of discrimination variables (including sex, marital status, race, age, location of property, neighborhood age, and racial composition of neighborhood).

The estimated equations for the five separate samples are reported in Appendix C. (Complete variable definitions are presented in Appendix A). All equations are linear and were estimated using ordinary least squares. As can be seen from the summary statistics presented in Table 8.1, sample size ranges from a low of 75 for the Rochester savings and loan association sample to a high of 616 for the New York-Nassau-Suffolk commercial bank sample. The fraction of variation explained (R-square) varies from 0.33 for the mutual savings bank sample in New York-Nassau-Suffolk to 0.64 for the savings and loan association sample in Rochester. All equations explain statistically significant proportions of the variation in the dependent variable.

The size of the requested loan (REQLOAN) and the requested-loan-to-appraised-value ratio (RLTOAV) are the key control variables. In all but the New York-Nassau-Suffolk commercial bank sample, both variables exert statistically significant and positive effects on the size of the downward modification, as expected.

The requested loan amount acts as a scale variable; for any given degree of loan risk as measured by the requested-loan-to-appraised-value variable and other control variables, the dollar amount of the modification depends on the size of the loan. The coefficients of REQLOAN are remarkably similar across the four samples other than the New York-Nassau-Suffolk commercial bank sample and imply that

Table 8.1
Summary statistics for downward-modification equations, New York State

Statistic	AST-ROCH-SYR COM	NYNS COM	MSB	SLA	ROCH SLA
Sample size	90	616	386	179	75
R-square	0.59	0.43	0.33	0.30	0.64
F-statistic	3.86	10.66	4.24	1.97	3.10
P-value	0.0001	0.0001	0.0001	0.0036	0.0003

The mutual savings bank equation is based on 1976–1977 mortgage applications data; the other equations are based on 1977–1978 applications. The abbreviations in the column headings are as follows: bank type: COM, commercial banks; MSB, mutual savings banks; SLA, savings and loan associations; metropolitan areas: AST, Albany-Schenectady-Troy; NYNS, New York-Nassau-Suffolk; ROCH, Rochester; SYR, Syracuse.

differences of $1,000 in the requested loan amount are associated with differences of approximately $100 in the amount by which loans are reduced.

A higher requested loan amount in relation to appraised value also increases the predicted magnitudes of the downward modifications in these four samples. A difference of 10 percentage points in the ratio of the requested loan to appraised value increases the loan reduction by $456 to $1,387 across samples, controlling for the size of the requested loan. Consider two applicants each requesting mortgage money for a home appraised at $55,000. If one requested $35,000 and the other $45,000 and if both requests are modified downward, the estimated equation suggests that on average the latter will receive $7,805 more than the former, *ceteris paribus*.[2] In other words, borrowers who ask for larger amounts in relation to appraised value obtain larger amounts, but they receive less than the full amount of the requested difference.

The results for the New York-Nassau-Suffolk commercial bank sample are harder to explain. Again the requested-loan variable enters positively as expected (and with a larger magnitude than in the other four samples), but the requested-loan-to-appraised-value variable exerts a statistically significant negative impact, contrary to expectations. The mean requested-loan-to-appraised-value ratio is lower and the size of the requested loan is higher on average and is characterized by greater variation in the New York-Nassau-Suffolk commercial bank sample than in the other four samples. The negative coefficient of RLTOAV may thus reflect a negative correlation between REQLOAN and RLTOAV and some nonlinearities not captured by the linear equation specification.[3]

Somewhat surprisingly, very few of the variables representing the financial characteristics of the borrower enter the MODOWN equations significantly. In other words, lenders appear to pay little attention to the income, net wealth, or employment stability of the applicant when deciding how much to reduce loans once it is decided that a loan reduction is in order. Even the size of the loan in relation to income appears to be relatively unimportant; the coefficient of the binary variable measuring whether the requested loan exceeds two times income is statistically insignificant in all but the New York-Nassau-Suffolk commercial bank sample, where it has an unexpected negative sign. Unlike the other samples, however, this New York-Nassau-Suffolk commercial bank sample simultaneously implies, consistent with expectations, that applicants with higher incomes have smaller modification, *ceteris paribus*. Again, the unexpected negative sign on the variable representing the requested loan in relation to income may reflect a pattern of correlation and nonlinearity not adequately captured by the model.

The final set of control variables, the characteristics of the neighborhood, also have little explanatory power. With the exception of the 1975–1970 change-in-income (DINC) variable, which enters positively in the New York-Nassau-Suffolk commercial bank equation, and the foreclosure rate (FORRATE), which enters positively in the New York-Nassau-Suffolk mutual savings bank equation, none of the neighborhood variables are significant in any of the equations.

Discrimination Results

The finding of a positive coefficient on a discrimination variable indicates that applicants who are members of the group in question, whether women, old people, blacks, or home buyers in allegedly redlined neighborhoods, experience larger loan reductions than comparable applicants from the baseline groups. Larger loan reductions translate directly into large down payments unless the borrower turns to an expensive second mortgage. In some cases, larger loan reductions may keep the applicant from purchasing the home at all and, thus, may be an indirect way for the bank to deny the loan. Provided the control variables in the MODOWN equations adequately represent the legitimate factors affecting the size of downward modifications, we can interpret statistically significant positive coefficients on any of the discrimination variables as support for the hypothesis of discriminatory behavior.

For each of the five samples, we have calculated the expected downward modification for a baseline application. This baseline application represents the type of application that bankers typically do not discriminate against; the applicants are a married, white, male-female couple; the wife is beyond childbearing age and not working; the applicant is between thirty-five and forty-four and the property is in the suburbs.[4] With respect to all other characteristics, the baseline application takes on average values for the particular MODOWN sample involved. In connection with each type of potential discrimination, the predicted downward modification for an application that differs from the baseline application in the discrimination dimension only is reported and compared to the baseline downward modification for that sample. In this way, similarly situated applicants can be compared, and the magnitude of the discriminatory differential can be put into perspective.

Sex and Marital Status   The results by sex and marital status are reported in Table 8.2. Each entry represents the predicted amount by which the bankers in each of the five samples reduce requested loan amounts for applications differing from baseline applications only in terms of sex or marital status. The numbers in parentheses represent the ratio of the predicted MODOWN for the indicated sex or marital status type to the type represented by the base. For example, the second entry in the second column indicates that commercial banks in the New York-Nassau-Suffolk metropolitan area reduce the actual loan below the requested loan on average by $4,139 for an application that differs from the base only in that the wife is working. The 1.39 in parentheses indicates that this loan reduction is 39 percent higher than that for the base application. The absence of asterisks with this entry indicates that the coefficient on which it is based is statistically insignificant at the 10 percent level. In general, one asterisk means that the relevant coefficient is significant at the 5–10 percent level, and two asterisks indicate the 5 percent or less significance level.

With respect to discrimination based on sex, we find limited statistically significant evidence of discriminatory behavior. The one significant finding consistent with discriminatory behavior relates to commercial banks in New York-Nassau-Suffolk, which appear to reduce loans for female-only applications with no women under thirty-four by more than twice the amount they reduce loans for baseline applications. Since this results in an additional down payment of $3,333, the magnitude is not negligible. Although not statistically significant, the results suggest that these same banks may treat younger female-only applicants adversely as well. Members of this group (FONLYCB, with the applicant between twenty-five and thirty-four) experience downward modifications 44 percent greater than those faced by baseline applicants.

The finding that commercial banks in the New York-Nassau-Suffolk area modify loans downward more for nonchildbearing female-only households than for baseline applications sheds additional light on the findings in Chapter 4 of a 0.47 denial ratio and a 1.42 modification ratio (neither of which is based on statistically significant coefficients) for these banks. The explanation appears to be that in many cases the

Table 8.2
Downward modifications (dollar amounts and ratios) by sex and marital status for baseline applications, New York State

Status	AST-ROCH-SYR	NYNS			ROCH
	COM	COM	MSB	SLA	SLA
Sex					
MFNCBNW (base)	8,249(1.00)	2,588(1.00)	6,481(1.00)	2,840(1.00)	4,403(1.00)
MFNCBW	5,101(0.62)*	4,139(1.39)	5,621(0.87)	4,242(1.52)	
MFCBW25–34[a]	3,636(0.44)	4,835(1.62)	4,459(0.68)	3,739(1.32)	1,445(0.33)**
MFCBNW25–34[a]	3,233(0.39)	5,860(1.96)	5,350(0.82)	3,886(1.37)	867(0.20)**
FONLYCB	8,751(1.06)	4,310(1.44)[a]	5,809(0.89)[a]	4,928(1.74)	1,829(0.42)**
FONLYNCB	6,521(2.11)*		5,628(0.87)		
MONLY	5,346(0.65)	3,721(1.25)	5,923(0.92)	4,529(1.40)	1,967(0.45)**
Marital Status					
MARRIED (base)	8,249(1.00)	2,588(1.00)	6,481(1.00)	2,840(1.00)	4,403(1.00)
SEP	10,156(1.23)	2,934(0.98)	8,777(1.35)*	2,288(0.81)	5,000(1.14)
UNMAR	3,153(1.06)		6,091(0.94)		

The mutual savings bank estimates are based on 1976–1977 mortgage applications data; the other equations are based on 1977–1978 applications. The abbreviations used in the column headings are defined in Table 8.1. The entries in the table represent the predicted downward modification (in dollars) for an applicant similar to the base application in all ways other than the characteristic listed. Numbers in parentheses represent the ratio of the downward modification for an application with the indicated characteristic to the downward modification for the baseline application. See text for definition of the baseline application. The asterisk (*) indicates that the numerator of the ratio is statistically significantly different from the denominator at the 5–10 percent level. Two asterisks (**) indicate that the difference is significant at the 5 percent or less level.
a. These estimates are constructed by adding the effect of reducing the age of the applicant from the baseline range of 35–44 to the 25–34-year-old range to the effect related specifically to the sex category of the application.

commercial banks have chosen not to deny mortgage loans to non-childbearing women but instead to modify requested loan amounts downward by amounts not justified by the objective characteristics of the application.

Although the New York-Nassau-Suffolk commercial bank FONLYNCB coefficient is the only statistically significant positive coefficient relating to the sex variables, the positive signs of many of the other female-only coefficients should be noted. Ignoring the Rochester savings and loan sample for which all the ratios are well below one, five out of the remaining six ratios for female-only applications exceed one.

No similarly consistent pattern emerges for any of the other related variables. On the one hand, upstate commercial banks, Rochester savings and loan associations, and New York-Nassau-Suffolk mutual savings banks appear to favor all six categories other than female-only relative to the base; just the reverse is true for the New York-Suffolk commercial banks and savings and loan associations.

Turning to the results relating to differential treatment based on marital status, we find evidence to support the view that mutual savings banks in the New York-Nassau-Suffolk metropolitan area discriminate against separated applicants. Specifically, separated applicants applying for mortgages from these banks experience downward modifications that average 35 percent larger than those of married couples. Thus, a separated applicant must raise, on average, an additional $2,296 to make the down payment just because of his or her marital status, given that the person is chosen for a downward modification in the first place.

No consistent pattern emerges across the other four samples in this regard. The pattern found for the New York-Nassau-Suffolk mutual savings bank sample (that is, a MODOWN ratio above one for separated applicants and below one for unmarried applicants) suggests that distinguishing between married and separated applicants may be important for the analysis. Unfortunately, data limitations prevent us from doing so in three of the five samples.

Race   The findings with respect to differential treatment based on race, summarized in Table 8.3, generally are inconsistent with the hypothesis of discriminatory behavior in the decision determining the amount by which the requested loan amount is to be reduced. Many of the ratios are less than one, implying that, if anything, lenders

Table 8.3
Downward modifications (dollar amounts and ratios) by race for baseline applications, New York State

Race	AST-ROCH-SYR	NYNS			ROCH
	COM	COM	MSB	SLA	SLA
White (base)	8,249(1.00)	2,938(1.00)	6,481(1.00)	2,840(1.00)	4,403(1.00)
Black	↑	3,673(1.23)	4,960(0.77)*	3,616(1.27)	↑
Hispanic	7,125(0.86)	2,539(0.84)	5,365(0.83)	1,951(0.69)	3,280(0.74)
Other minority	↓	1,910(0.64)	7,243(1.12)	2,814(0.99)	↓

The mutual savings bank estimates are based on 1976–1977 mortgage applications data; the other equations are based on 1977–1978 applications. The abbreviations used in the column headings are defined in Table 8.1. The entries in the table represent the predicted downward modification (in dollars) for an applicant similar to the base application in all ways other than the characteristic listed. Numbers in parentheses represent the ratio of the downward modification for an application with the indicated characteristic to the downward modification for the baseline application. See text for definition of the baseline application. The asterisk (*) indicates that the numerator of the ratio is statistically significantly different from the denominator at the 5–10 percent level. Two asterisks (**) indicate that the difference is significant at the 5 percent or less level.

modify loans downward by less for members of racial minorities than for similarly situated whites; furthermore, none of the three ratios greater than one is derived from a statistically significant coefficient. Recall, however, that minorities may be discriminated against in a more direct fashion; they may be differentially denied the loan (see Chapter 7).

When the results are combined with the denial and modification ratios discussed in Chapter 7, the following picture emerges. Bankers are more likely to modify the loan amount on applications from minorities than from whites, but once they decide to modify the loan, lenders do not reduce loan amounts excessively below requested amounts for members of racial minorities. Thus, the evidence presented here is not consistent with the view that bankers use the modification alternative to give minorities harsher loan terms than otherwise warranted. Given denial ratios for minorities consistently above one, we conclude that the evidence is consistent with the view that most bankers in New York State discriminate against minorities by denying loans outright rather than by imposing harsher terms.

Age Turning now to the results by age, we find evidence that some banks reduce loan amounts by more for applicants over forty-five than for otherwise comparable younger applicants. As summarized in Table 8.4, the results support the hypothesis that both commercial banks and savings and loan associations in the New York-Nassau-Suffolk metropolitan area discriminate against applicants between the ages of forty-five and fifty-four and against those over fifty-four. All four coefficients on which this conclusion is based are statistically significant at the 5 percent level or less. The direction of impact for applicants in these age groups in the New York-Nassau-Suffolk mutual savings bank sample is consistent with the hypothesis of discriminatory behavior as well, but the statistical insignificance of the relevant coefficients makes it impossible to reject the hypothesis that these banks treat older applicants the same as they treat younger applicants. Neither of the upstate samples give evidence of discrimination against older applicants either; indeed, the commercial banks in the Albany-Schenectady-Troy, Rochester, and Syracuse areas appear to reduce loans by less for older applicants relative to younger applicants.

For the New York-Nassau-Suffolk commercial banks and savings and loan associations samples, the magnitudes of the predicted downward modifications for applicants over forty-five who are otherwise

Table 8.4
Downward modifications (dollar amounts and ratios) by age for baseline applications, New York State

Age	AST-ROCH-SYR	NYNS			ROCH
	COM	COM	MSB	SLA	SLA
<25	5,704(0.69)**	3,768(1.26)	6,241(0.96)	3,371(1.19)	4,449(1.01)
25–34		4,036(1.35)	5,574(0.85)	2,855(1.01)	3,392(0.77)
35–44 (Base)	8,249(1.00)	2,980(1.00)	6,481(1.00)	2,840(1.00)	4,403(1.00)
45–54	5,358(0.65)**	6,083(2.04)**	7,223(1.11)	4,738(1.67)**	4,805(1.09)
>54		7,352(2.46)**	7,448(1.15)	6,098(2.15)**	2,475(0.56)

The mutual savings banks estimates are based on 1976–1977 mortgage applications data; the other equations are based on 1977–1978 applications. The abbreviations used in the column headings are defined in Table 8.1. The entries in the table represent the predicted downward modification (in dollars) for an applicant similar to the base application in all ways other than the characteristic listed. Numbers in parentheses represent the ratio of the downward modification for an application with the indicated characteristic to the downward modification for the baseline application. See text for definition of the baseline application. A single asterisk (*) indicates that the numerator of the ratio is statistically significantly different from the denominator at the 5–10 percent level. Two asterisks (**) indicate that the difference is significant at the 5 percent or less level.

comparable to the baseline applicant are substantial; they range from
$4,738 for 45- to 54-year-old applicants at savings and loan associations
to $7,352 for applicants over fifty-five at commercial banks. The dif-
ferences between the predicted downward modifications for the applicants over forty-five and those for the base applicants show that up to
60 percent of each predicted loan reduction for older applicants represents the effect of age alone.

These findings shed additional light on the denial and modification
ratios reported for these New York-Nassau-Suffolk banks in Chapter
7. Denial ratios close to one suggest that the commercial banks do not
discriminate against older applicants. However, the high modification
ratios for the two oldest age groups and the finding that the commercial
banks reduce loans more for older applicants than for younger applicants suggests that the modification ratios indicate discriminatory behavior. For the savings and loan associations, high denial ratios for
older applicants directly indicate age discrimination and the large
downward modifications on applications from older applicants lends
further support to the discriminatory behavior hypothesis, even though
the predicted probabilities of modification are low.

Because of the way the models are specified, the effect of age on
the size of the downward modification is invariant with respect to the
sex of the applicant. The specification does imply, however, that the
effects of sex and age are additive. This additivity is particularly
relevant for the New York-Nassau-Suffolk commercial bank sample
where larger than warranted downward modifications were found for
female-only applicants above childbearing age. Combining this finding
with the findings by age, the following implications emerge. Commercial banks would reduce the loan amount by $9,416, on average, on
applications, otherwise similar to the baseline application, from female
applicants between forty-five and fifty-four with no women of childbearing age and by $11,685 on applications from female applicants
over fifty-four. These modifications are 3.15 and 3.90 times the predicted downward modifications for the male-female baseline application. Thus, the allegation that older women are treated differently
from similarly situated younger male-female couples is supported for
New York-Nassau-Suffolk commercial banks.

For young applicants, we find little evidence of discriminatory behavior. The one possible exception is the almost statistically significant
positive effect for twenty-five to thirty-four year olds in the New York-
Nassau-Suffolk commercial bank sample. The direction of impact is

mixed across the five samples, and none of the positive coefficients are statistically significant at the 10 percent level.

Redlining Four of the five samples analyzed in this chapter have too few observations to permit examination of the hypothesis of differential downward modifications in neighborhoods alleged to be redlined. Only the New York-Nassau-Suffolk commercial bank sample permits such a test. As reported in Table 8.5, downward-modification ratios greater than one occur with respect to applications from only the alleged redlined areas and Manhattan. Although neither of the coefficients on which these ratios are based is statistically significant at the 10 percent (two-tail) level, their magnitudes and their significance at a 10 percent (one-tail) level suggest that they should not be dismissed completely. At most we can say that the evidence weakly supports the view that applicants from areas alleged to be redlined experience greater downward modifications than similarly situated suburban applicants.

Finally, the downward-modification data do not support allegations that bankers treat applications from older neighborhoods or from neighborhoods with high proportions of blacks differently than those

Table 8.5
Downward modifications (dollar amounts and ratios) by location for baseline applications at commercial banks in New York and Nassau-Suffolk SMSAs

Suffolk County (base)	2,988(1.00)
Alleged redlined areas	5,590(1.87)
Northeast Kings	1,076(0.36)
South Kings	2,002(0.67)
North Bronx	1,706(0.57)
Rest of Queens	2,513(0.84)
New York County (Manhattan)	5,381(1.80)
Richmond (Staten Island)	375(0.13)
Rockland	429(0.14)**
Westchester	1,616(0.54)
Nassau	1,916(0.64)

The estimates are based on 1977–1978 mortgage applications data. The entries in the table represent the predicted downward modification in dollars for an applicant similar to the base application in all ways other than the characteristic listed. Numbers in parentheses represent the ratio of the downward modification for an application with the indicated characteristic to the downward modification for the baseline application. See text for definition of the baseline application. A single asterisk (*) indicates that the numerator of the ratio is statistically significantly different from the denominator at the 5–10 percent level. Two asterisks (**) indicate that the difference is significant at the 5 percent or less level.

from other neighborhoods. The only possible exception to this conclusion is found in the Rochester savings and loan association sample, where a 10 percentage point increase in the percent black population is associated with a $1,299 increase in the average downward modification for a baseline applicant. The coefficient just misses statistical significance at the 10 percent level.

Interest Rate, Maturity, and Loan to Value Ratio

Although the New York data on applications does not contain the information necessary to estimate the terms model discussed in Chapter 4, a similar three-equation simultaneous model can be estimated from census-tract summaries. Unfortunately, this model cannot examine discrimination on the basis of the sex, race, or age of the individual applicants. It can, however, test allegations that lenders redline certain neighborhoods by imposing harsher mortgage terms (that is, higher interest rates, shorter maturities, and lower loan-to-value ratios) on borrowers with properties in these areas than similar borrowers with similar properties in other neighborhoods.

Under New York State Banking Department regulations, state-regulated lenders are required to report the average interest rate, maturity, and loan-to-value ratios of loans granted during their last fiscal year for each census tract within metropolitan areas. The first report covers the fiscal years that coincide approximately with calendar year 1975. Variations in the mortgage terms across census tracts in Bronx, Kings, and Queens counties at one point in time are studied with this data.

The model of the flow of mortgage funds developed in Chapter 3 contains equations for maturity period and loan-to-value ratio. An equation for interest rates can be obtained from the market-clearing constraint. The supply and demand equations are solved for the interest rate, which will be a function of the exogenous variables appearing in both equations. The three simultaneous equations are:

$$MAT = l(INT, LTV, RISK, LOC, OLD, PNW, DPNW) \qquad (8.1)$$

$$LTV = m(INT, MAT, RISK, PHI, PCINC, AVGVAL, LOC, \\ OLD, PNW, DPNW) \qquad (8.2)$$

$$INT = n(MAT, LTV, T, RISK, STOCK, LOC, OLD, PNW, \\ DPNW) \qquad (8.3)$$

The definitions of the variable vectors are given in Table 3.1.

In general, interest rates are expected to increase as risks of loss rise, and the maturity period and loan-to-value ratio are expected to fall when these risks rise. Since borrowers with relatively small amounts of net wealth are likely to demand high loan-to-value ratios, measures of neighborhood income and average property value are included as crude proxies for borrower resources.

Since high loan-to-value ratios and longer maturities represent greater risk of loss, lenders usually charge higher interest rates to compensate. On the other hand, credit rationing operates in periods of rising interest rates and frequently leads lenders to avoid higher loan-to-value ratios and long maturities. All borrowers can be expected to prefer lower interest rates. Consumers' preferences about the other two terms, however, cannot be so simply characterized. Some consumers may prefer higher loan-to-value ratios, others lower ones. Similarly, some consumers may prefer longer maturities, others shorter ones. For example, borrowers who prefer to own their house with a minimum of debt will prefer smaller loan-to-value ratios; borrowers who prefer to maximize the leverage of their own funds will prefer a larger loan-to-value ratio.

Estimates of Equations 8.1 to 8.3 with two-stage least squares are reported in Appendix C for two samples: conventional mortgages on one- to four-family houses and conventional mortgages on multifamily buildings.[5]

One- to Four-Family Mortgages

Only 15–22 percent of the variation in each mortgage term is explained by the model. Although the interest-rate equation has the highest explanation, it is the least satisfactory of the three because the neighborhood attributes, which are included as proxies for the risk of loss, indicate that interest rates decrease as the risk increases. Two neighborhood attributes show a statistically significant (10 percent level) negative relationship with interest rates: an increase in pending housing code violations on one- to four-family houses between 1972 and 1976, and the fraction of multifamily buildings that were vacant in 1969. An increase of 1 standard deviation in the value of these variables above their mean values would decrease the interest rate by 0.12 and 0.06 percentage points, respectively. Although these are small changes—the monthly payments on a twenty-five-year mortgage would decrease by less than 1 percent—the change is inconsistent with strong a priori reasoning that suggests that interest rates should increase as risk rises.

One reason for this inconsistent result is that the usury law restricts the interest rate on most one- to four-family houses. As a result, there is less opportunity to adjust the interest rate to reflect variations in risk. In fact, the interest rate varies much less across census tracts than the maturity and the loan-to-value ratio. Interest rates on multi-family mortgages, which are not covered by the usury law, also vary more than those on one- to four-family mortgages. It is also likely that much of the variation in the interest rates on one- to four-family mortgages is the result of variation in the fraction of this segment of the housing stock that is actually covered by the usury law. Another reason may be that these neighborhood attributes are poor proxies for the risk of loss in lending. There is reason to believe that the housing code variables are a weak proxy because of code enforcement policies that avoid the areas with the worst housing.

The age of housing stock and the racial composition variables are not statistically significantly related to interest rates. The property location variables indicate that Crown Heights has statistically significantly lower interest rates (−1.33 percentage points) and Park Slope has statistically significantly higher interest rates (+0.34 percentage points). Since both neighborhoods are alleged to be redlined and the results are in opposite directions, it is not possible to draw a firm conclusion regarding the hypothesis that redlining occurs through geographic price discrimination. The statistical insignificance and small size of the coefficients for other neighborhoods that are alleged to be redlined (South Bronx, Central Brooklyn, East Flatbush, and Southeast Queens) is further grounds for caution. As in the case of the risk variables, the relatively small variation in the interest-rate variable as a result of the usury law probably also restricts its usefulness as a redlining tactic. Unfortunately, the interest rate is the only one of the three terms that has an unambiguous interpretation. None of the remaining variables in the interest-rate equation show statistically significant (10 percent level) relationships with interest rates.

The neighborhood attributes perform better in the maturity and loan-to-value equations. Although a few of these variables have statistically significant coefficients with signs that disagree with theoretical expectations, most of the statistically significant coefficients indicate behavior consistent with rising risks leading to shorter maturities and lower loan-to-value ratios.

Neighborhoods with larger fractions of old housing stock receive shorter maturity periods for conventional mortgages on one- to four-family houses. The effect is statistically significant at the 5 percent level but relatively small. A neighborhood with 80 percent old housing receives a maturity period that is one year less than a neighborhood with 30 percent old housing. This is a 4.5 percent reduction from the average maturity and only increases the monthly payments by 1.2 percent. It could reflect a higher incidence of older borrowers who select maturity periods to match their retirement plans, neighborhood risks of loss that other variables have inadequately controlled for, or a form of redlining. One cannot separate out these effects with currently available data. In any case, the effect is quite small.

Neighborhoods with increasing nonwhite populations receive statistically significantly longer maturities than do racially stable neighborhoods. If the percentage nonwhite has increased by 50 percentage points between 1970 and 1974, the maturity period is three years longer. The difference in monthly payments between twenty-five and twenty-eight-year mortgages with an 8.5 percent interest rate is 3 percent. Although predominantly nonwhite neighborhoods that are racially stable tend to have shorter maturities than white neighborhoods, the effect is not statistically significant.

Five neighborhoods have statistically significantly shorter maturity periods than the portion of Queens County outside of Southeast Queens: North Bronx, Central Brooklyn, Crown Heights, Northeast Kings, and South Kings. Only two of these are alleged to be redlined: Central Brooklyn and Crown Heights. Although the results for these two neighborhoods are consistent with the redlining allegations, the results for the other allegedly redlined neighborhoods (South Bronx, East Flatbush, Park Slope, and Southeast Queens) are not. Furthermore, North Bronx and South Kings also received shorter maturities, yet they are not alleged to be redlined. On the other hand, the maturity period is 7.0 and 9.8 years shorter in Central Brooklyn and Crown Heights but only 1.7 and 1.1 years shorter in North Bronx and South Kings compared to Queens County outside of Southeast Queens. The differences are considerably larger for the neighborhoods that are alleged to be redlined. Although the results are mixed, they are consistent with allegations of redlining in at least two neighborhoods. Of course, it is important to bear in mind alternative explanations, such as borrower preferences and inadequate control for risk of loss.

Only one other variable (interest rate) has a statistically significant effect on the maturity period. Higher interest rates lead to lower maturities, which is consistent with both being used to compensate for additional risks of loss.

The final equation explains variations in the loan-to-value ratio. As in the maturity equation, the neighborhood attributes have coefficients that are more consistent with the risk-of-loss hypothesis than they are in the interest-rate equation. Four of these attributes have negative coefficients that are statistically significantly different from zero at the 10 percent level. Unfortunately, three other risk variables, which have coefficients that are statistically significantly different than zero at the 5 percent level, indicate that contrary to theoretical expectations, the loan-to-value ratio increases with risk.

The mixed performance for the neighborhood attributes may also be due to the fact that borrower preferences for loan-to-value ratios cannot be uniformly characterized as always favoring either higher or lower ratios. The average value of one- to four-family houses is included in the model to control for some of these preferences. Its coefficient indicates that loan-to-value ratios are slightly lower in census tracts that are wealthier, that is, have higher average sales prices, and is statistically significantly different from zero at the 5 percent level. A $10,000 increase in average sales price leads to only a 1.2 percentage point decrease in the loan-to-value ratio, which would raise the down payment by about 4 percent. Two income variables (per capita income and percent of households with high incomes) are also included to control for borrowers preferences, but the coefficients of both are small and statistically insignificant.

Neighborhoods with larger fractions of old housing stock have higher loan-to-value ratios. An increase of 0.5 in this fraction increases loan-to-value ratios by 2.3 percent, and the down payment required is lowered by approximately 9 percent.[6] This result is inconsistent with allegations that neighborhoods with older housing are redlined. It is nearly statistically significant at the 10 percent level.

Nonwhite neighborhoods receive statistically significantly lower loan-to-value ratios and, as a result, are required to make larger down payments. A neighborhood that is 80 percent nonwhite has a loan-to-value ratio that is 7 percentage points below an otherwise similar neighborhood that is 30 percent nonwhite. This is a substantial increase in the required down payment. On the other hand, racially changing neighborhoods (white to nonwhite) receive higher loan-to-value ratios and have lower down-payment requirements than racially stable neighborhoods. Neighborhoods with a 20 percentage point increase in the percent nonwhite between 1970 and 1974 have loan-to-value ratios that are 4.4 percent higher than racially stable neighborhoods. This effect is also substantial and statistically significant at the 10 percent level.

Large and statistically significant differences in loan-to-value ratios exist between neighborhoods. Central Brooklyn and Crown Heights have loan-to-value ratios that are 29 and 43 percentage points below those in Queens County after controlling for other factors such as risk of loss. Mortgages in the South Bronx also have lower loan-to-value ratios than those in Queens County—4 percentage points lower. All three of these areas are alleged to be redlined. Although mortgages in South Kings, which is not alleged to be redlined, also have lower loan-to-value ratios (6 percentage points) than mortgages in Queens County, the difference is much smaller than in Central Brooklyn and Crown Heights. The results of the analysis of loan-to-value ratios for conventional mortgages on one- to four-family houses are consistent with some of the allegations of redlining. Although borrower preferences may explain some of these differences, it seems unlikely that they would account for differences as large as those present in Central Brooklyn and Crown Heights.

Multifamily Mortgages
Each equation explains a higher percentage (41 to 45) of the variation in its dependent variable (interest rate, maturity, and loan-to-value ratio) than in the case of conventional mortgages on one- to four-family houses. However, the neighborhood attributes still exhibit a mixed pattern; that is, their coefficients cannot be consistently interpreted as indicating that mortgage prices rise along with risks of loss. The variables with statistically significant coefficients in each equation are discussed below.

Several of the variables measuring risk of loss have statistically significant coefficients in the interest-rate equation. Unfortunately, four of these coefficients have signs inconsistent with theoretical expectations, and only two indicate that increased risks of loss lead to higher interest rates.

As in the case of one- to four-family houses, the performance of the risk measures is disappointing. The measures, especially the housing code variables that the city acknowledges overstate housing quality in the worst neighborhoods, may be inadequate for the task.

Three other variables are important in the interest-rate equation. An extra five years lowers the interest rate by 1 percentage point. The relationship is consistent with expectations that high interest rates and shorter maturities should occur together in more risky loans. The magnitude of the effect is smaller than might have been expected. The monthly payments on a fifteen-year mortgage at 8.5 percent interest are 26 percent less than those on a ten-year mortgage of the same interest rate.[7] An interest rate of 8.5 percent would have to be cut in half to achieve the same percentage reduction in monthly payments on a fifteen-year mortgage.

Conventional multifamily mortgages have lower interest rates when the properties are in census tracts with more federally assisted multifamily mortgages. An increase of 1 standard deviation in this stock variable reduces the interest rate by 0.35 percentage points.

Finally, mortgages on properties in neighborhoods alleged to be redlined have interest rates that are 1.04 percentage points lower than those on properties in neighborhoods that are not alleged to be redlined. This is a large variation, but it is inconsistent with the allegation that these neighborhoods are redlined by charging higher interest rates.

In the maturity equation, four neighborhood attributes have coefficients that are statistically significantly different from zero at the 10 percent level. All but one have signs consistent with the hypothesis that maturities should decrease as risk of loss rises.

Neighborhoods with older multifamily housing have longer maturity periods. Although this effect is not statistically significant at the 10 percent level, it is inconsistent with allegations that lenders discriminate against older neighborhoods.

Conventional mortgages on multifamily buildings located in neighborhoods that are alleged to be redlined receive substantially shorter maturity periods—5.7 years shorter. This is a large and statistically significant modification in maturity. It increases the monthly payments by 22.6 percent on a mortgage with an 8.5 percent interest rate and is consistent with allegations that these neighborhoods are redlined by providing mortgages with less favorable terms (that is, shorter maturities) than in other locations having equal risk of loss. Unfortunately the mixed performance of the risk measures weakens one's confidence in this result.

Summary

The evidence from the analysis of downward modifications does not support the hypothesis that banks in New York State make widespread use of excessive loan reduction as a technique for discriminating against certain types of applications. On the other hand, the evidence supports the view that banks in the New York-Nassau-Suffolk area use this method to discriminate in some instances. The strongest finding is that commercial banks and savings and loan associations appear to discriminate against applicants over forty-five. When combined with the finding that the commercial banks also treat applications from female-only households with no woman of childbearing age adversely, this finding has particularly strong implications for the treatment of older women. Evidence of adverse treatment of separated applicants was found in the mutual savings bank sample. Although no discriminatory behavior based on the race of the applicant was discovered, the results weakly suggest that excessive modifications may occur for applicants purchasing properties in areas alleged to be redlined.

This chapter also tests the hypothesis that mortgage lenders subtly discriminate against borrowers in particular neighborhoods by requiring harsher terms (that is, higher interest rates, shorter maturities, lower loan-to-value ratios) in those neighborhoods than in otherwise similar neighborhoods. Because borrowers and lenders have preferences about each of the terms of the mortgage, and because all three terms are jointly determined in each mortgage transaction, this chapter uses a system of simultaneous equations to analyze the process by which all three terms are determined. We used data on the average terms on new mortgages in census tracts in Bronx, Kings, and Queens counties for 1975.

Higher risks of loss should lead lenders to impose harsher terms. Unfortunately, many of the measures of risk yield coefficients that directly contradict this hypothesis and are statistically significant. As a result, one cannot rule out the possibility that differences detected among neighborhoods in any of the terms may partially reflect differences in risk of loss that were not adequately controlled for by the measures of risk that were available.

In the models estimated using the census-tract data on mortgage terms, the age-of-housing-stock and racial-composition variables never make a statistically significant contribution to the interest-rate equations, and yield signs inconsistent with the discrimination hypothesis half the time. In the maturity and loan-to-value equations, these same variables are statistically significant factors in only one-third of the cases. Half of these instances are consistent with the discrimination hypotheses, and the other half are inconsistent with such hypotheses.

The coefficients on the neighborhood dummy variables in the interest-rate equations are statistically significant in only three of the twelve possible cases, and two of these significant coefficients contradict any discrimination hypothesis. In the maturity and loan-to-value equations, eleven of twenty-four coefficients are statistically significant. Five of these are coefficients for areas alleged to be redlined and have signs consistent with these allegations, while the remaining six are coefficients for areas not alleged to be redlined but have signs consistent with the hypothesis that they are redlined. In short, the pattern of empirical results on the variables whose purpose is to test redlining allegations is neither fully consistent with those allegations nor completely inconsistent with them. Although these results alone are inconclusive, the large differentials in terms between allegedly redlined and other neighborhoods in some cases (for example, higher interest rates in Park Slope, shorter maturities and lower loan-to-value ratios in Central Brooklyn and Crown Heights) cannot be entirely ignored.

Only three coefficients are statistically significant at the 10 percent level in the loan-to-value equation: pending housing-code violations per building for one- to four-family houses in 1972; the fraction of one- to four-family houses with more housing-code violations in 1976 than 1972; and the neighborhood variable for Northeast Kings. The two risk variables have substantial but opposing effects of approximately the same magnitude. One reason for the inconsistency in their relationship to loan-to-value ratios may be the tendency for the housing code data to overstate housing quality in neighborhoods with a high incidence of the poorest housing conditions.

Loan-to-value ratios are substantially lower (16 percentage points) in Northeast Kings than in other parts of the Bronx, Kings, and Queens counties. This area is not alleged to be redlined because it contains neighborhoods subject to such high risks of loss that persons and groups interviewed in the course of this study believed mortgage lenders could not be reasonably expected to make loans on the same terms as in other neighborhoods. The result is consistent with this characterization.

9
Appraisal Practices

When a mortgage is applied for on a particular property, the lending institution has an authorized person estimate the value of, or appraise, the property. The maximum loan amount that a lender will offer an applicant depends on the appraised value of the property, the lender's policies, and the regulatory restrictions on loan-to-value ratios. The applicant must provide the difference between the purchase price and the loan amount either from his or her own resources or from secondary sources of financing.

Some neighborhood organizations have alleged that properties in certain neighborhoods are systematically underappraised relative to their market value. If banks were underappraising properties in some neighborhoods relative to other neighborhoods, borrowers would have to make larger down payments on houses located in these underappraised neighborhoods. In some instances, the larger down payment requirements could prevent people from purchasing properties in these areas.

The proper test of discrimination is not whether appraised values are lower than market values, but whether the ratio of appraised value to market value varies systematically across locations. If appraisals reflected actual market conditions, the ratio of appraised value to market value would be one and should, on average, show no relationship to any particular variable. Therefore, it is important to ascertain the reasons, if any, for which appraised values may differ from market values.

Appraised values may systematically differ from market values for any of three reasons. First, appraisers may underappraise properties because the consequences of underestimating the value of a property are more acceptable to them than those of overestimating the value. An overestimation increases the chances of actual losses if the borrower defaults on the loan; underestimation decreases those chances.

Second, lenders face uncertainty that purchasers do not. Purchasers, as property owners, will make decisions on, for example, maintenance that affect the future market value of the property. This is a source of uncertainty for lenders because they have no control over these decisions. To compensate for this uncertainty, appraisers might value properties lower than their market values. Third, lenders may use a longer time horizon than the market when predicting events that might affect the future value of the property, which is a security for their long-term investment. These reasons would lead to appraised values being somewhat lower than market values.

Externalities such as the conditions of surrounding properties and the neighborhood affect the market value of any given property and are reflected in uncertainty factors that might lead an appraiser to view a property more conservatively than the market. These externalities should be spatially clustered. For example, building abandonment is more likely to occur in a specific area than in randomly distributed areas across the city. An increase in the number of abandoned buildings in an area may signal a future substantial drop in property values. Appraisers might give more weight to this trend than the market because they have a longer time horizon. One result would be a spatial variation in the appraised-value-to-market-value ratio.

Purchase prices are used to measure market value. Although the appraised value may differ from the purchase price in individual cases because of variations in the relative bargaining skills of buyers and sellers, these effects should average out in a large sample.

Appraisal practices in California and New York are analyzed. The California data are from the state's Loan Register of all mortgage applications at state savings and loan associations. The New York data are from the MIT–Harvard Joint Center for Urban Studies' Mortgage Loan Survey (MLS) of the mortgage portfolio of mutual savings banks. The California data have the advantage of including denied as well as approved applications and detailed information on the race and sex of the applicant that is not available for the New York MLS data. As a result, the New York analysis may underestimate discrimination through appraisal practices. If certain neighborhoods are systematically underappraised relative to other locations, however, data from loans actually granted and accepted in these areas should still reflect such appraisal practices.

Both the California and New York models of the appraisal process include variables related to uncertainty about future market values.

The California models include property characteristics (structure type and building age), neighborhood characteristics (percent high income, income level, and change in income and households in the recent past), and a set of binary variables representing the purchase price range of the property. These variables control for factors that legitimately might lead to appraised values that differ systematically from purchase prices because lenders recognize different risks or are more risk averse than the market. For example, lenders may undervalue condominiums because insufficient experience with such units leaves them uncertain about the strength of the future resale market. In addition, concern about the effects on housing values of neighborhood externalities may cause lenders to appraise properties in neighborhoods with potentially adverse externalities lower than the market. The purchase price ranges are included because appraisers may be unable to track price trends with equal accuracy for all price ranges in a rapidly changing real estate market.

The New York models include the age of the building, construction material, type of loan (FHA, VA, or conventional), type of structure, and the year of the loan as control variables. The year is included because the New York data cover a twenty-eight-year period (1950–1977), whereas the California models are estimated on data covering only a one-year interval. Unfortunately, measures of neighborhood conditions such as those employed in California are not available throughout the twenty-eight-year period.

The following variables are included to test allegations of discriminatory appraisal practices: age of the surrounding neighborhood, property location, racial composition of the neighborhood, and in California the age, race, and sex of the applicant.

Table 9.1 illustrates the relationship between the appraised-value-to-purchase-price ratio and the down-payment requirements. For example, the down payment would increase by 40 percent on an 80 percent loan-to-value-ratio mortgage when the property was underappraised by 10 percent (−0.100). The table helps to clarify the coefficients of the estimated models.

California Results

The models have been estimated with ordinary least squares in four California metropolitan areas (Fresno, Los Angeles-Long Beach, San Francisco-Oakland, and San Jose) in 1977 and 1978. Although the

Table 9.1
Relationship between the appraised-value-to-purchase-price ratio and down-payment requirements

Change in Appraised-Value-to-Purchase-Price Ratio	% Change in Loan Amount Granted	% Change in Down-Payment Requirements		
		70% Loan-to-Value Ratio	80% Loan-to-Value Ratio	90% Loan-to-Value Ratio
−0.001	−0.1	0.2	0.4	0.9
−0.010	−1.0	2.3	4.0	9.0
−0.100	−10.0	23.3	40.0	90.0
−0.200	−20.0	46.6	80.0	180.0

equations estimate apprasied-value-to-purchase-price ratios, we present the results here in terms of their impact on the down-payment requirement (see Appendix A for the definition of variable acronyms and Appendix B for the full equations).

Tables 9.2 and 9.3 summarize the results in terms of the percentage change in the down-payment requirements for a loan-to-appraised-value ratio of 80 percent. The asterisks indicate the statistical significance of the corresponding coefficient in the estimated equation. One asterisk indicates significance between the 5 and ten percent level and to indicate significance at the five percent or less level.

In general, the appraised value-to-purchase-price ratio varies substantially only with purchase price and building age. Higher-priced houses are systematically underappraised relative to houses priced below $30,001. Inspection of the last row in each table, which shows the appraised-value-to-purchase-price ratio for the equation's reference point, indicates that houses under $30,001 are overappraised. The amount of this overappraisal determines the general magnitude of the percentage changes in down payment; compare the parenthetical figures in the last row to those for the purchase price variables in the corresponding column. The percentage changes in downpayment show a distinct and regular pattern of increasing down payments as purchase price rises.

The building-age variables show that older buildings (at least one year old in 1977 and at least two years old in 1978) are systematically underappraised and show relatively small variations with building age beyond one year. Although there is a slight upward trend in down payment as building age rises above one year, it is not as pronounced as the purchase price relationship.

Table 9.2
Relationship between appraisal practices and down-payment requirements in four
California metropolitan areas, 1977

Variables	% Increase in Down Payment on an 80% Loan			
	Fresno	Los Angeles-Long Beach	San Francisco-Oakland	San Jose
Structure type				
CONDO	−3.6*	0.4	1.6**	0.4
Purchase price (relative to under $30,001)				
P30–50	6.8**	9.2**	5.2**	6.4**
P50–75	10.0**	12.8**	8.8**	12.4**
P75–100	12.8**	14.4**	11.2**	14.8**
P100–125	9.2**	15.6**	14.0**	18.0**
PGT125	18.8**	18.4**	17.2**	22.0**
Neighborhood characteristics[a]				
FHI (+0.20)	−0.3	−1.1**	−1.0**	−0.9**
INC1976 (+3.0)	−2.4	−0.1	−1.2**	1.2**
DINC7675 (+0.2)	2.0**	−0.0	0.1	−0.8**
DINC7570 (+0.9)	1.1	−0.4**	−0.0	0.4
DHH7675 (+1.0)	−0.2	−0.0	−0.8**	−0.8**
DHH7570 (+5.0)	−2.0**	0.0	0.2**	0.4
FVACANTSJ (+0.03)	—	—	—	0.1
Age of neighborhood[a]				
PRE1940 (+0.20)	−1.4**	−0.6**	0.6**	−1.0**
Building age relative to new buildings				
BA1–9	5.2**	2.4**	3.2**	10.0**
BA10–19	6.8**	2.4**	3.2**	9.2**
BA20–29	7.6**	2.4**	4.0**	9.2**
BA30–39	12.0**	3.2**	4.4**	10.0**
BA40–49	12.4**	3.2**	4.0**	11.6**
BAGE50	8.4**	6.0**	4.8**	16.0**
Age of applicant relative to 35–44 years				
ALT25	−0.8	0.4	−0.4	1.2
A25TO34	0.4	0.1	−0.1	0.8
A45TO54	0.4	0.1	1.2**	0.8
AGE55	1.2	0.4	0.8**	2.0**

Table 9.2 (cont.)

Variables	% Increase in Down Payment on an 80% Loan			
	Fresno	Los Angeles-Long Beach	San Francisco-Oakland	San Jose
Sex of applicant relative to MFNCB				
FONLYCB25–34	2.0	1.3**	1.1**	1.2
FONLYNCB	6.4**	0.8*	1.2**	2.4**
MFCB25–34	−0.4	−0.0	0.3	0.4
MONLY	1.2	−0.4**	0.1	−0.1
Race of applicant relative to white				
BLACK	−1.6	−0.1	−0.1	1.2
SPANISH	1.6	0.8**	−0.8*	0.8
ASIAN	3.2	0.4*	0.1	0.4
OMIN	1.2	0.4	0.1	−0.1
Racial composition of neighborhood[a]				
FBLACK (+0.1)	−4.2**	−0.1	−0.04	0.3
FSPANISH (+0.1)	0.6	0.4**	0.2	1.2**
FASIAN (+0.03)[b]	0.7*	−0.04	−0.3**	1.3'
Property location[c] relative to:	Suburbs	Suburbs	San Mateo	Suburbs
City of Fresno	0.8	—	—	—
Compton (AR)	—	−4.4	—	—
Covina-Azusa-West Covina (AR)	—	0.1	—	—
East L.A.-Boyle Heights-Echo Park (AR)	—	4.0**	—	—
Highland Park (AR)	—	0.8	—	—
Long Beach-Southwest (AR)	—	1.6	—	—
Pacoima-San Fernando (AR)	—	−0.0	—	—
Pasadena-North Central (AR)	—	−0.8	—	—
Pomona (AR)	—	3.2**	—	—
San Pedro (AR)	—	0.8	—	—
South Central L.A. (AR)	—	−0.1	—	—
Venice-Santa Monica (AR)	—	1.2	—	—

Table 9.2 (cont.)

| | % Increase in Down Payment on an 80% Loan | | | |
Variables	Fresno	Los Angeles-Long Beach	San Francisco-Oakland	San Jose
Rest of the City of Long Beach	—	−1.2**	—	—
Rest of the City of Los Angeles	—	−0.8**	—	—
Alameda County				
Alameda City	—	—	3.6**	—
Berkeley	—	—	2.4**	—
Central Oakland (AR)	—	—	4.4**	—
East Oakland	—	—	2.4**	—
West Oakland	—	—	2.0**	—
Rest of Alameda County	—	—	2.4**	—
Contra Costa County	—	—	0.8**	—
Marin County	—	—	0.4	—
San Francisco	—	—	−0.4	—
City of San Jose	—	—	—	−0.8*
Appraised value to purchase price for reference point constant from equation[d]	1.050 (−20.0)	1.034 (−13.6)	1.013 (−5.2)	1.065 (−26.0)

One asterisk (*) indicates that the appropriate coefficient is statistically significant at between the 5 and 10 percent level. Two asterisks (**) indicate that the appropriate coefficient is statistically significant at the 5 percent level or less. These are 2-tail tests. See Appendix A for explanation of the acronyms.

a. These are continuous variables and the numbers in parentheses after the variable name are the changes in value used to calculate the impact on down payment. These changes are approximately equal to the standard deviations of each variable.

b. The standard deviation for the Fresno SMSA is one-tenth that in the other SMSAs, and this smaller value has been used for Fresno.

c. An "AR" after a property location indicates the neighborhood has been alleged to be redlined.

d. These ratios apply to an application on a building that is new and neither a condominium nor cooperative with a purchase price under $30,001 located in a suburban neighborhood that has zero values of all the continuous variables and the applicants are a male-female couple with a woman beyond childbearing age who is 35–44 years old and white. The numbers in parentheses are the percentage change in down payment resulting from the overappraisal or underappraisal of the building.

Table 9.3
Relationship between appraisal practices and down-payment requirements in four California metropolitan areas, 1978

	% Increase in Down Payment on an 80% Loan			
	Fresno	Los Angeles-Long Beach	San Francisco-Oakland	San Jose
Structure type				
CONDO	4.4*	1.2**	2.0**	3.2**
Purchase price relative to under $30,001				
P30–50	17.6**	14.8**	9.6**	79.6**
P50–75	23.6**	19.2**	15.2**	86.8**
P75–100	32.4**	21.6**	18.4**	88.0**
P100–125	34.4**	22.8**	20.4**	90.8**
PGT125	39.2**	25.2**	24.0**	94.0**
Neighborhood characteristics[a]				
FHI (+0.2)	−0.7	−1.3**	−1.4**	−1.0**
INC1976 (+3.0)	2.4	−0.2	−0.2	1.2**
DINC7675 (+0.2)	−1.8	−0.1	−0.2*	−0.2
DINC7570 (+0.9)	1.8	−0.2*	0.0	0.0
DHH7675 (+1.0)	2.8**	−0.1**	0.0	0.4
DHH7570 (+5.0)	−6.0**	−0.0	−0.1	0.0
FVACANTSJ (+0.03)	—	—	—	−0.2
Age of neighborhood[a]				
PRE1940 (+0.20)	−1.4**	−0.6**	−0.2	−0.1
Building age relative to new and 1-year-old buildings				
BA2–10	13.2**	1.2**	2.4**	2.4**
BA11–20	13.6**	1.2**	2.0**	2.8**
BA21–30	14.4**	2.0**	3.6**	4.0**
BA31–40	14.8**	2.0**	3.2**	6.0**
BA41–50	15.2**	3.6**	4.4**	7.6**
BAGE51	24.8**	5.6**	3.6**	6.8**
Age of applicant relative to 35–44 years				
ALT25	−0.4	0.8*	0.8*	−1.2
A25TO34	2.0	0.4	0.4**	−0.4
A45TO54	1.2	0.8**	0.8**	−0.4
AGE55	−0.8	0.4	0.8*	0.4

Table 9.3 (cont.)

	% Increase in Down Payment on an 80% Loan			
	Fresno	Los Angeles-Long Beach	San Francisco-Oakland	San Jose
Sex of applicant relative to MFNCB				
FONLYCB25–34	5.2	0.8	2.0**	−2.4**
FONLYNCB	0.4	0.8**	0.8*	2.0**
MFCB25–34	2.8	0.4	−0.0	−0.8
MONLY	2.0	−0.0	−0.4	−0.4
Race of applicant relative to white				
BLACK	−2.8	−0.1	0.8	1.6
SPANISH	3.6**	1.6**	0.8**	0.2
ASIAN	1.6	0.8**	0.8**	−0.4
OMIN	1.2	0.4	−0.4	−1.2
Racial composition of neighborhood[n]				
FBLACK (+0.1)	−5.8**	0.0	0.2*	0.2
FSPANISH (+0.1)	0.4	0.6**	0.4**	0.9**
FASIAN (+0.03)[b]	2.1**	−0.1	−0.2**	0.3
Property location[c] relative to:	Suburbs	Suburbs	San Mateo	Suburbs
City of Fresno	2.8**	—	—	—
Compton (AR)	—	5.6*	—	—
Covina-Azusa-West Covina (AR)	—	−0.8	—	—
East L.A.-Boyle Heights-Echo Park (AR)	—	6.4**	—	—
Highland Park (AR)	—	5.2**	—	—
Long Beach-Southwest (AR)	—	0.4	—	—
Pacoima-San Fernando (AR)	—	1.6*	—	—
Pasadena-North Central (AR)	—	−1.6	—	—
Pomona (AR)	—	6.8**	—	—
San Pedro (AR)	—	2.8*	—	—
South Central L.A. (AR)	—	3.2**	—	—

Table 9.3 (cont.)

	% Increase in Down Payment on an 80% Loan			
	Fresno	Los Angeles-Long Beach	San Francisco-Oakland	San Jose
Venice-Santa Monica (AR)	—	−4.0**	—	—
Rest of the City of Long Beach	—	−0.8	—	—
Rest of the City of Los Angeles	—	−0.8**	—	—
Alameda County				
Alameda City	—	—	1.6	—
Berkeley	—	—	0.8	—
Central Oakland (AR)	—	—	4.8**	—
East Oakland	—	—	2.4**	—
West Oakland	—	—	6.0**	—
Rest of Alameda County	—	—	1.2**	—
Contra Costa County	—	—	2.0**	—
Marin County	—	—	1.2**	—
San Francisco	—	—	−1.2**	—
City of San Jose	—	—	—	−0.4
Appraised value to purchase price for reference point, constant from equation[d]	1.136 (−54.4)	1.052 (−20.8)	1.043 (−17.2)	1.236 (−94.4)

One asterisk (*) indicates that the appropriate coefficient is statistically significant at between the 5 and 10 percent level. Two asterisks (**) indicate that the appropriate coefficient is statistically significant at the 5 percent level or less. These are 2-tail tests. See appendix A for explanation of the acronyms.

a. These are continuous variables and the numbers in parentheses after the variable name are the changes in value used to calculate the impact on down payment. These changes are approximately equal to the standard deviations of each variable.

b. The standard deviation for the Fresno SMSA is one-tenth that in the other SMSAs, and this smaller value has been used for Fresno.

c. An "AR" after a property location indicates the neighborhood has been alleged to be redlined.

d. These ratios apply to an application on a building that is new and neither a condominium nor cooperative with a purchase price under $30,001 located in a suburban neighborhood that has zero values of all the continuous variables and the applicants are a male-female couple with a woman beyond childbearing age who is 35–44 years old and white. The numbers in parentheses are the percentage change in down payment resulting from the overappraisal or underappraisal of the building.

With one exception (1977 Fresno), condominiums and cooperative dwelling units are systematically underappraised. As a result, down payments on these units are 0.4 to 4.4 percent higher than down payments on otherwise similar single-family dwellings.

Appraisal practices do not vary greatly with the neighborhood characteristics. Most of these variables have the expected negative relationship with the appraised-value-to-purchase-price ratio. DINC7570 is the only substantial deviant, but its positive values are close to zero and statistically insignificant at the 10 percent level. Although a little less than half the neighborhood coefficients are statistically significant, all but one imply down-payment changes with magnitudes below 2.5 percent. The exception is DHH7570 for 1978 Fresno (−6.0 percent). A 2 percent change in down payment on a $100,000 house with a loan-to-appraised-value ratio of 80 percent is $400. Nearly two-thirds of the changes in down payment, which are based on standard deviations in the samples, are under 1.0 percent (less than $200 for the $100,000 house).

Sex

Male-female applicants with a woman of childbearing age (MFCB) and male-only applicants (MONLY) receive approximately the same treatment in the appraisal process as male-female applicants where the woman is not of childbearing age (MFNCB). Only one of these sixteen coefficients is statistically significant (1977 Los Angeles-Long Beach), and it (MONLY) is so small in magnitude that down payment increases by only 0.4 percent, or $40 on a $100,000 house.

The evidence, however, does indicate that the properties of female-only applicants not of childbearing age (FONLYNCB) are systematically underappraised. All of its coefficients are positive and all but one are statistically significant at the 5 to 10 percent level. Although most of them are relatively small in magnitude, one is quite large (1977 Fresno) and results in a 6.4 percent increase in the down payment with an 80 percent loan-to-appraised-value ratio. On a $100,000 house, this would be $1,280. The other coefficients lead to a 0.8 to 2.4 percent increase in down payment.

Female-only applicants with someone of childbearing age (FONLY-CB25–34) face statistically significant underappraisal in three cases: 1977 Los Angeles-Long Beach, and 1977 and 1978 San Francisco-Oakland. However, they face significant overappraisals on San Jose properties in 1978. The changes in down payment are between a 2.0 percent decrease and a 1.6 percent increase.

It is also important to assess the impact of such differentials on the probability of denial. One approach is to assume a constant down payment and to adjust the requested loan-to-appraised-value ratio. In this way, a 2.5 percent underappraisal, which would have increased down payment by 10 percent, translates into a requested loan-to-appraised-value ratio of 82.05 instead of 80 percent. As a result, the chances of denial would rise. Using results from the lender-decision models (Chapter 5), a 2.05 percentage point increase in the requested loan-to-appraised-value ratio would lead to a denial ratio that is 1.13 times that of the typical applicant in the Los Angeles-Long Beach area. None of the sex or other discrimination variables produce changes in down payment as large as 10 percent; the largest is 6.4 percent, which would increase the requested loan-to-value ratio by 1.3 percentage points and lead to a denial ratio of 1.08 in the Los Angeles-Long Beach metropolitan area. The 2 percent increases in down payment that are more common for the discrimination variables in Tables 9.2 and 9.3 would increase the requested ratio by only 0.4 percentage points and lead to a denial ratio of 1.02 in the same metropolitan area, indeed a small effect on the chance of denial.

Race

Appraised-value-to-purchase-price ratios for black applicants are not significantly different from those for similarly situated white applicants.

The properties of Spanish applicants, however, tend to be systematically underappraised relative to those of similar white applicants. The largest differential, a 3.6 percent increase in the down payment, occurs in the Fresno metropolitan area in 1978. The other differentials are smaller. In the San Francisco-Oakland metropolitan area, the evidence is consistent with systematic underapprisal in 1978 but inconsistent in 1977; both coefficients are statistically significant at the 10 percent level and approximately equal in magnitude.

The results for Asian applicants parallel those for Spanish applicants, but the coefficients are smaller and fewer of them are statistically significant.

There is no support for the proposition that the properties of other minorities are either systematically overappraised or underappraised relative to those of similar white applicants.

Age of Applicant
Although a few of the age coefficients are statistically significant, their magnitudes are small and no pattern of age related underappraisal or overappraisal is evident.

Redlining
Allegations that specific neighborhoods are redlined were available to use for the Los Angeles-Long Beach and San Francisco-Oakland, but not the Fresno and San Jose, metropolitan areas. The Los Angeles-Long Beach allegations are based on a report reviewing the entire metropolitan area; those for the San Francisco–Oakland area are based on a study restricted to the City of Oakland.[1]

The results for both years are consistent with these allegations in four cases: East Los Angeles-Boyle Heights-Echo Park, Highland Park, Pomona, and Central Oakland. Systematic underappraisal of properties in these neighborhoods increases down payments by 3.2 to 6.8 percent.

Properties in older neighborhoods are systematically overappraised, which results in slightly lower down payments. Although nearly all of the coefficients are statistically significant, their magnitudes are small.

The racial composition of the neighborhood affects appraisal practices in both directions. Although a 10 percentage point increase in the fraction of the population that is Spanish leads to underappraisal and slight (0.4 to 1.2 percent) increases in down-payment, the same increase in the fraction that is black leads to overappraisal and as much as a 5.8 percent reduction in down payment. The effect of changes in the fraction that is Asian are small except in Fresno where there is very little variation in this variable.

New York Results

Appraisal models have been estimated for five metropolitan areas in New York: Albany-Schenectady-Troy, Buffalo, New York-Nassau-Suffolk, Rochester, and Syracuse. The equations are presented in Appendix C. The following discussion reviews these results with a focus on the aspects most relevant to discrimination. Tables 9.4 to 9.8 illustrate the estimated effect of each variable on the down payment required to purchase a house when the mortgage is 80 percent of the value. The magnitude of each effect varies with the loan-to-value ratio,

Table 9.4
Relationship between appraisal practices and down-payment requirements for 1- to 4-family houses in the Albany-Schenectady-Troy SMSA

Variable from Appraised-Value-to-Purchase-Price Model	% Increase in Down Payment on an 80% Loan
Age of housing stock	
(increase by 1 standard deviation equal to 27.1 percentage points)	0.00
Age of building relative to new construction (years)	
1–9	2.06
10–19	3.58
20–29	6.87
30–39	−1.50
40–49	2.05
≥50	3.56
Construction material relative to nonwood	
Wood	3.64
Structure type relative to 2- to 4-unit buildings	
Single-family house	4.36
Type of loan relative to conventional	
FHA	−4.96
VA	1.92
Property location[a]	
City of Albany	
Arbor Hill and Hudson-Park (AR)	−9.82
West Hill (AR)	−9.00
South End (AR)	[b]
Rest of City of Albany	5.38
Albany County outside City of Albany	1.50
City of Schenectady	
Central State Street (AR)	4.42
Hamilton Hill (AR)	−2.18
Rest of City of Schenectady	−4.83

Table 9.4 (cont.)

Variable from Appraised-Value-to-Purchase-Price Model	% Increase in Down Payment on an 80% Loan
Schenectady County outside City of Schenectady	7.68
City of Troy	
Hillside and North Central (AR)	−1.72
Central South (AR)	b
Rest of City of Troy	−4.68
Rensselaer County outside City of Troy	−0.99
Montgomery County	b

None of the coefficients in this equation are significant at the 10 percent level or less.
a. The location coefficients measure the average percentage difference in the down payment on an 80 percent loan between properties located in the area specified and those located in Saratoga County. The "AR" in parentheses after some of the neighborhoods indicates that those are alleged to be redlined.
b. No observations reported.

Table 9.5
Relationship between appraisal practices and down-payment requirements for 1- to 4-family houses in the Buffalo SMSA

Variable from Appraised-Value-to-Purchase-Price Model	% Increase in Down Payment on an 80% Loan
Age of housing stock	
(increase by 1 standard deviation equal to 33.7 percentage points)	−0.27
Age of building relative to new construction (years)	
1–9	4.14
10–19	7.76
20–29	3.66
30–39	0.68
40–49	10.03
≥50 years	9.26
Construction material relative to nonwood	
Wood	6.46

Table 9.5 (cont.)

Variable from Appraised-Value-to-Purchase-Price Model	% Increase in Down Payment on an 80% Loan
Structure type relative to 2- to 4-unit buildings	
Single-family house	−4.36
Type of loan relative to conventional	
FHA	−3.83
VA	0.32
Property location[a]	
City of Buffalo	
Black Rock and West Side (AR)	−0.76
Broadway and Shiller	−8.21
Center City and Industrial (AR)	−17.15**
East Elmwood and North Buffalo	1.68
Fillmore-Leroy (AR)	−10.96
South Buffalo	−5.24
University	−7.16
West Elmwood (AR)	0.24
City of Lackawanna	−31.42**
City of Niagara Falls	0.89
Niagara County outside City of Niagara Falls	−0.04

A single asterisk (*) indicates that the appropriate coefficient is significant at between the 5 and 10 percent levels. Two asterisks (**) indicate that the appropriate coefficient is significant at the 5 percent level or less.

a. The location coefficients measure the average percentage difference in the down payment on an 80% loan between properties located in the area specified and those located in Erie County outside the cities of Buffalo and Lackawanna. The "AR" in parentheses after some of the neighborhoods indicates that these are alleged to be redlined.

Table 9.6
Relationship between appraisal practices and down-payment requirements for 1- to 4-family houses in Bronx, Kings, Nassau, Queens, Suffolk, and Westchester counties

Variable from Appraised-Value-to-Purchase-Price Model	% Increase in Down Payment on an 80% Loan
Age of housing stock	
(increase by 1 standard deviation equal to 28.8 percentage points)	0.81
Age of building relative to new construction (years)	
1–9	3.08
10–19	6.08*
20–29	10.61**
30–39	2.97
40–49	4.67
≥50	−4.54
Construction material relative to nonwood	
Wood	−3.21
Structure type relative to 2- to 4-unit buildings	
Single family house	−6.44*
Type of loan relative to conventional	
FHA	3.80
VA	1.77
Property location relative to Suffolk County[a]	
Allegedly redlined areas	
South Bronx	7.15
Northwest Kings	21.17**
Southeast Queens	1.25
Other areas	
North Bronx	22.88**
Northeast Kings	11.53*

Table 9.6 (cont.)

Variable from Appraised-Value-to-Purchase-Price Model	% Increase in Down Payment on an 80% Loan
South Kings	17.96**
Nassau	−7.12
Rest of Queens	7.95**
Westchester	13.04**

One asterisk (*) indicates that the appropriate coefficient is significant at the 5–10 percent level. Two asterisks (**) indicate that the appropriate coefficient is significant at the 5 percent level or less.

a. South Bronx contains all the census tracts south of Fordham Road and Pelham Parkway. Northwest Kings consists of Boerum Hill, Brooklyn Heights, Carroll Gardens, Clinton Hill, Cobble Hill, Crown Heights, Downtown Brooklyn, East Flatbush, Fort Greene, Gowanus, and Park Slope properties. Southeast Queens contains Brookville, Cambria Heights, Laurelton, and Rosedale properties. In addition, loans made in Northeast Kings have been separated because the housing market is substantially different in these neighborhoods. Northeast Kings contains Bedford-Stuyvesant, Brownsville, Bushwick, East New York, Greenpoint, and Williamsburg properties.

Table 9.7
Relationship between appraisal practices and down-payment requirements for 1- to 4-family houses in the Rochester SMSA

Variable from Appraised-Value-to-Purchase-Price Model	% Increase in Down Payment on an 80% Loan
Age of housing stock	
(increase by 1 standard deviation equal to 34.5 percentage points)	0.14
Age of building relative to new construction (years)	
1–9	−8.23*
10–19	0.59
21–29	−9.02
30–39	0.06
40–49	−10.64
≥50	−20.11**
Construction material relative to nonwood	
Wood	−5.77
Structure type relative to 2- to 4-unit buildings	
Single-family house	−5.11

Table 9.7 (cont.)

Variable from Appraised-Value-to-Purchase-Price Model	% Increase in Down Payment on an 80% Loan
Type of loan relative to conventional	
FHA	−2.70
VA	−7.20
Property location[a]	
Dutchtown (AR)	14.92
Edgerton/Brown Square, Cornhill, Park/Oxford, South Wedge/Swillburg, rest of the primary target area	9.26
Zip code area 14621 (AR)	10.35
16th Ward area (AR)	18.00*
Ward 19	13.01
Rest of the City of Rochester	13.58**

One asterisk (*) indicates that the appropriate coefficient is significant at the 5–10 percent level. Two asterisks (**) indicate that the appropriate coefficient is significant at the 5 percent level or less.

a. The location coefficients measure the average percentage difference in the down payment on an 80 percent loan between properties located in the area specified and those located outside the City of Rochester but within the Rochester SMSA. The "AR" in parentheses after some of the neighborhoods indicates that these are alleged to be redlined.

Table 9.8
Relationship between appraisal practices and down-payment requirements for 1- to 4-family houses in the Syracuse SMSA

Variable from Appraised-Value-to-Purchase-Price Model	% Increase in Down Payment on an 80% Loan
Age of housing stock	
(increase by 1 standard deviation equal to 27.7 percentage points)	−1.00
Age of building relative to new construction (years)	
1–9	−6.68
10–19	−2.50

Table 9.8 (cont.)

Variable from Appraised-Value-to-Purchase-Price Model	% Increase in Down Payment on an 80% Loan
20–29	5.52
30–39	3.71
40–49	−3.21
≥50	−12.85
Construction material relative to nonwood	
Wood	−8.51
Structure type relative to 2- to 4-unit buildings	
Single-family house	4.18
Type of loan relative to conventional	
FHA	5.19
VA	3.26
Property location[a]	
City of Syracuse	
Brighton and part of Near Northeast (AR)	−1.46
North Side and Far West Side	1.48
Salt Spring and part of Near Northeast	−5.23
Strathmore	−2.07
Syracuse Southwest	1.85
Rest of the City of Syracuse	−3.52
Oswego County	−14.43**
Madison County	11.63

A single asterisk (*) indicates that the appropriate coefficient is significant at between the 5 and 10 percent levels. Two asterisks (**) indicate that the appropriate coefficient is significant at the 5 percent level or less.

a. The location coefficients measure the average percentage difference in the down payment on an 80 percent loan between properties located in the area specified and those located within Onondaga County but outside the city of Syracuse. The "AR" in parentheses after some of the neighborhoods indicates that these are alleged to be redlined.

and the reader can examine these variations with the help of Table 9.1.

In general, there is little evidence that New York appraisal practices vary with factors alleged to be criteria for redlining neighborhoods. If an area were redlined through the appraisal process, its properties would have to be systematically underappraised relative to other areas, which would result in higher down payments. Property appraisals in older neighborhoods are virtually identical to those of similar properties in newer neighborhoods in all five metropolitan areas. The results are similar for construction material and type of loan.

The age of the building does not have a significant effect on appraised values in three of the areas (Albany-Schenectady-Troy, Buffalo, and Syracuse). In the Rochester area, 1- to 9-year-old and over fifty-year-old buildings are significantly overappraised and, as a result, have 8 and 20 percent lower down-payment requirements than new buildings. The only significant underappraisal with respect to building age occurs in the New York-Nassau-Suffolk area; 10- to 29-year-old buildings have 6 to 10 percent higher down payments than newly constructed buildings.

Single-family houses are significantly overappraised in the New York-Nassau-Suffolk area, leading to a 6 percent decrease in the down-payment requirement relative to multiunit buildings. There is no significant relationship in any of the other four metropolitan areas.

Appraisal practices appear to adversely affect allegedly redlined neighborhoods in the New York-Nassau-Suffolk and Rochester areas. As a result, borrowers on properties in Northwest Kings County, an area including Central Brooklyn, Crown Heights, and East Flatbush, face down-payment requirements that are 21 percent higher than those in Suffolk County. In the 16th Ward area of Rochester, down payments are 18 percent higher than in the surrounding suburbs. In both areas, however, neighborhoods that are not alleged to be redlined are also significantly underappraised. Mortgages on properties in North Bronx, Northeast Kings, South Kings, Queens, and Westchester counties have down payments that are 8–22 percent above those in Suffolk County. And the rest of the City of Rochester has down payments that are nearly 14 percent above those in the suburbs.

The results in Buffalo indicate that the allegedly redlined neighborhoods are favored by appraisal practices. Three of the four are overappraised and have down-payment requirements that are below those of the Buffalo suburbs. In one case (Center City and Industrial) the differential is large and significant (17 percent). Borrowers in the City of Lackawanna, which some organizations believed might be redlined, also had significantly smaller (31 percent) down payments.

The only other significant geographic variation occurs in the Syracuse area. Oswego County borrowers have down payments 14 percent lower than those in the Onondaga County suburbs.

Although geographic variations in the ratio of appraised value to purchase price are large and statistically significant, they do not correspond with the allegedly redlined neighborhoods. Allegedly redlined areas should have lower appraisal-value-to-purchase-price ratios and higher down-payment requirements than other neighborhoods if redlining is practiced through systematic underappraising. Only one of the six locations in the greater New York area with large and significant increases in down-payment requirements relative to Suffolk County is an alleged redlined area (Northwest Kings). The other two areas that are allegedly redlined (South Bronx and Southeast Queens) have relatively small and statistically insignificant increases in down-payment requirements. In the Rochester area, only one of the three allegedly redlined neighborhoods has significantly higher down payments.

Location-Specific Estimates

The preceding analysis assumes that the effects of age of the neighborhood's housing stock, the building age, the construction materials, the structure type, and the year of transaction on the appraised-value-to-purchase-price ratio are the same for all property locations. Although the model allows for overall differences across locations, it does not allow the effects of the other independent variables to vary by location.

The possibility of interactions between location and year of transaction is of particular interest because redlining may exist in an area during one period but not during another. Prior to any period during which systematic underappraisal occurs, all areas should have approximately the same appraised-value-to-purchase-price ratios. If an area is redlined through systematic underappraisal of property values, appraised-value-to-purchase-price ratios should begin to fall below the ratios in nonredlined areas and should remain below those in the other areas as long as systematic underappraisal is being practiced.

Separate models of the appraised-value-to-purchase-price ratio are estimated in four of the metropolitan areas (Albany-Schenectady-

Troy, Buffalo, New York-Nassau-Suffolk, and Syracuse). Each area is divided into areas alleged to be redlined and areas not so alleged. The results are displayed in Figures 9.1 to 9.4. These figures show that the time paths for the areas alleged to be redlined are not systematically below those for the rest of their metropolitan areas. The graphs illustrate the point made by the statistical analysis; namely, neighborhoods alleged to be redlined do not appear to be systematically underappraised relative to those areas not so alleged in any of the four metropolitan areas.

Summary

In California, the major differentials in appraisal practices vary with the purchase price and building age. New buildings or buildings selling for less than $30,001 are overappraised. Higher-priced buildings are increasingly underappraised relative to those priced under $30,001

Although there are many types of California households who receive statistically significant underappraisals of their properties, the magnitudes are generally small and result in less than 2 percent increases in down-payment. Female-only applicants with no one of childbearing age are an exception; underappraisal of their properties raises their down payments by 6.4 percent in the Fresno metropolitan area in 1977. Some of the neighborhoods alleged to be redlined are another exception. Properties in the East Los Angeles-Boyle Heights-Echo Park, Highland Park, and Pomona areas of Los Angeles and in Central Oakland are sufficiently underappraised to raise down payments by 3.2 to 6.8 percent.

The empirical results for New York also provide little evidence that certain neighborhoods or types of neighborhoods or structures are systematically underappraised. However, the omission of mortgage applications that were denied by the banks or withdrawn by the applicants restricts the ability to generalize these results. Data on these omitted applications are not available in New York, but they are the ones most likely to be relatively underappraised, if such practice exists. As such, the evidence is not conclusive. Although this evidence indicates that underappraisal is not the rule, there are two exceptions: the statistically significant underappraisal of properties located within Northwest Kings in New York City and the 16th Ward of the City of Rochester.

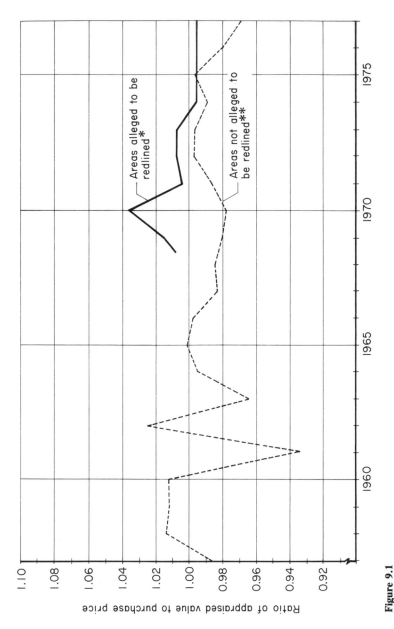

Figure 9.1

Trends in the ratio of appraised value to purchase price for 1- to 4-family houses in Albany-Schenectady-Troy neighborhoods, 1957–1977.

*Arbor Hill, Hudson-Park, West Hill, South End, Hamilton Hill, Central State Street, Hillside, North Central, "567," and Central South.

**All other portions of the cities of Albany, Schenectady, and Troy and of the counties of Albany, Schenectady, and Rensselaer, plus the counties of Saratoga and Montgomery.

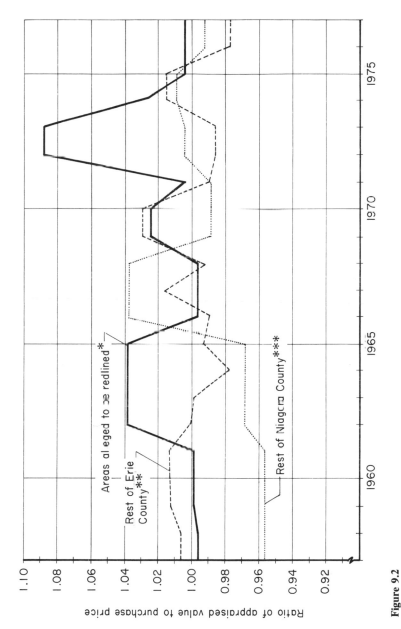

Figure 9.2
Trends in the ratio of appraised value to purchase price for 1- to 4-family houses in Buffalo neighborhoods, 1957–1977.
*Center City, Industrial, West Side, Blackrock, West Elmwood, and Fillmore-Leroy.
**All of Erie Countie outside the cities of Buffalo and Lackawanna.
***All of Niagara County outside the city of Niagara.

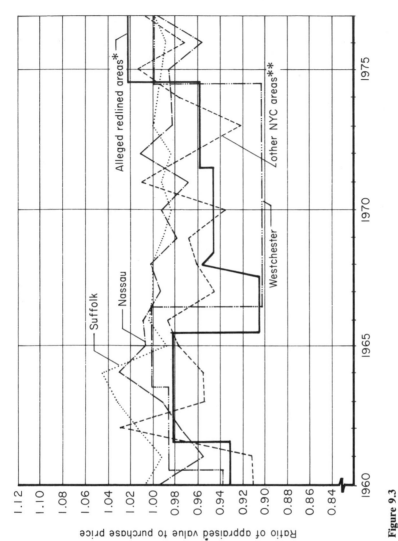

Figure 9.3
Trends in the ratio of appraised value to purchase price for 1- to 4-family houses in each of five locations, 1960–1977.
*South Bronx, Northwest Kings, and Southeast Queens.
**North Bronx, Northeast Kings, South Kings, and rest of Queens.

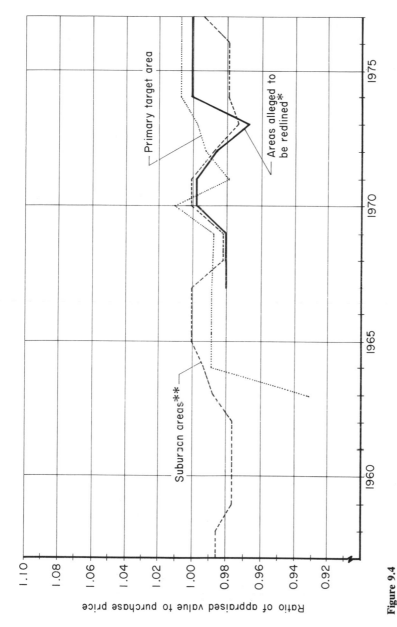

Figure 9.4
Trends in the ratios of appraised value to purchase price for 1- to 4-family houses in Rochester neighborhoods, 1957–1965.
*ZIP Code area 14621, 16th Ward, Dutchtown.
**Those parts of Monroe County outside the city of Rochester, plus the counties of Ontario, Orleans, Livingston, and Wayne.,

10
Summary of Results

Introduction

Many federal and state statutes currently makes it illegal for banking institutions, when granting mortgage loans, to discriminate against certain borrowers on the basis of personal characteristics such as race, sex, or marital status or on the basis of the arbitrary use of certain characteristics of the property they wish to buy such as its age or location. These laws reflect two social concerns. One pertains to individual justice and the other to the viability of urban neighborhoods.

Generally accepted concepts of justice demand that individuals not be treated adversely just because they happen to have certain characteristics in common. Membership in certain groups, especially those defined by the color of a person's skin, has in the past resulted in differential treatment. This concept of justice and its historic violations have led to laws that prohibit discriminatory lending on the basis of certain unacceptable categories while allowing differentiation based on other, more objective, factors related to the riskiness of the loan, such as the income of the applicant or the applicant's net wealth. The federal Equal Credit Opportunity Act (as amended, March 23, 1976) embodies this concept of fairness:

It shall be unlawful for any creditor to discriminate against any applicant, with respect to any aspect of a credit transaction—
(1) on the basis of race, color, religion, national origin, sex, or marital status, or age (provided the applicant has the capacity to contract);
(2) because all or part of the applicant's income derives from any public assistance program; or
(3) because the applicant has in good faith exercised any right under the Consumer Credit Protection Act.[1]

Community activist groups have been instrumental in the development of laws that require disclosure of mortgage lending by census tract or zip code, that encourage financial institutions to "help meet the credit needs of the local communties in which they are chartered consistent with the safe and sound operation of such institutions," [2] or that make discrimination on the basis of the age or location of a building illegal.[3] These groups believe that lending institutions contribute to the declining quality of life in certain urban neighborhoods by refusing to grant mortgages even though demand exists, or by granting mortgages with less favorable terms even though the expected yield and risk of loss are the same as in other neighborhoods. They allege that older or largely minority neighborhoods are usually the target of these practices, which are commonly known as "redlining."

This study uses mortgage application data to examine the extent to which urban mortgage lenders discriminate on the basis of borrower characteristics that are illegal and the extent to which allegations by antiredlining groups are valid. Its focus on the lender's decision to lend, rather than on the aggregate volume of lending by geographic area, differentiates this study from most previous studies.

The banker's mortgage lending decision is only one link in a chain of decisions that determines the extent to which decent housing is accessible to women and minorities. Other actors in the urban housing market have a major role in determining whether or not women and minorities can buy homes. Among them are real estate brokers who may steer buyers away from or toward certain neighborhoods because of their race, sex, or martial status: real estate appraisers who may underappraise certain types of property for discriminatory reasons; or insurance companies who may refuse to sell fire insurance to certain geographic areas or categories of home owners. The analysis of the role of these actors (with the exception of appraisers) is beyond the scope of this study. One must keep their interactions with mortgage lenders in mind, however, when interpreting the results of this study. For example, if banks do not appear to discriminate against minorities in making mortgage loans, their actions may be only a result of advance screening by real estate brokers who discourage their minority clients from even applying for a bank loan.

The Nature of the Study

Lenders may limit or restrict the access to mortgage credit of women, minorities, the elderly, and those trying to purchase homes in allegedly redlined areas in at least four ways. First, a lender may discourage certain potential borrowers from submitting a formal application for a mortgage. Second, the person authorized by the lending institution to estimate the value of, or appraise, the property may differentially and systematically underappraise certain types of properties relative to others. (Underappraisal of this type reduces the maximum loan amount below what it would be with non-discriminatory appraisal.) Third, the lender may use criteria to evaluate loan applications that result in systematic discrimination against certain types of applicants with the result that such applicants face higher probabilities of loan denial or adverse modification than other applicants. Fourth, the lender may arbitrarily impose harsher mortgage terms (for example, higher interest rates, shorter maturity periods, or higher loan fees) on some applicants than on others. If the potential borrower cannot afford the harsher terms, this practice is tantamount to the outright denial of the loan.

This study deals with three of these four ways that lenders may limit the access to mortgage credit. Since our data base includes only formal applications, we are unable to examine the first method, pre-screening by lenders. This is unfortunate; many allege that prescreening, although illegal, is a widely used way for lenders to practice discrimination. To the extent that our results provide evidence of discrimination at the subsequent stages of the lending process, they suggest that discriminatory prescreening may exist as well. The reverse is not true, however; absence of evidence supporting charges of discrimination related to formal applications does not imply a lack of discrimination at the preapplication stage.

This summary reports on the examination of allegations of lender discrimination on the basis of one or more of the following prohibited criteria:

- sex of applicant
- race of applicant
- age of applicant
- age of neighborhood
- racial composition of neighborhood
- location of property

By estimating models that control for the credit worthiness of the applicant, the security offered by the property, and the risk of loss to the lender, we test for discriminatory behavior in connection with the following types of lender practices:

• decision to approve, modify, or deny a mortgage application
• setting of mortgage terms (interest rate, maturity period, loan-to-value ratio, and loan fees)
• appraisal practices

Lenders have several options when they receive a mortgage application. They can approve the application with the terms requested by the applicant, they can approve it after modifying the terms, or they can deny it altogether. Modifications can take several forms. Lenders can reduce the loan amount below the requested value, they can increase the loan amount above the requested value, or they can shorten or lengthen the maturity period. We analyze lending decisions by examining the likelihood that lenders will deny or modify a loan application given its characteristics. Higher chances that applications from women or minorities will be denied or approved with a loan amount below the requested amount indicate discrimination against these groups.

We use several approaches in analysing mortgage credit terms. First, we study the terms of the mortgage contract (interest rate, maturity period, and loan-to-value ratio). Since borrowers prefer lower interest rates and lenders prefer higher rates for any given combination of the other terms, our summary focuses on the results with regard to interest-rate discrimination. Higher interest rates for women and minorities are evidence of discrimination against women and minorities, respectively. Second, we analyze the dollar amount of the reductions in requested loan amounts (downward modifications). Above average reductions in requested loan amounts are another piece of evidence consistent with discrimination. Third, we examine the variation in the loan fees lenders charge for processing loans. Disproportionately high loan fees for women or racial minorities indicate discrimination against members of these groups.

Finally, we analyze the fairness of appraisal practices. Underappraisal of properties in certain locations or of properties being purchased by women or racial minorities is evidence of discrimination against these locations or persons.

Study Areas

Analysis of discrimination in mortgage lending requires detailed information on objective factors such as the credit worthiness of individual applicants and the security value of the property that legitimately affect the mortgage lending decision, and information on those characteristics of the applicant or the property that constitute illegal discrimination. Fortunately, because California and New York state laws require state-regulated banks to maintain detailed information on all mortgage applications, we were able to obtain the necessary data from state-regulated savings and loan associations in California and all state-regulated lenders in New York State. New York regulates three types of lenders: commercial banks, mutual savings banks, and savings and loan associations.

We study mortgage lending separately for each type of lender in each metropolitan area. In addition, we examine California state-chartered savings and loan associations for each metropolitan area separately for each of the years 1977 and 1978. The New York information covers the period from May 1977 to October 1978 for commercial banks and savings and loan associations. The mutual savings bank data cover the period May 1976 to October 1977. Tables 10.1 and 10.2 summarize the number of mortgage applications analyzed in each study area.

Table 10.1
Number of mortgage applications by metropolitan area and year: California savings and loan associations

Study Area	1977	1978
Anaheim-Santa Ana-Garden Grove	16,672	12,542
Bakersfield	1,722	1,646
Fresno	3,173	2,850
Los Angeles-Long Beach	38,398	34,792
Modesto	1,885	1,558
Oxnard-Ventura	4,631	3,970
Sacramento	5,163	4,884
Salinas-Monterey	1,860	1,530
San Bernardino-Riverside-Ontario	2,606	2,038
San Diego	7,628	7,508
San Francisco-Oakland	24,766	21,608
San Jose	9,887	7,691
Santa Barbara	1,401	1,254
Santa Rosa	3,419	3,307
Stockton	2,432	2,381
Vallejo-Napa	1,884	1,866

Table 10.2
Number of mortgage applications by bank type and metropolitan area: New York
State

Study Area	Number
Albany-Schenectady-Troy SMSA	
Mutual savings banks	6,173
Albany-Schenectady-Troy, Rochester, and Syracuse SMSAs	
Commercial banks	2,586
Buffalo SMSA	
Commercial banks	1,434
Mutual savings banks	7,408
New York and Nassau-Suffolk SMSAs	
Commercial banks	4,919
Mutual savings banks	
Large sample without sex and marital status	18,696
Small sample with sex and marital status	4,131
Savings and loan associations	2,170
Rochester SMSA	
Mutual savings banks	3,047
Savings and loan associations	1,304
Syracuse SMSA	
Mutual savings banks	2,695

Sex and marital-status information is available for a sufficient number of applications at
all commercial banks and savings and loan associations, but at only the mutual savings
banks in the New York-Nassau-Suffolk metropolitan area.

The California and New York data sets are not identical; each has
its own strengths and weaknesses. The New York recording form
includes, for example, marital status, net wealth, and years at present
occupation, all of which are omitted from the California form. However, the New York form records house purchase price and income in
interval form only, while California provides much more precise and
detailed information on these items, including the separate incomes of
the applicant and co-applicant. In addition, the California form provides information on the building's age and the final terms of the
mortgage contract, which, except for the loan-to-value ratio, are not
available in New York. By relying on both data sources, this study
can focus on a broader range of issues than would be possible with a

single data set. In particular, the New York information makes possible a test of discrimination on the basis of marital status, while the California data set permits an examination of discriminatory behavior in the treatment accorded secondary income, the setting of mortgage terms, and appraisal practices.

Other major advantages derive from the use of two separate data sets. First, the data cover a wide variety of lending institutions. Second, the data cover a wide range of economic conditions. The rapid economic growth and booming housing market in California contrast sharply with the situation in New York State. In addition, the data allow a wide variety of metropolitan areas to be studied in both states, allowing large areas to be compared with small and rapidly growing areas with those that are growing slowly. For example, the San Jose metropolitan area is growing more rapidly than the rest of California because of the influx of high technology firms in the "Silicon Valley." In New York, the Rochester area's economy is better off than that of the rest of the state.

Another important consequence of the variety of banks and economic conditions covered by the two data sources is the potential generalizability of the results. Results that are consistent across such a wide variety of circumstances will provide a firm foundation for the formulation of national policy.

The number of separate study areas we analyze varies with the lender practice being examined. In some cases data availability limitations reduce the number of study areas. For example, inadequate sample sizes keep us from separating downward and upward modifications in some study areas, thereby reducing the number of California study areas from thirty-two (sixteen geographic areas each for 1977 and 1978) to twenty-two between the denial and downward-modification models. In addition, in California we selected four metropolitan areas (Fresno, Los Angeles-Long Beach, San Francisco-Oakland, and San Jose) for intensive study. Only in these four areas do we analyze mortgage credit terms and appraisal practices. Since we separately study two years in each, the credit terms and appraisal model results are based on a total of eight study areas.

Findings

The analysis indicates that, as expected, objective factors such as the ratios of requested loan amount to income and to appraised value explain the vast majority of lending decisions. Applications are more likely to be denied or modified downward as either or both of these ratios increase. Similarly, applicants with more income or more net wealth, and properties located in relatively risk-free neighborhoods (for example, with little likelihood of being adjacent to vacant buildings) are more likely to be approved. At the same time, the evidence supports several of the allegations that lenders discriminate on the basis of the race, sex, or age of the applicant, the age or racial composition of the neighborhood, and the geographic location of the property. The remainder of this summary describes our findings on the extent to which lenders in California and New York provide equal opportunity in mortgage lending.

Sex and Marital Status
Testing for discrimination on the basis of sex is complicated by the fact that lenders, to the extent they discriminate, may not discriminate equally against all members of a particular sex. For example, they may discriminate against female applicants who are of childbearing age (under thirty-five) but not other female applicants. The allegations relating to sex discrimination indicate that the preferable method of analysis would include a detailed breakdown of household categories that takes into account whether the female applicant is of childbearing age or is employed. The distinction between working and nonworking female applicants reflects the allegation that lenders discriminate against applications where at least part of the income comes from a supposedly unreliable source, the earnings of the working woman. The breakdown between women of childbearing and nonchildbearing age captures a potential distinction made by lenders who believe that possible pregnancy increases the probability that a woman will leave the labor force or will incur additional expenses.

Various organizations also allege that lenders use marital status as a basis for discrimination. To test whether lenders treat marital status differently depending on the sex of the applicant, it is important to examine the sex and marital status of the applicant simultaneously. Unfortunately, marital status information is only available in our New York data set.

In general, we compare various types of applicants to a type that is least likely to be discriminated against; in this case, it is the joint application of a male-female couple with the woman beyond childbearing age. The employment status of women applicants is treated differently in the New York and California data sets. In New York, we know only whether the female applicant works; in California we know the actual income earned by both the applicant and the co-applicant. Therefore, in New York we analyze the working status of women by adding this fact to the description of the types of applicants; the base for comparison becomes a joint application from a male-female couple with a nonworking woman beyond childbearing age.

The allegation of income discounting can be tested more explicitly in California where information on the separate incomes of the applicant and the co-applicant is available. With such data, we can allow explicitly for differential treatment of the income of the primary and secondary workers in each household. In addition, we can test the hypothesis that lenders treat the income of secondary female workers differently from secondary male workers.

The California and New York analyses have sufficient differences in the definition of the sex variables that we summarize the results of each separately.

California In California, we define the following categories of applications:

- male-female couples with no woman of childbearing age (base for comparison)
- male-female couples with a woman of childbearing age
- female-only households with no women of childbearing age
- female-only households with at least one woman of childbearing age
- male-only households

We present the results for these categories separately for households with only one worker and for those with two workers earning equal incomes. Table 10.3 contains a summary of the number of study areas with significant findings consistent with allegations of discrimination for each of six measures of discrimination.

There is limited evidence of sex discrimination in some study areas, but no pattern exists across a large number of areas. We summarize first the results in the upper half of Table 10.3, those for single-wage-earner households.

Male-female couples with a woman of childbearing age have higher chances of denial or downward modification than male-female couples with no woman of childbearing age in two of thirty-two and one of twenty-two study areas, respectively. In these three areas, applications from couples with women of childbearing age are roughly 1.35

Table 10.3
Number of areas with a finding consistent with discrimination on the basis of sex or secondary-income sources in California

Type of Household	Higher Chance of Denial	Higher Chance of Downward Modification	Higher Interest Rates	Larger Dollar Amount of Downward Modification	Higher Loan Fees	Under-appraisal
One wage earner						
Male-female couples with a woman of childbearing age	2	1	0	1	2	0
Female-only households with no women of childbearing age	4	2	3	0	0	7
Female-only households with at least one woman of childbearing age	3	0	3	0	2	3
Male-only households	3	2	5	0	4	0
Two wage earners with equal income[a]						
Male-female couples with no woman of childbearing age	4	3	1	0	b	b
Male-female couples with a woman of childbearing age	1	0	1	0	b	b
Female-only households with no women of childbearing age	4	4	4	1	b	b
Female-only households with at least one woman of childbearing age	1	0	3	0	b	b
Male-only households	2	4	5	0	b	b
Number of areas studied	32	22	8	8	8	8

A finding is viewed as consistent with discriminatory behavior if applicants from the indicated group have a statistically significantly harder time receiving a mortgage or receive mortgages that have statistically significantly harsher terms The indicated groups of applicants are compared to male-female couples with no woman of childbearing age and only one wage earner.
a. We have selected two wage earners with equal incomes to illustrate our findings. The findings, however, apply to two-wage-earner households with all possible divisions of income between the two workers.
b. The income source variable did not have a role in these models.

times as likely to result in an adverse decision. These same couples pay higher loan fees in two of eight study areas, but the fees average only 1 percent higher.

Female-only households with no women of childbearing age face higher chances of denial and downward modification in four of thirty-two and two of twenty-two study areas, respectively. The differentials are large: adverse action on these applications is 2.5 to 3.0 times as likely as adverse action on applications from male-female couples with no woman of childbearing age. In addition, these borrowers pay higher interest rates in three of the four 1977 study areas but, interestingly, in none of the four 1978 study areas. Finally, we find the properties of these applicants to be underappraised in seven of eight study areas. These underappraisals result in down payments that are as much as 6.4 percent above normal, or an increase of $1,000 in the case of a $60,000 mortgage with an 80 percent loan-to-appraised-value ratio.

Female-only households with at least one woman of childbearing age are discriminated against less frequently and less severely than female-only households without women of childbearing age. Like their older counterparts, they pay slightly higher interest rates in three 1977 study areas but in none of the 1978 areas.

Male-only households face discrimination through a higher chance of denial and downward modification in three of thirty-two and two of twenty-two study areas. More striking is the conclusion that they pay higher interest rates and loan fees than any of the other sex categories. Their higher interest rates add about $11 a year to the payments on a $60,000 mortgage with a 9.75 percent interest rate and a thirty-year maturity period. Their fees are 2–6 percent above average.

The lower half of Table 10.3 shows the results for applications with two wage earners with equal incomes compared with the treatment received by male-female couples having no women of childbearing age and only one wage earner. In many cases, state savings and loan associations in California apparently favor rather than disfavor secondary income. Perhaps they believe that two sources of income reduce the uncertainty about the continuity of future income. Differences in the treatment of secondary income that do exist across sex categories are similar to those for one-earner households. The results from the interest rate analyses, however, are consistent with income discounting and imply that secondary income earned by men is discounted more than that earned by women.

To summarize, two apparent patterns of sex discrimination by California savings and loan associations emerge: one is the treatment of male-only applicants in the setting of mortgage terms; the other is the underappraisal of the properties of female-only applicants. Although we find evidence of other instances of discrimination against female-only applicants, especially in the 1977 study areas, against certain types of male-female households, no other patterns emerge across study areas.

New York In New York, we can examine sex categories separately for the two marital status categories of married and unmarried or separated. The categories of married applicants are:

• male-female couples with a nonworking woman beyond childbearing age (base for comparison)
• male-female couples with a working woman beyond childbearing age
• male-female couples with a nonworking woman of childbearing age
• male-female couples with a working woman of childbearing age
• female-only households
• male-only households

The categories for unmarried or separated applicants are similar except for the division of the female-only households into those with no women of childbearing age and those with at least one woman of childbearing age. Table 10.4 summarizes the New York results.

We find only limited evidence of discrimination against married male-female couples who differ from the reference group solely in terms of the childbearing age or working status of the woman. For the three married male-female categories, we find evidence of a higher chance of denial in only one study area: commercial banks in Buffalo are twice as likely to deny male-female couples with a working woman beyond childbearing age than similar households with a nonworking woman.

Stronger evidence of discriminatory lending emerges with respect to the treatment of unmarried or separated male-female households. These applicants face chances of mortgage denial 1.4 to 3.9 times as high as those faced by the married male-female household with a nonworking woman beyond childbearing age in either two or three of the six study areas, depending on the working status or childbearing age of the woman. Regardless of martial status, male-female households are more likely to receive modified approvals from savings and loan associations in the New York metropolitan area if the woman is either working or in her childbearing years.

Table 10.4
Number of areas with findings consistent with discrimination on the basis of sex, marital status, and work status of the woman in New York

Status of Woman	Higher Chance of Denial	Higher Chance of Downward Modification	Larger Dollar Amount of Downward Modification
Married			
Male-female couples with a working woman beyond childbearing age	1	1	0
Male-female couples with a nonworking woman of childbearing age	0	1	0
Male-female couples with a working woman of childbearing age	0	1	0
Female-only households	2	0	1
Male-only households	3	2	0
Unmarried or separated			
Male-female couples with a nonworking woman beyond childbearing age	2	0	[a]
Male-female couples with a working woman beyond childbearing age	3	1	[a]
Male-female couples with a nonworking woman of childbearing age	2	1	[a]
Male-female couples with a working woman of childbearing age	2	1	[a]
Female-only households with no women of childbearing age	0	1	[a]
Female-only households with at least one woman of childbearing age	0	0	[a]
Male-only households	4	0	[a]
Number of areas studied	6	6	5

A finding is viewed as consistent with discriminatory behavior if the applicants from the indicated group have a statistically significantly harder time receiving a mortgage or receive mortgages that have statistically significantly harsher terms. The indicated groups of applicants are compared to male-female married couples with a nonworking woman beyond childbearing age.
a. Small sample size prevented the examination of the same sex and marital-status interactions that were possible for the chance of denial and downward-modification models. However, the analysis we were able to conduct indicated that separated persons, as opposed to married or unmarried households, receive significantly larger dollar amounts of downward modifications in one of the five areas.

Married female-only applicants are more than twice as likely to be denied as married male-female applicants with a nonworking woman beyond the childbearing age in two of the six study areas. In addition, these applicants experience larger downward modifications in one of five study areas. Unmarried or separated female-only households with no woman of childbearing age experience higher chances of downward modifications in one of six study areas.

Unexpectedly, the strongest evidence points to discrimination against male-only households, regardless of their marital status. They are over twice as likely to be denied as the married male-female household with a nonworking woman beyond childbearing age in two-thirds of the study areas.

In summary, our analysis of lending decisions in New York State provides only limited support for allegations that lenders discriminate against female-only or certain types of male-female applicants. In contrast, the results support the hypothesis that lenders in many areas discriminate against male-only and against unmarried or separated male-female households. Since all but one of the mutual savings bank samples exclude data on sex and marital status, these findings relate to New York commercial banks and savings and loan associations with the following exceptions. Married female-only and married, unmarried, or separated male-only applicants are more likely to be denied by mutual savings banks in the New York-Nassau-Suffolk metropolitan area. In addition, these mutual savings banks also exact above-average downward modifications from separated applicants regardless of their sex or work status.

Race
We study the treatment of four groups of racial minorities and compare them with the treatment of white applicants. The groups are:

• blacks
• Spanish or Hispanics
• Asians (only in California)
• other minorities

The results, which are summarized in Table 10.5, indicate that discrimination against racial minorities is widespread.

Black applicants have significantly higher chances of denial than whites in similar circumstances in eighteen of the thirty-two California study areas and six of the ten New York study areas. Moreover, the

Table 10.5
Number of areas with a finding consistent with discrimination on the basis of race of applicant in California (CA) and New York (NY)

Race of Applicant	Higher Chance of Denial		Higher Chance of Downward Modification		Higher Interest Rates	Larger Dollar Amount of Downward Modification		Higher Loan Fees	Under-appraisal
	CA	NY	CA	NY	CA	CA	NY	CA	CA
Black	18	6	2	2	5	0	0	5	0
Spanish or Hispanic	10	1[a]	1	1[a]	6	0	0[b]	4	4
Asian	3	[c]	1	[c]	4	0	[c]	3	3
Other minority	11	1	0	2	1	0	0	0	0
Number of areas studied	32	10	22	10	8	8	5	8	8

A finding is viewed as consistent with discriminatory behavior if applicants from the indicated group have a statistically significantly harder time receiving a mortgage or receive mortgages that have statistically significantly harsher terms. The indicated groups of applicants are compared to white applicants.
a. Because of small sample sizes, Spanish or Hispanic applicants are grouped with other minorities in six of the ten study areas. Therefore, there are only four New York study areas where we could test for discrimination against Spanish or Hispanic applicants.
b. Because of small sample sizes, Spanish or Hispanic applicants could only be separately identified in three of the five study areas. They are grouped with other minorities in the two remaining areas.
c. Included in other minorities in New York because of small sample size.

differences are large; black applicants are 1.58 to 7.82 times as likely to be denied as are similar white applicants. Although blacks and whites are treated similarly with respect to loan modifications and in the appraisal process, blacks are charged higher interest rates and higher loan fees in five of eight areas studied. We emphasize that we find no evidence that New York commercial banks discriminate against blacks. We find, however, that they discriminate against minorities other than blacks or Hispanics.

In California, savings and loan associations consistently discriminate against Spanish applicants. These applicants face higher chances of denial in ten of thirty-two study areas, higher interest rates in six of eight areas, and higher loan fees in four of eight areas than whites in similar circumstances. In addition, their properties tend to be systematically underappraised in four of eight study areas. The estimated magnitudes suggest that Spanish applicants are about twice as likely to be denied as are otherwise similar white applicants; that interest rates are higher by 0.03 percentage points, which amounts to $16 in the annual payments on a 9.75 percent $60,000 mortgage with a thirty-year maturity period and that loan fees are 3 percent higher.

In New York, Hispanic applicants receive approximately the same treatment as white applicants with some important exceptions. Hispanics in the New York City metropolitan area are nearly twice as likely to receive modifications at the hands of savings and loan associations as similar white applicants.

Lenders in California treat Asians approximately the same as white applicants with respect to loan denials and downward modifications. Asians have a higher chance of denial in only three of thirty-two study areas, and higher chances of downward modification in only one of twenty-two study areas. However, their mortgages carry slightly higher interest rates (0.02 percentage points above norm) and are based on small (less than 0.2 percent) underappraisals of the property.

The final category consists primarily of applicants who chose to classify themselves as "other minorities." In New York, we include Asians in this category as well. There is substantial support for the view that these other minorities are discriminated against in California; their chances of denial are higher than similar white applicants in eleven of thirty-two study areas. The difference is large, ranging from 1.37 to 5.95 times as likely to be denied. This group does not appear to be discriminated against through loan modification, loan fees, or appraisal practices. They do pay slightly higher interest rates (0.02 percentage points above norm) in only one of eight study areas.

In New York, other minorities receive treatment similar to that of whites with a few exceptions. New York City metropolitan area commercial banks and Buffalo commercial and mutual savings banks are 1.80 to 4.23 times as likely to modify the loan applications of these minorities than those of white applicants in similar circumstances.

Age

Applicants are grouped into one of five age categories to test for discrimination on the basis of age. The categories are:

• under twenty-five years
• twenty-five to thirty-four years
• thirty-five to forty-four years (base for comparison)
• forty-five to fifty-four years
• fifty-five or more years

We selected the middle-age group (thirty-five to forty-four) as the basis of comparison because applicants in that group are considered least likely to be discriminated against. The results are summarized in Table 10.6. Contrary to our expectations, the middle-age (thirty-five to forty-four) applicants have higher chances of denial in nearly half of the thirty-two California study areas. In a few areas, however, applicants under thirty-five or over forty-four have higher chances of denial than 35- to 44-year-old applicants. New York State savings and loan associations make it harder for 45- to 54-year-old applicants to obtain a mortgage; these applicants are 1.7 times as likely to be denied by these lenders as are 35- to 44-year-old applicants.

We have substantial evidence that older applicants receive adverse treatment through the modification process. Although the summary of results presented in Table 10.6 indicates that older applicants (over forty-four) have higher chances of downward modification than 35- to 44-year-old applicants in only six of twenty-two California study areas, they have significantly higher chances of such adverse action than the youngest applicants (under twenty-five) in fifteen of the twenty-two areas. Applicants over fifty-four are 1.25 to 2.80 times as likely to receive downward modifications as are applicants under twenty-five. Furthermore, applicants over forty-five receive larger dollar amount reductions in their requested loan amounts when they are modified

Table 10.6
Number of areas with findings consistent with discrimination on the basis of age of applicant in California (CA) and New York (NY)

Age of Applicant (years)	Higher Chance of Denial		Higher Chance of Downward Modification		Higher Interest Rates	Larger Dollar Amount of Downward Modification		Higher Loan Fees	Under-appraisal
	CA	NY	CA	NY	CA	CA	NY	CA	CA
<25	0	0	0	1	5	0	0	5	2
25–34	2	0	1	1		1	0	1	1
45–54	2	2	3	2		5	2	0	3
>54	0	0	3	1	0	2	2	1	3
Number of areas studied	32	6	22	5	8	8	5	8	8

A finding is viewed as consistent with discriminatory behavior if applicants from the indicated group have a statistically significantly harder time receiving a mortgage or receive mortgages that have statistically significantly harsher terms. The indicated groups of applicants are compared to 35–44 year old applicants.

downward than do similar but younger applicants; the differences range from 12 to 163 percent.

New York State lenders seem only slightly more likely to modify older than younger applicants, but it is the older applicants who receive the larger dollar amount reductions in their requested loan amounts. The difference in reductions ranges from 67 to 146 percent.

Young applicants (those under twenty-five) receive slightly higher interest rates than those in the middle age range. The differential would add about $13 to the annual payments on a $60,000 mortgage with a 9.75 percent interest rate and a thirty-year maturity period. In addition, these young applicants face the highest loan fees. Applicants under twenty-five pay loan fees that are 2–3 percent above those paid by 35- to 44-year-old applicants.

The properties of older applicants are underappraised in three of eight study areas, but the differential is small. The required down payment would rise by only 0.8–2.0 percent on a mortgage with an 80 percent loan-to-appraised-value ratio. This would amount to less than $300 with a $60,000 mortgage.

Redlining

Various organizations allege that lenders discriminate against certain mortgage applicants because of the neighborhood in which the property they wish to purchase is located. Our analysis focuses on three types of neighborhoods alleged to receive adverse treatment:

• specific neighborhoods that community groups have alleged to be redlined
• older neighborhoods
• largely minority neighborhoods

We summarize our findings with respect to each type of allegation in the following subsections.

Property Location   In all the New York and a few of the California metropolitan areas, we are able to examine local allegations that certain neighborhoods are redlined by lenders. In the other metropolitan areas in California, we are only able to compare lending decisions in the central cities with those in the surrounding suburbs. In all cases, lending decisions on applications for mortgages on properties in allegedly redlined neighborhoods or in the central city are compared with decisions on otherwise similar applications on suburban properties. In addition, we are able to study the probability of default and the appraisal-to-purchase-price ratios of granted mortgages at mutual savings banks and the quantity of funds and the average credit terms provided by state-regulated lenders in New York State.

In California, we have information containing allegations that lenders redline twelve neighborhoods in Los Angeles County, one in the city of Oakland, and one in the city of Sacramento. The evidence does not support the allegation in Sacramento.

Although lenders are not more likely to deny or modify downward applications for mortgages on properties in the Central Oakland neighborhood than similar applications on suburban San Mateo County properties, they tend to underappraise the properties and, in 1977, to impose higher interest rates on the mortgages. The underappraisals increase the down payment by 4.5 percent with a mortgage for 80 percent of the appraised value. The higher interest rates raise the annual payment by $38 on a $60,000 mortgage with a 9.75 percent interest rate and a thirty-year maturity period.

In Los Angeles County, at least one piece of evidence is consistent with the redlining allegations in all but two neighbhorhoods. The results are summarized in Table 10.7. There are two study areas for each type of potential adverse action because of the separate analysis of the 1977 and 1978 data. The following paragraphs describe in more detail findings consistent with redlining allegations.

If a property is located in the East Los Angeles-Boyle Heights-Echo Park or San Pedro neighborhoods, the mortgage application has a higher chance of denial (1.68 and 2.00 times as likely, respectively) than a similar application on a property located in the suburbs. In addition, properties in these neighborhoods are underappraised so that the down payments are 3–6 percent higher than average. Mortgages on San Pedro properties also have higher interest rates, adding $32 to the annual payments on a $60,000 mortgage with a 9.75 percent interest rate and a thirty-year maturity period.

Applications on properties in the Covina-Azusa, Pacoima-San Fernando, and Venice-Santa Monica neighborhoods have higher chances of downward modification (1.58 to 2.62 times as likely). Applicants wishing to buy properties in the Covina-Azusa and West Covina neighborhoods combined are additionally burdened by having to pay 22 percent higher loan fees than if the property were located in the suburbs. Properties in the Pacoima-San Fernando neighborhood are slightly underappraised.

Mortgages on Compton properties have higher interest rates, adding

Table 10.7
Number of areas with a finding consistent with discrimination on the basis of property location: Los Angeles-Long Beach SMSA

Location	Higher Chance of Denial	Higher Chance of Downward Modification	Higher Interest Rates	Larger Dollar Amount of Downward Modification	Higher Loan Fees	Under-appraisal
Compton	0	0	1	a	0	1
Covina-Azusa	0	1	0	a	2	0
East L.A.-Boyle Heights-Echo Park	1	0	0	a	0	2
Highland Park	0	0	0	a	1	1
Long Beach-Southwest	0	0	0	a	0	0
Pacoima-San Fernando	0	2	0	a	0	1
Pasadena-North Central	0	0	0	a	0	0
Pomona	0	0	1	a	2	2
San Pedro	1	0	1	a	0	1
South Central L.A.	0	0	0	a	1	1
Venice-Santa Monica	0	1	0	a	0	0
West Covina	0	0	1	a	b	b
All alleged redlined neighborhoods together	NA	NA	NA	0	NA	NA
Number of areas studied	2	2	2	2	2	2

A finding is viewed as consistent with discriminatory behavior if applicants from the indicated group have a statistically significantly harder time receiving a mortgage or receive mortgages that have statistically significantly harsher terms. The indicated property locations are compared to the remaining part of suburban Los Angeles County.
a. Because of insufficient observations, all the allegedly redlined neighborhoods had to be grouped together for the analysis of the dollar amount of downward modifications.
b. In these models, West Covina was grouped with Covina-Azusa.

$65 to the annual payments on a $60,000 mortgage with a 9.75 percent interest rate and a thirty-year maturity. Properties in Compton are also underappraised, so that the down payment is 5 percent above average.

Mortgages in the Highland Park, Pomona, and South Central Los Angeles neighborhoods have higher loan fees and lower appraisals. In addition, mortgages in Pomona bear higher interest rates, adding $49 to the annual payments on a $60,000 mortgage with a 9.75 percent interest rate and a thirty-year maturity period. Together with evidence of 20 percent higher loan fees and underappraisals (adding up to 6.8 percent to the down payment) in both years, the evidence supports the allegation that Pomona is redlined. Applicants with properties in the South Central Los Angeles and Highland Park neighborhoods pay loan fees that are about 5 percent above average. Highland Park properties are sufficiently underappraised to increase the down payment by 5.2 percent on average. Finally, mortgages in West Covina have higher interest rates.

In summary, the findings with respect to discrimination on the basis of property location in the Los Angeles-Long Beach metropolitan area suggest that two areas, Long Beach-Southwest and Pasadena-North Central receive no adverse treatment by lenders. Pomona, on the other hand, receives substantial adverse treatment, although not in the form of higher chances of mortgage denial or downward modification. Many of the areas experience adverse treatment of more than one type.

Community organizations allege that lenders redline twenty-five neighborhoods in the five largest metropolitan areas in New York State. The evidence is consistent with nine of these allegations. Mutual savings banks are more likely to deny mortgage applications if the property is located in the Hudson-Park neighborhood of Albany, the Hillside neighborhood in Troy, or the Fort Greene and Southeast Queens neighborhoods of New York City than in a suburb. The evidence also supports the conclusion that commercial banks are more likely to deny mortgage applications on properties from the combined Central Brooklyn and Fort Greene neighborhoods than on suburban properties. Evidence of redlining from the modification results are weaker. They indicate that mutual savings banks are more likely to modify mortgage applications on properties in the Center City neighborhood in Buffalo, and the Central Brooklyn, Fort Greene, Park Slope, Crown Heights, and East Flatbush neighborhoods in New York City than applications on suburban properties. However, since applications on properties in New York-Nassau-Suffolk neighborhoods that are not alleged to be redlined are also more likely to be modified, these modification results offer little support for the redlining allegations in New York City.

After accounting for the characteristics of the borrower, the loan, and the property, neither the risk of loss nor the appraisal practices of mutual savings banks are consistently associated with the location of the property in an area alleged to be redlined. Although the average credit terms of state-regulated lenders vary across geographic areas, there is no consistent relationship between areas alleged to be redlined and unfavorable mortgage terms. However, the analysis of the quantity of funds provided by state-regulated lenders indicates that allegations that the South Bronx, Crown Heights, East Flatbush, and Southeast Queens are redlined may be correct.

Age of Neighborhood Table 10.8 summarizes the number of areas with significant findings consistent with the allegation that lenders discriminate against mortgage applications on properties in older neighborhoods. In New York, the results may be ambiguous because the age-of-neighborhood measure is associated with objective measures of the risk of loss (such as the condition of the property) that were excluded from the models because of inadequate information. Fortunately, the California models include the age of the property, and therefore, the age-of-neighborhood measure (fraction of housing built before 1940) probably provides a reasonably clear test of discrimination against old neighborhoods. At the same time, the exact meaning of the building-age results is probably ambiguous because they could represent risk factors (building condition) or discrimination (against old buildings). Tests of the effect of the building-age variables in California indicate that they are important; their absence from the New York analysis is thus a significant limitation on the New York findings.

In California, applications for mortgages on properties in older neighborhoods are more likely to be denied in eight of thirty-two study areas. A neighborhood that has ten additional percentage points of old housing (built before 1940) is 1.09 to 1.33 times more likely to be denied in these eight study areas. In addition, such applications are 1.05 to 1.20 times as likely to be modified downward in four of twenty-two California study areas. The size of the downward modification averages 4–5 percent above reductions in applications on properties in neighborhoods with average proportions of old housing. There is

Table 10.8

Number of areas with findings consistent with discrimination on the basis of the age or racial composition of neighborhood in California (CA) and New York (NY)

Neighborhood Type	Higher Chance of Denial		Higher Chance of Downward Modification		Higher Interest Rates	Larger Dollar Amount of Downward Modification		Higher Loan Fees	Under-appraisal	
	CA	NY	CA	NY	CA	CA	NY	CA	CA	NY
Older neighborhoods	8/32	4/10	4/22	7/10	0	2	0	1	0	0
Largely Black neighborhoods	7/30	1/10	2/22	0/10	4	2	0	4	1	a
Largely Spanish neighborhoods	9/32	a	4/22	a	6	1	a	2	5	a
Largely Asian neighborhoods	3/12	a	1/12	a	0	0	a	2	2	a
Number of areas studied	b	b	b	b	8	8	5	8	8	5

A finding is viewed as consistent with discriminatory behavior if applicants from the indicated group have a statistically significantly harder time receiving a mortgage or receive mortgages that have statistically significantly harsher terms.

a. These types of neighborhoods were not studied in New York because of data limitations.

b. The number of areas studied varies with the variable because of data limitations and is indicated after the slash in these four columns.

no evidence that mortgages on properties in older neighborhoods have higher interest rates or that the properties are systematically under-appraised; there is also very little evidence that applicants for such mortgages pay higher loan fees.

In New York, applications for mortgages on properties in older neighborhoods are more likely to be denied in four of ten study areas. If the older neighborhood has ten percent more old housing than average, the chance of denial is 1.08 to 1.17 times as likely than in the average neighborhood. The chance of modification is higher in older neighborhoods in seven of ten study areas. If the difference in age of old housing between two neighborhoods is 10 percent, the chance of modification is 6–19 percent higher in the older neighborhood. Mutual savings banks are responsible for six of the eleven significant findings that applications on properties in older neighborhoods have higher chances of adverse action. There is no evidence that properties in older neighborhoods are systematically underappraised by mutual savings banks.

Racial Composition of the Neighborhood   The number of significant findings consistent with allegations that lenders discriminate against applications for mortgages on properties in largely minority neighborhoods is also summarized in Table 10.8.

The chances of denial are higher if the property is located in a largely black neighborhood in seven of thirty California study areas. The differences in these seven areas are large; applications are usually more than twice as likely to be denied compared with similar applications in a largely white neighborhood. There is less evidence of discrimination against largely black neighborhoods through downward modifications. But mortgages in these neighborhoods carry interest rates that are 0.05 to 0.13 percentage points higher than similar mortgages in largely white neighborhoods in four of eight study areas. These higher interest rates add about $49 to the annual payments on a $60,000 mortgage with a 9.75 percent interest rate and a thirty-year maturity period. Applicants for mortgages on properties in largely black areas pay an extra $27 to $50 in loan fees, about a 5 percent markup. There is little evidence that properties in largely black neighborhoods are underappraised; the one significant finding would only raise the down payment by 0.2 percent with a mortgage for 80 percent of the appraised value.

In New York, only one finding is consistent with the allegation that lenders redline largely black neighborhoods. Commercial banks in the greater New York City area are more likely to deny applications for mortgages in predominantly black neighborhoods than in neighborhoods with mostly white residents.

In California, we have findings on two additional measures of the racial composition of the neighborhood: largely Spanish and largely Asian. Applications for mortgages on properties in predominantly Spanish neighborhoods have higher chances of denial than similar applications in mostly white neighborhoods in nine of thirty-two study areas. The chances of denial in these Spanish neighborhoods are 1.27 to 6.13 times those for similar applications in the white neighborhoods. Furthermore, downward modification is 1.25 to 1.70 times more likely in largely Spanish neighborhoods in four of twenty-two study areas. Interest rates are 0.03 to 0.12 percentage points higher when the property is in a largely Spanish neighborhood in six of eight study areas. As a result, the annual payments on a $60,000 mortgage with a 9.75 percent interest rate and a thirty-year maturity period are as much as $65 higher than average. The loan fees are also 6–11 percent higher in two of eight study areas. And finally, properties are systematically underappraised in five of eight study areas, but the differences are small. For example, the down payment required to accompany a mortgage for 80 percent of the appraised value increases by no more than 1.2 percent, or $180 for a purchase price of $75,000.

The evidence is consistent with allegations of discrimination against largely Asian neighborhoods in only a few study areas. Applications on properties in largely Asian neighborhoods have a higher chance of denial or downward modification in three of twelve and one of twelve study areas, respectively. Higher loan fees and underappraisals were found in largely Asian neighborhoods in two of eight study areas.

Conclusions

Our major findings of mortgage lending discrimination in New York and California are:

• We find only limited evidence of discrimination on the basis of the sex or marital status of the applicant. In particular, our findings do not support allegations of widespread discrimination against female-only applicants or of the widespread discounting of the incomes of secondary workers. The results support the view that lenders discriminate against male-only applicants and against unmarried or separated applicants.

- Discrimination on the basis of the race of the applicant is widespread in both New York and California. This discrimination takes many forms and has substantial adverse impacts on black, Spanish, and other minority applicants.
- We find some evidence that lenders treat older applicants adversely relative to younger applicants, especially in connection with loan modifications.
- The results are mixed with regard to allegations that lenders redline specific neighborhoods; some neighborhoods appear to be redlined and others do not. In addition, some support is found for allegations that lenders redline older or largely minority neighborhoods.

11
Recommendations

The mortgage-lending practices of banks have been the subject of considerable criticism during the last several years. The critics believe that lending institutions contribute to neighborhood decay by withdrawing mortgage credit even though demand exists. In the ensuing debate, serious questions regarding the allocation of mortgage credit have been raised. For example, do the terms of mortgages vary according to property location or age of housing stock? Do mortgage-lending decisions vary according to the race of the applicant? In an attempt to answer some of these questions, this study provides a careful, scientific analysis of mortgage-lending practices. This analysis can then be used as a basis for constructive public and private action.

This chapter discusses recommendations for public and private action to improve the flow of mortgage funds and to ensure equitable treatment of similarly situated mortgage applicants. The recommendations are categorized as those designed to enhance competitive market forces, those designed to counter risk, and those designed to eliminate discrimination.

Enhancing Competitive Market Forces

Public policies are needed to enhance competitive forces in the mortgage market. Two distinctly different, and complementary, approaches should be jointly undertaken in response to this need. First, public policies should encourage in-state institutional lenders to compete in the in-state mortgage market by removing unnecessary and counterproductive constraints. Second, various actions should be undertaken to increase the sophistication of mortgage seekers such that they are able to shop around for the best set of mortgage terms available.

Encourage In-State Competition

States should enhance competitive forces in the in-state mortgage market by ensuring that public policies do not place unnecessary constraints on the ability of in-state institutional lenders to compete in this market. Specifically, states should judiciously relax existing constraints, such as restrictive usury ceilings, and avoid imposing any new constraints.

Usury ceilings are an inappropriate and counterproductive means of protecting unsophisticated mortgage seekers.[1] It is inappropriate because it does not provide the information, skills, or incentives that would help unsophisticated mortgage seekers find the best mortgage terms available; it is counterproductive because it leads to credit rationing, that is, the restriction of in-state credit, whenever the usury ceiling falls below the market yield. The lower-income and less-sophisticated borrowers bear the burden of his law through reduced opportunities for mortgage credit.

The state could better protect unsophisticated borrowers by setting the usury ceiling sufficiently above the prevailing market yield to allow lenders to vary the interest rates they offer mortgage borrowers in accordance with the riskiness of the mortgage, but not so far above the market rate that lenders could set an exorbitant rate for any given borrower. For example, a usury ceiling that is 2 percentage points above the Ten-Year Constant Maturity Yield Index of United States Treasury Securities would satisfy these two criteria. In fact, New York modified its usury ceiling in response to a portion of this study that focused on usury ceilings.[2] Although the legislation provides for the above 2 percentage point differential, it does not allow the ceiling to reach market yields. The legislation severely restricts the movement of the ceiling from its 1978 value of 8.5 percent toward the market yield. The ceiling was immediately increased by only 1 percentage point and further increases are limited to 0.25 percentage points per quarter. As a result, New York's ceiling is still 2 percentage points below the market yield. The law should be amended to allow the ceiling to catch up with the realities of today's money market.

In addition, states should evaluate a new program designed to benefit moderate-income home seekers. Specifically, when a borrower's income is less than 80 percent of the median family income in the metropolitan area in which the property is located, the interest rate could be limited to a lower figure, such as the 1978 figure of 8.5 percent in New York, provided the state adopts a program to reimburse lenders for the difference between that lower interest rate and the market rate.[3] This reimbursement program should allow a lump-sum payment to the lender at the time the mortgage is closed that is equal to the discount necessary to equate the yield on the mortgage to the market rate. The lending institution would retain the mortgage in its portfolio and assume all of the risks of default. This approach assists moderate-income households, as well as encourages state-regulated lenders to lend in the state by allowing them to earn a fair rate of return on their investments.

A usury ceiling is only one example of publicly imposed constraints that can ultimately lead to a decrease in the availability of mortgage credit. Another constraint is the geographic lending quotas that have been proposed by several organizations around the country including the New York Public Interest Research Group. A more detailed discussion of these proposed quotas appears in the last section of this chapter. Here, it is important to note that the ultimate effect of such a proposal will be to decrease the amount of investment funds available from lenders who are subject to the constraint.

A requirement that lenders maintain at least a specified fraction of their portfolio in any particular class of investments, such as in-state mortgages, would decrease the overall yield on funds held by investors if the specified fraction were greater than the fraction that would otherwise exist. This lower yield would lead to a decrease in funds available to lenders because savers will turn to other financial intermediaries that can offer them higher returns for their savings. The end result of geographic lending quotas would be a net decrease in the availability of investment funds for precisely those investments that the restriction was intended to increase.

Increase Sophistication of Mortgage Seekers
There are several direct actions that states should undertake to help "borrowers of limited means who are unsophisticated and lacking in financial knowledge."[4] Each of these actions would make it easier and more efficient for such potential borrowers to shop around for the best set of mortgage terms available.

If the usury law conforms to the above recommendation, the state should conduct a monthly survey of all state-regulated lenders within each metropolitan area to identify the interest rate and other fees being charged. The results of this survey should be published and widely distributed (for example, in local newspapers). The interest rates for mortgages with several different combinations of maturity period and loan-to-appraised-value ratios should be reported, as well as information on discounts, closing costs, and other fees charged by the lender.[5] By publishing this data, the state would enable mortgage seekers within each metropolitan area to more easily identify those lenders offering the best mortgage terms. Easy access to this information would substantially reduce the level of effort required for each applicant to find his or her most preferred lender. By helping to increase the efficiency of the mortgage search process, this policy would help increase the quality of competition in the mortgage market.

However, to effectively evaluate various mortgage terms, mortgage seekers also need to know how each institution's lending criteria will affect both their own chance of obtaining a mortgage and the terms under which a mortgage is likely to be granted. Therefore, lending institutions should provide all prospective borrowers with a written statement of the criteria they use to evaluate an application and the relative importance of each criterion. If necessary, lenders should be required to develop these statements and make them available to the public. These statements should also include an estimate of the length of time required to process applications for typical mortgages (conventional, FHA, VA, one- to four-family house, multifamily building). This information would allow mortgage seekers to evaluate their chances of success, the type of terms they are likely to receive, and the amount of time that will probably be required to file an application and have it acted upon at each lending institution. Such information would greatly aid mortgage seekers in their selection of lenders. Because completing formal mortgage applications is time-consuming, it is important that mortgage seekers be able to realistically select a set of lenders with whom to formally apply.

The preceding requirements would serve three distinct purposes. First, they would facilitate the mortgage seeker's preapplication search for the most promising lenders. Second, in doing so, they would provide an incentive for individual lending institutions to offer the most competitive mortgage lending criteria and terms possible. Third, the second requirement should aid in the detection and prevention of discrimination in mortgage lending, as it requires lenders to make public their lending criteria.

Some mortgage seekers, especially those who are neither new to the mortgage market or unsophisticated, will need more guidance than just information on interest rates, other fees, and lending criteria if they are to locate the best terms available. For these applicants, lenders and state or federal regulatory agencies should publish a brochure explaining what to look for in a mortgage loan and how to evaluate each of the terms of the mortgage, as well as the various fees that must be paid when the mortgage is closed.[6]

The brochure should address the following issues:

1. *finding the right house*
- what to look for in the neighborhood
- what questions to ask about insurance
- what to look for in the interior of the structure
- what to look for and questions to ask about the exterior of the structure
- whom to contact if the owner does not have the answers

2. *getting the money*
- choosing a lender
- understanding which factors the lender considers important in a mortgage application and why
- determining how much the applicant can afford to borrow
- deciding which type of mortgage to obtain (conventional, FHA or VA)
- identifying, understanding and evaluating the terms of the mortgage
  the downpayment
  the interest rate
  any prepayment penalties
  any discount points
  the mortgage contract and note

3. *the purchase and sale agreement*
- finding a lawyer
- understanding all the provisions of the purchase and sale agreement

4. *the closing*
- transferring the deed and the money
- paying the closing fees or closing costs
  legal fees
  title search
  recording the new title

Lenders or regulatory agencies should also provide technical assistance, advice, and counseling to individual mortgage seekers.[7] Such a program might take the form of neighborhood seminars for prospective home buyers. A regulatory agency could create a mortgage-seeker seminar team that would establish and maintain contacts with mortgage lenders, real estate brokers, and neighborhood or community groups around a state. The seminar team would, with the aid of these contacts, set up periodic seminars for mortgage seekers within particular neighborhoods. At these seminars, prospective house buyers could ask specific questions about searching for and evaluating the terms of a mortgage loan. This program should focus primarily on those neighborhoods in which mortgage seekers are most likely to be "unsophisticated and lacking in financial knowledge."

Countering Risk

The results of this study strongly suggest that variation in risk is an important cause of variation in mortgage lending across neighborhoods. To the extent that these variations in risk are caused by externalities, it is appropriate that the public sector design policies to help counter those external causes. The public sector may also want to create subsidy programs designed to decrease investor risk or increase demand within certain neighborhoods or by certain types of property purchasers.

A neighborhood that is only beginning to decline may be assisted through new neighborhood decision-making arrangements, a Neighborhood Housing Services (NHS) program, or a coinsurance program. On the other hand, a neighborhood that has deteriorated may require a much larger public-sector commitment if it is to be rejuvenated. In this section, only policies aimed at declining neighborhoods are discussed; discussion of larger policies designed to improve deteriorated neighborhoods, such as urban renewal, is beyond the scope of this study.

Neighborhood Decision-Making Arrangements
One way to protect property investors against the effects of negative neighborhood externalities is to allow the investors to participate in certain types of decisions that are likely to affect neighborhood property values. Condominium-ownership agreements are a good example of such an arrangement. Each condominium owner may maintain the interior of his or her apartment as he or she sees fit, so long as no harm is done to the structural integrity of the building. The entire set of owners within a single development, however, is responsible for

maintenance of the common spaces and the exterior condition of the apartments. Typically, an individual condominium owner can alter the exterior of his or her apartment only with permission of all owners. Such arrangements are designed specifically to deal with the fact that structural and exterior-maintenance decisions affect the values of all condominiums within the development.

Although this type of joint decision making is of particular importance when all units share a common structure, it need not be and, in fact, is not restricted to dwelling-unit ownership within a common structure. For example, in High Park Green, a development in Toronto, Canada, a similar type of arrangement exists for several city blocks of one- and two-family condominum houses. Neighborhood, structural, and exterior-maintenance decisions are made and underwritten collectively by all condominium owners within the neighborhood.

The public sector should encourage joint decision-making arrangements in neighborhoods that are threatened with deterioration because of externalities. An appropriate public response would be to enact enabling legislation that would prescribe the conditions under which a neighborhood could create a joint decision-making arrangement, the legal steps necessary to establish such an arrangement, and the legal rights and responsibilities of property owners within a neighborhood before, during, and after the implementation of such an arrangement.

Neighborhood Housing Services

The Neighbhorhood Housing Services (NHS) program is an alternative means of dealing with the effects of neighborhood externalities on mortgage risk and demand within a neighborhood. The first NHS was established in the Central North Side (CNS) community of Pittsburgh in 1968. This NHS "has directed its activities toward the preservation and revitalization of the CNS using, as its major tool, a revolving high-risk loan fund provided by foundation grants."[8]

This idea was later adopted by the federal government, which created the Urban Reinvestment Task Force (the Task Force) to encourage the formation of NHS programs in other neighborhoods throughout the United States. The Task Force was created on April 22, 1974, by the Department of Housing and Urban Development and the Federal Home Loan Bank Board. As of June 14, 1976, new NHS programs were operating in twenty-three cities, including several in New York State. William A. Whiteside, staff director of the Task

Force and director of the Office of Neighborhood Reinvestment of the
Federal Home Loan Bank Board (FHLBB), provided a clear summary
of this program and its requirements in his testimony before the Senate
Committee on Banking, Housing, and Urban Affairs.

We found that a successful NHS program must operate in a neighborhood in which the housing stock is beginning to show signs of deterioration but yet remains basically sound, and where there is a high
degree of home ownership. The program has five basic elements: (1)
residents who want to preserve their neighborhood, improve their
homes, and who are willing to make an effort to establish and operate
an NHS program; (2) local government which seeks to improve the
neighborhood by making the necessary improvements in public amenities and by conducting an appropriate housing code inspection and
compliance program coordinated with NHS activities; (3) group of
financial institutions which agree to reinvest in the neighborhood by
making market rate loans for qualified borrowers and tax deductible
contributions to the NHS to support its operating cost; (4) high risk
revolving loan fund to make loans at flexible rates and terms to residents not meeting commercial credit standards; the funds are provided
by private foundations, industry or government; and (5) an NHS organization, which is a state-chartered, private, non-profit corporation
having a board of directors of which a majority are community residents, along with significant representation from financial institutions,
and a three-member staff.
   Neighborhood Housing Services programs represent a blend of pri-
vate-public-community involvement in a working partnership, with
each group strongly represented and respectful of the others' positions.
This partnership must be constructed with the greatest care.[9]

In 1978, the demonstration activities of the Task Force were trans-
ferred to the National Neighborhood Reinvestment Corporation, a new
corporation established by an act of Congress.[10] The new corporation
has been charged with implementing and expanding the activities of
the Task Force.

An NHS program can only be effective in neighborhoods that have
begun to decline, but that have not yet completely deteriorated. This
program also requires considerable trust and cooperation among neighborhood residents, local financial intermediaries, and local government
agencies, such as the housing code enforcement agency. Although the
success of such a program is never easily documented, the NHS
program does provide an excellent and well-thought-out approach to
increasing the availability of mortgage funds to neighborhoods that are
threatened with decline. Local financial intermediaries should take
steps to encourage the formation of local NHS programs wherever

neighborhood property owners exhibit strong interest in such a program.

Coinsurance

A properly designed mortgage coinsurance program could help make mortgage credit more readily available in declining, but basically sound, neighborhoods. The importance of careful design of a coinsurance program is illustrated by recent experience in the FHA mortgage insurance program. Specifically, the FHA program has been accused of hastening the decline of certain urban neighborhoods. Although the rationale behind these accusations is not entirely clear, a major problem with the FHA program is that it fully insures mortgage loans. One hundred percent coverage removes the main incentive for lenders to carefully review prospective borrowers and properties. According to community leaders:

The FHA/VA system presents a myriad of problems for the home buyer and the neighborhood. Right from the beginning forms are falsified by realtors, minimal downpayments are required, and home-buying counseling is virtually nonexistent. Defective and unsound houses are sold and servicing of the mortgagor by the broker is very minimal. Forebearance is an unknown word to the new homeowner.[11]

Critics of the FHA/VA program assert that these practices have led to abandonment of properties and deterioration of neighborhoods.

To avoid these results, a coinsurance program should be structured so that lenders have an incentive to carefully review mortgage applicants and to service mortgages with a view toward helping borrowers to keep their payment current, rather than toward assigning delinquent mortgages to FHA or VA as rapidly as possible.

Lenders will carefully review applications and helpfully service mortgages, only if they share some of the risk. Partial insurance coverage of the outstanding mortgage balance forces the lender to bear some of the risk and thereby provides an incentive for the lender to carefully review mortgage applications. At the same time, the insurance allows the lender to make somewhat riskier loans than would be made if no insurance existed.

Coverage of risk-related expenses will also alter the lender's incentives. By insuring some fraction of the costs of rearranging terms to bring a delinquent account up to date, the public insuring agency can provide an incentive for lenders to help borrowers through periods of delinquency. If foreclosure costs are at the same time uninsured, the public insurance agency can discourage unnecessary foreclosures.

Borrowers must also share some of the risk, or they may lose their incentive to maintain either the property or the mortgage. A common way of ensuring that borrowers share some of the risk is to restrict coinsurance eligibility to mortgage amounts of less than some administratively determined fraction of the property's market value. For instance, eligibility for coverage could be restricted to mortgages of less than 90 percent of the average of the purchase price and the appraised value.

The manner in which benefits are paid will also affect the incentives of lenders and borrowers. For example, if the public sector insured 50 percent of the outstanding balance of a mortgage loan and the outstanding balance were $10,000, the public sector could pay the lender as much as $5,000. The amount of benefits actually paid the lender, should the mortgage be foreclosed, depends on both the difference between the sales price of the property at foreclosure and the outstanding balance and the way in which the benefit payment schedule is arranged. For instance, if the collateral on this mortgage sold for $5,000, a $5,000 loss would have to be shared by the lender and the public insuring agency. If the insurance paid 100 percent of the first $5,000 in losses, lenders would have no incentive to avoid foreclosure, since their losses would be zero. If, on the other hand, lenders were required to pay 100 percent of the first $5,000 in losses, they would treat this mortgage in the same manner as an uninsured mortgage, because they would have to absorb the total $5,000 loss. Compromises between these two extremes are possible; insurance could pay 50 percent of any losses up to the outstanding balance. This arrangement would act as an incentive to lenders to make higher risk loans, and the dollar value of that incentive per dollar of outstanding loan commitment would not vary with the size of the loan. This arrangement would also provide lenders with some incentive to avoid foreclosure in those instances when such action would lead to losses. In this example, the dollar value of this incentive would be exactly half the dollar value of the incentive facing the lender had the same mortgage not been insured.

Eligibility criteria for state-subsidized mortgage coinsurance should be designed to meet four key demands. First, the eligibility criteria should not simply identify particular neighborhoods as eligible, as this frequently leads to the accusation that the public sector is institutionalizing or legitimizing redlining. Eligibility for coinsurance should also depend on the riskiness of the proposed mortgage.

Second, the eligibility criteria should provide incentives to lenders to make somewhat riskier-than-normal loans, but to turn down proposed loans that are too risky. These incentives, then, must encourage lenders to carefully and accurately evaluate the riskiness of each mortgage application.

Third, the eligibility criteria should provide incentives to mortgage seekers to shop around for the most advantageous terms available in the mortgage market. In this manner, mortgage seekers who could obtain a mortgage without the aid of such a program could do so and not simply take advantage of the publicly supported coinsurance program.

Fourth, the eligibility criteria should benefit lower-income households.

Eliminating Discrimination

Legislation prohibiting most forms of discrimination already exists at both the state and federal level. For example, federal law provides that mortgage credit cannot be denied because of:

race, color, religion, national origin, sex, marital status, or age (provided that the applicant has the capacity to enter into a binding contract); the fact that all or part of the applicant's income derives from any public assistance program, or the fact that the applicant has in good faith exercised any right under the Consumer Credit Protection Act or any [applicable state law].[12]

New York statutes prohibit discrimination against any applicant for mortgage credit "because of the race, creed, color, national origin, sex, marital status, or disability" of the applicant(s).[13] Such discrimination is explicitly prohibited in "the granting, withholding, extending, or renewing, or in the fixing of the rates, terms, or conditions of" mortgage credit.[14] Creditors are also prohibited from refusing

to consider sources of an applicant's income or to subject an applicant's income to discounting, in whole or in part, because of the applicant's race, creed, color, national origin, sex, marital status, childbearing potential or disability.[15]

The redlining debate has focused on one essentially discriminatory criterion that is not covered by any of these laws. Specifically, various persons and organizations have alleged that properties in certain neighborhoods are either denied mortgage credit even though the risks of loss do not justify such action or are offered mortgage credit with more onerous terms than properties in other neighborhoods with the same risks of loss. When based on the racial composition of the neighborhood, such geographic distinctions are prohibited by existing equal credit opportunity legislation. It is alleged, however, that neighborhoods are also singled out on the basis of the age of their housing stock or the use of streets or other geographic boundaries that are not highly correlated with the racial composition of the neighborhood.

This study has found evidence that supports some of the specific redlining allegations, contradicts others, and is ambiguous for still others. Some support is found for the allegation that older neighborhoods are discriminated against. In most cases, the results contradict the allegation that a neighborhood is redlined. In other cases, the evidence supports the allegation that a neighborhood is discriminated against because of its location. For example, the results support the allegations that the Hudson-Park neighborhood in Albany and the Hillside neighborhood in Troy are redlined. Chapter 10 contains a detailed summary of the results.

Each mortgage application should be evaluated on its own merits. A mortgage application is not being evaluated on its merits if the decision is based on its location without regard to the credit worthiness of the applicant or the risk of loss associated with the specific property. Although this study has found only limited evidence of redlining on the basis of the age of the housing stock or geographic location, this evidence is sufficient to justify legislation outlawing such arbitrary lending decisions. Such legislation should require that each mortgage application be reviewed on its own merits by prohibiting the use of an area-specific standard operating policy. However, the legislation should explicitly recognize that neighborhood characteristics such as fires, vacant buildings, housing code violations, and property tax arrears are relevant factors in determining the market value of the property and assessing the risk of loss on a loan. Lenders should be allowed to use specific relevant facts about neighboring properties and actual movements in market values when making lending decisions. An area the size of a census tract is probably an appropriate definition of the neighborhood for the development of such specific facts.

The fair-housing laws require that lenders use objective measures of each application's risk of loss. Such measures must have a causal relationship with risk, not just a correlation. Society has correctly identified certain personal characteristics, such as race and sex, as having no causal relationship to risk of loss. Any observed correlation is purely spurious. Similarly, aggregate measures of these characteristics, such as the racial composition of the neighborhood, are also unconditionally prohibited from use in the lending process. Other neighborhood and location factors, however, should not be prohibited if there is a causal relationship with the risk of loss. A very likely candidate for such a causal link is the incidence of housing code violations and vacant buildings.

The FHLBB has recently adopted a regulation that prohibits member institutions from discrimination in lending "on the basis of the age or location of the dwelling."[16] FHLBB goes on to state that:

these restrictions are intended to prohibit use of unfounded or unsubstantiated assumptions regarding the effect upon loan risk of the age of a dwelling or the physical or economic characteristics of an area. Loan decisions should be based on the present market value of the property offered as security (including consideration of specific improvements to be made by the borrower) and the likelihood that the property will retain an adequate value over the term of the loan. Specific factors which may negatively affect its short-range future value (up to 3–5 years) should be clearly documented. Factors which in some cases may cause the market value of a property to decline are recent zoning changes or a significant number of abandoned homes in the immediate vicinity of the property. *However, not all zoning changes will cause a decline in property values, and proximity to abandoned buildings may not affect the market value of a property because of rehabilitation programs or affirmative lending programs, or because the cause of abandonment is unrelated to high risk. Proper underwriting considerations include the condition and utility of the improvements, and various physical factors such as street conditions, amenities such as parks and recreation areas, availability of public utilities and municipal services, and exposure to flooding and land faults.* However, arbitrary decisions based on age or location are prohibited, since many older, soundly constructed homes provide housing opportunities which may be precluded by an arbitrary lending policy.[17]

Many of the public comment letters on FHLBB's proposed version of this regulation expressed concern that the prohibition of the use of the age and location of the dwelling in lending decisions might require institutions to eliminate all location-related factors (including location next to or near abandoned buildings) from the appraisal process, and, hence, to make unsafe loans. FHLBB responded that the effect of the regulation is only to prohibit the arbitrary use of age and location. In the preface to the final regulations, FHLBB states that "conditions of the area which may be reliably related to risk" may be considered.[18] Unfortunately, the fact that such conditions may be considered is not made sufficiently clear in the regulation.

The FHLBB statement that "proximity to abandoned buildings may not affect the market value of a property" can be interpreted as further weakening the cautiously worded preceding sentence (abandonment "may" cause decline of property values "in some cases"). In addition, the FHLBB statement that lists proper underwriting considerations should explicitly include the conditions of adjacent buildings and buildings on both sides of the street, as well as those behind the property. It is difficult to justify excluding this factor while including such factors as street conditions. Some of the reasons given for why abandonment does not always reduce market value are also valid for street conditions. For example, potholes can be repaved by a city program at least as easily as abandoned buildings can be rehabilitated by a city program. The FHLBB's policy statement would be clearer if building conditions were included in the list of proper underwriting considerations, or if the sentences, "However . . . ," and, "Proper underwriting considerations . . . ," were eliminated.

California has regulations prohibiting the use of the age of the residential structures in the neighborhood and the location of the property in mortgage-lending decisions. These are probably the most detailed and carefully written regulations in the country.[19] In general, these factors cannot be considered unless the "financial institution can demonstrate that such consideration in a particular case is required to avoid an unsafe and unsound business practice." The regulations recognize only two situations in which neighborhood or location factors can be deemed to be required to avoid an unsafe and unsound business practice:

1. natural or other hazardous conditions
2. documentation that "factors relating to the geographic area closely surrounding the . . . property are likely to cause the fair market value of the . . . property to decrease during the early years (three to five years) of the mortgage term."

The regulations, however, provide that lenders may consider the physical condition of the housing and the "properly appraised fair market value of the property." In defining nondiscriminatory appraisals, neighborhood characteristics or trends can be used in arriving at an appraised value apparently without showing that they are necessary to avoid an unsafe or unsound business practice.

Although the California regulations reflect concern with only prohibiting the arbitrary use of location, they are too broad. Requiring a documented relationship between the neighborhood characteristic and an unsafe and unsound business practice in each "particular case" considered by a lender is too demanding and unnecessarily burdensome. The lender should not be required to establish a correlation in each case when there is a persuasive case for a causal relationship.

In response to the results of this study, New York State passed a law prohibiting lenders from refusing to make a "prudent loan" because of the geographic location of the property.[20] According to this law, acceptable banking standards determine the prudency of a loan. The legislation should have clearly stated that it is the arbitrary use of location that is prohibited.

Detection

New York's Equal Housing Opportunity Lender (EHOL) form and California's loan register provide information on the subject property, the requested loan, the lender action, and the socioeconomic characteristics of all applicants. The analysis of this data if the best approach, short of "testing" (see below), for detecting the existence of any form of discrimination. New York and California provide regulatory agencies and the public with the minimum amount of information necessary to ascertain through multivariate statistical procedures whether discrimination occurred.

The disclosure of lending activity required by the Home Mortgage Disclosure Act of 1975 provides data wholly inadequate to analyze discrimination.[21] It provides information only on the aggregate amount of lending in local geographic areas (census tracts or zip code areas). The Home Mortgage Disclosure Act should be repealed because it requires the maintenance of nearly useless records. It should be replaced with a law requiring the maintenance and disclosure of detailed information on each and every serious mortgage inquiry. The FHLBB has taken some tentative steps in this direction, but has been unwilling to impose a requirement to report sufficiently detailed information other than in a demonstration program in three metropolitan areas.

"Testing" is a procedure by which an enforcement agency sends minority and majority group members, who are equal in all relevant respects, to the same lender to apply for a loan on the same or similar property. The treatment of each group is then compared. Testing is generally viewed as slightly preferable to the analysis of EHOL-type data because it theoretically allows for more control of the character-istics of the minority and majority group members being compared. It does, however, have an obvious limitation in assessing geographic and other forms of neighborhood discrimination because of the difficulty of matching properties in different locations for comparison. In this situation, statistical analysis of EHOL-type data may be preferable. The EHOL-based approach is also more economical than the employ-ment of a sufficient number of testers. In addition, a property must be available for appraisal to adequately test the mortgage application process. Limited use of testers, however, may prove to be valuable in some situations, especially in assessing the extent to which discrimi-nation occurs through screening prior to an application.

Several steps need to be taken to effectively use the EHOL-type information in detecting discrimination. First, the regulatory agency should develop an affirmative monitoring program. This program should require that all the form's information be sent directly to the agency. In New York, this means that all three parts of the EHOL form ("personal economic data," "descriptive data", and "disposi-tions of mortgage loan applications") should be kept together with a copy sent directly to the state on a monthly basis. The regulatory agency should then code, computerize, and analyze these forms. Cal-ifornia does code and computerize the data. The analysis should follow the general outline of the analysis described in Chapters 5 to 8. The agency should then take any appropriate action as required by the specific results of its analysis.

Second, information should be available for all serious mortgage inquiries. In New York, this would require that coverage of the EHOL forms be expanded. Presently, every state-regulated banking organi-zation with over $50 million in assets is required to maintain an EHOL form on:

all written applications received for conventional, FHA, FmHA, and VA mortgage loans obtained for the purpose of financing the purchase or construction, or refinancing the ownership, of one to four family residential real estate.[22]

The reporting procedure could be improved by specifying when a lender must accept a written application. It should be made clear that the EHOL form is to be completed when a potential home buyer makes serious oral inquiries. This requirement would act to minimize the potential for discrimination in informal screening procedures. It is important that every applicant have the right to file a written application and that lenders be required to inform all applicants of this right. In addition, situations currently exempt from the EHOL requirements, such as telephone applications, should require the completion of the EHOL form. Finally, because some New York lenders appear to have ignored the EHOL requirement, all lenders should be regularly monitored to ensure full compliance.

Third, the information that is gathered should:

1. Provide detailed information on income, assets, debts, purchase price, and appraised value. As in California, the exact amounts rounded to the nearest hundred dollars should be provided. At a minimum, the New York form should have more categories, and the categories of response should be consistent across questions, especially in the case of assets and debts.

2. Include all loan terms including loan-to-value ratio, interest rate, term, loan fees, and type of loan. This information should include the requested as well as the granted terms. California's loan register provides most of this information.

3. Clearly identify the bank action and applicant response perhaps along the line indicated in Figure 11.1.

4. Inquire as to the applicant's status as a depositor, including the length of time he or she has been a depositor. This information may be valuable in explaining lending decisions across time because of variations in the availability of funds, especially in states with restrictive usury laws.

5. Obtain information on any credit report that the lender has received.

6. Obtain information on the number of persons in the applicant's household.

7. Specify the more frequent reasons for bank action and gather these data for approvals, as well as denials and modifications.

Finally, the form should be standardized to facilitate computerizing. All lenders should be required to use exactly the same format. As a result, the regulatory agency's data-processing expenses would be considerably reduced.

BANK ACTION

☐ Approved as applied for

☐ Approved with modifications to
(check all applicable categories and
provide the approved values in the
space to the right of the category)

☐ term   _____

☐ loan amount   _____

☐ loan-to-value ratio   _____

☐ interest rate   _____

☐ type of loan   _____

☐ other (describe)   _____

☐ Denied

☐ Cancelled because of failure to complete application within
90 days.

Describe missing information

_____

_____

_____

☐ Still pending

☐ Withdrawn by applicant prior to bank action.

APPLICANT RESPONSE

☐ Accept loan

☐ Refuse loan

Figure 11.1
Proposed bank action and applicant response section for the EHOL form.

Prevention and Enforcement

Lenders have a major responsibility to increase efforts to eliminate racial discrimination in mortgage lending. They should develop written standards for evaluating loan applications, institute an affirmative marketing program, employ more minority group members as mortgage loan officers, conduct seminars to train loan officers to treat all applicants fairly, and expand opportunities for private redress in individual cases of discrimination.

Written standards for underwriting will facilitate each lender's effort to ensure that similarly situated mortgage applicants receive equal treatment. These written standards can also be used to identify the objective lending factors that need to be incorporated in an analysis aimed at determining if discrimination is occurring. Regulatory agencies may want to delineate appropriate lending criteria to increase the effectiveness of their monitoring process.

Lenders and regulatory agencies should develop a mortgage applicant credit evaluation system. This system will ensure that applicants of all races will be treated equally in terms of denial, approval after modification, or approval. A credit evaluation system delineates the precise weight that should be accorded to the objective measures of credit worthiness, such as income, net wealth, employment experience, credit history, and loan-to-appraised-value ratio. Each objective measure is weighted consistently for all applicants. The sum of the products of each weight and the value of its corresponding measure is the mortgage credit score. The score will determine if the application is approved. Each lending institution should be able to establish its own cutoff point on the mortgage credit scale so that it can respond to the variations in net new money (deposits less withdrawals). However, the value a lender selects must be used for all applications received during the period of time it is in effect.

Lenders should also take steps to seek out applications from minority persons by developing an affirmative marketing strategy. This strategy should include advertising clearly stating that there will be no discrimination. Media that serve minority group members should be employed.

Because the results of the analysis suggest that lenders are not treating similarly situated minority applicants the same as white applicants, a concerted effort is necessary to modify their employees' attitudes. Increasing the number of minority persons who have customer contact and are involved in the decision-making process is an essential step. In addition, lenders should organize a series of regular seminars aimed at increasing employee awareness of subjective, and probably subconscious, factors that enter lending decisions. Once employees are aware of such factors, they are more likely to eliminate those that are discriminatory or inconsistent with other lending policies. It may be advisable to employ appropriate outside consultants to develop and conduct these seminars. Top-management personnel should attend these sessions and make their commitment clear to all other participants.

Most of the New York State mutual savings banks participate in an internal review process known as the Mortgage Review Fund (MRF).[23] Persons who have been refused a mortgage loan by one of the ninety-three participating savings banks may apply to the MRF for a mortgage loan. The MRF will make an independent evaluation of the application, and if a mortgage loan is justified under normal bank-lending criteria, the MRF will approve a loan from its funds. Regional committees, which are composed of three public members selected by a commission appointed by the governor and three members elected by savings banks, review the applications and make nonbinding recommendations to the MRF. The fund has been in operation since March 1977. During its first year, the MRF received 262 requests for applications, but only seventy-five completed applications were returned. More than half (forty-two) received a favorable recommendation by the regional committees.[24] Of these, eleven were withdrawn prior to final action by the MRF, six received loans from participating savings banks, nineteen were approved for an MRF loan, four were declined loans by the MRF, and two were in process at the end of the year.

Although the establishment of the MRF has been a useful contribution to eliminating discrimination, it can be improved. At present, only persons who have had their applications denied by a participating savings bank are eligible to apply. Other possible forms of discrimination should be addressed. In particular, the review procedure should consider applicants who have been offered a mortgage but complain that its terms are unlawfully differentiated from those of other mortgages granted similarly situated applicants. The procedure should also provide some relief for persons who complain that they have not been allowed to file a written application. In this situation, the MRF could be structured to require that the participating savings bank that is closest to the property accept and process a written application.

A second problem is the length of time it takes the MRF to process an application. Much of this is the result of the multitiered review process that was established at the request of some members of the New York State Legislature. A procedure to expedite the processing of those applications that are likely to receive a favorable decision would be useful. Perhaps the regional committees could allow the secretary of the fund to forward an application to the MRF without regional committee action if the secretary finds that there is a strong case for approving the application. Because the MRF should not deny any loan without the participation of the regional committee, applications should be returned to the regional committees when the MRF disagrees with the judgment of its secretary.

Finally, much of the literature implies that the opportunity to receive an MRF mortgage is limited to cases in which the reason for denial is the person's belief that "the property they're interested in is in the wrong place." In view of the findings of this study, all literature describing the MRF should make it clear that the denial of equal mortgage credit on any unlawful basis (for example, race and sex) is a sufficient basis for MRF involvement.

Another attempted deterrent to discrimination is the Bank Reinvestment Act, proposed by the New York Public Interest Research Group (NYPIRG). According to this proposal:

> Each state-chartered bank would be required to meet a "standard requirement factor" to be set annually by the Superintendent of Banks but not to be less than 50 percent. That is, at least 50 percent of the amount deposited by residents of a given census tract or zip code area would have to be reinvested there in the form of mortgage, home improvement or small business loans.
> . . . In those cases where the standard reinvestment factor was not met, the Department would be required to investigate the situation. The Department would determine whether demand was artificially depressed by lack of advertising, difficulty of obtaining loan applications, high down payments, low appraisals, etc.[25]

There are three very serious objections to this approach. First, it sets an arbitrary figure that is unrelated to the neighborhood demand for mortgage monies. In some neighborhoods, the demand for mortgage funds may be nearly nonexistent because the residents have paid off their mortgages and are happy where they live.

Second, this approach presumes that government action is justified in a broad range of situations. However, the criterion triggering such action is unrelated to any finding of unlawful discriminatory behavior on the part of any institution. In short, the remedy is not responsive to unlawful lending behavior, which is presumably defined to include discrimination on the basis of property location.

Third, the administrative action that this proposal would require would be extensive and very costly. New York's Banking Department would be required to review thousands of census tracts, nearly all of which would fall below the standard reinvestment factor because of the legitimate lack of demand. Such an expenditure of scarce tax dollars cannot be justified when there is a clear need to increase enforcement efforts aimed at eliminating the race of the applicant as a lending criterion.

The proposed Banking Reinvestment Act is a weak response to a complex problem. As such, it should not be enacted into law.

If a regulatory agency finds a pattern of unlawful discrimination during the course of its audit of a particular institution's reporting forms, it should have the power to take one or more of the following actions:

1. Require the creditor to cease and desist from unlawful discrimination.
2. Impose a fine.
3. Award compensatory damages to specific individuals.
4. Establish lending targets for lending to members of the group that has been discriminated against on the basis of that institution's treatment of members of groups that have not been discriminated against.
5. Postpone decisions on applications for branches and mergers until a lending institution's pattern of discrimination has been eliminated.
6. Require other affirmative action that will achieve the objectives of eliminating unlawful discrimination from mortgage-credit decisions.

Appendix A
Variable Definitions

The variables used in the California and New York analyses are defined in this appendix.

California

Financial Characteristics

RLTOINC
Requested loan amount divided by total income less 2.5 when positive; otherwise, zero.

FSECINC
Fraction of secondary income to total income.

FSIFCB
Variable equal to FSECINC if the secondary wage earner is a female of childbearing age (under thirty-five); otherwise, zero.

FSIFNCB
Variable equal to FSECINC if the secondary wage earner is a female beyond the childbearing age (thirty-five or older); otherwise, zero.

RLTOAV
Requested loan amount divided by the appraised value.

Neighborhood Characteristics

FHI
Fraction of households with annual income greater than $15,000 in the census tract of the subject property in 1969.

INC1976

1976 mean income in the zip code area containing the subject property (based on IRS returns) (thousands).

DINC7675

1976 mean income less the 1975 mean income in the zip code area containing the subject property (based on IRS returns) (thousands).

DINC7570

1975 mean income (based on IRS returns) less the 1970 mean income (based on the census) in the zip code area containing the subject property (thousands).

DHH7675

Number of households in 1976 less the number in 1975 in the zip code area containing the subject property (based on IRS returns) (thousands).

DHH7570

Number of households in 1975 (based on IRS returns) less the number in 1970 (based on the census) in the zip code area containing the subject property (thousands).

Age of Neighborhood

PRE1940

Fraction of housing units built before 1940 in the census tract containing the subject property.

Building Age

BA1–9

Dummy variable equal to one if the building is one to nine years old; otherwise, zero.

BA10–19

Dummy variable equal to one if the building is ten to nineteen years old; otherwise, zero.

BA20–29

Dummy variable equal to one if the building is twenty to twenty-nine years old; otherwise, zero.

BA30–39

Dummy variable equal to one if the building is thirty to thirty-nine years old; otherwise, zero.

BA40–49
Dummy variable equal to one if the building is forty to forty-nine years old; otherwise, zero.

BAGE50
Dummy variable equal to one if the building is fifty or more years old; otherwise, zero.

Age of Applicant

ALT25
Dummy variable equal to one if the applicant is under twenty-five years of age; otherwise, zero.

A25TO34
Dummy variable equal to one if the applicant is twenty-five to thirty-four years of age; otherwise, zero.

A45TO54
Dummy variable equal to one if the applicant is forty-five to fifty-four years of age; otherwise, zero.

AGE55
Dummy variable equal to one if the applicant is fifty-five or more years of age; otherwise, zero.

Sex

FONLYCB
Dummy variable equal to one if all applicants are female and at least one is of childbearing age; otherwise, zero.

FONLYNCB
Dummy variable equal to one if all applicants are female and none are of childbearing age; otherwise, zero.

MFCB
Dummy variable equal to one if the application is from a male-female couple and the woman is of childbearing age; otherwise, zero.

MFNCB
This is the reference group for the sex-based dummy variables. It includes applications from male-female applicants with no women of childbearing age.

MONLY

Dummy variable equal to one if all applicants are male; otherwise, zero.

FONLY

Dummy variable equal to one if all applicants are female; otherwise, zero. This is only used when there are too few observations to separate female applications into FONLYCB and FONLYNCB.

Race

BLACK

Dummy variable equal to one if at least one applicant is black; otherwise, zero.

SPANISH

Dummy variable equal to one if at least one applicant is Spanish and none are blck; otherwise, zero.

ASIAN

Dummy variable equal to one if at least one applicant is Asian and none are black or Spanish; otherwise, zero.

OMIN

Dummy variable equal to one if at least one applicant is a minority and none are black, Spanish or Asian; otherwise, zero.

Racial Composition of the Neighborhood

FBLACK

Fraction of the population that is black in the census tract containing the subject property (1970).

FSPANISH

Fraction of the population that is Spanish in the census tract containing the subject property (1970).

FASIAN

Fraction of the population that is Asian in the zip code area containing the subject property (1970).

Neighborhood Characteristics for the Anaheim-Santa Ana-Garden Grove SMSA

FHIASG
Fraction of households with annual income greater than or equal to $15,000 in the census tract of the subject property in 1975 (special census).

INC1975ASG
Median household income from a January 1976 special census for the census tract containing the subject property (thousands).

DINC7570ASG
1976 median income (based on special census) less the 1970 mean income (based on the census) in the census tract containing the subject property (thousands).

DPOP7670ASG
1976 population (based on special survey) less the 1970 population (based on the census) in the census tract containing the subject property (thousands).

Neighborhood and Racial Composition Characteristics for the Sacramento SMSA

FHISAC
Fraction of households with $15,000 or more in annual income during 1975 in the census tract containing the subject property (special census).

INC1976SAC
Median household income during 1975 in the census tract containing the subject property (special census).

DINC7570SAC
1975 median income (based on the special census) less the 1970 mean income (based on the census) in the census tract containing the subject property (thousands).

DPOP7570SAC
1975 population (based on the special census) less the 1970 population (based on the census) in the census tract containing the subject property (thousands).

FBLACKSAC

Fraction of the population that is black in the census tract containing the subject property (1975 special census).

FSPANISHSAC

Fraction of the population that is Spanish in the census tract containing the subject property (1975 special census).

FASIANSAC

Fraction of the population that is Asian in the census tract containing the subject property (1975 special census).

Additional Neighborhood Characteristics for the City of Los Angeles

ASP7677LAC

Average sales price in 1976 and 1977 in the census tract of the subject property (thousands). Two years have been combined to increase the number of transactions in a census tract. At least five transactions were required before an observation was included in the Los Angeles City analysis.

DSP7774LAC

Average sales price in 1976 and 1977 less the average sales price in 1973 and 1974 in the census tract of the subject property (thousands).

Some Substitute Neighborhood Characteristics for the San Diego SMSA

FHISD

Fraction of households with $15,000 or more annual income in 1975 (special census) in the census tract containing the subject property. In those census tracts where the special census data was missing, IRS zip code data were substituted.

INC1975SD

1975 median income in the census tract of subject property (special census with use of IRS zip code data for missing census tracts) (thousands).

DINC7570SD

1975 median income (based on the special census) less the 1970 mean income (based on the census) in the census tract containing the subject property (thousands).

Additional or Substitute Neighborhood Characteristics in San Jose

FHISJ

Fraction of households with annual incomes of $16,000 or more in 1975 (special census) in the census tract containing the subject property.

FVACANTSJ

Fraction of housing units vacant in January 1976 (special census) in the census tract containing the subject property.

FBLACKSJ

Fraction of the population that is black in the census tract containing the subject property (1976 special census).

FSPANISHSJ

Fraction of the population that is Spanish in the census tract containing the subject property (1976 special census).

FASIANSJ

Fraction of the population that is Asian in the census tract containing the subject property (1976 special census).

Neighborhood Characteristics in the Stockton SMSA

DPOP7570STK

1975 population (based on special census) less 1970 population (based on the census) in the census tract containing the subject property (thousands).

AVESP77STK

Average sales price for 1977 in the census tract containing the subject property (thousands).

DSP7776STK

1977 average sales price less 1976 average sales price in the census tract containing the subject property (thousands).

FVACANTSTK

Fraction of housing units vacant in 1975 in the census tract containing the subject property.

DVAC7570STK

1975 fraction of housing units vacant less 1970 fraction vacant in the census tract containing the subject property (expressed as a percentage).

FBLACKSTK
Fraction of the population that is black in 1975 for the census tract containing the subject property.

FOTHERSTK
Fraction of the population that is neither white nor black in 1975 for the census tract containing the subject property.

Additional Variables

REQLOAN
Requested loan amount (thousands).

MODOWN
Requested loan amount less the granted loan amount.

INT
Interest rate (percent).

MAT
Maturity period (years).

LTOAV
Granted loan amount divided by the appraised value.

VRM
Dummy variable equal to one if the interest rate is variable over the life of the mortgage; otherwise, zero.

CONDO
Dummy variable equal to one if the housing unit is a condominium, cluster type or cooperative apartment development; otherwise, zero.

P30–50
Dummy variable equal to one if the purchase price is $30,001 to $50,000; otherwise, zero.

P50–75
Dummy variable equal to one if the purchase price is $50,001 to $75,000; otherwise, zero.

P75–100
Dummy variable equal to one if the purchase price is $75,001 to $100,000; otherwise, zero.

P100–125
Dummy variable equal to one if the purchase price is $100,001 to 125,000; otherwise, zero.

PGT125
Dummy variable equal to one if the purchase price is greater than $125,000; otherwise, zero.

AV
Appraised value (thousands).

LOANAMT
Granted loan amount (thousands).

SPACE
Square feet of living area (thousands).

New York

The information on the Equal Housing Opportunity Lender (EHOL) forms is transformed into a series of variables designed to explain lender decisions. The principle technique for making these transformation is to create a set of variables that have a value of either one or zero. Such variables are commonly referred to as dummy variables. Any applicant response not specifically included in one of these dummy variables becomes the base against which the effect of other responses is measured. The New York analysis requires a greater use of dummy variables than California because nearly all questions on the EHOL form call for categorical responses. In each case the categorical responses to a question lead to several dummy variables. The maximum detail permitted by the sample size has been incorporated into each model. The variable definitions follow.

Financial Characteristics

INC10–15
Dummy variable equal to one if the gross annual income of the applicant(s) was reported to be in the $10,001 to $15,000 interval; otherwise, zero.

INC15–25
Dummy variable equal to one if the gross annual income of the applicant(s) was reported to be in the $15,001 to $25,000 interval; otherwise, zero.

INCGT25

Dummy variable equal to one if the gross annual income of the applicant(s) was reported to be in the greater than $25,000 range; otherwise, zero.

BNW

Dummy variable equal to one if the applicant's asset category is one less than the debt category; otherwise, zero.

SATNW

Dummy variable equal to one if the applicant's asset and debt categories are the same; otherwise, zero.

GNW

Dummy variable equal to one if the applicant's asset category is exactly one more than debt category; otherwise, zero.

VGNW

Dummy variable equal to one if the asset category is at least two categories in excess of the debt category; otherwise, zero.

OCC3–5

Dummy variable equal to one if the number of years at present occupation is in the three- to five-year interval; otherwise, zero.

OCCGT5

Dummy variable equal to one if the number of years at present occupation is in the more than five-year range; otherwise, zero.

RLGT2*INC

Dummy variable equal to one if the amount of the requested loan is clearly greater than two times income. Because of the categorical nature of the responses to the income question, some loan requests exceeding two times income are not covered by this variable.

RLTOAV

Requested loan amount divided by the appraised value.

Neighborhood Characteristics

FHI

Fraction of households with income greater than $15,000 in the census tract containing the subject property (1970 census).

DINC
Change in average household income (1976 less 1969) in the census tract containing the subject property (thousands). (1970 census and National Planning Data Corporation estimate for 1976).

DPOP
Population change (1977 less 1960) in the census tract containing the subject property (thousands). (1960 census and National Planning Data Corporation estimate for 1977).

FORRATE
The dollar value of the outstanding principal of foreclosures in the last five years divided by the dollar value of active mortgages on one-to-four-family houses in the census tract containing the subject property expressed as a percentage. (New York State Banking Department, Supervisory Procedure G-107, Appendix 8, for fiscal years ending prior to May 31, 1976).

DELRATE
The dollar value of the outstanding balance of mortgages that are sixty or more days delinquent divided by the dollar value of active mortgages on one- to four-family houses in the census tract containing the subject property expressed as a percentage. (same as for foreclosure rate).

PRE1940
Fraction of housing built before 1940 in the census tract containing the subject property. (1970 census).

Age of Applicant

ALT25
Dummy variable equal to one if the applicant is under twenty-five years of age; otherwise, zero.

A25TO34
Dummy variable equal to one if the applicant is between twenty-five and thirty-four years of age; otherwise, zero.

A45TO54
Dummy variable equal to one if the applicant is between forty-five and fifty-four years of age; otherwise, zero.

AGE55

Dummy variable equal to one if the applicant is fifty-five or more years of age; otherwise, zero.

Sex and Marital Status

MFCBW

Dummy variable equal to one if the application is from a male and female couple with the woman working and of childbearing age (under thirty-five years of age); otherwise, zero.

MFCBNW

Dummy variable equal to one if the application is from a male and female couple with the woman of childbearing age but not working; otherwise, zero (no female workers among the two applicants).

MFNCBW

Dummy variable equal to one if the application is from a male and female couple with a working woman who is past childbearing age; otherwise, zero (no females of childbearing age among the two applicants).

FONLY

Dummy variable equal to one if all applicants are female; otherwise, zero.

FONLYCB

Dummy variable equal to one if all applicants are female and at least one is of childbearing age; otherwise, zero.

FONLYNCB

Dummy variable equal to one if all applicants are female and none are in the childbearing years; otherwise, zero.

MONLY

Dummy variable equal to one if all applicants are male; otherwise, zero.

SEP

Dummy variable equal to one if at least one of the applicants is separated; otherwise, zero.

UNMAR

Dummy variable equal to one if at least one of the applicants is unmarried (single, divorced, or widowed); otherwise, zero.

UNSMONLY
Dummy variable equal to one if at least one applicant is unmarried or separated and all applicants are male; otherwise, zero.

UNSFONLY
Dummy variable equal to one if at least one applicant is unmarried or separated and all applicants are female; otherwise, zero.

UNSFCB
Dummy variable equal to one if at least one applicant is unmarried or separated and all applicants are female but at least one female is in her childbearing years; otherwise, zero.

UNSFNCB
Dummy variable equal to one if at least one applicant is unmarried or separated and all applicants are female but none are in their child-bearing years; otherwise, zero.

UNSMF
Dummy variable equal to one if two applicants are of opposite sex and at least one is unmarried or separated; otherwise, zero.

MARFONLY
Dummy variable equal to one if married but no males reported among the applicants; otherwise, zero.

Race

BLACK
Dummy variable equal to one if at least one applicant is black; otherwise, zero.

HISPANIC
Dummy variable equal to one if at least one applicant is Hispanic and none are black; otherwise, zero.

OTHERMIN
Dummy variable equal to one if at least one applicant is a member of a minority group and none are black or Hispanic; otherwise, zero.

Racial Composition of Neighborhood

FBLACK
Fraction of the population that is black in the census tract containing the subject property (1970 census).

Additional Variables

REQLOAN
Requested loan amount (thousands).

Additional Neighborhood Characteristics for Bronx, Kings and Queens Counties

HCV1472
Pending housing code violations per building on one- to four-family buildings in 1972 in the census tract containing the subject property.

BHCV14
Fraction of one- to four-family buildings with fewer pending housing code violations in 1976 than in 1972 in the census tract containing the subject property.

WHCV14
Fraction of one- to four-family buildings with more pending housing code violations in 1976 than in 1972 in the census tract containing the subject property.

HCVG472
Pending housing code violations per building on greater than four-unit buildings in 1972 in the census tract containing the subject property.

BHCVG4
Fraction of greater than four-unit buildings with fewer pending housing codes violations in 1976 than in 1972 in the census tract containing the subject property.

WHCVG4
Fraction of greater than four-unit buildings with more pending housing code violations in 1976 than in 1972 in the census tract containing the subject property.

VAC1469
Fraction of one- to four-unit buildings vacant in 1969 in the census tract containing the subject property.

DVAC14
Change in the fraction of one- to four-unit buildings vacant in the census tract containing the subject property: 1975 less 1969.

VACG469

Fraction of greater than four-unit buildings vacant in 1969 in the census tract containing the subject property.

DVACG4

Change in the fraction of greater than four-unit buildings vacant in the census tract containing the subject property: 1975 less 1969.

TAX1472

Property tax arrearage (dollars of tax arrears per dollar of assessed value) for one- to four-unit buildings in the census tract containing the subject property in 1972.

DTAX14

Change in property tax arrearage (see TAX1472 definition): 1975 less 1972.

TAXG472

Property Tax arrearage (dollars of tax arrears per dollar of assessed value) for greater than four-unit buildings in the census tract containing the subject property in 1972.

DTAXG4

Change in property tax arrearage (see TAXG469 definition): 1975 less 1972.

FIRE70

Serious structural fires per building in the census tract containing the subject property in 1970.

DFIRE

Change in serious structural fires per building (see FIRE70 definition): 1975 less 1970.

PCWEL70

Per capita welfare payments in the census tract containing the subject property in 1970.

DWEL

Change in per capita welfare (see PCWEL70 definition): 1974 less 1970.

DPNW

Change in percent nonwhite in the census tract containing the subject property: 1974 less 1970.

Appendix B
Model Estimates for
California Savings and Loan
Associations

All the tables could not be printed because of space limitations. The following pages contain one example of each model estimated. A copy of Appendix B containing all of the tables can be obtained from the Joint Center for Urban Studies of MIT and Harvard University for a reasonable fee to cover reproduction costs. Write to the Joint Center for Urban Studies of MIT and Harvard University, 53 Church Street, Cambridge, MA 02138.

List of Tables

B.1
Decision model in the Los Angeles-Long Beach SMSA, 1977

B.2
Modified loan amount model in the Los Angeles-Long Beach SMSA, 1977

B.3
Mortgage credit terms (interest rate, maturity, and loan-to-value ratio) in the Los Angeles-Long Beach SMSA, 1977

B.4
Loan-fees model in the Los Angeles-Long Beach SMSA, 1977

B.5
Appraisal practices in the Los Angeles-Long Beach SMSA, 1977

Table B.1

Multinomial logit estimation of actions on applications for conventional mortgages on owner-occupied single-family houses in the Los Angeles-Long Beach SMSA, 1977

Variable	Denial	Modified Down	Modified Up
Financial characteristics			
RLTOINC	0.98	0.72	−0.36
	(14.22)	(13.44)	(−2.58)
FSECINC	0.36	−0.11	0.32
	(2.50)	(−1.01)	(2.13)
FSIFCB	−0.63	−0.09	−0.00
	(−3.11)	(−0.59)	(−0.02)
FSIFNCB	−1.42	−0.01	−0.12
	(−4.85)	(−0.04)	(−0.39)
RLTOAV	6.08	6.42	−6.58
	(54.06)	(55.25)	(−47.99)
Neighborhood characteristics			
FHI	−1.45	1.46	0.25
	(−11.95)	(14.41)	(1.91)
INC1976	−0.09	−0.04	0.05
	(−24.42)	(−18.32)	(14.73)
DINC7675	0.68	0.38	−0.37
	(22.10)	(14.16)	(−11.21)
DINC7570	0.06	0.03	−0.05
	(3.65)	(2.01)	(−2.71)
DHH7675	0.02	0.04	−0.04
	(1.24)	(3.32)	(−2.14)
DHH7570	0.02	0.01	−0.00
	(4.85)	(2.80)	(−0.04)
Age of neighborhood			
PRE1940	−0.82	0.85	0.56
	(−5.49)	(6.54)	(2.82)
Property location (relative to the rest of Los Angeles County)			
Compton (AR)	−13.01	1.04	−10.21
	(−7.93)	(0.83)	(−5.83)
Covina-Azusa (AR)	−12.58	0.96	−0.93
	(−20.74)	(2.20)	(−1.50)
East L.A.-Boyle Heights-Echo Park (AR)	−0.51	−0.20	0.83
	(−1.07)	(−0.56)	(1.64)
Highland Park (AR)	0.33	−1.72	0.37
	(0.71)	(−4.31)	(0.68)

Table B.1 (continued)

Variable	Denial	Modified Down	Modified Up
Long Beach-Southwest (AR)	0.90	0.17	−10.18
	(1.50)	(0.17)	(−7.41)
Pacoima-San Fernando (AR)	−0.40	1.03	0.80
	(−1.13)	(4.78)	(2.24)
Pasadena-North Central (AR)	0.17	0.42	−0.31
	(0.30)	(0.99)	(−0.51)
Pomona (AR)	0.71	−0.18	−0.13
	(1.47)	(−0.47)	(−0.26)
San Pedro (AR)	0.36	0.39	−10.46
	(0.65)	(0.79)	(−14.70)
South Central L.A. (AR)	0.11	−0.54	−0.55
	(0.36)	(−2.13)	(−1.55)
Venice-Santa Monica (AR)	0.19	−0.63	−0.08
	(0.32)	(−1.35)	(−0.12)
West Covina (AR)	0.11	0.13	0.46
	(0.13)	(0.19)	(0.46)
Rest of the City of Long Beach	−0.07	−0.19	−0.29
	(−0.40)	(−1.36)	(−1.52)
Rest of the City of Los Angeles	0.05	0.27	−0.05
	(0.75)	(5.65)	(−0.80)
Building age (relative to new buildings)			
BA1–9	−0.78	−0.51	−1.49
	(−8.52)	(−7.00)	(−14.09)
BA10–19	−0.39	−0.73	−1.79
	(−4.20)	(−9.70)	(−16.40)
BA20–29	−0.66	−0.95	−2.04
	(−9.58)	(−18.03)	(−23.61)
BA30–39	−0.32	−0.60	−2.09
	(−3.00)	(−6.73)	(−16.24)
BA40–49	−0.25	−0.58	−1.99
	(−2.11)	(−5.94)	(−13.62)
BAGE50	−0.04	−0.51	−2.20
	(−0.24)	(−3.84)	(−11.38)

Table B.1 (continued)

Variable	Denial	Modified Down	Modified Up
Age of applicant (relative to 35–44 years)			
ALT25	−0.52	−0.12	0.06
	(−3.68)	(−1.09)	(0.41)
A25TO34	0.08	−0.03	0.08
	(1.49)	(−0.74)	(1.31)
A45TO54	−0.39	0.33	−0.29
	(−4.28)	(4.82)	(−2.99)
AGE55	−0.46	0.29	−1.04
	(−3.66)	(3.00)	(−7.51)
Sex of applicant (relative to MFNCB)			
FONLYCB	−0.45	−0.11	−0.50
	(−2.49)	(−0.80)	(−2.51)
FONLYNCB	−0.52	−0.08	−0.53
	(−3.43)	(−0.66)	(−3.18)
MFCB	−0.57	−0.10	0.11
	(−10.22)	(−2.13)	(1.55)
MONLY	−0.38	−0.19	0.14
	(−4.52)	(−3.04)	(1.40)
Race of applicant			
BLACK	0.44	−0.30	−0.07
	(2.54)	(−2.19)	(−0.37)
SPANISH	0.17	−0.00	0.17
	(1.92)	(−0.03)	(1.82)
ASIAN	−0.20	0.04	−0.20
	(−1.62)	(0.40)	(−1.54)
OMIN	0.25	0.03	−0.56
	(1.35)	(0.21)	(−2.80)

Table B.1 (continued)

Variable	Denial	Modified Down	Modified Up
Racial composition of neighborhood			
FBLACK	−0.86	0.48	0.59
	(−3.06)	(2.20)	(1.91)
FSPANISH	0.36	0.36	−1.06
	(1.75)	(2.08)	(−4.74)
FASIAN	4.65	1.16	−1.01
	(4.78)	(1.54)	(−0.96)
Constant	−7.09	−8.56	2.28
	(−75.18)	(−63.25)	(17.78)
Sample size		38,398	
Likelihood ratio statistic		1,884.43	
Degrees of freedom		141	
Probability		0.0	
Corresponding standard normal deviate		44.63	

The numbers in parentheses are t-statistics. An "AR" after a property location indicates the neighborhood is alleged to be redlined.

Table B.2
Downward loan modifications on applications for conventional mortgages on owner-occupied single-family houses in the Los Angeles-Long Beach SMSA, 1977

Variable	1977
Financial characteristics	
RLTOINC	3,142
	(5.57)
FSECINC	−1,684
	(−0.70)
FSIFCB	3,172
	(1.08)
FSIFNCB	38
	(0.01)
RLTOAV	5,045
	(2.07)
REQLOAN	120
	(13.78)
Neighborhood characteristics	
FHI	2,135
	(0.94)
INC1976	287
	(1.67)
DINC7675	−2,774
	(−2.33)
DINC7570	30
	(0.12)
DHH7675	−140
	(−0.91)
DHH7570	−31
	(−0.57)
Age of neighborhood	
PRE1940	3,484
	(1.64)
Building age (relative to new buildings)	
BA1–9	−2,109
	(−2.14)
BA10–19	−728
	(−0.69)
BA20–29	−1,256
	(−1.33)
BA30–39	−2,109
	(−1.82)
BA40–49	−1,111
	(−0.87)

Table B.2 (continued)

Variable	1977
BAGE50	−3,510
	(−2.20)

Property location (relative to the rest of Los Angeles County)

Alleged redlined area	−1,140
	(−0.85)
Rest of the City of Long Beach	−814
	(−0.43)
Rest of the City of Los Angeles	−764
	(−1.17)

Age of applicant (relative to 35–44 years)

ALT25	−1,514
	(−1.11)
A25TO34	−677
	(−0.89)
A45TO54	1,485
	(1.82)
AGE55	3,058
	(2.95)

Sex of applicant (relative to MFNCB)

FONLYCB	−539
	(−0.32)
FONLYNCB	−343
	(−0.27)
MFCB	−942
	(−0.96)
MONLY	−596
	(−0.64)

Race of applicant

BLACK	2,784
	(1.56)
SPANISH	−715
	(−0.83)
ASIAN	−1,038
	(−1.05)
OMIN	155
	(0.11)

Table B.2 (continued)

Variable	1977
Racial composition of neighborhood	
FBLACK	−5,414
	(−1.78)
FSPANISH	5,773
	(2.09)
FASIAN	4,497
	(0.41)
Constant	−4,942
	(−1.74)
Sample size	1,325
R-squared	0.30
F-statistic	15.15
P-value	0.0001
Mean of dependent variable	8,666

The numbers in parentheses are t-statistics.

Table B.3
Interest rate, maturity, and loan-to-value ratio for conventional mortgages on owner-occupied single-family homes in the Los Angeles-Long Beach SMSA, 1977

Variable	Interest Rate (%)	Maturity (years)	Loan-to-Value Ratio (%)
Mortgage terms			
INT[a]	—	—	−3.70
			(−5.61)
LTOAV[a]	0.001	—	—
	(10.29)		
MAT	−0.008	—	0.12
	(−8.49)		(10.03)
Financial characteristics			
REQLOAN	0.001	0.003	—
	(19.69)	(11.20)	
VRM	−0.01	—	—
	(−3.59)		
RLTOAV	—	1.34	95.11
		(18.60)	(481.35)
RLTOINC	−0.003	−0.03	−0.96
	(−0.61)	(−0.96)	(−15.88)
FSECINC	0.03	0.07	0.33
	(3.29)	(1.29)	(2.43)
FSIFCB	−0.00	0.00	−0.10
	(−0.19)	(0.05)	(−0.60)
FSIFNCB	−0.03	0.03	−0.25
	(−1.91)	(0.34)	(−1.25)
Neighborhood characteristics			
FHI	−0.18	0.11	−1.04
	(−16.15)	(1.91)	(−7.01)
INC1976	−0.002	−0.00	−0.02
	(−2.11)	(−0.82)	(−1.58)
DINC7675	−0.00	−0.03	0.13
	(−0.26)	(−0.97)	(1.84)
DINC7570	−0.009	0.02	−0.03
	(−7.01)	(2.79)	(−1.89)
DHH7675	−0.002	−0.00	−0.01
	(−3.67)	(−0.64)	(−1.38)
DHH7570	−0.001	0.004	−0.05
	(−2.52)	(3.41)	(−0.19)
Age of neighborhood			
PRE1940	−0.06	0.13	−0.63
	(−6.21)	(2.37)	(−4.85)

Table B.3 (continued)

Variable	Interest Rate (%)	Maturity (years)	Loan-to-Value Ratio (%)
Building age (relative to new buildings)			
BA1–9	0.05	0.00	0.33
	(9.83)	(0.12)	(4.56)
BA10–19	0.08	−0.05	0.52
	(14.81)	(−1.80)	(6.31)
BA20–29	0.08	−0.00	0.49
	(16.16)	(−0.01)	(6.39)
BA30–39	0.09	−0.18	0.50
	(14.85)	(−5.74)	(5.54)
BA40–49	0.09	−0.45	0.54
	(12.93)	(−12.69)	(5.50)
BAGE50	0.11	−1.24	0.68
	(13.22)	(−28.75)	(5.61)
Property location (relative to rest of Los Angeles county)			
Compton (AR)	−0.05	−0.21	−1.62
	(−0.83)	(−0.69)	(−2.33)
Covine-Azusa (AR)	0.01	0.07	−0.18
	(0.53)	(0.64)	(−0.71)
East Los Angeles-Boyle Heights-Echo Park (AR)	0.02	0.41	0.43
	(0.99)	(4.03)	(1.81)
Highland Park (AR)	−0.04	0.15	0.16
	(−1.86)	(1.20)	(0.56)
Long Beach-Southwest (AR)	0.04	0.38	−0.42
	(0.76)	(−1.49)	(−0.71)
Pacoima-San Fernando (AR)	−0.01	0.13	−0.65
	(−0.96)	(1.74)	(−3.89)
Pasadena-North Central (AR)	0.01	−0.88	0.23
	(0.72)	(−8.21)	(0.92)
Pomona (AR)	0.09	−0.32	0.42
	(5.32)	(−3.56)	(1.96)
San Pedro (AR)	0.06	0.14	0.27
	(2.51)	(1.14)	(0.93)
South Central Los Angeles (AR)	−0.01	−0.62	0.09
	(−0.51)	(−8.12)	(0.51)
Venice-Santa Monica (AR)	0.02	−0.03	0.35
	(0.79)	(−0.30)	(1.33)
West Covina (AR)	0.08	0.14	0.61
	(2.61)	(0.82)	(1.52)

Table B.3 (continued)

Variable	Interest Rate (%)	Maturity (years)	Loan-to-Value Ratio (%)
Rest of the City of Long Beach	0.01	0.01	0.13
	(1.81)	(0.18)	(1.57)
Rest of the City of Los Angeles	−0.02	0.07	−0.09
	(−6.66)	(4.01)	−2.39
Age of applicant (relative to 35–44 years)			
ALT25	0.02	−0.67	0.26
	(4.31)	(−2.21)	(3.57)
A25TO34	0.004	0.01	0.10
	(1.27)	(0.78)	(2.26)
A45TO54	−0.00	−0.07	−0.19
	(−0.96)	(−3.36)	(−3.70)
AGE55	−0.10	−0.05	−0.34
	(−1.30)	(−1.68)	(−5.31)
Sex of applicant(s) (relative to MFNCB)			
FONLYCB	0.02	0.07	0.10
	(2.73)	(1.64)	(1.04)
FONLYNCB	0.03	0.05	0.05
	(4.31)	(1.60)	(0.73)
MFCB	−0.01	0.01	0.04
	(−2.06)	(0.32)	(0.73)
MONLY	0.01	−0.06	0.20
	(3.22)	(−2.28)	(3.56)
Race of applicant			
BLACK	0.05	0.04	0.35
	(6.99)	(0.94)	(3.45)
SPANISH	0.03	−0.07	0.21
	(8.58)	(−3.31)	(4.07)
ASIAN	0.01	−0.01	0.10
	(3.11)	(−0.55)	(1.69)
OMIN	0.00	−0.05	−0.05
	(0.02)	(−1.33)	(−0.66)

Table B.3 (continued)

Variable	Interest Rate (%)	Maturity (years)	Loan-to-Value Ratio (%)
Racial composition of neighborhood			
FBLACK	0.10 (6.68)	−0.13 (−1.53)	0.65 (3.21)
FSPANISH	0.01 (0.80)	−0.70 (−9.86)	−0.18 (−1.08)
FASIAN	−0.23 (−4.71)	0.96 (3.62)	−1.44 (−2.34)
Constant	9.15 (297.47)	28.75 (371.82)	33.60 (5.72)
Sample size	37,606	37,606	37,606
Standard error of the equation	0.24	1.29	2.99
Mean value of the dependent variable	9.06	29.78	77.30

Two-stage least squares were used to estimate the interest rate and loan-to-value equations. Ordinary least squares were used to estimate the maturity equation. *t*-statistics are in parentheses. The "AR" after a property location indicates that the neighborhood is alleged to be redlined.

a. Predicted values from the first stage of the two-stage least squares estimation technique.

Table B.4
Loan fees on conventional mortgages granted on owner-occupied single-family houses in the Los Angeles-Long Beach SMSA, 1977

Variable	1977
Loan and property characteristics	
LOANAMT	10.60
	(85.56)
AV	0.42
	(4.52)
SPACE	−3.10
	(−1.37)
Neighborhood characteristics	
FHI	−72.79
	(−7.11)
INC1976	−5.37
	(−6.84)
DINC7675	19.16
	(3.64)
DINC7570	0.22
	(0.18)
DHH7675	0.08
	(0.15)
DHH7570	0.10
	(0.48)
Age of neighborhood	
PRE1940	−56.61
	(−5.74)
Building age (relative to new buildings)	
BA1–9	18.79
	(4.01)
BA10–19	8.47
	(1.78)
BA20–29	8.75
	(1.98)
BA30–39	13.57
	(2.52)
BA40–49	20.65
	(3.40)
BAGE50	18.32
	(2.46)

Table B.4 (continued)

Variable	1977
Property location (relative to the rest of Los Angeles County)	
Compton (AR)	72.23
	(1.48)
Covina-Azusa and West Covina (AR)	156.92
	(10.07)
East L.A.-Boyle Heights-Echo Park (AR)	4.49
	(0.25)
Highland Park (AR)	16.34
	(0.85)
Long Beach-Southwest (AR)	22.86
	(0.35)
Pacoima-San Fernando (AR)	−18.77
	(−1.64)
Pasadena-North Central (AR)	−8.55
	(−0.47)
Pomona (AR)	163.06
	(10.48)
San Pedro (AR)	25.79
	(1.24)
South Central L.A. (AR)	−26.07
	(−1.97)
Venice-Santa Monica (AR)	−36.64
	(−1.76)
Rest of the City of Long Beach	−1.41
	(−0.21)
Rest of the City of Los Angeles	−22.30
	(−7.76)
Age of applicant (relative to 35–44 years)	
ALT25	11.62
	(2.13)
A25TO34	0.58
	(0.17)
A45TO54	−3.96
	(−1.04)
AGE55	−0.00
	(−0.00)

Table B.4 (continued)

Variable	1977
Sex of applicant (relative to MFNCB)	
FONLYCB	11.86
	(1.73)
FONLYNCB	−0.02
	(−0.00)
MFCB	7.89
	(2.12)
MONLY	9.29
	(2.40)
Race of applicant	
BLACK	23.59
	(3.25)
SPANISH	13.51
	(3.62)
ASIAN	9.35
	(2.16)
OMIN	2.87
	(0.46)
Racial composition of neighborhood	
FBLACK	44.55
	(3.04)
FSPANISH	−5.31
	(−0.41)
FASIAN	−84.77
	(−1.75)
Constant	151.32
	(16.56)
Sample size	29,937
R-square	0.75
F-statistic	1,850
P-value	0.0001
Mean value of the dependent variable	698

The numbers in parentheses are t-statistics. An "AR" after a property location indicates the neighborhood is alleged to be redlined.

Table B.5
Appraised-value-to-purchase-price ratio in the Los Angeles-Long Beach SMSA, 1977
(ordinary least squares)

Variable	1977
Structure type	
CONDO	−0.001
	(−1.57)
Purchase price (relative to less than $30,001)	
P30–50	−0.023
	(−20.76)
P50–75	−0.032
	(−27.32)
P75–100	0.036
	(−27.50)
P100–125	−0.039
	(−25.23)
PGT125	−0.046
	(−29.87)
Neighborhood characteristics	
FHI	0.014
	(6.95)
INC1976	0.000
	(0.68)
DINC7675	0.000
	(0.04)
DINC7570	0.001
	(3.40)
DHH7675	0.000
	(0.26)
DHH7570	−0.000
	(−0.92)
Age of neighborhood	
PRE1940	0.007
	(3.86)
Building age (relative to new buildings)	
BA1–9	−0.006
	(−6.50)
BA10–19	−0.006
	(−6.16)
BA20–29	−0.006
	(−6.30)
BA30–39	−0.008
	(−7.24)

Table B.5 (continued)

Variable	1977
BA40–49	−0.008
	(−6.92)
BAGE50	−0.015
	(−10.62)

Property location (relative to rest of Los Angeles County)

Compton (AR)	0.011
	(1.15)
Covina-Azusa and West Covina (AR)	−0.000
	(−0.08)
East L.A.-Boyle Heights-Echo Park (AR)	−0.010
	(−3.24)
Highland Park (AR)	−0.002
	(−0.49)
Long Beach-Southwest (AR)	−0.004
	(−0.56)
Pacoima-San Fernando (AR)	0.000
	(0.03)
Pasadena-North Central (AR)	0.002
	(0.51)
Pomona (AR)	−0.008
	(−2.51)
San Pedro (AR)	−0.002
	(−0.59)
South Central L.A. (AR)	0.000
	(0.09)
Venice-Santa Monica (AR)	−0.003
	(−0.91)
Rest of the City of Long Beach	0.003
	(2.35)
Rest of the City of Los Angeles	0.002
	(3.48)

Age of applicant (relative to 35–44 years)

ALT25	−0.001
	(−0.90)
A25TO34	−0.000
	(−0.56)
A45TO54	−0.000
	(−0.33)
AGE55	−0.001
	(−1.60)

Table B.5 (continued)

Variable	1977
Sex of applicant (relative to MFNCB)	
FONLYCB	−0.003
	(−2.28)
FONLYNCB	−0.002
	(−1.87)
MFCB	0.000
	(0.52)
MONLY	0.001
	(2.06)
Race of applicants	
BLACK	0.000
	(0.18)
SPANISH	−0.002
	(3.14)
ASIAN	−0.001
	(−1.73)
OMIN	0.001
	(−1.08)
Racial composition of neighborhood	
FBLACK	0.002
	(0.82)
FSPANISH	−0.009
	(3.64)
FASIAN	0.003
	(0.35)
Constant	1.034
	(514.75)
Sample size	38,231
R-squared	0.03
F-statistic	28.18
P-value	0.00
Mean value of the dependent variable	1.004

The numbers in parentheses are *t*-statistics. An "AR" after a property location indicates that the neighborhood is alleged to be redlined.

**Appendix C
Model Estimates for State-
regulated Lenders in New
York**

All the tables could not be printed because of space limitations. The following pages contain one example of each model which we estimated. A copy of Appendix C containing all of the tables can be obtained from the Joint Center for Urban Studies of MIT and Harvard University for a reasonable fee to cover reproduction costs. Write to the Joint Center for Urban Studies of MIT and Harvard University, 53 Church Street, Cambridge, MA 02138.

List of Tables

C.1
Decision model for mutual savings banks in the New York-Nassau-Suffolk SMSAs, 1976–1977

C.2
Modified loan amount model for mutual savings banks in the New York-Nassau-Suffolk SMSAs, 1976–1977

C.3
Mortgage credit terms (interest rate, maturity and loan-to-value ratio) for Bronx, Kings, and Queens counties, 1975 (state-regulated lenders)

C.4
Default models: Probability of delinquency in mutual savings banks

C.5
Quantity of mortgage funds provided by state-regulated lenders:
Conventional mortgages on 1- to 4-family houses in Bronx, Kings,
and Queens counties, 1975

C.6
Appraisal practices of mutual savings banks in the New York-Nassau-Suffolk SMSAs

Table C.1
Multinomial logit estimation of actions by mutual savings banks on applications for
conventional mortgage loans on owner-occupied 1- to 4-family houses in the New
York-Nassau-Suffolk SMSA, 1976–1977

Variable	Denial	Modification	Withdrawal
Financial characteristics			
INC15–25	−0.26	−0.09	0.01
	(−1.98)	(−0.47)	(0.05)
INCGT25	−0.80	−0.28	−0.02
	(−6.59)	(−1.46)	(−0.18)
SATNW	−0.39	−0.92	−0.48
	(−1.02)	(−1.84)	(−0.96)
GNW	−0.48	−0.24	−0.84
	(−1.44)	(−0.52)	(−1.90)
VGNW	−0.88	−0.25	−0.96
	(−2.88)	(−0.56)	(−2.53)
OCC3–5	−0.02	0.18	0.12
	(−0.16)	(1.35)	(0.65)
OCCGT5	−0.34	0.10	−0.27
	(−3.58)	(1.01)	(−2.47)
RLGT2*INC	0.52	0.22	−0.68
	(1.76)	(0.71)	(−1.48)
RLTOAV	4.97	6.39	0.45
	(19.09)	(20.71)	(3.03)
Neighborhood characteristics			
FHI	−0.70	0.59	0.78
	(−1.53)	(2.35)	(3.35)
DINC	−0.03	0.01	−0.03
	(−1.87)	(0.73)	(−2.36)
DPOP	0.03	−0.01	−0.08
	(1.49)	(−0.66)	(−3.11)
FORRATE	−0.00	0.01	0.00
	(−0.01)	(1.19)	(0.24)
DELRATE	−0.01	−0.00	0.01
	(−1.24)	(−0.18)	(0.70)
Age of neighborhood			
PRE1940	0.26	1.53	0.25
	(1.30)	(8.52)	(1.60)
Property location (relative to Suffolk County)			
Bronx County			
North	−0.12	−0.32	1.30
	(−0.19)	(−0.57)	(2.30)
South (AR)	0.15	−0.85	0.25
	(0.27)	(−1.36)	(0.30)

Table C.1 (continued)

Variable	Denial	Modification	Withdrawal
Kings County			
Central Brooklyn and	−0.47	0.52	1.11
Fort Greene (AR)	(−0.92)	(1.30)	(2.33)
Crown Heights and East	−0.34	0.52	−0.47
Flatbush (AR)	(−0.52)	(1.07)	(−0.55)
Northeast Kings	−0.19	0.97	1.26
	(−0.37)	(2.42)	(2.50)
Park Slope (AR)	−0.72	0.45	0.70
	(−1.34)	(1.10)	(1.23)
South Kings	0.17	0.26	0.08
	(0.63)	(1.11)	(0.24)
Nassau	0.21	−0.11	−0.09
	(1.00)	(−0.62)	(−0.44)
New York (Manhattan)	−0.82	0.41	0.68
	(−1.61)	(0.96)	(1.32)
Queens County			
Southeast Queens	0.76	0.52	−7.26
	(0.95)	(0.66)	(−5.25)
Rest of Queens	0.28	−0.05	−0.17
	(1.19)	(−0.23)	(−0.61)
Richmond	−0.70	−0.62	−1.66
	(−3.82)	(−3.96)	(−6.30)
Rockland	−1.29	−0.68	0.08
	(−2.82)	(−2.50)	(−0.21)
Westchester	−0.64	−1.10	−0.09
	(−3.08)	(−7.28)	(−0.50)
Age of applicant (relative to 35–44 years)			
ALT25	−0.44	0.12	−0.07
	(−1.64)	(0.50)	(−0.20)
A25TO34	−0.34	−0.11	−0.21
	(−3.42)	(−1.17)	(−1.38)
A45TO54	−0.34	−0.30	−0.31
	(−2.20)	(−2.25)	(−1.55)
AGE55	−0.30	0.11	−0.26
	(−1.39)	(0.61)	(−0.95)
Sex of applicant (relative to male-female couples with nonworking woman past the childbearing age of 34)			
MFCBW	−0.05	−0.72	−0.07
	(−0.24)	(−4.24)	(−0.46)

Table C.1 (continued)

Variable	Denial	Modification	Withdrawal
MFCBNW	−0.09	−0.30	0.34
	(−0.37)	(−1.53)	(1.49)
MFNCBW	0.17	−0.22	−0.33
	(0.92)	(−1.45)	(−1.87)
MONLY	1.01	−0.18	−0.35
	(4.89)	(−0.97)	(−1.71)
Marital status of applicant (relative to married male-female couple or married male-only application)			
UNSFCB	0.29	−0.39	−0.60
	(0.63)	(−1.00)	(−1.05)
UNSFNCB	0.37	−0.23	−0.19
	(1.06)	(−0.78)	(−0.45)
UNSMF	0.24	−0.06	−0.78
	(0.78)	(−0.24)	(−1.92)
UNSMONLY	−0.28	0.02	0.14
	(−1.35)	(0.09)	(0.48)
MARFONLY	1.24	0.28	1.06
	(2.15)	(0.54)	(1.72)
Race of applicant			
BLACK	0.60	0.47	−0.11
	(2.70)	(2.43)	(−0.35)
HISPANIC	0.75	0.17	0.14
	(2.78)	(0.69)	(0.36)
OTHERMIN	0.32	0.09	−0.34
	(1.16)	(0.36)	(−0.91)
Racial composition of neighborhood			
FBLACK	−0.22	−0.64	0.87
	(−0.48)	(−1.60)	(1.48)
Constant	−4.06	−6.58	−1.92
	(−9.44)	(−10.00)	(−6.99)

Sample size	4,131
Likelihood ratio statistic	791.02
Degrees of freedom	138
Probability	0.0
Corresponding standard normal deviate	23.19

The numbers in parentheses are t-statistics. An "AR" after a property location indicates the neighborhood is alleged to be redlined.

Table C.2
Downward loan modifications in loan amount on applications for conventional
mortgage loans on owner-occupied 1- to 4-family houses by mutual savings banks in
the New York-Nassau-Suffolk SMSA, 1976–1977

Financial characteristics	
INC15–25	−827
	(−0.79)
INCGT25	−1,174
	(−1.01)
GNW	1,992
	(1.62)
VGNW	1,926
	(1.73)
OCC3–5	449
	(0.55)
OCCGT5	390
	(0.53)
REQLOAN	114
	(6.79)
RLGT2*INC	1,839
	(1.55)
RLTOAV	6,568
	(2.90)
Neighborhood characteristics	
FHI	235
	(0.11)
DINC	−45
	(−0.50)
DPOP	−98
	(−1.04)
FORRATE	96
	(3.98)
DELRATE	−47
	(−1.37)
Age of neighborhood	
PRE1940	645
	(0.62)
Property location (relative to Suffolk County)	
Alleged redlined areas	−224
	(−0.22)
Northeast Kings	304
	(0.22)
South Kings	−420
	(−0.26)

Table C.2 (continued)

Nassau	−183
	(−0.20)
New York (Manhattan)	288
	(0.18)
Rest of Queens	−1,069
	(−1.06)
Richmond	−1,524
	(−1.60)
Rockland	−650
	(−0.44)
Westchester	−2,611
	(−2.68)
Age of applicant (relative to 35–44 years)	
ALT25	−240
	(−0.20)
A25TO34	−908
	(−1.33)
A45TO54	742
	(1.10)
AGE55	967
	(1.12)
Sex of applicant (relative to MFNCBNW)	
FONLYCB	233
	(0.15)
FONLYNCB	−853
	(−0.61)
MFCBW	−1,135
	(−1.15)
MFCBNW	−225
	(−0.20)
MFNCBW	−860
	(−0.97)
MONLY	−548
	(−0.56)
Marital status of applicant (relative to a married male-female couple, married male-only, or married female-only application)	
SEP	2,296
	(1.69)
UNMAR	−391˙
	(−0.54)

Table C.2 (continued)

Race of applicant	
BLACK	−1,222
	(−1.71)
HISPANIC	−1,116
	(−1.16)
OTHERMIN	761
	(0.73)
Racial composition of neighborhood	
FBLACK	801
	(0.40)
Constant	−5,280
	(−2.22)
Sample size	386
R-squared	0.33
F-statistic	4.24
P-value	0.0001
Mean value of the dependent variable	$4,557

The numbers in parentheses are t-statistics.

Table C.3
Interest rate, maturity, and loan-to-value ratio for conventional mortgages on 1- to 4-family houses in Bronx, Kings, and Queens counties, 1975 (two-stage least-squares estimation technique)

Explanatory Variables	Dependent Variables		
	Interest Rate (%)	Maturity (years)	Loan-to-Value Ratio (%)
Mortgage prices			
Predicted interest rate (%)[a]	—	−5.79 (−1.66)	−31.62 (−1.78)
Predicted maturity (years)[a]	−0.007 (−0.19)	—	−0.07 (−0.06)
Predicted loan-to-value ratio (%)[a]	−0.029 (−1.11)	−0.01 (−0.15)	—
Neighborhood attributes			
Pending housing code violations per building: 1- to 4-family buildings in 1972	0.316 (1.42)	4.38 (2.07)	23.83 (2.36)
Fraction of 1- to 4-family buildings with fewer pending housing code violations in 1976 than in 1972	−1.037 (−0.71)	−11.94 (−0.99)	−103.86 (−2.54)
Fraction of 1- to 4-family buildings with more pending housing code violations in 1976 than in 1972	−1.697 (−3.04)	−17.19 (−2.45)	−57.54 (−1.52)
Pending housing code violations per building: >4-unit buildings in 1972	0.001 (0.20)	−0.00 (−0.05)	−0.20 (−1.47)
Fraction of >4-unit buildings with fewer pending housing code violations in 1976 than in 1972	−0.057 (−0.34)	0.08 (0.06)	2.99 (0.77)
Fraction of >4-unit buildings with more pending housing code violations in 1976 than in 1972	−0.050 (−0.71)	0.37 (0.93)	1.78 (1.42)
Fraction of 1- to 4-unit buildings vacant, 1969	−8.805 (−0.91)	−235.88 (−3.40)	−465.09 (−1.23)
Change in fraction of 1- to 4-unit buildings vacant, 1975 less 1969	−1.293 (−0.53)	−17.18 (−0.83)	−59.15 (−0.86)
Fraction of >4-unit buildings vacant, 1969	−2.963 (−1.86)	−27.54 (−1.55)	−134.88 (−1.74)

Table C.3 (continued)

Explanatory Variables	Dependent Variables		
	Interest Rate (%)	Maturity (years)	Loan-to-Value Ratio (%)
Change in fraction of >4-unit buildings vacant, 1975 less 1969	−2.090 (−1.48)	−19.95 (−1.37)	−108.42 (−1.78)
Tax arrearage on 1- to 4-unit buildings, 1972 (fraction of buildings three-quarters or more in arrears)	1.394 (1.28)	−0.72 (−0.07)	50.01 (1.33)
Change in tax arrearage on 1- to 4-unit buildings, 1975 less 1972	−1.890 (−1.33)	5.32 (0.52)	−22.08 (−0.65)
Tax arrearage on >4-unit buildings, 1972	0.514 (1.29)	−1.52 (0.63)	−4.02 (−0.55)
Change in tax arrearage on >4-unit buildings, 1975 less 1972	−0.048 (−0.25)	−1.07 (−0.71)	−6.66 (−1.35)
Serious structural fires per building, 1970	5.277 (0.89)	80.09 (1.64)	283.22 (1.41)
Change in serious structural fires per building, 1975 less 1970	−8.377 (−1.37)	−123.65 (−2.09)	−548.48 (−1.90)
Per capita welfare, 1970 (thousands)	−0.978 (−1.58)	−6.65 (−1.05)	−56.81 (−2.02)
Change in per capita welfare, 1974 less 1970 (thousands)	0.029 (0.03)	−2.34 (−0.38)	69.52 (3.16)
Change in per capita income, 1974 less 1970 (thousands)	0.036 (1.33)	0.31 (2.07)	0.22 (−0.36)
Change in population, 1977 less 1960 divided by the average population	−0.049 (−0.62)	0.48 (0.96)	2.03 (1.34)
Risk of loss in mortgage lending			
Ratio of foreclosure ($) in last 5 years to total loans ($): conventional mortgages on 1- to 4-unit buildings—first G-107 reporting period	−2.935 (−0.73)	44.75 (2.19)	117.30 (1.58)
Ratio of 60-day delinquencies ($) to total loans ($): conventional mortgages on 1- to 4-unit buildings—first G-107 reporting period	−0.390 (−1.36)	−0.55 (−0.29)	1.99 (0.35)

Table C.3 (continued)

Explanatory Variables	Dependent Variables		
	Interest Rate (%)	Maturity (years)	Loan-to-Value Ratio (%)
Income and assets			
Per capita income, 1970 (thousands)	—	—	−0.29 (−0.64)
Percent of households with incomes ≥$15,000 in 1970	—	—	0.09 (1.03)
Average property value, 1975 (thousands)	—	—	−0.12 (−2.49)
Mortgage stocks			
Stock of conventional 1- to 4-family mortgages (thousands of $ per building)	0.000 (0.25)	—	—
Stock of conventional multifamily mortgages (thousands of $ per building)	0.000 (0.40)	—	—
Stock of federally insured or guaranteed 1- to 4-family mortgages (thousands of $ per building)	−0.034 (−1.43)	—	—
Stock of federally insured or guaranteed multifamily mortgages (thousands of $ per building)	0.000 (0.83)	—	—
Predicted transactions[a]			
1- to 4-family buildings (thousands of $ per building)	−0.013 (−0.32)	—	—
Age of housing stock			
Fraction of 1- to 4-unit buildings built in 1939 or earlier as of 1970	−0.136 (−0.81)	−2.07 (−2.85)	4.61 (1.63)
Racial composition			
Percent of population nonwhite, 1974	−0.001 (−0.04)	−0.02 (−1.40)	−0.14 (−2.52)
Change in percent of population nonwhite, 1974 less 1970	0.004 (0.96)	0.06 (2.00)	0.22 (1.72)

Table C.3 (continued)

Explanatory Variables	Dependent Variables		
	Interest Rate (%)	Maturity (years)	Loan-to-Value Ratio (%)
Neighborhoods			
North Bronx	0.100	−1.70	−2.99
	(0.79)	(−2.72)	(−1.23)
South Bronx[b]	0.001	−0.72	−4.09
	(0.01)	(−0.92)	(−1.69)
Central Brooklyn in Kings[b]	−0.312	−7.00	−29.42
	(−0.88)	(−2.44)	(−2.08)
Crown Heights in Kings[b]	−1.330	−9.75	−43.67
	(−6.58)	(−1.93)	(−1.69)
East Flatbush in Kings[b]	−0.122	−1.19	−1.08
	(−1.13)	(−1.46)	(−0.35)
Park Slope in Kings[b]	0.341	0.90	6.61
	(1.85)	(0.58)	(1.11)
Northeast Kings	0.260	−1.59	−1.24
	(1.49)	(−2.11)	(−0.47)
South Kings	0.144	−1.08	−5.93
	(0.87)	(−1.88)	(−3.93)
Southeast Queens[b]	−0.042	0.12	3.88
	(−0.34)	(0.13)	(1.52)
Constant	6.767	73.56	334.22
	(3.66)	(2.41)	(2.00)
R-squared	0.22	0.17	0.15
Sample size	801	801	801
F-statistic	5.23	4.35	3.31
P-value	0.0	0.0	0.0
Mean value of dependent variable	8.395	22.10	64.82

The numbers in parentheses are t-statistics.
a. Predicted values from the first stage of the two-stage least-squares estimation technique.
b. These neighborhoods are alleged to be redlined.

Table C.4
Probability of delinquency for mortgages on 1- to 4-family houses, mutual savings banks (ordinary least squares estimation technique)

Variables	Albany-Schenectady-Troy SMSA	New York-Nassau-Suffolk SMSA	Rest of Upstate SMSAs
Economic burden factors			
Ratio of mortgage payments to income	0.051	0.150	−0.034
	(0.61)	(2.05)	(−0.62)
Ratio of monthly income (thousands) to household size	−0.023	0.021	−0.008
	(−1.88)	(1.23)	(−0.82)
Borrower's net wealth (thousands)	−0.001	0.000	0.000
	(−1.81)	(0.05)	(0.07)
Equity factors			
Down payment (thousands)	−0.280	−1.060	−0.250
	(−0.29)	(−1.74)	(−0.52)
Age of loan as a percentage of maturity period relative to greater than 50%			
0–5%	0.001	0.007	0.000
	(0.08)	(0.89)	(0.07)
5–10%	0.007	0.019	0.000
	(0.64)	(1.75)	(0.01)
10–15%	0.008	0.020	0.002
	(0.87)	(2.37)	(0.35)
15–20%	0.001	0.028	0.008
	(0.16)	(3.13)	(0.31)
20–25%	0.008	0.028	0.005
	(0.82)	(2.99)	(1.92)
25–30%	0.001	0.010	0.000
	(0.11)	(0.77)	(0.08)
30–35%	0.003	0.017	−0.001
	(0.32)	(1.85)	(−0.09)
35–40%	0.005	0.014	−0.005
	(0.52)	(1.37)	(−0.76)
40–50%	−0.000	0.005	0.002
	(−0.02)	(0.58)	(0.33)
Expectations of future property value			
Condition of building relative to good condition	0.009	0.018	0.008
	(1.30)	(2.12)	(1.70)
Age of building relative to new construction			
1–9 years	0.009	0.006	−0.002
	(1.16)	(0.89)	(−0.31)

Table C.4 (continued)

Variables	Albany-Schenectady-Troy SMSA	New York-Nassau-Suffolk SMSA	Rest of Upstate SMSAs
10–19 years	0.011	−0.015	−0.000
	(1.34)	(−1.86)	(−0.02)
20–29 years	0.019	−0.008	0.001
	(2.02)	(−0.87)	(0.18)
30–39 years	0.011	−0.005	−0.006
	(1.00)	(−0.42)	(−0.70)
40–49 years	0.019	−0.002	0.002
	(1.92)	(−1.17)	(0.27)
≥50 years	0.013	−0.018	0.001
	(1.56)	(−1.66)	(0.09)
Age of housing stock			
Fraction of housing units built in 1939 or earlier (as of 1970)	0.023	0.003	0.003
	(1.86)	(0.26)	(0.34)
Personal factors			
Age of borrower relative to less than 28 years			
28–33 years	−0.001	−0.006	0.002
	(−0.11)	(−0.97)	(0.41)
34–39 years	−0.003	−0.004	0.013
	(−0.41)	(−0.54)	(2.74)
40–45 years	0.015	0.005	−0.001
	(1.55)	(0.61)	(−0.12)
46–49 years	0.014	−0.016	−0.009
	(1.20)	(−1.66)	(−1.16)
≥50 years	0.002	−0.015	−0.005
	(0.21)	(−1.47)	(−0.54)
Borrower married	0.010	0.008	IV
	(0.86)	(0.70)	
Prior home ownership	0.008	0.010	0.002
	(1.48)	(1.51)	(0.50)
Self-employed	0.004	0.009	−0.002
	(0.43)	(1.22)	(−0.32)
Multiple wage-earner household	0.007	0.004	0.002
	(1.23)	(0.80)	(0.42)
2- to 4-family house	−0.005	0.019	−0.000
	(−0.51)	(2.11)	(−0.05)
Other test and control variables			
FHA mortgage	0.013	0.024	0.001
	(1.83)	(3.48)	(0.28)

Table C.4 (continued)

Variables	Albany-Schenectady-Troy SMSA	New York-Nassau-Suffolk SMSA	Rest of Upstate SMSAs
VA mortgage	0.013	0.015	0.001
	(1.32)	(2.27)	(0.16)
Female borrower	IV	−0.008	IV
		(−0.61)	
Property located in area alleged to be redlined	−0.011	−0.013	0.001
	(−1.08)	(−1.30)	(0.15)
Change in neighborhood population between 1969 and 1976 on a per capital basis	0.019	0.000	−0.002
	(2.06)	(0.06)	(−0.56)
Change in neighborhood median income between 1969 and 1976 (thousands)	0.000	−0.004	−0.003
	(0.02)	(−0.70)	(−0.59)
Constant	−0.020	−0.018	0.013
	(−0.94)	(−0.90)	(1.20)
R-squared	0.39	0.27	0.20
Sample size	144	274	198
F-statistic	1.88	2.39	1.12
P-value	0.068	0.00	>0.25
Mean value of the dependent variable[a]	0.0225	0.0290	0.0133

The numbers in parentheses are t-statistics; IV = insufficient variation.
a. All coefficients have been scaled by a factor that adjusts the mean value of the binary dependent variable to equal the actual delinquency rate for mortgages of this type in the MLS.

Region	Mean Value of Binary Dependent Variable	Scaling Factor	MLS Delinquency Rate
Albany-Schenectady-Troy	0.417	0.0541	0.0225
New York-Nassau-Suffolk	0.401	0.0723	0.0290
Rest of upstate New York	0.318	0.0417	0.0133

Table C.5
Quantity of conventional mortgages on 1- to 4-family houses in Bronx, Kings, and Queens counties, 1975 (OLS estimation technique)

| Variable | Dependent Variable: Mortgage Lending ($) per Building[a] during 1 Year | |
	Alleged Redlined Neighborhoods	Other Neighborhoods[b]
Transactions		
1- to 4-family buildings	90.97	16.32
(thousands of $ per building)[a]	(3.11)	(9.27)
Mortgage prices (conventional)		
Interest rate (%)	43.30	73.14
	(1.15)	(1.90)
Maturity (years)	−5.35	−1.61
	(−0.67)	(−0.37)
Loan-to-value ratio (%)	−3.31	−0.92
	(−1.12)	(−0.67)
Mortgage stocks		
Stock of conventional 1- to 4-family mortgages (thousands of $ per building)[a]	36.79 (4.35)	−0.09 (−0.36)
Stock of conventional multifamily mortgages (thousands of $ per building)[a]	−0.14 (−0.71)	0.05 (2.57)
Stock of federally insured or guaranteed 1- to 4-family mortgages (thousands of dollars per building)[a]	−4.52 (−0.26)	−4.51 (−0.57)
Stock of federally insured or guaranteed multifamily mortgages (thousands of dollars per building)[a]	3.28 (1.23)	−0.22 (−1.07)
Neighborhood attributes related to risk of loss		
Pending housing code violations per building: 1- to 4-family buildings in 1972	246.07 (2.45)	441.12 (1.60)
Fraction of 1- to 4-family buildings with fewer pending housing code violations in 1976 than in 1972	−3,621.00 (−3.08)	−4,378.90 (−2.82)
Fraction of 1- to 4-family buildings with more pending housing code violations in 1976 than in 1972	743.51 (1.74)	−3,019.30 (−2.42)

Table C.5 (continued)

Variable	Dependent Variable: Mortgage Lending ($) per Building[a] during 1 Year	
	Alleged Redlined Neighborhoods	Other Neighborhoods[b]
Pending housing code violations per building: >4-unit buildings in 1972	−16.85 (−0.89)	6.98 (1.63)
Fraction of >4-unit buildings with fewer pending housing code violations in 1976 than in 1972	1,489.80 (2.68)	−121.94 (−0.98)
Fraction of >4-unit buildings with more pending housing code violations in 1976 than in 1972	22.82 (0.21)	−51.05 (−0.97)
Fraction of 1- to 4-unit buildings vacant, 1969	6,093.80 (0.45)	−8,249.40 (−0.92)
Change in fraction of 1- to 4-unit buildings vacant, 1975 less 1969	6,265.70 (1.44)	−2,056.30 (−0.83)
Fraction of >4-unit buildings vacant, 1969	4,931.70 (1.49)	180.53 (0.11)
Change in fraction of >4-unit buildings vacant, 1975 less 1969	2,643.40 (1.17)	−139.46 (−0.09)
Tax arrearage on 1- to 4-unit buildings, 1972 (fraction of buildings three-quarters or more in arrears)	−4,853.40 (−3.01)	1,683.90 (1.59)
Change in tax arrearage on 1- to 4-unit buildings, 1975 less 1972	275.22 (0.21)	−35.33 (−0.03)
Tax arrearage on >4-unit buildings, 1972	−238.25 (−0.28)	−40.24 (−0.18)
Change in tax arrearage on >4-unit buildings, 1975 less 1972	133.99 (0.19)	−109.65 (−0.78)
Serious structural fires per building, 1970	5,941.50 (0.50)	3,918.70 (0.70)
Change in serious structural fires per building, 1975 less 1970	2,359.70 (0.28)	−6,285.00 (−1.43)
Change in per capita income, 1974 less 1970	−0.07 (−1.09)	−0.00 (−0.42)
Per capita welfare, 1970	0.59 (0.90)	1.52 (3.04)

Table C.5 (continued)

Variable	Dependent Variable: Mortgage Lending ($) per Building[a] during 1 Year	
	Alleged Redlined Neighborhoods	Other Neighborhoods[b]
Change in per capita welfare, 1974 less 1970	0.69 (1.00)	−1.04 (−2.44)
Change in population, 1977 less 1960 divided by the average population	−135.50 (−1.09)	−10.71 (−0.21)
Risk of loss in mortgage lending		
Ratio of foreclosures ($) in last 5 years to total loans ($): conventional mortgages on 1- to 4-unit buildings (first G-107 reporting period)	−5,528.30 (−0.76)	−1,233.70 (−0.68)
Ratio of 60-day delinquencies ($) to total loans ($): conventional mortgages on 1- to 4-unit buildings (first G-107 reporting period)	−32.44 (−0.09)	−605.70 (−3.29)
Age of housing stock		
Fraction of 1- to 4-unit buildings built in 1939 or earlier as of 1970	94.74 (0.60)	86.63 (1.40)
Racial composition		
Percent of population nonwhite, 1974	1.58 (0.78)	−3.43 (−3.24)
Change in the percent of population nonwhite, 1974 less 1970	−8.74 (−2.03)	3.51 (1.08)
Constant	−39.12 (−0.11)	−398.87 (−0.19)
R-squared	0.68	0.25
Sample size	110	640
F-statistic	4.88	6.07
P-value	0.00	0.00
Mean value of dependent variable	292.53	352.67

The numbers in parentheses are t-statistics.
a. The phrase "per building" indicates that the variable has been divided by the number of 1- to 4-family buildings in the census tract.
b. Includes Bronx, Kings, and Queens counties, except the alleged redlined neighborhoods and Northeast Kings.

Table C.6
Appraised-value-to-purchase-price ratio on 1- to 4-family houses in Bronx, Kings, Queens, Westchester, Nassau, and Suffolk counties, 1951–1977 (OLS estimation technique)

Explanatory Variables	Dependent Variable: Ratio of Appraised Value to Purchase Price
Age of housing stock	
Percent of housing units built in 1939 or earlier (1970 census)	−0.000 (−0.51)
Age of building relative to new construction	
1–9 years	−0.008 (−1.12)
10–19 years	−0.015 (−1.87)
20–29 years	−0.027 (−2.62)
30–39 years	−0.007 (−0.66)
40–49 years	−0.012 (−0.98)
≥50 years	0.011 (0.82)
Construction material relative to nonwood	
Wood	0.008 (1.38)
Structure type relative to 2- to 4-unit buildings	
Single-family house	0.016 (1.90)
Type of loan relative to conventional	
FHA	−0.009 (−1.52)
VA	−0.004 (−0.67)
Property location relative to Suffolk County	
North Bronx	−0.057 (−3.10)
South Bronx[a]	−0.018 (−0.80)
Northeast Kings	−0.029 (−1.64)
Northwest Kings[a]	−0.053 (−2.67)

Table C.6 (continued)

Explanatory Variables	Dependent Variable: Ratio of Appraised Value to Purchase Price
South Kings	−0.045
	(−3.26)
Nassau	0.002
	(0.26)
Southeast Queens[a]	−0.003
	(0.18)
Rest of Queens	−0.020
	(−1.96)
Westchester	−0.033
	(−2.85)
Year of transaction relative to prior to 1951	
1951	−0.016
	(−0.62)
1952	−0.010
	(−0.34)
1953	0.006
	(0.22)
1954	−0.033
	(−1.35)
1955	−0.018
	(−0.81)
1956	−0.051
	(−2.17)
1957	−0.052
	(−1.98)
1958	0.031
	(1.22)
1959	−0.045
	(−1.83)
1960	−0.011
	(−0.46)
1961	−0.017
	(−0.74)
1962	0.014
	(0.60)
1963	0.009
	(0.38)
1964	0.025
	(1.11)

Table C.6 (continued)

Explanatory Variables	Dependent Variable: Ratio of Appraised Value to Purchase Price
1965	0.005 (0.21)
1966	0.014 (0.62)
1967	−0.011 (−0.48)
1968	0.001 (0.04)
1969	−0.011 (−0.50)
1970	−0.021 (−0.92)
1971	0.002 (0.08)
1972	−0.006 (−0.26)
1973	−0.010 (−0.45)
1974	0.000 (0.00)
1975	0.011 (0.47)
1976	−0.011 (−0.49)
1977	0.038 (1.61)
Constant	0.993 (43.80)
R-squared	0.16
Sample size	1,032
F-statistic	3.83
P-value	0.0
Mean value of the dependent variable	0.982

The numbers in parentheses are t-statistics.
a. Areas that are allegedly redlined.

Notes

Chapter 1

1. Equal Credit Opportunity Act (as amended March 23, 1976), Public Law 93-495, Title VII; Federal Home Loan Bank Board, CFR Title 12, chap. 5, subchap. B, pt. 528 (effective July 1, 1978); California Business and Transportation Agency, Department of Savings and Loan, Chap. 3, subchap. 4, Title 21, "Regulations Pursuant to the Housing Financial Discrimination Act of 1977" (May 13, 1979); and New York, *Executive Law* Sec. 296-9 (1976).

2. Equal Credit Opportunity Act, Public Law 93-495, Title VII, sec. 701 (March 1976).

3. Public Law 95-128, 95th Cong., 1st sess., October 12, 1977.

4. Federal Home Loan Bank Board, C.F.R. Title 12, chap. 5, subchap. B, pt. 528.

5. Two major exceptions are G. C. Lowry, *An Analysis of Discrimination in Mortgage Lending*, Banking Research Center, Working Paper, no. 42 (Evanston, Ill.: Northwestern University Press, 1977); and R. Schafer, *Mortgage Lending Decisions: Criteria and Constraints* (Cambridge: MIT-Harvard Joint Center for Urban Studies, 1978).

6. There is some evidence that each of these actors participate in discriminatory behavior. See U.S. Department of Housing and Urban Development, "Background and Initial Findings of the Housing Market Practices Survey," Washington, D.C., 1978; U.S. Department of Housing and Urban Development, *Insurance Crisis in America*, Washington, D.C., 1978; and *United States* v. *American Institute of Real Estate Appraisers, et al.*, Civil Action, no. 76 C1448 (N.D. Ill., 1976) (complaint and settlement agreement with the American Institute of Real Estate Appraisers and the National Association of Realtors).

7. See, for example, W. Bryant, *Mortgage Lending* (New York: McGraw-Hill, 1962), chap. 5; and U.S. Commission on Civil Rights, *Mortgage Money: Who Gets It? A Case Study of Mortgage Lending Discrimination in Hartford, Connecticut*, Chap. 3, Clearinghouse Publication 48, June 1974.

8. A 1971 Federal Home Loan Bank survey of savings and loans found that more than half the respondents would count less than 50 percent of the income of a wife, age twenty-five, with two school-age children and a full-time secretarial position. A 1972 U.S. Saving and Loan League survey found that only 28 percent of the surveyed lenders would count a wife's income fully. Only six of fourteen respondents from nine lending institutions in the Hartford, Connecticut, area said they would fully count the wife's income even under favorable conditions. These surveys are cited or reported in a variety of sources, including National Council of Negro Women, Inc. *Women and Housing: A Report on Sex Discrimination in Five American Cities* (U.S. Department of Housing and Urban Development, June 1975), and U.S. Commission on Civil Rights, *Mortgage Money: Who Gets It?*

9. U.S. Commission on Civil Rights, *Mortgage Money: Who Gets It?*, chap. 4, table 8.

10. *Ibid.*, p. 42.

11. See, for example, testimony by W. L. Taylor, "Economic Problems of Women," *Hearings before the Joint Economic Committee*, U.S. Congress, 93rd Cong. 1st sess., 1973), pp. 176, 196.

12. U.S. Department of Housing and Urban Development, *Mortgage Credit Analysis Handbook for Mortgage Insurance on One to Four-Family Properties*, 1972, sec. 1–22.

13. For example, see Taylor, *Hearings Before the JEC*.

14. U.S. Department of Housing and Urban Development, *Women in the Mortgage Market* (Washington, D.C.: U.S. Government Printing Office, 1976). Even though the study gives insufficient attention to the variance of income, its general conclusion that realistic projections would lead to less than 50 percent discounting is probably valid.

15. Between 1947 and 1964, the labor force participation rate of women in the age group twenty-five to thirty-four increased about 0.03 percent a year. Between 1964 and 1977, the participation rate rose at a rate of 1.7 percent a year. See R. E. Smith, *Women in the Labor Force in 1990* (Washington, D.C.: The Urban Institute, March 1979), p. 11 and *passim*.

16. Federal Reserve Board, Regulation B, 12 C.F.R. 202.6 (effective March 23, 1977).

17. Federal Home Loan Bank Board, Nondiscrimination Guidelines, C.F.R. Title 12, chap. V, pt. 531.8.

18. National Council of Negro Women, *Women and Housing*, pp. 53, 63, 66.

19. *Ibid.*, pp. 61–65.

20. Federal Reserve Board, Regulation B, 12 C.F.R. 202.6 (effective March 23, 1977).

21. National Council of Negro Women, *Women and Housing*, pp. 64–66.

22. See, for example, Taylor, *Hearings before the JEC*; and U.S. Commission on Civil Rights, *Mortgage Money: Who Gets It?*, chap. 4.

23. The U.S. Court of Appeals for the District of Columbia has ruled that the Equal Credit Opportunity Act requires a savings and loan association to aggregate the incomes of an unmarried couple in determining their credit worthiness in processing a joint mortgage application. *Markham* v. *Colonial Mortgage Service Co., Associates, Inc.* (August 2, 1979) as reported in the *Housing and Development Reporter*, August 20, 1979, pp. 279–280.

24. See C. Abrams, *Forbidden Neighbors* (New York: Harper, 1956); and D. McEntire, *Residence and Race* (Berkeley, Calif.: University of California Press, 1960).

25. Lowry, *An Analysis of Discrimination in Mortgage Lending*.

26. For a thorough review of the redlining literature, see A. T. King, *Redlining: A Critical Review of the Literature with Suggested Research*, Federal Home Loan Bank Board, draft, 1978.

27. California, Business and Transportation Agency, Department of Savings and Loan, *Loan Register Report*; New York, Banking Department, Supervisory Procedure G-107.

28. See A. Thomas King, "Discimination in Mortgage Lending: A Study of Three Cities," Research Working Paper No. 91, Federal Home Loan Bank Board, Washington, D.C., February 1980.

The comptroller of the currency and the FDIC conducted a large survey of mortgage-lending applications at 300 lending institutions around the country, but the quality of the data was disappointing. For example, participation was voluntary and only 176 of the 300 institutions actually participated. The survey consisted of a two-part form; one part to be completed by the lender; the other, by the applicant. Although banks sent in 13,613 parts and applicants 10,287, only 5,107 matched. And only 138 of the matches were rejected applications.

Since March 23, 1977, the Federal Reserve Board (Regulation B) has required member banks to "request "information on the race, national origin, sex, marital status, and age of applicants for "consumer credit relating to the purchase of residential real property." Unfortunately, Regulation B only requires that the applicant and joint applicant be "asked, but not required" to supply this information.

Chapter 2

1. The MLS includes a sample of active and satisfied mortgages from the portfolios of mutual savings banks. In general, data were collected on various loan, property, neighborhood, and borrower characteristics on a sample of 4,392 mortgages on properties located throughout the Albany-Schenectady-Troy, Buffalo, Nassau-Suffolk, New York, Rochester, and Syracuse metropolitan areas.

2. J. S. Earley and J. P. Herzog, *Home Mortgage Delinquency and Foreclosure* (New York: National Bureau of Economic Research, 1970), R. II. Edelstein, "Improving the Selection of Credit Risks: An Analysis of a Commercial Bank Minority Lending Program," *Journal of Finance* (March 1975), pp. 37–55; R. J. Green, and G. M. von Furstenberg, "The Effects of Race and Age of Housing on Mortgage Delinquency Risk," *Urban Studies* (Feb. 1975), pp. 85–89; R. E. Knight, "The Quality of Mortgage Credit: Part I," *Federal Reserve Bank of Kansas City: Monthly Review* (March 1969), pp. 13–20; R. E. Knight, "The Quality of Mortgage Credit: Part II," *Federal Reserve Bank of Kansas City: Monthly Review* (April 1969), pp. 10–18; R. L. Sandor and H. B. Sosin, "The Determinants of Mortgage Risk Premiums: A Case Study of the Portfolio of a Savings and Loan Association," *Journal of Business* (Jan. 1975), pp. 27–38; G. M. von Furstenberg, "Default Risk on FHA-Insured Home Mortgages as a Function of the Terms of Financing: A Quantitiative Analysis," *Journal of Finance* (June 1969), pp. 459–477; G. M. von Furstenberg, "Interstate Differences in Mortgage Lending Risks: An Analysis of the Causes," *Journal of Financial and Quantitative Analysis* (June 1970), pp. 229–242; G. M. von Furstenberg, "Risk Structures and the Distribution of Benefits within the FHA Home Mortgage Insurance Program," *Journal of Money, Credit, and Banking* (Aug. 1970), pp. 303–322; G. M. von Furstenberg, "The Investment Quality of Home Mortgages," *Journal of Risk and Insurance* (Sept. 1970), pp. 437–445; G. M. von Furstenberg, and R. J. Green, "Estimation of Delinquency Risk for Home Mortgage Portfolios," *AREUEA Journal* (Spring 1974), pp. 5–19; G. M. von Furstenberg and R. J. Green, "Home Mortgage Delinquencies: A Cohort Analysis," *Journal of Finance* (Dec. 1974), pp. 1545–1548; and G. M. von Furstenberg and R. J. Green, "The Effect of Income and Race on the Quality of Home Mortgages: A Case for Pittsburgh," in *Patterns of Racial Discrimination, Vol. 1: Housing* ed. G. M. von Furstenberg, B. Harrison, and A. R. Horowitz (Lexington, Mass.: Lexington Books, 1974).

3. R. J. Green and G. M. von Furstenberg, "The Effects of Race and Age of Housing on Mortgage Delinquency Risk," *Urban Studies* (Feb. 1975), pp. 85–89; and von Furstenberg and Green, "Home Mortgage Delinquencies."

4. Because the MLS sample covers an extended period of time, all variables measured in dollar figures have been deflated to 1967 dollars using the consumer price index.

5. Almost all loans in the MLS sample were closed after 1950.

6. D. J. Levinson, *The Seasons of a Man's Life* (New York: Alfred A. Knopf, 1978).

7. Building condition categories used in the MLS questionnaire are good, fair, fair-to-poor, and poor.

8. Delinquency risk is expected to respond to changes in the age of the borrower. In particular, adults are believed to experience periods of crisis between twenty-eight and thirty-three years of age and again between forty and forty-five years. A test for the effects of the age of borrower on delinquency risk is to measure the borrower's age at the time of delinquency or nondelinquency, rather than at the time of closing. Separate models were estimated with this substitution in the age-of-borrower variables. None of the coefficients were statistically significant. In the New York-Nassau-Suffolk region the two largest increases in probability of delinquency occur in the twenty-eight to thirty-three and forty to forty-five age categories, a pattern that is consistent with the adult crisis hypothesis. In the other regions, however, the relative magnitudes of the coefficients do not support the hypothesis. Some of the other default models discussed below provide statistically significant support for this hypothesis.

9. Unfortunately, a sizable number (twenty-eight) of the delinquent loans used to estimate the model of the probability of delinquency are dropped from the analysis of the frequency of delinquency because of missing information on the dependent variables. Almost all eliminated mortgages are recorded as being "chronically" delinquent.

10. This measure could not be included in the analysis of one- to four-family mortgage default because of high correlation with down payment.

11. J. Kirlin is developing such models using the MLS data. See "A Credit Risk Model for Single-Family Conventional Mortgages," Ph.D. dissertation, Harvard University (forthcoming).

Chapter 3

1. See E. A. Hanushek and J. E. Jackson, *Statistical Methods for Social Science* (New York: Academic Press, 1977).

2. The lending data is available under a disclosure regulation of the New York State Banking Department. See Supervisory Procedure G-107. In principal, federally assisted mortgages on multifamily buildings could also be analyzed, but census tracts with new mortgages of this type were too few to estimate a multivariate model.

3. *Federal Reserve Bulletin,* 64 (Feb. 1978): A41.

4. Information on transactions could not be obtained for any other counties in the four largest metropolitan areas in upstate New York. In addition, the supplementary data such as measures of risk of loss, is much less detailed for upstate areas.

5. As the lagged values of stock required for this model are not available, they have been approximated by subtracting mortgages made during the year (1975) from the stock at the end of the year.

6. The housing code violations data came with the following disclaimer: "The number of pending violations is normally a better indicator of building condition than total violations. . . . HDA [Housing Development Authority] tends to concentrate code enforcement in good and transient areas, consequently the file overstates housing quality in bad areas."

7. The interest rate can vary because it is based on mortgages covering one- to four-family houses, whereas the usury law principally restricts the interest rate on one- and two-family houses. See Chapter 2.

8. Because dollar value of mortgage lending cannot be negative or exceed the dollar value of transactions, predicted values less than zero have been set equal to zero and

those greater than transactions have been set equal to transactions. See D. S. Huang, *Regressions and Econometric Methods* (New York: John Wiley, 1970), p. 170; and R. S. Pindyck and D. L. Rubinfeld, *Econometric Models and Forecasts* (New York: McGraw-Hill, 1976) pp. 241–242. Although a log-linear specification would avoid exceeding the lower bound on mortgage lending, it would not eliminate predictions in excess of transactions. In addition, a log-linear specification would require that the zero value of independent variables be arbitrarily set to some nonzero value, another reason for not relying on a log-linear specification. The logarithmic-reciprocal transformation has both a lower and an upper bound, but the upper bound is fixed, whereas in this analysis it is variable. It should also be noted that the forecast error increases as the difference between the observed values of the independent variables and their mean values increases in the estimated equation. As a result, the forecast error is probably largest when the other-neighborhoods equation is used to predict lending in the riskier areas. The areas alleged to be redlined are those with the highest risk.

9. A *t*-statistic is used to test the difference between the two coefficients. The combined standard error is the square root of the sum of the variances of each coefficient. This assumes that the covariance between the coefficients is relatively small.

10. Estimates are based on mean values of all other independent variables in each equation.

11. This difference has a *t*-statistic of 1.54, indicating that the result has only a 12.3 percent chance of being random.

12. Estimates are based on mean values of all other independent variables in each equation.

13. Estimates as in note 12.

14. U.S. Congress, Senate Committee on Housing, Banking and Urban Affairs, *Neighborhood Preservation Hearings*, 94th Cong., 2nd sess., 1976, p. 105–116; and Urban-Suburban Investment Study Group, *Redlining and Disinvestment as a Discriminatory Practice in Residential Mortgage Loans* (Washington, D.C.: U.S. Government Printing Office, HUD-EO-235, June 1977) pp. 64–75.

15. The separate equation is not reported here because of the similarity of the results. It is available in R. Schafer, *Mortgage Lending Decisions: Criteria and Constraints* (Cambridge: MIT-Harvard Joint Center for Urban Studies, 1978) pp. 5-52 to 5-58.

16. Only three of the twenty-three observations in the reference area are located in North Bronx.

17. The mean and standard deviation of the transactions variable are 11.05 and 21.14, respectively. This and other estimates of impact are evaluated using the mean value of all variables.

Chapter 4

1. A logistic relationship would be preferable to this simple linear relationship but is difficult to deal with mathematically.

2. This can be proved as follows:

$$\bar{R}_t = ER_t = X - (X - X')EP_t$$
$$= X - (X - X')E(a - bY_t)$$
$$= X - a(X - X') + b(X - X')\bar{Y}_t$$

and

$$\begin{aligned}
\mathrm{Var}R_t &= E(R_t - ER_t)^2 \\
&= E[X - (X - X')P_t - X + (X - X')EP_t]^2 \\
&= E[X - (X - X')(a - bY_t) - X + (X - X')(a - b\overline{Y}_t)]^2 \\
&= b^2(X - X')^2 E(Y_t - \overline{Y}_t)^2
\end{aligned}$$

It should be noted that the link between the variance of income and the variance of the portfolio return is more complex in a nonlinear probability-of-default function.

3. Note that we are simplifying the analysis by ignoring the covariances between Y_t and Y_j for all years of the contract $t \neq j$.

4. It should be noted that the variance of household income for a two-earner household may be lower than that for a single-earner household. For example, consider a two-earner male-female household where the income of the male in year t is Y_m and that for the female is Y_f. Then the variance of total household income in year t can be expressed as:

$$\mathrm{Var}\ (Y_m + Y_f) = \mathrm{Var}\ Y_m + \mathrm{Var}\ Y_f + 2\ \mathrm{Cov}\ (Y_m Y_f)$$

A negative covariance between Y_m and Y_f will reduce the variance of the sum below the sum of the individual variances.

5. The statement in the text should be qualified to exclude loan fees. See the discussion of the loan-fee model.

6. In some instances in the empirical work, blacks cannot be separated out, and in others, Asians are included in the base.

7. It should be noted that the term "risk" is being used slightly differently here than in the portfolio model. Here, it refers to all objective factors influencing either the expected return or the variance of that return; in the portfolio model, it is used specifically to refer to the variance.

Chapter 5

1. In New York, the decision-to-lend models were estimated with and without measures of net wealth and employment stability. The findings were virtually unaffected by leaving out these variables.

2. In the Stockton metropolitan area the fraction Spanish also includes all nonblack minorities.

3. These probabilities can be calculated from the logit estimate using the following relationships.

$$\sum_{j=0}^{c} P_j = 1 \tag{7.1}$$

$$\lambda_j = Ln(P_j/P_0) = \alpha_j + B_j X \qquad j = 1, \ldots, c \tag{7.2}$$

$$P_j = \exp(\lambda_j)/[1 + \sum_{k=1}^{c} \exp(\lambda_k)] \tag{7.3}$$

$$P_0 = 1/[1 + \sum_{k=1}^{c} \exp(\lambda_k)] \tag{7.4}$$

where P_j is the conditional probabilities of the jth outcome given a vector of explanatory variables (X), $c + 1$ represents the total number of possible outcomes, and the probability of one outcome is arbitrarily selected as the reference base (P_0).

4. The 1978 ratio for Anaheim-Santa Ana-Garden Grove is greater than one (1.24) but not statistically significant.

5. These ratios are not reported in Table 5.8.

6. The 1977 San Diego and 1978 Santa Barbara denial ratios for MFNCB are also greater than one but the underlying secondary-income coefficients are not statistically significant.

7. The City of Los Angeles results are not presented in the text, but the underlying equations are reported in Appendix B.

8. We also estimated versions of the multivariate model without the building-age variables. Comparison of the two results suggests that an age-of-neighborhood variable will capture a significant portion of the effect of the building-age variables when these are excluded.

Chapter 6

1. The order condition is a necessary but insufficient condition for identification. See, for example, Robert S. Pyndyck and Daniel L. Rubinfeld, *Econometric Models and Economic Forecasts* (New York: McGraw-Hill, 1976), Ch. 5.

2. Although savings and loan associations report information on the month of the application for the *Loan Register*, this information was deleted from the data made available to us.

3. A recent Federal Home Loan Bank Board study of mortgage lending provides limited empirical support for this new specification. Based on individual mortgage data collected from federally insured savings and loan associations in three SMSA's, A. Thomas King estimated simultaneous models of mortgage terms. The availability of information on the borrowers' requested maturity allowed him to estimate equations of the basic form presented in Equations 4.7–4.9. For two of the three samples, both LTOAV and INT are statistically insignificant in the MAT equation when REQMAT is included. In the Toledo sample, however, the interest rate variable is significant at the 10 percent (two-tailed) level. See A. Thomas King, "Discrimination in Mortgage Lending: A Study of Three Cities," Office of Policy and Economic Research, Federal Home Loan Bank Board, Washington, D.C. (February 1980).

An imperfect test of the assumption for one of our study areas, San Jose (1978) also yields results that are consistent with our approach; both INT and LTOAV are statistically insignificant explanatory variables in the MAT equation when estimated by ordinary least squares. We used ordinary least squares because use of REQLOAN and RLTOAV as proxies for the unobserved REQMAT means the MAT equation is no longer identified.

In an earlier version of this study, we dealt with this identification problem in a less satisfactory way. Namely, we included REQLOAN as a proxy for REQMAT in the MAT equation and excluded it from the INT equation. This solution led to large standard errors in some cases and is inconsistent with our current view that REQLOAN belongs in the interest rate equation. See Robert Schafer and Helen F. Ladd, *Equal Credit Opportunity: Accessibility to Mortgage Funds by Women and by Minorities*, Vol. 1, ch. 4 (Joint Center for Urban Studies of the Massachusetts Institute of Technology and Harvard University, 1980).

4. The MAT equation and the two equation block, INT and LTOAV, fall into the category of seemingly unrelated equations. Single equation estimating methods can be improved upon when the correlations of the error terms across equations are high. See, for example, Jan Kmenta, *Elements of Econometrics* (New York: The MacMillan Company, 1971), pp. 517–529 and J. Johnston, *Econometric Methods* revised edition (New York: McGraw-Hill Book Company, Inc., 1972).

5. Fresno (1977) is the one exception; the coefficient of REQLOAN is small and insignificant in the interest rate equation.

6. Fresno (1978) is the only study area for which the requested loan-to-income variable has a statistically significant impact on the maturity period. The finding that this financial variable plays no direct role in the maturity equation in the other seven study areas is consistent with our two-stage view of the lending process. According to this view, maturity periods are set prior to the full evaluation of the loan application.

7. The same interpretation holds for a male secondary earner in a male-female household.

8. The insignificant differentials for Asians and blacks in Fresno may reflect their relatively small sample sizes. This is not the case for Asians in San Jose who are well represented in the sample.

9. This conclusion is generally consistent with the downward-modification equations.

10. A "high" proportion of a minority group is calculated as the maximum value of the racial composition variable minus two standard deviations. The values of "high" minority populations used in Table 6.6 are presented in Table 5.32.

11. When interpreting these results, it should be remembered that the racial composition variables are based on 1970 data.

12. The redlining allegations for Los Angeles County are derived from *Where the Money Is: Mortgage Lending, Los Angeles County* (Los Angeles: The Center for New Corporate Priorities, 1975). This report is reprinted in *Hearings on the Home Mortgage Disclosure Act of 1975*, U.S. Senate, Committee on Banking, Housing and Urban Affairs, 94th Congress, 1st Session (May 5–8, 1975). For the San Francisco-Oakland area, the redlining allegation is based on a study examining mortgage lending in Oakland only. See William M. Frej, "Discriminatory Lending Practices in Oakland," in *Hearings on the Home Mortgage Disclosure Act of 1975*, U.S. Senate, Committee on Banking, Housing and Urban Affairs, 94th Congress, 1st Session (May 5–8, 1975).

13. The baseline reference locations are: the suburbs in Fresno, the portions not alleged to be redlined and non-central city portions of Los Angeles County in Los Angeles-Long Beach, San Mateo County in San Francisco-Oakland, and the suburbs in San Jose.

14. The calculated impact reflects the effects of both the sex and age of the applicants. See footnote b, Table 6.9.

15. See footnote 10, this chapter.

16. The reference suburban locations are the same as those for the downward-modification results. See footnote 13, this chapter.

17. The San Jose 1978 result just misses statistical significance.

18. See footnote 10, this chapter.

19. See footnote 12, this chapter.

Chapter 7

1. See R. Schafer, *Mortgage Lending Decisions, Criteria and Constraints* (Cambridge: Joint Center for Urban Studies of MIT and Harvard, 1978), chaps. 7, 11, and 12.

2. Unfortunately, the question asking for the information on years at present occupation is vague. It appears that some applicants gave the number of years at the present position and others, the number of years in their present occupation. The possible responses on the form added confusion by having a "not-employed" category. As a

result, this variable does not perform as consistently as we would like. However, it is an improvement over the California data, which lacks any measure of the stability (or variance) of the individual applicant's credit worthiness.

3. Because of the categorical nature of the responses to the income question, some loan requests in excess of two times income are not covered by this variable.

4. See Schafer, *Mortgage Lending Decisions*; chaps. 7, 11, and 12, for a discussion of the mutual savings bank samples.

5. Applications at commercial banks in the Albany-Schenectady-Troy, Rochester, and Syracuse metropolitan areas had nearly equal incidences of incomes in the $15,001 to $25,000 and over $25,000 ranges, 42 and 45 percent, respectively, and applications at commercial banks in the New York-Nassau-Suffolk area had most of their applications in the highest income range (74 percent versus 23 percent in the $15,001 to $25,000 range).

6. See Chap. 2, footnote 3.

7. For the mutual savings bank model for Rochester, see Schafer, *Mortgage Lending Decisions*, table 12-7.

8. The Central Brooklyn-Fort Greene coefficient is significant at the 5 percent level.

9. The results are the same in the Bronx-Kings-Queens mutual savings banks sample with the more detailed measures of neighborhood externalities.

10. In the Bronx-Kings-Queens mutual savings banks sample, only applications on properties in East Flatbush, Fort Greene, Park Slope, and Northeast Kings are more likely to be modified than ones on properties located in the portion of Queens County that is not alleged to be redlined.

11. Mutual savings banks in the Bronx-Kings-Queens sample are also significantly (5 percent level) more likely to deny applications on older properties. The denial ratio is 1.06.

12. The modification results for mutual savings banks in the Bronx-Kings-Queens sample are similar to those shown in Table 7.19.

13. However, mutual savings banks in the Bronx-Kings-Queens sample are more likely to modify applications on properties in largely black neighborhoods; the modification ratio is 1.49. Furthermore, these same banks are also more likely to modify applications on properties in neighborhoods that have had an increase in their nonwhite population. A 20-percentage-point increase leads to a modification ratio of 1.25. Both of these effects are statistically significant at the 5 percent level.

14. This also occurs in the mutual savings banks Bronx-Kings-Queens sample. The withdrawal ratio is small: 1.01.

Chapter 8

1. Since New York State's usury law was binding during our study period, analysis of interest rates would not be fruitful.

2. This calculation is based on a weighted average of the coefficients across the four samples. The 10,000 difference in requested loan increases the downward modification by $960; the increase in RLTOAV from 0.63 to 0.82 increases the modification by $1235. Hence, the additional amount granted is $7,805 ($10,000 − $2,195) instead of $10,000.

3. Because of this unexpected sign of RLTOAV, a variety of alternative model specifications, including nonlinear specifications, were estimated for the New York-Nassau-

Suffolk commercial bank sample. The results for the discrimination variables were remarkably stable across specifications.

4. In the New York-Nassau-Suffolk metropolitan area, the baseline suburb is Suffolk County; in the Rochester area, Monroe County. The combined upstate data base requires two modifications to the baseline application; first, the baseline application is expanded to include those married male-female couples where the wife is beyond childbearing age and is working, and second, since no location variables are included in the equation, the base location is the entire study area.

5. Similar analysis for federally assisted mortgages is not presented because the Supervisory Procedure G-107 data do not provide information on discounts, if any, which are required to convert the stated interest rate into an effective interest rate. This is especially important in those periods when the federal interest-rate ceilings are binding.

6. Impact on down payment is estimated for loan-to-value ratios that start at 80 percent.

7. The short maturity periods are used because they are typical of conventional multi-family mortgages in Bronx, Kings, and Queens counties.

Chapter 9

1. The redlining allegations are derived from *Where the Money Is: Mortgage Lending, Los Angeles County* (Los Angeles: Center for New Corporate Priorities, 1975) as reprinted in U.S. Senate, Committee on Banking, Housing and Urban Affairs, *Hearings on the Home Mortgage Disclosure Act of 1975*, 94th Cong., 1st sess., May 5–8, 1975; and W. M. Frej, "Discriminatory Lending Practices in Oakland," also in U.S. Senate, *Hearings*.

Chapter 10

1. Public Law 93-495, Title VII, Section 701.

2. Public Law 95-128 (October 12, 1977).

3. Federal Home Loan Bank Board, CFR Title 12, Chapter V, Subchapter B, Part 528.

Chapter 11

1. See R. Schafer and G. Reid, "Impact of Usury Ceilings on Mortgage Lending," Working Paper No. 60 (Cambridge: Joint Center for Urban Studies of MIT and Harvard University, 1979).

2. *Ibid.*

3. The income cutoff point has been selected because it is the one employed in several federal programs. See Housing and Community Development Act of 1974, Title II, sec. 201(a)(8), 42 USC sec. 1401, and 24 CFR secs. 880–883.

4. This phrase describes the rationale underlying New York's usury laws. See E. Kohn, C. J. Carlo, and B. Kaye, *The Impact of New York's Usury Ceiling on Local Mortgage Lending Activity* (New York State Banking Department, Jan. 1976), p. 1.

5. The mortgages should be standardized for those characteristics of the property, neighborhood, and requested loan that play a legitimate and important role in determining the effective interest rate through their impact on risk.

6. A good example of such a brochure is the one prepared by the Quincy Savings Bank in Massachusetts, "How to Buy a House." It is the source of the outline that is given in the text.

7. The First American Bank for Savings in Boston, Massachusetts, gives approximately four-week courses on "How to Buy a House." *First Fund Report* (May 11, 1978).

8. R. S. Ahlbrandt, Jr., and P. C. Brophy, *An Evaluation of Pittsburgh's Neighborhood Housing Services Program* (March 1975), through U.S. Department of Housing and Urban Development, under contract no. H-2214R. (ACTION-Housing, Inc., Pittsburgh, Pennsylvania), p. 1.

9. U.S. Congress, Senate Committee on Banking, Housing, and Urban Affairs, *The Cause of Neighborhood Decline and the Impact, Positive or Negative, of Existing Programs, Policies and Laws on Existing Neighborhoods, Hearings*, 94th Cong., 2nd sess. June 14, 1976, pp. 11–12.

10. Public Law 95-557, Title VI.

11. Statement of M. Foster, Buckeye Woodland Community Congress, Cleveland, Ohio, U.S. Congress, Senate Committee on Banking, Housing, and Urban Affairs, *The Cause of Neighborhood Decline*, p. 107.

12. Federal Reserve Board, "Equal Credit Opportunity," Regulation B, 12 CFR 202.2(z) (March 23, 1977). See also, Equal Credit Opportunity Act, 15 USC sec. 1601 *et seq.*, 1977.

13. New York, *Executive Law* sec. 296 9, 1976.

14. *Ibid.*

15. *Ibid.*

16. 12 CFR 528.2(a), 43 *Federal Register* 22335, May 25, 1978.

17. 12 CFR 531.8(c)(6), 43 *Federal Register* 22339, May 25, 1978 (emphasis added).

18. 43 *Federal Register* 22333, May 25, 1978.

19. California Administrative Code, Title 21, chap. 3, subchap. 4.

20. New York Laws of 1978, chap. 788, Dec. 8, 1978.

21. Public Law 94-200, Title III.

22. New York State Banking Department, Supervisory Procedure G-107, Aug. 31, 1976.

23. See, generally, Mortgage Review Fund, *Annual Report. 1977*, March 31, 1978.

24. One of the seventy-five applications was still being processed at the end of the reporting period.

25. R. M. Golden, "Redlining: What Is To Be Done?" New York Public Interest Research Group Report, 1977, pp. 17–18.

Publications of the Joint Center for Urban Studies

The Joint Center for Urban Studies, a cooperative venture of the Massachusetts Institute of Technology and Harvard University, was founded in 1959 to organize and encourage research on urban and regional problems and family and social policy. Participants have included scholars from the fields of anthropology, architecture, business, city planning, economics, education, engineering, history, law, philosophy, political science, and sociology.

The findings and conclusions of this book are, as with all Joint Center publications, solely the responsibility of the authors.

Published by Harvard University Press

The Intellectual versus the City: From Thomas Jefferson to Frank Lloyd Wright, by Morton and Lucia White, 1962

Streetcar Suburbs: The Process of Growth in Boston, 1870–1900, by Sam B. Warner Jr., 1961

City Politics, by Edward C. Banfield and James Q. Wilson, 1963

Law and Land: Anglo-American Planning Practice, edited by Charles M. Haar, 1964

Location and Land Use: Toward a General Theory of Land Rent, by William Alonso, 1964

Poverty and Progress: Social Mobility in a Nineteenth Century City, by Stephan Thernstrom, 1964

Boston: The Job Ahead, by Martin Meyerson and Edward C. Banfield, 1966

The Myth and Reality of Our Urban Problems, by Raymond Vernon, 1966

Muslim Cities in the Later Middle Ages, by Ira Marvin Lapidus, 1967

The Fragmented Metropolis: Los Angeles, 1850–1930, by Robert M. Fogelson, 1967

Law and Equal Opportunity: A Study of the Massachusetts Commission Against Discrimination, by Leon H. Mayhew, 1968

Varieties of Police Behavior: The Management of Law and Order in Eight Communities, by James Q. Wilson

The Metropolitan Enigma: Inquiries into the Nature and Dimensions of America's "Urban Crisis," edited by James Q. Wilson, revised edition, 1968

Traffic and the Police: Variations in Law-Enforcement Policy, by John A. Gardiner, 1969

The Influence of Federal Grants: Public Assistance in Massachusetts, by Martha Derthick, 1970

The Arts in Boston, by Bernard Taper, 1970

Families Against the City: Middle Class Homes of Industrial Chicago, 1872–1890, by Richard Sennett, 1970

The Political Economy of Urban Schools, by Martin T. Katzman, 1971

Origins of the Urban School: Public Education in Massachusetts, 1870–1915, by Marvin Lazerson, 1971

The Other Bostonians: Poverty and Progress in the American Metropolis, 1880–1970, by Stephan Thernstrom, 1973

Published by the MIT Press

The Image of the City, by Kevin Lynch, 1960

Housing and Economic Progress: A Study of the Housing Experience of Boston's Middle-Income Families, by Lloyd Rodwin, 1961

The Historian and the City, edited by Oscar Handlin and John Burchard, 1963

The Federal Bulldozer: A Critical Analysis of Urban Renewal, 1949–1962, by Martin Anderson, 1964

The Future of Old Neighborhoods: Rebuilding for a Changing Population, by Bernard J. Frieden, 1964

Man's Struggle for Shelter in an Urbanizing World, by Charles Abrams, 1964

The View from the Road, by Donald Appleyard, Kevin Lynch, and John R. Myer, 1964

The Public Library and the City, edited by Ralph W. Conant, 1965

Regional Development Policy: A Case Study of Venezuela, by John Friedmann, 1966

Urban Renewal: The Record and the Controversy, edited by James Q. Wilson, 1966

Transport Technology for Developing Regions: A Study of Road Transportation in Venezuela, by Richard M. Soberman, 1966

Computer Methods in the Analysis of Large-Scale Social Systems, edited by James M. Beshers, 1968

Planning Urban Growth and Regional Development: The Experience of the Guayana Program of Venezuela, by Lloyd Rodwin and Associates, 1969

Build a Mill, Build a City, Build a School: Industrialization, Urbanization, and Education in Ciudad Guayana, by Noel F. McGinn and Russell G. Davis, 1969

Land-Use Controls in the United States, by John Delafons, second edition, 1969

Beyond the Melting Pot: The Negroes, Puerto Ricans, Jews, Italians, and Irish of New York City, by Nathan Glazer and Daniel Patrick Moynihan, revised edition, 1970

Bargaining: Monopoly Power versus Union Power, by George de Menil, 1971

Housing the Urban Poor: A Criticial Evaluation of Federal Housing Policy, by Arthur P. Solomon, 1974

The Politics of Neglect: Urban Aid from Model Cities to Revenue Sharing, by Bernard J. Frieden and Marshall Kaplan, 1975

Planning a Pluralist City: Conflicting Realities in Ciudad Guayana, by Donald Appleyard, 1976

The Environmental Protection Hustle, by Bernard J. Frieden, 1979

The Urban Transportation System: Politics and Policy Innovation, by Alan A. Altshuler with James P. Womack and John R. Pucher, 1979

Seasonal Cycles in the Housing Market: Patterns, Costs, and Policies, by Kenneth T. Rosen, 1979

The Prospective City: Economic, Population, Energy, and Environmental Developments, edited by Arthur P. Solomon, 1979

Discrimination in Mortgage Lending, by Robert Shafer and Helen F. Ladd, 1981

The Joint Center also publishes reports and working papers.

Index

Abandonment of property, 18, 248
Adult-crisis hypothesis, 22, 26–27,
  380n8
Age of borrower. *See also* Adult-crisis
  hypothesis
and credit terms
  in California, 149, 151–154, 163–166,
    183, 284, 300
  in New York, 230, 234–237, 245, 292,
    300
and decision to lend
  in California, 107–110, 134, 290–292
  in New York, 207–209, 223, 236, 292
and default risk, 22, 380n8
and delinquency probability in New
  York, 25
detection of treatment by, 75–76
and downward modification in New
  York, 230, 234–237, 245, 292
and maturity period in New York, 241
and modification of credit terms in
  California, 300
and property appraisal
  in California, 259
  in New York, 292
and severity of delinquency in New
  York, 26–27
treatment by
  in California, 101–110, 134, 151–154,
    163–166, 174–177, 183, 259, 290–
    292, 300
  in New York, 207–209, 223, 266,
    234–237, 290–292, 300
Age of mortgage. *See also* Maturity
  periods
and delinquency probability in New
  York, 23–24
Age of neighborhood
and conventional mortgage lending
  in California, 121–127, 135, 300
  in New York, 45, 48, 58, 59, 60, 217,
    220, 224, 296, 300

and credit terms in California, 154,
  183–184, 298
and decision to lend in New York,
  217, 220, 224, 298
and default risk in New York, 30, 31–
  32
and delinquency probability in New
  York, 23
and denial probability
  in California, 121–127, 296
  in New York, 217, 218, 244, 296
and downward modification
  in California, 166, 296
  in New York, 237–238
and federally-assisted mortgage lending in New York, 51–52, 61
and foreclosure probability in New
  York, 28
and interest rates in New York, 240,
  245–246
and loan fees in California, 177, 298
and loan-to-value ratio in New York,
  242, 246
and maturity period in New York,
  241, 244, 246
and modifications in New York, 217,
  219, 224, 296
and property appraisal
  in California, 259, 298
  in New York, 267
and severity of delinquency in New
  York, 26
Age of property. *See* Building age
Albany, treatment by property location
  in, 14–15, 32, 58, 210, 216, 223, 260,
  270, 295
Albany-Schenectady-Troy. *See also*
  Upstate region
borrower characteristics in, 26
building conditions in, 28
default risk in, 23–26, 28, 32

Albany-Schenectady-Troy (cont.)
  denial probability in, 197, 202, 216,
    223, 295
  downward modification in, 234
  federally-assisted mortgages in, 25
  property appraisal in, 267
  treatment by
    age in, 207–209, 234
    age of neighborhood in, 26, 58, 217–
      220
    building age in, 24, 32, 267
    property location in, 14–15, 32, 58,
      210, 216, 223, 260, 270, 295
    race in, 202–207, 222
    racial composition of neighborhoods
      in, 58, 220
  and withdrawal probability, 220
Anaheim-Santa Ana-Garden Grove
  denial probability in, 96, 101, 107, 111,
    127, 133, 135
  downward modification in, 107, 127,
    134
  income discounting in, 107, 134
  treatment by
    age of neighborhood in, 127, 135
    neighborhood characteristics in, 96
    race in, 111
  treatment of
    female-headed households in, 107,
      134
    male-headed households in, 101, 107,
      133
Appraisal of property. See Property
  appraisal
Appraisal practices
  in California, 249–259, 269
  in New York, 259–269
Appraised value, of property, 3, 247–
  249. See also Property appraisal;
  Overappraisal: Underappraisal
  in California, 169, 182
  and market value differences, 247–248
Appraised-value-to-purchase-price
  in California, 250, 257, 258
  in New York, 268–269
Asian neighborhoods in California,
  131–132, 156, 177, 259, 299
Average income
  and loan fees in California, 171
  and probability of denial in California,
    95
Average sales price. See Sales price,
  average

"baby letter," 5
Bakersfield
  decision to lend in, 131, 133, 135
  denial probability in, 115, 121, 127,
    135
  treatment by
    age of neighborhood in, 127, 135
    property location in, 121
    racial composition of neighborhood
      in, 131, 135
    race in, 115
    sex in, 133
Bank Reinvestment Act, 321–322
Black neighborhoods
  in California, 127–131, 135, 154–156,
    166, 177, 184, 259, 299
  in New York, 237–238, 298–299,
    385n13
Borrower characteristics. See also Age
  of borrower; Financial characteristics, of a borrower; Sex of borrower
  and delinquency probability in New
    York, 24–25
  and default risk, 312–313
  and foreclosure in New York, 17–18
  and portfolio-choice model, 64–66
  and severity of delinquency in New
    York, 26
Buffalo
  denial probability in, 196, 197, 198,
    201, 202, 207, 217, 221, 222, 223,
    224, 285
  modification probability in, 201, 204,
    207, 216, 223, 224, 290
  property appraisal in, 267–268
  requested loan amount in, 196
  treatment by
    age in, 207, 209, 223, 285
    age of neighborhood in, 217, 224
    building age in, 267
    marital status in, 198, 201, 221, 222,
      285
    property location in, 216, 224, 267–
      268
    race in, 202, 204, 222
    sex in, 198, 201, 221, 222, 285
  treatment of
    female-headed households in, 201,
      221, 285
    male-headed households in, 198, 201,
      221, 222
  withdrawal probability in, 209
Building age, 296
  and appraised value in New York, 267
  and appraised-value-to-purchase-price
    in California, 250, 269
  in California, 296
  and credit terms in California, 144–146
    154, 183–184

and decision to lend in California,
121–127, 135
and default risk in New York, 32
and delinquency probability in New
York, 24
and delinquency rates, 19
and denial probability in California,
121
and downward modification in California, 160
and loan fees in California, 169–171,
183–184
and maturity periods in California, 146
Building condition, 217, 296
and default risk
in California, 184
in New York, 30, 31
and delinquency probability in New
York, 24
and foreclosure in New York, 18–19,
31
and foreclosure probability in New
York, 28

Change in household. See Population
change
Change in sales price. See Sales price,
change in
Civil Rights Act (1968), 8
Coinsurance, 306, 309–311
Collateral, 68–69
and default risk, 3
Combined upstate region. See Upstate
region (New York)
Commercial banks (New York), 186,
190, 225
and denial probability, 196, 197, 198,
201, 202–204, 207, 215, 217, 221,
222, 223, 224, 285, 295, 299
and downward modification, 230–232,
234–237, 245
and employment stability, 196
and foreclosure rate, 229
and modification probability, 201, 204,
207, 223, 290
and net wealth, 196
and requested loan amount, 196, 227–
229
and requested-loan-to-appraised value,
227–228
and requested-loan-to-income, 228–229
and treatment by
age, 207–209, 223, 230–232, 234–237,
245, 285
age of neighborhood, 217, 220, 224
marital status, 198, 201, 202, 221,
222, 230–232, 236, 245, 285, 287

property location, 215, 217, 223, 237,
295
race, 202–204, 206–207, 222, 289
racial composition of neighborhoods,
224, 299
sex, 198, 201, 202, 221, 222, 230–232,
236, 245, 285, 287
and treatment of
female-headed households, 201, 221,
230–232, 236, 245, 285
male-headed households, 198, 201,
202, 221, 222
and withdrawal probability, 202, 206–
207, 209, 217, 220
Condominiums, 249, 257, 306–307
Construction material and property appraisal in New York, 267
Conventional mortgage lending in New
York, 22–28, 28–30, 42–50, 54–55,
56–59, 59–61, 239–244
Conventional mortgages and delinquency rates in New York, 14
Credit evaluation, 4–5, 7, 62–76, 304,
319. See also Creditworthiness, of a
borrower; Future income estimation; Prescreening
by property location, 8
regulation of, 7
Credit evaluation system, establishment
of, 304, 319
Credit rationing, 38, 68, 239, 302
Credit terms, 62, 69–70, 137. See also
Downward modification; Interest
rates; Maturity periods; Loan fees;
Loan-to-value ratio
and default risk, 141–142, 239, 245
and discrimination, 8
models of, 76–80, 138–141, 238–239
modification of. See Modification of
credit terms
and older applicants in New York, 245
and racial discrimination in California,
149–151, 182–183
Credit worthiness, of a borrower. See
also Borrower characteristics;
Credit evaluation; Future income
estimation; Financial characteristics, of a borrower
and default risk, 3, 239
determinants of, 3, 4
evaluation of, 5–7, 312, 319
measured by financial characteristics
in California, 85, 92–95
in New York, 187, 220–221

Decision to lend model, 71–76
Deed restrictions, 7–8

Default. *See* Foreclosure
Default risk, 3, 19–22. *See also*
    Delinquency
and building age in California, 144–146
and interest rates in New York, 239,
    243–244
and loan repayment, 20
measures of, 41–42, 60
in New York, 31–32
and property appraisal, 247–248
and redlining, 14
and supply of mortgage credit, 34
Delinquency, in mortgage payments.
    See also Default risk
duration of, 26
frequency of, 26
probability of, 23–25, 30, 31
severity of, 25–27, 31
Delinquency rates, 19
and conventional mortgage lending in
    New York, 44, 57, 59
and denial probability in New York,
    197
in New York, 14–15, 44, 57, 59, 197
Demand for mortgage credit
determinants of, 33
Demographic change. *See* Population
    change
Denial probability
and age of neighborhood in California,
    121–127
and building age in California, 121
and financial characteristics in Califor-
    nia, 92–95
and race in California, 110–115
and racial composition of neighbor-
    hoods in California, 127–132
and property location in California,
    116–121
and requested-loan-to-appraised value,
    280–281
and requested-loan-to-income, 280–281
and secondary income in California,
    102–107
and sex of applicant in California, 96–
    107, 258
Discrimination, 275–287. *See also* Age,
    treatment by: Age of borrower;
    Credit worthiness, of a borrower;
    Female-headed households, treat-
    ment of; Income discounting; Male-
    headed households, treatment of:
    Marital status, treatment by; Pre-
    screening; Property location; Racial
    discrimination; Redlining; Sex
    discrimination

on the basis of borrower characteris-
    tics, 4–8, 72–76, 281–292
in California, 101–116, 133–134, 146–
    154, 160–168, 171–177, 181–183,
    257–259, 269, 282–285, 287–292
in New York, 194–209, 221–223,
    230–237, 285–292
in conventional mortgage lending, 61
detection of, 72–76, 79, 101, 138–139,
    146, 160, 171–172, 217, 221, 226,
    229–230, 247, 248, 267, 277, 281–
    282, 304, 315
on a geographic basis, 8–10, 76, 281,
    292–299, 312
in California, 116–132, 134–136, 154–
    157, 166–171, 171–180, 183–184,
    259, 269, 292–295
in New York, 42–61, 209–220, 223–
    224, 237–246, 267–269, 292, 295–
    299, 385n11, 395n13
Down payment, 226, 229, 247, 248
and appraised-value-to-purchase-price,
    249
in California, 146, 250, 257–259, 269,
    284, 295
and delinquency probability in New
    York, 23
in New York, 230, 242, 259, 267, 268
Downward modification, 77, 158, 277
in California, 91, 158–168, 289
and older applicants in California,
    163–166, 183
in New York, 189, 225–226, 229–230
and requested-loan-to-appraised value,
    280–281
and requested-loan-to-income, 280–281
and sex discrimination in California,
    102–107,133–134
Downward-modification probability
and age of applicant in California,
    107–110, 134
and age of neighborhood in California,
    121–127
by building age in California, 121
by property location in California,
    116–121
by race in California, 115–116
and racial composition of neighbor-
    hoods in California, 127–132
by sex in California, 96–107
Duration of delinquency. *See* Delin-
    quency, duration of

ECOA. *See* Equal Credit Opportunity
    Act
EHOL form. *See* Equal Housing Op-
    portunity Lender form

Employment stability
and decision to lend in New York, 196
and modification of credit terms in
New York, 228
Equal Housing Opportunity Lender
(EHOL) form, 185–186, 316–317
Equal Credit Opportunity Act (ECOA)
and discrimination by marital status, 7
as an expression of social justice, 1,
274
and income discounting, 6
and sex discrimination, 6, 7
Equity
and default risk, 20–21
and default risk in New York, 31
and delinquency probability in New
York, 23
in foreclosure models, 27–28

Fair housing laws, 312
Federal Home Loan Bank, 10, 383n3
Federal Home Loan Bank Board, 307–
308, 313–314, 315
and income discounting, 6
Federal Housing Administration
(FHA), 52
loan policy of, 5–6, 52, 61
mortgage insurance program, 309
Federal Reserve Board Regulation B,
6, 7, 189
Federally-assisted mortgage lending in
New York, 50–56, 59–61
Federally-assisted mortgages, 52
and delinquency probability in New
York, 25
Female-headed households
and credit terms in California, 181, 284
and decision to lend in California,
133–134, 284
and denial probability
in California, 101–102, 107
in New York, 198–201, 221, 287
and downward modification
in California, 102–107, 133–134
in New York, 230–232, 236, 245
and income discounting in California,
107
and interest rates in California, 147–
149, 181–182, 284
and loan fees in California, 172–174,
182
and modification probability in New
York, 201
and property appraisal in California,
257–258, 269, 284, 285
treatment of (See also Marital status;
Sex discrimination)

in California, 299–300
in New York, 299–300
and withdrawal probability in New
York, 201–202
FHA. See Federal Housing
Administration
FHA mortgages. See Federally-assisted
mortgages
FHLBB. See Federal Home Loan
Bank Board
Financial characteristics, of a borrower. See also Borrower
characteristics
in California, 92–95
and decision to lend
in California, 92–95, 132–133
in New York, 194–196, 220–221,
228–229
Flow of mortgage funds, 33–36. See
also Supply of mortgage credit
and interaction of supply and demand
factors
in New York, 38, 45, 56, 58, 50
FmHA mortgages. See Federally-assisted mortgages
Foreclosure, 4, 19–22, 27–28
causes for, 16–19
and denial probability in New York,
197
and modification of credit terms in
New York, 229
in New York, 14–19, 57
probability of, in New York, 27 28, 30
Frequency of delinquency. See Delinquency, frequency of
Fresno
credit terms in, 143
denial probability in, 127–135
downward modification in, 161, 163,
166
downward modification probability in,
107, 131, 134, 135
income discounting in, 107, 133, 134,
163
interest rates in, 143, 144, 147, 151,
182, 184
loan fees in, 171, 174, 183
loan-to-income ratio in, 384n6
loan-to-value in, 154
maturity period in, 151, 384n6
property appraisal in, 257, 258, 259,
269
treatment by
age of applicant in, 151, 154, 166
age of neighborhood in, 127, 135
building age in, 144, 171
marital status in, 257, 269

Fresno (cont.)
  neighborhood characteristics in, 143
  race in, 151, 174, 182, 183, 258
  racial composition of neighborhood
    in, 131, 135, 184, 259
  sex in, 257, 269
  treatment in high-income neighbor-
    hoods in, 143
  treatment of
  female-headed households in, 107,
    147, 182, 257, 269
  male-headed households in, 107, 134,
    147, 161, 182
  variable rate mortgages in, 143
Future income, estimation of, 5, 66
Future market value
  and default risk, 21, 248
  estimation of, 68–69
  measures of, 21

High-income neighborhoods
  and denial probability in New York,
    196–197
  and loan fees in California, 171
  and interest rates in California, 143
  and loan-to-value ratio in New York,
    242
  and maturity period in California, 143
  and probability of denial in California,
    95
Home Mortgage Disclosure Act, 315
Housing code violation
  and conventional mortgage lending in
    New York, 43–44
  and interest rates in New York, 239
  and loan-to-value in New York, 246
Housing obsolescence, 10. See also
    Building age
HUD. See U.S. Department of Hous-
    ing and Urban Development

Income, and modification of credit
    terms in New York, 228–229
Income change
  and credit terms in California, 143
  and decision to lend in California, 95
and denial probability
  in California, 95
  in New York, 196–197
  and loan fees in California, 171
  and modification of credit terms in
    New York, 229
Income discounting, 5–7, 282, 300,
    377n8. See also Female-headed
    households, treatment of; Male-
    headed households, treatment of;

Marital status, treatment by; Sex
  discrimination
  in California, 102–107, 133–134, 163,
    149, 182, 284
  detection of, 74–75
  in New York, 299–300
  regulations against, 6
Informal screening, 84, 186, 317. See
    also Prescreening
Insurance. See Coinsurance
Insurance companies, 2, 9, 275
Interest rates 79–80, 138–140, 238–239
  and age of applicant in California, 183
  in California, 141–143, 284, 289
  and maturity period in New York,
    241–242, 244
  in New York, 45, 48, 188, 239–240,
    241–242, 243–244, 246, 380n8

Joint Center for Urban Studies, 11
Joint Center Mortgage Loan Survey.
    See Mortgage Loan Survey

Loan characteristics. See Credit terms
Loan fees, 80–82, 168–169, 277
  and age of applicants in California,
    183
  in California, 168–180, 284, 289
  and racial discrimination in California,
    174, 183
Loan-fees model, 80–82
Loan modification. See Modification of
    credit terms
Loan Register Report, 83–84, 248
Loan repayment
  and delinquency probability in New
    York, 23
  and default risk, 20, 30, 31
  and foreclosure probability in New
    York, 28
Loan-to-appraised value, in California,
    141, 258
Loan-to-value
  and age of applicant in California, 154,
    183
Loan-to-value ratios, 78–80, 138–140,
    238–239
  and building age in California, 146
  in California, 142–143
  and male-headed households in Cali-
    fornia, 147
  in New York, 36–38, 50, 239, 240,
    242–243, 246, 259–267
Location of property. See Property
    location
Los Angeles, City of
  denial probability in, 102, 134

downward-modification probability in,
115
treatment of male-headed households
in, 102, 134
treatment by race in, 115
Los Angeles–Long Beach,
appraised value in, 169
credit terms in, 143
denial probability in, 96, 127, 131–132,
135, 136
downward modification in, 160, 163–
166, 166–168, 183
downward-modification probability in,
127, 130–131, 132, 135
income discounting in, 149
interest rates in, 143, 144, 147–149,
154, 155–156, 182, 184
loan fees in, 169–171, 174–177, 182,
183, 184
loan-to-appraised-value in, 151
loan-to-value ratio in, 146
maturity period in, 151–154, 156
property appraisal in, 257
requested-loan-to-income in, 143
treatment by
age of applicant in, 151–154, 163–
166, 174–177
age of neighborhood in, 127, 166, 183
building age in, 144, 146, 160, 169–
171
marital status in, 257
neighborhood characteristics in, 96,
143
property location in, 168
race in, 151, 174, 182, 183
racial composition of neighborhoods
in, 127, 130–131, 132, 135, 136, 154,
155–156, 166–168, 177, 184
sex in, 257
treatment in high-income neighborhoods in, 171
treatment of
female-headed households in, 174,
182, 257
male-headed households in, 147–149,
257
variable rate mortgages in, 143

Male-headed households
and credit terms in California, 181–
182, 284–285
and decision to lend
in California, 133–134, 282–285
in New York, 221–222
and denial probability
in California, 101, 102, 107, 133–134,
282–284

in New York, 198–201, 221–222, 285,
287
and downward modification
in California, 102–107, 133–134, 182,
282–284
in New York, 232
and income discounting in California,
102, 107, 133–134, 149, 182, 284
and interest rates in California, 147,
181–182, 284
and loan fees in California, 174, 182,
284
and loan-to-value ratios in California,
147, 182
and modification probability in New
York, 201
and property appraisal in California,
257
and withdrawal probability in New
York, 201–202
treatment of, 299–300 (see also Marital status, treatment by; Sex
discrimination)
Marital status. See also Female-headed
households, treatment of; Income
discounting; Male-headed households, treatment of
and decision to lend in New York,
198–202, 221–222
and denial probability in New York,
198–201, 221–222, 285, 287
detection of treatment by, 75
and downward modification in New
York, 230–232, 245
and foreclosure probability in New
York, 28
and modification probability in New
York, 201
and property appraisal in California,
257, 269
treatment by, 5–7, 281–287
in New York, 198–202, 221–222,
230–232, 245, 285–287, 300
and withdrawal probability in New
York, 201–202
Maturity periods, 78–80, 138–140, 238–
239
in California, 142
and conventional mortgage lending in
New York, 56, 58, 240–242, 244, 246
and delinquency probability in New
York, 23–24
Modesto
decision to lend in, 131, 136
denial probability in, 96, 101, 107, 127,
133, 134, 135
income discounting in, 107, 134

Modesto (cont.)
  and requested-loan-to-income ratio, 93
  treatment by
    neighborhood characteristics in, 96
    racial composition of neighborhoods
      in, 127, 131, 135, 136
  treatment of
    female-headed households in, 101,
      133
    male-headed households in, 101, 107,
      133, 134
Modification of credit terms, 70, 76–82,
    277, 300. *See also* Downward
    modification.
  in New York, 188–189, 204–206, 217,
    221, 224, 245–246
Modification of loans. *See* Modification
    of credit terms
Monterey
  denial probability in, 121
  treatment by property location in, 121
Mortgage. *See* Age of mortgage; Credit
    terms; Conventional mortgage lend-
    ing; Delinquency rate; Downward
    modification; Federally-assisted
    mortgages; Foreclosure; Downpay-
    ment; Interest rates; Loan Fees;
    Loan-to-value ratios; Maturity peri-
    ods; Multiple unit mortgage; Supply
    of mortgage credit; Variable rate
    mortgage
  determinants of demand for, 12
Mortgage default. *See* Foreclosure
Mortgage loan survey (MLS), 12, 16–
    17, 248, 379n1, 379n4, 379n5
Mortgage price, 34
Mortgage Review Fund, 320–321
Mortgage terms. *See* Credit Terms
MRF. *See* Mortgage Review Fund
Multifamily buildings, and property ap-
    praisal in New York, 267
Multiple unit mortgages, 28–30, 239–
    244
  and delinquency probability in New
    York, 25
  and foreclosure probability in New
    York, 28
Mutual savings banks (New York), 16,
    30, 186, 190, 225, 320
  and decision to lend, 298
  and denial probability, 194, 196, 197,
    201, 202–204, 207, 216, 217, 221,
    222, 223, 224, 287, 295
  and downward modification, 232, 234,
    245, 287
  and employment stability, 196
  and foreclosure rate, 229

  and modification-acceptance probabil-
    ity, 204
  and modification probability, 204, 207,
    216, 220, 222–223, 224, 290, 295,
    385n11, 385n13
  and modification-withdrawal probabil-
    ity, 204
  and property appraisal, 296, 298
  and requested loan amount, 196
  and requested-loan-to-appraised-value,
    194
  and treatment by
    age, 207, 223, 224
    age of neighborhood, 217, 220, 224,
      298
    marital status, 201, 202, 221, 222,
      232, 245, 287
    property location, 216, 223–224, 295,
      296
    race, 202–204, 206, 207, 222–223
    racial composition of neighborhoods,
      220, 385n13
    sex, 201, 202, 221, 222, 232, 287
  and treatment of
    female-headed households, 201, 202,
      221, 287
    male-headed households, 201, 222,
      287
  and withdrawal probability, 202, 206–
    207, 220
National Neighborhood Reinvestment
    Corporation, 308
Neighborhood change
  and delinquency probability in New
    York, 25
  and loan-to-value ratio in New York,
    242–243
  and maturity period in New York,
    241, 244
Neighborhood characteristics
  and appraisal practices in New York,
    267
  and appraised-value-to-purchase-price
    in California, 257
  and conventional mortgage lending in
    New York, 48, 57, 58, 59, 60, 217–
    220, 223–224, 239–244, 385n13
  and credit terms
    in California, 143–146
    in New York, 240–246
  and decision to lend
    in California, 85–86, 95–96
    in New York, 188, 196–197, 217–220,
      223–224, 385n13
  and downward modification in New
    York, 229, 237–238

and federally-assisted mortgage lending in New York, 51
and interest rates in New York, 239, 246
and loan-to-value ratio in New York, 242, 246
and maturity period in New York, 240–241, 246
and modification of credit terms in New York, 229
and probability of denial in California, 96
and property appraisal in California, 257, 259
Neighborhood decision-making, 306–307
Neighborhood decline, 2, 52, 275, 309
and mortgage default in New York, 31
and redlining, 9–10
Neighborhood Housing Services (NHS), 306, 307–309
Neighborhoods alleged to be redlined
and conventional mortgage lending in New York, 42–50, 58
and default risk in New York, 32
and delinquency probability in New York, 23
and delinquency rates in New York, 14–15
and downward modification in New York, 237, 245
and federally-assisted mortgage lending in New York, 50–56, 61
and foreclosure probability, 28
and maturity period in New York, 244
and severity of delinquency in New York, 26
Net wealth
and modification of credit terms in New York, 228
in New York, 196
New York-Nassau-Suffolk
appraisal of multi-family buildings in, 267
borrower characteristics in, 26, 32
default risk
and age of borrower in, 26, 32
and age of mortgage in, 23–24
and building age in, 24
and building condition in, 24
and down payment in, 23
and federally-assisted mortgages in, 25
and marital status in, 28
and multiple unit mortgages in, 25
and payment-to-income ratio in, 23
delinquency, duration of, in, 26

delinquency probability in, 23, 24, 25, 32
delinquency rate in, 197
denial probability in, 196, 197, 198, 201, 202–204, 207, 215, 216, 217–220, 221, 222, 223, 224, 236, 287, 299
downward modification in, 230–232, 234–237, 245, 287
employment stability, 196
foreclosure probability in, 28
foreclosure rate in, 229
high-income neighborhoods in, 196–197
income change in, 229
modification acceptance probability in, 204
modification probability in, 201, 204, 207, 216–217, 222–223, 224, 285, 290, 295 296
modification-withdrawal probability in, 204
net wealth in, 196
property appraisal in, 267
requested loan amount in, 227–229
requested-loan-to-appraised-value in, 227–228
requested-loan-to-income in, 228–229
severity of delinquency in, 26, 32
treatment by
age in, 207, 223, 226, 230–232, 234–237, 245, 285
age of neighborhood in, 217, 224
building age in, 267
income in, 196
marital status in, 198, 201, 202, 221, 222, 230–232, 236, 287
property location in, 215, 216–217, 223–224, 237, 295–296
race in, 202–204, 222–223
racial composition of neighborhoods in, 217–220, 224, 299
sex in, 198, 201, 202, 221, 222, 226, 230–232, 236, 285, 287
treatment of
female-headed households in, 201, 202, 221, 226, 230–232, 236, 285, 287
male-headed households in, 198, 201, 222, 287
withdrawal probability in, 202, 206–207, 217
New York Public Interest Research Group, 303, 321–322
New York State Banking Department, 38, 186, 238

NHS. *See* Neighborhood Housing Services
Nonowner occupancy and delinquency probability in New York, 25
NYPIRG. *See* New York Public Interest Research Group

Other minority neighborhoods in California, 131–132
Overappraisals, 247–248
in California, 257–258, 259, 269
in New York, 267
Oxnard-Ventura
decision to lend in, 133
denial probability in, 127, 135
treatment by
racial composition of neighborhoods in, 127, 135
sex in, 133

Payment-to-income ratio, in New York, 23
Per capita income, and loan-to-value ratio in New York, 242
Personal characteristics, of borrower or applicant. *See* Borrower characteristics
Population change
and conventional mortgage lending in New York, 59
and credit terms in California, 143
and denial probability in New York, 197
and loan fees in California, 171
and probability of denial in California, 95–96
Portfolio-Choice Model, 63–71
Pregnancy, and credit worthiness, 5, 281
Prejudice, 6–8
Prescreening, 62–63, 276. *See also* Informal screening
Probability of delinquency. *See* Delinquency, probability of
Probability of foreclosure. *See* Foreclosure, probability of
Property appraisal, 8–9, 68–69, 247–249, 277. *See also* Appraised value of property; Overappraisal; Underappraisal
in California, 249–259, 269, 289
criteria used for, 9, 247–249
Property location
and conventional mortgage lending in California, 116–121, 300
in New York, 58, 59, 60, 209–220, 223–224, 300

and credit terms
in California, 154–157, 184, 293–295
in New York, 296
and decision to lend
in California, 293, 295
in New York, 209–217, 223–224, 295–296
and denial probability in California, 293
and downward modification
in California, 168, 293
in New York, 237
and interest rates in New York, 240, 244
and loan fees in California, 177–180, 293, 295
and loan-to-value ratio in New York, 243, 246
and maturity periods in New York, 241, 244
and property appraisal
in California, 259, 269, 293, 295
in New York, 267–269
Property transactions, 33–34
and conventional mortgage lending in New York, 43, 48, 56, 58, 59
and federally-assisted mortgage lending in New York, 50
volume of, in New York, 36–38
Purchase price. *See* Sales price

Racial composition of neighborhood
and conventional mortgage lending
in California, 127–132, 135, 300
in New York, 45, 48, 58, 59, 60, 217–220, 224, 300, 385n13
and credit terms in California, 154–156, 184
and decision to lend
in California, 127–132, 135
in New York, 217–220, 224, 298–299, 385n13
and delinquency rates, 19
and denial probability in California, 298, 299
and downward modification
in California, 166–168, 184
in New York, 237–238
and federally-assisted mortgage lending in New York, 61
and interest rates
in California, 298, 299
in New York, 240, 245–246
and loan fees in California, 177, 298–299
and loan-to-value ratio in New York, 242–243, 246

and maturity periods in New York, 241, 246
and modification probability in California, 298, 299
and property appraisal in California, 259, 298, 299
Racial discrimination, 7–8. *See also* Racial composition of neighborhoods
against Asians in California, 114–115, 116–117, 134, 151, 174, 182–183, 258, 289, 300
against blacks
in California, 110–111, 115, 135, 151, 174, 182–183, 258, 287–289, 300
in New York, 202–206, 222–223, 287–289, 300
in California, 110–116, 134, 149–151, 174, 182–183, 258, 287, 289–290, 300
and credit terms, 289
deed restrictions as a form of, 7–8
and denial probability
in California, 287, 289
in New York, 287, 289
detection of, 75, 204–206
and downward modification in New York, 232–234, 245
against Hispanics in New York, 202–206, 222–223, 289, 300
and modification probability, 289
and modification probability in New York, 234, 289, 290
in New York, 202–207, 222–223, 232–234, 245, 287–290, 300
against other minorities
in California, 111–114, 116, 134, 258, 289–290, 300
in New York, 202–207, 222, 223, 289–290, 300
and property appraisal in California, 258, 289–290
against Spanish in California, 111–114, 115, 134, 151, 174, 182 183, 258, 289, 300
against whites
in California, 163, 183
in New York, 232–234
Racial transition in neighborhoods
and conventional mortgage lending in New York, 45, 60
and federally-assisted mortgage lending in New York, 52, 53, 61
Ratio of federal to conventional lending in New York, 54–56
Real estate brokers, 2, 275
Recommendations, 301–322
to counter risk, 306–311
to eliminate discrimination, 304, 311–322
to enhance market forces, 301–306
Redlining, 2, 8–10, 14, 33, 275, 292–299, 311–312.
See also Neighborhoods alleged to be redlined; Property location
in California, 116–132, 134–136, 154–157, 166–168, 177–180, 183–184, 259, 269, 293–295, 300
in California cities, 116, 118–121, 135, 156–157, 168, 179–180, 184, 293–295
definition of, 9
detection of, 76, 121
institutionalization of, 52, 61, 309, 310–311
in New York, 31, 32, 45–48, 48–49, 53–54, 55–56, 57, 59–61, 209–220, 223–224, 237–238, 238–246, 267, 268, 269, 295–299, 300, 385n11, 385n13
in New York cities, 57–58, 60, 209–217, 223–224, 237, 241, 243, 267–268, 295–296
subtle forms of, 8
Refinancing, of mortgages on multi-family properties, 28–29
Regulation. *See also* specific acts; Usury ceilings
of banking investments, 3, 303
of banks in New York, 186, 238
of credit evaluation, 7
against income discounting, 6, 311
of interest rates, 302
of savings and loan associations in California, 84
against treatment by
building age 313, 314–315
marital status, 7, 311
possibility of pregnancy, 6, 311
property location, 313, 314–315
race, 8, 311
sex, 6, 311
Rental income and delinquency probability in New York, 25
Requested loan amount
in California, 142–143, 159–160
and denial probability in New York, 196
and modification of credit terms in New York, 227–229
Requested-loan-to-appraised-value, 280–281
in New York, 194–196
and modification of credit terms in New York, 227–228

Requested-loan-to-appraised-value-ratio
in California, 92–93, 95, 142
Requested-loan-to-income, 280–281
Requested-loan-to-income ratio in California, 93–95, 142–143, 159–160
Residential lending, process of, 3–4,
62–63, 70
Risk, 382n7
lenders' attitudes toward, 66–67
measurement of in California, 141
Risk of default. *See* Default risk
Rochester. *See also* Upstate region
denial probability in, 194, 196, 198,
201, 202, 207, 216, 217, 222, 223,
224
downward modification in, 232, 234,
238
modification probability in, 204, 207,
220, 223
property appraisal in, 267, 268
requested loan amount in, 196
requested-loan-to-appraised-value in,
194
treatment by
age in, 207, 223, 234
age of neighborhood in, 217, 224
building age in, 267
marital status in, 198, 201, 222, 232
property location in, 216, 223, 268
race in, 202–204, 207, 222
racial composition of neighborhoods
in, 220, 238
sex in, 198, 201, 222, 232
treatment of
female-headed households in, 201,
232
male-headed households in, 201, 222
withdrawal probability in, 206–207,
220

Sacramento
denial probability in, 96, 101, 102,
131–132, 133, 134, 136
treatment by
neighborhood characteristics in, 96
racial composition of neighborhoods
in, 131–132, 136
treatment of
female-headed households in, 101,
133
male-headed households in, 101, 102,
134
Sales price, and appraised-value-to-purchase-price in California, 250–269
Sales price, average
and loan-to-value ratio in New York,
242

and probability of denial in California,
96
Sales price, change in and decision to
lend in California, 96
Salinas-Monterey
decision to lend in, 133
denial probability in, 127, 135
requested-loan-to-appraised-value ratio
in, 92–93
treatment by
racial composition of neighborhoods
in, 127, 135
sex in, 133
San Bernardino-Riverside-Ontario
decision to lend in, 131, 136
denial probability in, 101–102, 107,
133, 134
downward-modification probability in,
107, 115, 116, 134
income discounting in, 107, 134
treatment by
race in, 115, 116
racial composition of neighborhoods
in, 131, 136
treatment of
female-headed households in, 101–
102, 133, 134
male-headed households in, 101, 107,
134
San Diego
denial probability in, 96, 101, 102, 107,
127, 134, 135
downward-modification probability in,
115
income discounting in, 107, 133, 134
requested-loan-to-income ratio in, 93
treatment by
neighborhood characteristics in, 96
race in, 115
racial composition of neighborhoods
in, 127, 135
treatment of
female-headed households in, 101,
134
male-headed households in 102, 107,
134
San Francisco-Oakland
credit terms in, 143, 151
decision to lend in, 153
denial probability in, 96, 115, 127, 135
downward-modification probability in,
130–131, 135, 163–166, 183
income discounting in, 149
interest rates in, 143, 154, 156, 182,
184
loan fees in, 169, 171, 174–177, 182,
183, 184

loan-to-appraised-value in, 151
maturity periods in, 151–154
maturity periods in, 151–154
property appraisal in, 257–258
requested-loan-to-income in, 143
treatment by
  age of applicant in, 151–154, 163–
    166, 174–177
  age of neighborhood in, 127, 135,
    166, 183
  building age in, 169
  marital status in, 257
  neighborhood characteristics in, 96,
    143
  race in, 115, 151, 174, 182, 183, 258
  racial composition of neighborhoods
    in, 130–131, 135, 154, 156, 166, 177,
    184
  sex in, 133, 257
treatment in high-income neighborhoods in, 171
treatment of female-headed households in, 174, 182, 257
variable rate mortgages in, 143
San Jose
  credit terms in, 143, 151, 182
  decision to lend in, 131, 136
  denial probability in, 96, 115, 121, 127,
    135
  downward modification in, 160, 166
  downward-modification probability in,
    107, 131, 134, 136
  income discounting in, 107, 134, 149
  interest rates in 141, 143–144, 156,
    182, 184
  loan fees in, 171, 174–177, 183, 184
  loan-to-appraised-value in, 141
  loan-to-value ratio, 146
  maturity periods in, 151–154, 156
  property appraisal in, 257–258
  treatment by
    age of applicant in, 151–154, 166,
      174–177
    age of neighborhood in, 127, 135,
      177, 183
    building age in, 146, 160
    marital status in, 257–258
    neighborhood characteristics in, 96,
      143
    property location in, 121
    race in, 115, 151, 174, 182, 183
    racial composition of neighborhoods
      in, 127, 131, 135, 136, 156, 177, 184
    sex in, 257–258
    vacancy rate in, 143–144
  treatment in high-income neighbor-
    hoods in, 171

treatment of
  female-headed households in, 107,
    134, 257–258
  male-headed households in, 107
  variable rate mortgages in, 143
Santa Ana
  denial probability in, 121
  treatment by property location in, 121
Santa Barbara
  decision to lend in, 131, 136
  denial probability in, 92, 101, 107,
    133–134
  income discounting in, 107, 134
  requested-loan-to-income ratio in, 93
  treatment by racial composition of
    neighborhoods in, 131, 136
  treatment of
    female-headed households in, 101,
      133–134
    male-headed households in, 107
Santa Rosa
  decision to lend in, 131, 136
  denial probability in, 96, 111, 115
  downward-modification probability in,
    102, 107, 116, 133, 134
  income discounting in, 107, 134
  treatment by
    neighborhood characteristics in, 96
    race in, 111, 115, 116
    racial composition of neighborhoods
      in, 131, 136
  treatment of
    female-headed households in, 102,
      107, 133, 134
    male-headed households in, 102, 107,
      134
Savings and loan associations (California), 83, 132, 181
Savings and loan association (New
  York), 186, 190, 225
  and delinquency rate, 197
  and denial probability, 196, 197, 198,
    201, 202, 207, 216, 217–220, 222,
    223, 224, 290
  and downward modification, 232, 234–
    236, 238, 245
  and high-income neighborhoods, 196–
    197
  and income of a borrower, 196
  and modification probability, 201, 204,
    207, 222–223, 285, 289
  and treatment by
    age, 207, 223, 234–236, 245, 285, 290
    age of neighborhood, 217, 224
    marital status, 198, 201, 222, 232, 287
    property location, 216, 217, 223

Savings and loan (N.Y.) (cont.)
  race, 202–204, 206–207, 222–223, 289
  racial composition of neighborhoods,
    217–220, 238
  sex, 198, 201, 222, 232, 285, 287
  and treatment of
    female-headed households, 201, 232,
      285
    male-headed households, 198, 201,
      222
  and withdrawal probability, 206–207,
    217
Secondary income discounting. See Income discounting
Severity of delinquency. See Delinquency, severity of
Sex discrimination 5–7, 281–287. See
  also Female-headed households,
  treatment of; Income discounting;
  Male-headed households, treatment
  of; Sex of borrower
  in California, 101–107, 133–134, 147–
    149, 161–163, 172–174, 181–182,
    257–258, 269, 282–285, 229–300
  detection of, 73–75
  in New York, 198–202, 221–222, 226,
    230–232, 245, 299–300
  regulations against, 6
  subtle forms of, 7
Sex of borrower
  and decision to lend
    in California, 96–107, 133–134, 258,
      282–285
    in New York, 198–202, 221–222
  and delinquency probability in New
    York, 25
  and denial probability in New York,
    198–201, 221–222
  and downward modification in New
    York, 230–232, 245
  and modification probability in New
    York, 201
  and property appraisal in California,
    257–258, 269
  and withdrawal probability in New
    York, 201–202
Social justice, 1, 5, 6, 274
Spanish neighborhoods, in California,
  127–131, 135, 156, 166–168, 177,
  184, 259, 299
Stock of conventional mortgages, and
  conventional mortgage lending in
  New York, 43, 48, 58
Stock of federally-assisted mortgages
  and conventional mortgage lending in
  New York, 58, 59, 244

and federally-assisted mortgage lending in New York, 50–51
and interest rates in New York, 244
Stockton
  change in vacancy rate in, 96
  denial probability in, 96, 101, 111, 131,
    133–134, 136
  requested-loan-to-income ratio in, 93
  treatment by
    race in, 111
    racial composition of neighborhoods
      in, 131, 136
  treatment of female-headed house-
    holds in, 101, 133–134
Supply of federally-assisted mortgage
  credit in New York, 50–56
Supply of mortgage credit
  for conventional mortgages in New
    York, 42–50, 54–55, 56–59
  determinants of, 12, 34
  in New York, 59–61, 296
Syracuse. See also Upstate region
  denial probability in, 222, 223
  downward modification in, 234
  property appraisal in, 267, 268
  treatment by
    age in, 234
    building age in, 267
    property location in, 268
    race in, 222
The Task Force, 307–308
Tax arrearage
  and conventional mortgage lending in
    New York, 44
  and federally-assisted mortgage lend-
    ing in New York, 51
Tenant problems, and foreclosure in
  New York, 19
Terms of loan. See Credit terms
"testing" for discrimination, 315–316
Time path and redlining in New York,
  268–269
Troy
  denial probability in, 295
  treatment property location in, 295

Underappraisal, 8–9, 62, 247–248, 276,
  277
  in California, 250, 257, 259, 269, 284–
    285, 293, 295, 299
  in New York, 267, 268, 269, 298
Underwriting standards, 319
Upstate region (Albany-Schenectady-
  Troy, Rochester and Syracuse)
  default risk
    and age of borrower in, 25
    and age of neighborhood in, 28

and building condition in, 24
and neighborhoods alleged to be redlined in, 26
delinquency frequency in, 26
delinquency probability in, 24, 25
denial probability in, 196, 197, 202,
207, 217, 223, 224
downward modification in, 232, 234
foreclosure probability in, 28
modification probability in, 207, 223
requested loan amount in, 196
treatment by
age in, 207, 223, 234
age of neighborhood in, 217, 220, 224
marital status in, 199, 202, 232
race in, 202
sex in, 199, 202, 232
treatment of male-headed households
in, 199, 202
withdrawal probability in, 202, 220
Urban Reinvestment Task Force. See
The Task Force
U.S. Commission on Civil Rights, 5
U.S. Department of Housing and Urban Development (HUD), 6, 307
Usury ceilings, 302–303
in New York, 38, 80, 188, 240, 302,
380n7, 385n1

VA. See Veterans Administration
VA mortgages. See Federally-assisted
mortgages
Vacancy
and conventional mortgage lending in
New York, 57
and interest rates in New York, 239
Vacancy rate
and decision to lend in California, 96
and interest rates in California, 143–
144
Vacancy rate, change in California, 96
Vallejo-Napa
denial probability in, 96
downward-modification probability in,
102, 107, 115, 116, 127, 131, 134,
136
income discounting in, 107, 134
treatment by
age of neighborhood in, 127
neighborhood characteristics in, 96
race in, 115, 116
racial composition of neighborhoods
in, 131, 136
treatment of male-headed households,
102, 107, 134
Variable rate mortgages, 79
in California, 143

Ventura
denial probability in, 121
downward-modification probability in,
121
treatment by property location in, 121
Veterans Administration (VA), 52, 309
loan policy, 5, 52, 61

Welfare payments
and conventional mortgage lending in
New York, 44
Welfare payments
and conventional mortgage lending in
New York, 44
and federally-assisted mortgage lending in New York, 51
Whiteside, William A., 307–308

About the authors

Robert Schafer practices law in Boston. From 1971 to 1979, he was a professor of urban public policy at Harvard University and a faculty associate at the Joint Center for Urban Studies of the Massachusetts Institute of Technology and Harvard University. He received his J.D. from Harvard Law School and has a Ph.D. in urban planning and economics, also from Harvard.

Helen F. Ladd is Associate Professor at the Kennedy School of Government, Harvard University. She received her Ph.D. in economics from Harvard, her master's degree from the London School of Economics, and her undergraduate degree from Wellesley College.